Unequal Protection

Also by Thom Hartmann

Unequal Protection

How Corporations Became "People"
—and You Can Fight Back

2nd Edition, Revised and Expanded

By Thom Hartmann

BK

Berrett–Koehler Publishers, Inc.
San Francisco
a BK Currents book

Berrett-Koehler Publishers, Inc.
235 Montgomery Street, Suite 650, San Francisco, CA 94104-2916
Tel: (415) 288-0260   Fax: (415) 362-2512   www.bkconnection.com

Ordering Information

Quantity sales. Special discounts are available on quantity purchases by corporations, associations, and others. For details, contact the "Special Sales Department" at the Berrett-Koehler address above.

Individual sales. Berrett-Koehler publications are available through most bookstores. They can also be ordered directly from Berrett-Koehler:
Tel: (800) 929-2929; Fax: (802) 864-7626; www.bkconnection.com.

Orders for college textbook/course adoption use. Please contact Berrett-Koehler:
Tel: (800) 929-2929; Fax: (802) 864-7626.

Orders by U.S. trade bookstores and wholesalers. Please contact Ingram Publisher Services, Tel: (800) 509-4887; Fax: (800) 838-1149; E-mail: customer.service@ ingrampublisherservices.com; or visit www.ingrampublisherservices.com/Ordering for details about electronic ordering.

Berrett-Koehler and the BK logo are registered trademarks of Berrett-Koehler Publishers, Inc.

Printed in the United States of America

Berrett-Koehler books are printed on long-lasting acid-free paper. When it is available, we choose paper that has been manufactured by environmentally responsible processes. These may include using trees grown in sustainable forests, incorporating recycled paper, minimizing chlorine in bleaching, or recycling the energy produced at the paper mill.

Library of Congress Cataloging-in-Publication Data
Hartmann, Thom, 1951–
    Unequal protection : how corporations became "people"—and you can fight back / Thom Hartmann.
        p. cm.
    Includes bibliographical references and index.
    ISBN 978-1-60509-559-2 (pbk. : alk. paper)
1. Industrial policy—United States—History. 2. Corporation law—United States—History. 3. Business and politics—United States—History. 4. Corporations—Moral and ethical aspects—United States. 5. Human rights—United States—History. I. Title.
    HD3616.U46H317 2009
    338.0973—dc22

                                                                    2009040845

Second Edition

15   14   13   12   11   10   10 9 8 7 6 5 4 3 2 1

Cover design by Richard Adelson. Interior design and composition by Gary Palmatier. Elizabeth von Radics, copyeditor; Mike Mollett, proofreader; Medea Minnich, indexer.

To my favorite Zen Master, Mike Dirkx

History has informed us that bodies of men, as well as individuals, are susceptible to the spirit of tyranny.

—Thomas Jefferson, *A Summary View of the Rights of British America,* 1774

Contents

Introduction:
The Battle to Save Democracy

It's really a wonder that I haven't dropped all my ideals, because they seem so absurd and impossible to carry out. Yet I keep them, because in spite of everything I still believe people are really good at heart.

—Anne Frank, from her diary, July 15, 1944

ON SEPTEMBER 2, 2009, THE TRANSNATIONAL PHARMACEUTICAL GIANT Pfizer pled guilty to multiple criminal felonies. It had been marketing drugs in a way that may well have led to the deaths of people and that definitely led physicians to prescribe and patients to use pharmaceuticals in ways they were not intended.

Because Pfizer is a corporation—a legal abstraction, really—it couldn't go to jail like fraudster Bernie Madoff or killer John Dillinger; instead it paid a $1.2 billion "criminal" fine to the U.S. government—the biggest in history—as well as an additional $1 billion in civil penalties. The total settlement was more than $2.3 billion—another record. None of its executives, decision-makers, stockholders/owners, or employees saw even five minutes of the inside of a police station or jail cell.

Most Americans don't even know about this huge and massive crime. Nor do they know that the "criminal" never spent a day in jail.

But they do know that in the autumn of 2004, Martha Stewart was convicted of lying to investigators about her sale of stock in another pharmaceutical company. Her crime cost nobody their life, but she famously was escorted off to a women's prison. Had she been a corporation instead of a human being, odds are there never would have even been an investigation.

Yet over the past century—and particularly the past forty years—corporations have repeatedly asserted that they are, in fact, "persons" and therefore eligible for the human rights protections of the Bill of Rights.

In 2009 the right-wing advocacy group Citizens United argued before the Supreme Court that they had the First Amendment right to "free speech"

1

and to influence elections through the production and the distribution of a slasher "documentary" designed to destroy Hillary Clinton's ability to win the Democratic nomination. (Some political observers assert that they did this in part because they believed that a Black man whose first name sounded like "Osama" and whose middle name was Hussein could never, ever, possibly win against a Republican, no matter how poor a candidate they put up.)

In that, they were following on a 2003 case before the Supreme Court in which Nike claimed that it had the First Amendment right to lie in its corporate marketing, a variation on the First Amendment right of free speech. (Except in certain contract and law enforcement/court situations, it's perfectly legal for human persons to lie in the United States. Nobody ever went to jail for saying, "No, of course you don't look fat in those pants!")

Corporations haven't limited their grasp to the First Amendment; pretty much any and virtually every amendment that could be used to further corporate interests has been fair game. (They haven't yet argued the Third Amendment—you can't force citizens to quarter soldiers in their homes—although Blackwater's activities in New Orleans during the aftermath of Hurricane Katrina could have provided an interesting test.)

As you'll learn in this book, in previous decades a chemical company took to the Supreme Court a case asserting its Fourth Amendment "right to privacy" from the Environmental Protection Agency's snooping into its illegal chemical discharges. Other corporations have asserted Fifth Amendment rights against self-incrimination as well as asserted that the Fourteenth Amendment—passed after the Civil War to strip slavery from the Constitution—protects their right "against discrimination" by a local community that doesn't want them building a toxic waste incinerator, commercial hog operation, or superstore.

If this trend continues, it's probably just a matter of time before a corporation (maybe one of the many mercenary forces that emerged out of George W. Bush's Iraq War?) claims the Second Amendment right to bear arms anywhere, anytime, and your credit card company's bill collector shows up at your home with a sidearm.

This legal situation is not only bizarre but also quite the opposite of the vision for this country held by the Founders of the nation and the Framers of the Constitution. They were sufficiently worried about corporate power that they didn't even include in the Constitution the word *corporation*, intending instead that the states tightly regulate corporate behavior (which the states did quite well until just after the Civil War).

The American Revolution, you'll learn in this book, was in fact provoked by the misbehavior of a British corporation; our nation was founded in an anti-corporate-power fury.

Corporate Personhood in the Making

The most significant and oft-quoted precedent to the turning point of corporate power in America began just after the Civil War. It rested on a Constitutional Amendment successfully written and passed by a group of "Radical Republicans" after the Civil War to take slavery out of the Constitution.

Given that today's Republican Party has—largely since the Robber Baron Era of the 1880s—been the party of big business and the very rich, it's a bit difficult for some people to get their minds around the possibility that the Republican Party started out as a reform party that for nearly seventy years (from before Abraham Lincoln until just after Theodore Roosevelt left the party to start a third party) had a strong progressive wing. But it did.

Although Lincoln was by today's standards a "moderate" Republican, he was still anti-slavery, pro–middle class, and pro-labor (he famously said, "Labor is superior to capital because it precedes capital"—nobody was wealthy until somebody made something—and was the first president both to use the word "strike" and to actually stop police and private armies from killing and beating strikers).

And just like in today's mainstream Democratic Party, where there's a progressive minority that always seems to be pushing the edges, in the Republican Party of the 1800s there was a very—even by today's standards—progressive faction.

The Radical Republicans were a splinter group that emerged in a big way from the Republican Party at its founding in 1854; and just after the Civil War, in 1866, they gained a majority among Republicans in the House of Representatives, where they had a powerful influence until the faction disintegrated in the 1870s during the presidency of Republican Ulysses S. Grant. They supported the absolute right of freed slaves to vote and participate in all aspects of government and society, and they pushed hard for the punishment of former Confederates (and Democrats in the South) and fought with the more moderate mainstream Republicans.

After Lincoln's assassination they had so much power in the House that they were able to push through the Civil Rights Act of 1866 and override President Andrew Johnson's veto of it (and a dozen other bills). They drove the impeachment of Johnson and missed by a single vote.

They also realized that if they wanted to really free Blacks, it wasn't enough to just pass a law. They had to get the implicit approval of slavery out of the Constitution itself, so they proposed three Constitutional amendments—what we now call the Thirteenth, Fourteenth, and Fifteenth Amendments, or the Reconstruction Amendments.

The Thirteenth Amendment explicitly abolishes slavery, saying, "Neither slavery nor involuntary servitude, except as a punishment for crime whereof the party shall have been duly convicted, shall exist within the United States, or any place subject to their jurisdiction." The Fifteenth Amendment explicitly forbids any government within the United States to prevent Blacks from voting, saying, "The right of citizens of the United States to vote shall not be denied or abridged by the United States or by any State on account of race, color, or previous condition of servitude."

Both of these changed the face of America, but the Fourteenth Amendment has proved the most radical—just not in the way its authors intended.

The main goal of the Fourteenth Amendment was to reverse the 1857 *Dred Scott v. Sanford* decision of the U.S. Supreme Court, which had excluded African Americans from access to the protections of the Constitution and the Bill of Rights (the first ten amendments to the Constitution).

Section 1 explicitly made them citizens (assuming they were born or naturalized here) and explicitly entitled them to the same "equal protections" under the law that White citizens enjoyed.

Sections 2 through 4 also made sure that Black Americans were counted as a full person (and not three-fifths of a person) for the purpose of determining congressional districts, and it took a swipe at the former Confederates and their sympathizers by, in Section 3, excluding them from participation in holding public office. The language was quite straightforward, reflecting the Radical Republican agenda:

The Fourteenth Amendment

Section 1. All persons born or naturalized in the United States, and subject to the jurisdiction thereof, are citizens of the United States and of the State wherein they reside. No State shall make or enforce any law which shall abridge the privileges or immunities of citizens of the United States; nor shall any State deprive any person of life, liberty, or property, without due process of law; nor deny to any person within its jurisdiction the equal protection of the laws.

Section 2. Representatives shall be apportioned among the several States according to their respective numbers, counting the whole number of persons in each State, excluding Indians not taxed. But when the right to vote at any election for the choice of electors for President and Vice President of the United States, Representatives in Congress, the Executive and Judicial officers of a State, or the members of the Legislature thereof, is denied to any of the male inhabitants of such State, being twenty-one years of age, and citizens of the United States, or in any way abridged, except for participation in rebellion, or other crime, the basis of representation therein shall be reduced in the proportion which the number of such male citizens shall bear to the whole number of male citizens twenty-one years of age in such State.

Section 3. No person shall be a Senator or Representative in Congress, or elector of President and Vice President, or hold any office, civil or military, under the United States, or under any State, who, having previously taken an oath, as a member of Congress, or as an officer of the United States, or as a member of any State legislature, or as an executive or judicial officer of any State, to support the Constitution of the United States, shall have engaged in insurrection or rebellion against the same, or given aid or comfort to the enemies thereof. But Congress may by a vote of two-thirds of each House, remove such disability.

Section 4. The validity of the public debt of the United States, authorized by law, including debts incurred for payment of pensions and bounties for services in suppressing insurrection or rebellion, shall not be questioned. But neither the United States nor any State shall assume or pay any debt or obligation incurred in aid of insurrection or rebellion against the United States, or any claim for the loss or emancipation of any slave; but all such debts, obligations and claims shall be held illegal and void.

Section 5. The Congress shall have power to enforce, by appropriate legislation, the provisions of this article.

As revolutionary as this amendment was, many Radical Republicans— who deeply opposed tyranny of all kinds—felt that it didn't sufficiently protect human beings from oppression. When the Fourteenth Amendment was first introduced to the House of Representatives on June 13, 1866, that body's Republican floor leader, Radical Republican Thaddeus Stevens, expressed reluctance at endorsing "so imperfect a proposition." Like many of his colleagues, he

**Radical Republican
Thaddeus Stevens**
(April 4, 1792–August 11, 1868)

thought the Reconstruction Amendments didn't go far enough in solidifying the rights of African Americans and poor Whites and in punishing the southern Democrats and Ku Klux Klansmen who still held sympathy with the vanquished Confederacy. In the end, however, Stevens urged his colleagues to endorse the bill on the grounds that he and they both "live among men and not among angels; among men as intelligent, as determined and as independent as myself, who, not agreeing with me, do not choose to yield up their opinions to mine. Mutual concessions is our only resort, or mutual hostilities."*[1]

---

*Here's the part of Stevens's speech that precedes the quote above:

> In my youth, in my manhood, in my old age, I had fondly dreamed that when any fortunate chance should have broken up for awhile the foundation of our institutions, and released us from obligations the most tyrannical that ever man imposed in the name of freedom, that the intelligent, pure and just men of this Republic, true to their professions and their consciences, would have so remodeled all our institutions as to have freed them from every vestige of human oppression, of inequality of rights, of the recognized degradation of the poor, and the superior caste of the rich.

> This bright dream has vanished "like the baseless fabric of a vision."

> Do you inquire why, holding these views and possessing some will of my own, I accept so imperfect a proposition?

Given all this context and history, a reasonable person would probably conclude that the Reconstruction Amendments—particularly the Fourteenth Amendment—were designed to grant rights exclusively to human beings. There's no discussion at all of corporations in the Amendment itself, and nobody in that day would have dared propose that the Civil War was fought to "free" corporations. (If anything, many residents of the southern states to this day believe that it was corporate power in New England—particularly the bankers and the commodity traders in New York—who triggered the Civil War by asserting their economic power to bring the White plantation owners and agricultural commodity traders in the South into servitude to the northern banks.) And when it comes to the intentions of the authors of the Amendment, that reasonable person would be right.

But here's the problem: the particular choice of words used in the Fourteenth Amendment created a loophole that corporations continue to exploit to this day—to our collective detriment as a democracy.

American constitutional law is, in many ways, grounded in British common law, which goes back to the sixth century. In common law there are two types of "persons": "natural persons," like you and me, and "artificial persons," which include governments, churches, and corporations. The creation of a category for governments, churches (and other nonprofits), and for-profit corporations was necessary so that the law (and taxes) could reach them.

Without some sort of category, they couldn't enter into contracts, be held accountable to the law, or be assessed and made to pay taxes, among other things. Knowing this, most laws having to do with just human beings used the phrase "natural persons"; and those laws that were designed to reach only governments, churches, or corporations would specify them or their type by name or refer to "artificial persons."

The Fourteenth Amendment, however, does not draw any distinction between "natural" and "artificial" personhood, and twenty years later corporate lawyers would seize upon that to turn corporations from mere ways of organizing a business into the transnational superpersons that they are today.

Of course, such sweeping ramifications never occurred to Thaddeus Stevens or his colleagues who drafted the Fourteenth Amendment. The clause that grants all "persons" equal protection under the law, in context, seems to apply pretty clearly only to human beings "born or naturalized" in the United States of America.

But fate and time and the conspiracies of great wealth and power often have a way of turning common sense and logic on its head, as you'll learn in just a few pages.

What Is a "Person"?

In today's America when a new human is born, the child is given a Social Security number and is instantly protected by the full weight and power of the U.S. Constitution and the Bill of Rights. Those rights, which have been fought for and paid for with the blood of our young men and women in uniform, grace the child from the moment of birth.

This is the way we designed it; it's how we all agreed it should be. Humans are born with human rights. Those human rights are *inherent*—part of the natural order to deists like Thomas Jefferson, given to us by God in the minds of the more religious of the Founders. And those rights are not to be lightly infringed upon by government in any way. They're explicitly protected by the Constitution *from* the government. We are, after all, fragile living things that can be suppressed and abused by the powerful.

For example, in 2001 then–state senator Barack Obama said in a radio interview on Chicago's WBEZ,[2] speaking of the charges that the Supreme Court under Chief Justice Earl Warren had been a radical or activist court, pointed out that the Constitution was designed not to give us rights but to prevent government from taking our rights. He noted:

> To that extent, as radical as I think people try to characterize the Warren Court, it wasn't that radical. It didn't break free from the essential constraints that were placed by the Founding Fathers in the Constitution, at least as it's been interpreted, and the Warren Court interpreted in the same way, that generally *the Constitution is a charter of negative liberties.* [It] says what the states *can't* do to you. [It] says what the federal government *can't* do to you, but doesn't say what the federal government or state government must do on your behalf. [Italics added.]

His 2001 reference to the Constitution as a "charter of negative liberties" was loudly criticized by his political opponents in 2008 when the tape of the radio interview was publicized, but as a constitutional law professor and scholar he was right. The Constitution doesn't give us rights: it restrains government from infringing on rights we acquire at birth by virtue of being human beings, "natural rights" that are held by "natural persons." The Constitution holds back (restraining government) rather than gives forward (granting rights to people).

While Thomas Jefferson felt it important to add a Bill of Rights to the Constitution (he wrote its first outline in a letter to James Madison), Alexander Hamilton spoke and wrote strongly against it, for exactly the same reasons President Obama had mentioned.

"The truth is, after all the declamations we have heard, that the Constitution is itself, in every rational sense, and to every useful purpose, A BILL OF RIGHTS"[3] (capitals Hamilton's), he wrote in the Federalist Papers (No. 84). His concern was that if there were a few rights specified in the Constitution, future generations may forget that those are just examples and that the Constitution itself protects *all* human rights.

Those few examples may become the only rights to survive into future times, an outcome the reverse of the intention of the Framers of the Constitution. Instead of defining a few rights, Hamilton wrote in Federalist No. 84, "Here, in strictness, the people surrender nothing, and as they retain everything, they have no need of particular reservations."

Hamilton pointed out that England needed a Bill of Rights because the king had absolute power, but in the United States that power was reserved to the people themselves. Thus, he said, "I go further, and affirm that bills of rights, in the sense and in the extent in which they are contended for, are not only unnecessary in the proposed constitution, but would even be dangerous."

An example he gave, particularly relevant today in the light of the recent *Citizens United v. Federal Election Commission* Supreme Court case, was the freedom of the press written into the First Amendment. "What is the liberty of the press?" Hamilton demanded. "Who can give it any definition which would not leave the utmost latitude for evasion? I hold it to be impracticable"[4] to try to define it or any right narrowly in a Bill of Rights.

But Hamilton lost the day, Jefferson won, and we have a Bill of Rights built into our Constitution that, as Hamilton feared, has increasingly been used to limit, rather than expand, the range of human rights American citizens can claim. And because it's in our Constitution, the only way other than a Supreme Court decision to make explicit "new" rights (such as a right to health care) is through the process of amending that document.

And in American democracy, like most modern democracies, our system is set up so that it takes a lot of work to change the Constitution, making it very difficult to deny its protections to the humans it first protected against King George III and numerous other threats—internal and external—since then.

Similarly, when papers called articles of incorporation are submitted to state governments in America, another type of new "person" is brought forth into the nation. Just like a human, that new "person" gets a government-assigned number. (Instead of a Social Security number, it's called a federal employer identification number, or EIN.)

Thanks to a century and a half of truly bizarre Supreme Court decisions (never bills passed by the elected legislature), however, today's new corporate "person" is instantly endowed with many of the rights and protections of human beings.

The modern corporation is neither male nor female, doesn't breathe or eat, can't be enslaved, can't give birth, can live forever, doesn't fear prison, and can't be executed if found guilty of misdoings. It can cut off parts of itself and turn them into new "persons," can change its identity in a day, and can have simultaneous residences in many different nations. It is not a human but a creation of humans. Nonetheless, today a corporation gets many of the constitutional protections America's Founders gave humans in the Bill of Rights to protect them against governments or other potential oppressors:

- Free speech, including freedom to influence legislation

- Protection from searches, as if their belongings were intensely personal

- Fifth Amendment protections against double jeopardy and self-incrimination, even when a clear crime has been committed

- The shield of the nation's due process and anti-discrimination laws

- The benefit of the constitutional amendments that freed the slaves and gave them equal protection under the law

Even more, although they now have many of the same "rights" as you and I—and a few more—they don't have the same fragilities or responsibilities, under both the law and the realities of biology.

What most people don't realize is that this is a fairly recent agreement, a new cultural story, and it hasn't always been this way. Traditional English, Dutch, French, and Spanish law didn't say that corporations are people. The U.S. Constitution wasn't written with that idea; corporations aren't mentioned anywhere in the document or its Amendments. For America's first century, courts all the way up to the Supreme Court repeatedly said, "No, corporations do not have the same rights as humans."

In fact, the Founders were quite clear (as you can see from Hamilton's debate earlier) that *only humans* inherently have *rights*. Every other institution created by humans—from governments to churches to corporations—has only *privileges*, explicitly granted by government on behalf of the people with the rights.

In the Founders' and the Framers' views, rights are human and inherent; privileges are granted conditionally. For example, deducting the cost of a business lunch from corporate income taxes is not a right; it's a privilege granted by laws that create and regulate the corporate form. Not being imprisoned without due process of law is a right with which every human is born. Even the "right" to incorporate is actually a privilege, since at its core it's simply a petition for a specific set of rules to do business by, which limits liabilities and changes tax consequences of certain activities.

But the Supreme Court has gradually—since the first decade of the nineteenth century in the *Trustees of Dartmouth College v. Woodward* case— been granting corporations *privileges* that looked more and more like *rights*. And, particularly since 1886, the Bill of Rights has been explicitly applied to corporations.

Perhaps most astoundingly, no branch of the U.S. government ever formally enacted corporate personhood "rights":

- The public never voted on it.

- It was never enacted into law by any legislature.

- It was never even stated by a decision after arguments before the Supreme Court.

This last point will raise some eyebrows because for one hundred years people have believed that the 1886 case *Santa Clara County v. Southern Pacific Railroad* did in fact conclude that "corporations are persons." But this book will show that the Court never stated this: it was added by the court reporter who wrote the introduction to the decision, a commentary called a headnote. And as any law student knows, headnotes have no legal standing.

It's fashionable in America right now—as it was during the Gilded Age—to equate unrestrained, "free market" laissez faire capitalism with democracy, even going so far as to suggest that democracy can't exist without unrestrained capitalism.

China, Singapore, and other free-market capitalist dictatorships give the lie to this notion: their markets are among the most robust and vibrant in the world—and in Singapore's case has been so for more than half a century. And this myth, promulgated by "free market" think tanks funded by big corporations and individuals who got rich using the corporate form, even goes so far as to suggest that democratic socialism—a regulated marketplace, a strong social safety net, and democratic institutions of governance—will inevitably lead to the loss of "freedom." Democratic socialist states like Sweden, Norway, and Denmark give the obvious lie to that, although most Americans are blissfully ignorant of it.

But far more interesting is the inverse: Is it possible that what's *really* incompatible with democracy isn't socialism or a regulated marketplace but, instead, is the ultimate manifestation of corporate power—*corporate personhood?* And, if so—a case I'll build in this book—how do We the People take back our democratic institutions like the Congress from their current corporate masters?

Corporations Take Over

The 20th century has been characterised by three developments of great political importance. The growth of democracy; the growth of corporate power; and the growth of corporate propaganda as a means of protecting corporate power against democracy.

—Alex Carey (1922–1988), Australian author and psychologist

CHAPTER 1

The Deciding Moment?

The first thing to understand is the difference between the natural person and the fictitious person called a corporation. They differ in the purpose for which they are created, in the strength which they possess, and in the restraints under which they act.

Man is the handiwork of God and was placed upon earth to carry out a Divine purpose; the corporation is the handiwork of man and created to carry out a money-making policy.

There is comparatively little difference in the strength of men; a corporation may be one hundred, one thousand, or even one million times stronger than the average man. Man acts under the restraints of conscience, and is influenced also by a belief in a future life. A corporation has no soul and cares nothing about the hereafter....

—William Jennings Bryan, in his address to the
Ohio 1912 Constitutional Convention

Part of the American Revolution was about to be lost a century after it had been fought. At the time probably very few of the people involved realized that what they were about to witness could be a counterrevolution that would change life in the United States and, ultimately, the world over the course of the following century.

In 1886 the Supreme Court met in the U.S. Capitol building, in what is now called the Old Senate Chamber. It was May, and while the northeastern states were slowly recovering from the most devastating ice storm of the century just three months earlier, Washington, D.C., was warm and in bloom.

In the Supreme Court's chamber, a gilt eagle stretched its 6-foot wingspan over the head of Chief Justice Morrison Remick Waite as he glared down

**Supreme Court Chief Justice
Morrison Remick Waite**
(November 29, 1816–
March 23, 1888)

at the attorneys for the Southern Pacific Railroad and the county of Santa Clara, California. Waite was about to pronounce judgment in a case that had been argued over a year earlier, at the end of January 1885.

The chief justice had a square head with a wide slash of a mouth over a broomlike shock of bristly graying beard that shot out in every direction. A graduate of Yale University and formerly a lawyer out of Toledo, Ohio, Waite had specialized in defending railroads and large corporations.

In 1846 Waite had run for Congress as a Whig from Ohio but lost before being elected as a state representative in 1849. After serving a single term, he had gone back to litigation on behalf of the biggest and wealthiest clients he could find, this time joining the Geneva Arbitration case suing the British government for helping outfit the Confederate Army with the warship *Alabama*. He and his delegation won an astounding $15.5 million (close to $200 billion in today's dollars) for the United States in 1871, bringing him national attention in what was often referred to as the Alabama Claims case.

In 1874, when Supreme Court Chief Justice Salmon P. Chase died, President Ulysses S. Grant had real trouble selecting a replacement, in part because his administration was embroiled in a railroad bribery scandal. His first two choices withdrew, his third was so patently political that it was certain to be rejected by the Senate, and three others similarly failed to pass muster. On his seventh try, Grant nominated attorney Waite.

Waite had never before been a judge in any court, but he passed Senate confirmation, instantly becoming the most powerful judge in the most powerful court in the land. It was a position and a power he relished and promoted, even turning down the 1876 Republican nomination for president to stay on the Court and to serve as a member of the Yale [University] Corporation.

Standing before Waite and the other justices of the Supreme Court that spring day were three attorneys each for the railroad and the county.

The chief legal adviser for the Southern Pacific Railroad was S. W. Sanderson, a former judge. He was a huge, aristocratic bear of a man, more than 6 feet tall, with neatly combed gray hair and an elegantly trimmed white goatee. For more than two decades, Sanderson had made himself rich, litigating for the nation's largest railroads. Artist Thomas Hill included a portentous and dignified Sanderson in his famous painting *The Last Spike* about the 1869 transcontinental meeting of the rail lines of the Union Pacific and Central Pacific railroads at Promontory Summit, Utah.

The lead lawyer for Santa Clara County was Delphin M. Delmas, a Democrat who later went into politics and by 1904 was known as "the Silver-tongued Orator of the West" when he was elected a delegate from California to the Democratic National Convention. Whereas Waite and Sanderson had spent their lives serving the richest men in America, Delmas had always worked on behalf of local California governments and, later, as a criminal defense attorney. For example, he passionately and single-handedly argued pro bono before the California legislature for a law to protect the nation's last remaining redwood forests.

Fiercely defensive about "the rights of natural persons," Delmas was a fastidious, unimposing man, known to wear "a frock coat, gray-striped trousers,

Attorney Delphin M. Delmas
(April 14, 1844– August 1, 1928)

a wing collar and an Ascot tie," whose "voice thrummed with emotion," and he was nationally known as the master dramatist of America's courtrooms. He had a substantial nose and a broad forehead only slightly covered in its center with a wispy bit of thinning hair. In the courtroom he was a brilliant lawyer, as the nation would learn in 1908 when he successfully defended Harry K. Thaw for murder in what was the most sensational case of the first half of the century, later made into the 1955 movie *The Girl in the Red Velvet Swing,* starring Ray Milland and Joan Collins (Delmas was played by Luther Adler).

The case about to be decided in the Old Senate Chamber before Justice Waite's Supreme Court was about the way Santa Clara County had been taxing the land and rights-of-way owned by the Southern Pacific Railroad. Claiming the taxation was improper, the railroad had refused for six years to pay any taxes levied by Santa Clara County, and the case had ended up before the Supreme Court, with Delmas and Sanderson making the main arguments.

Although the case on its face was a simple tax matter, having nothing to do with due process or human rights or corporate personhood, the attorneys for the railroad nonetheless used much of their argument time to press the issue that the railroad corporation was, in fact, a "person" and should be entitled to the same right of equal protection under the law that was granted to former slaves by the Fourteenth Amendment.

The Mystery of 1886 and Chief Justice Waite

In the decade leading up to this May day in 1886, the railroads had lost every Supreme Court case that they had brought seeking Fourteenth Amendment rights. I've searched dozens of histories of the time, representing a wide variety of viewpoints and opinions, but only two have made a serious attempt to answer the question of what happened that fateful day—and their theories clash.

No laws were passed by Congress granting corporations the same treatment under the Constitution as living, breathing human beings, and none has been passed since then. It was not a concept drawn from older English law. No court decisions, state or federal, held that corporations were or should be considered the same as *natural* persons instead of *artificial* persons. The Supreme Court did not rule, in this or any other case, on the issue of corporate personhood.

In fact, to this day there has been no Supreme Court ruling that explicitly explains why a corporation—with its ability to continue operating forever, its being merely a legal agreement that can't be put in jail and doesn't need fresh water to drink or clean air to breathe—should be granted the same constitutional rights our Founders fought for, died for, and granted to the very mortal human beings who are citizens of the United States, to protect them against the perils of imprisonment and suppression they had experienced under a despot king.

But something happened in 1886, even though nobody to this day knows exactly what or why.

That year Sanderson decided to again defy a government agency that was trying to regulate his railroad's activity. This time he went after Santa Clara County, California. His claim, in part, was that because a railroad corporation was a "person" under the Constitution, local governments couldn't discriminate against it by having different laws and taxes in different places. It was a variation on the Fourteenth Amendment argument made by civil rights advocates in the 1960s that if a White man could sit at a Woolworth's lunch counter, a Black man should receive the same privilege. In 1885 the case came before the Supreme Court.

In arguments before the Court in January 1885, Sanderson asserted that corporate persons should be treated the same as natural (or human) persons. He said, "I believe that the clause [of the Fourteenth Amendment] in relation to equal protection means the same thing as the plain and simple yet sublime words found in our Declaration of Independence, 'all men are created equal.' Not equal in physical or mental power, not equal in fortune or social position, but equal before the law."[1]

Sanderson's fellow lawyer for the railroads, George F. Edmunds, added his opinion that the Fourteenth Amendment leveled the field between artificial persons (corporations) and natural persons (humans) by a "broad and catholic provision for universal security, resting upon citizenship as it regarded political rights, and resting upon humanity as it regarded private rights."

But that wasn't actually what the case was about—that was just a minor point. The county was suing the railroad for back taxes, and the railroad refused to pay, claiming six different defenses. The specifics are not important because the central concern is whether the Court ruled on the Fourteenth Amendment issue. As will be shown below, the Supreme Court's decision clearly says it did not. But to put the railroad's complaint in perspective, consider this:

- On property with a $30 million mortgage, the railroad was refusing to pay taxes of about $30,000. (That's like having a $10,000 car and refusing to pay a $10 tax on it—and taking the case to the Supreme Court.)

- One of the railroad's defenses was that when the state assessed the value of the railroad's property, it accidentally included the value of the fences along the right-of-way. The county, not the state, should have assessed the fences, so the tax being paid in Santa Clara County was different—unequal—from the tax paid in other counties that did their own assessment instead of using the state's. To make their point (and to make the case a bigger deal), the railroad withheld *all* its taxes from the county.

All the tax was still due to Santa Clara County; the railroad didn't dispute that. But it said that the wrong assessor assessed the fences—a tiny fraction of the whole amount—so it refused to pay any of the tax and fought it all the way to the U.S. Supreme Court.

And as it happens, the Supreme Court of the United States (SCOTUS) agreed: "the entire assessment is a nullity, upon the ground that the state board of equalization included...property [the fences] which it was without jurisdiction to assess for taxation..."

The Court rejected the county's appeal, and that was the end of it. Except for one thing. One of the railroad's six defenses involved the Fourteenth Amendment. As it happens, because the case was decided based on the fence issue, the railroad didn't need those extra defenses, and the Court never ruled or commented in its ultimate decision on any of them. But one of them—related to the Fourteenth Amendment—still crept into the written record, even though the Court specifically did not rule on it.

Here's how the matter unfolded. First, the railroad's defense.

The Treatment That the Railroad Claimed Was Unfair

In the Fourteenth Amendment part of its defense, the railroad said:

> That the provisions of the constitution and laws of California...*are in violation of the Fourteenth Amendment of the Constitution,* in so far as they require the assessment of their property at its full money value, without making deduction, as in the case of railroads [that are only] operated in one county, and of other corporations [that operate in only one county], and of natural persons [who can physically reside in only one county], for the value of the mortgages... [Italics added.]

The italic portions say, in essence, "The state is taxing us in a different way from how it taxes other corporations and real live human beings. That's not fair, and it violates our corporate right to equal protection that is the same as all other 'persons' under the tax laws."

The implication, of course, is that the state has no right to decide that corporations get different tax rates than humans. And the railroad was using the former slaves' equal protection clause (the Fourteenth Amendment) as its shield.

The Legal Difference between Artificial and Natural Persons

In the Supreme Court at that time, cases were typically decided a year after arguments were presented, allowing the justices time to research and prepare their written decisions. So it happened that on January 26, 1885 (a year before the 1886 decision was handed down), Delphin M. Delmas, the attorney for Santa Clara County, made his case before the Supreme Court. I searched for the better part of a year for copies of the arguments made in the case—the Supreme Court kept no notes—and finally discovered, in an antiquarian book shop in San Francisco, a copy of *Speeches and Addresses* by D. M. Delmas.[2] It was a hardbound collection of Delmas's speeches and his *Santa Clara County* arguments before the Supreme Court, which he had personally paid to self-publish in 1901. It's incredibly rare to have such a time-machine look back into the past, and—even more exciting—Delmas's arguments were as brilliant and persuasive as any of the words that Erle Stanley Gardner ever put into the mouth of Perry Mason.

"The defendant claims [that the state's taxation policy]...violates that portion of the Fourteenth Amendment which provides that no state shall deny to any person within its jurisdiction the equal protection of the laws," Delmas said, standing before the assembled justices while reading from the notes he would later self-publish. He added that such an argument, "if tenable, would place the organic law of California in a position ridiculous to the extreme."

Winding himself up into full-throated outrage, Delmas rebuked the railroad's lawyers with a pure and honest fury:

> The shield behind which [the Southern Pacific Railroad] attacks the Constitution and laws of California is the Fourteenth Amendment. It argues that the amendment guarantees to every person within the jurisdiction of the State the equal protection of the laws; that a corporation is a person; that, therefore, it must receive the same protection as that accorded to all other persons in like circumstances....

> To my mind, the fallacy, if I may be permitted so to term it, of the argument lies in the assumption that corporations are entitled to be governed by the laws that are applicable to natural persons. That, it is said, results from the fact that corporations are [artificial] persons, and that the last clause of the Fourteenth Amendment refers to all persons without distinction.

This was the crux of the argument that the railroad had been putting forth and on which, in the Ninth Circuit Court in California, Judge Stephen J. Field had kept ruling. Because the Fourteenth Amendment says no "person" can be denied equal protection under the law, and corporations had been considered a type of person (albeit an artificial person) for several hundred years under British common law, the railroad was now trying to get that recognition under American constitutional law.

Delmas said: "The defendant has been at pains to show that corporations are persons, and that being such they are entitled to the protection of the Fourteenth Amendment....The question is, Does that amendment place corporations on a footing of equality with individuals?"

He then quoted from the bible of legal scholars—the book that the Framers of our Constitution had frequently cited and referenced in their deliberations in 1787 in Philadelphia—Sir William Blackstone's 1765 *Commentaries on the Laws of England*: "Blackstone says, 'Persons are divided by the law into either natural persons or artificial. Natural persons are such as the God of nature formed us; artificial are such as are created and devised by human laws for the purposes of society and government, which are called corporations or bodies politic.'"[3]

Delmas then moved from quoting the core authority on law to pleading common sense. If a corporation was a "person" legally, why couldn't it make out a will or get married, for example?

> This definition suggests at once that it would seem unnecessary to dwell upon, that though a corporation is a person, it is not the same kind of person as a human being, and need not of necessity—nay, in the very nature of things, cannot—enjoy all the rights of such or be governed by the same laws. When the law says, "Any person being of sound mind and of the age of discretion may make a will," or "any person having arrived at the age of majority may marry," I presume the most ardent advocate of equality of protection would hardly contend that corporations must enjoy the right of testamentary disposition or of contracting matrimony.

It's about real human people, Delmas said. Any idiot who looked at the history or purpose of the Fourteenth Amendment could figure that out: "The whole history of the Fourteenth Amendment demonstrates beyond dispute that its whole scope and object was to establish equality between men—an attainable result—and not to establish equality between natural and artificial beings—an impossible result."

As a good liberal California Democrat (as distinct from the southern Democrats), Delmas was furious. He'd spent much of his life fighting for the little guy, agreed strongly with the Radical Republicans (who had mostly become Democrats a decade earlier) about civil rights, and knew—as did anybody who read the newspapers of that era—the history of the Fourteenth Amendment.

The railroad lawyer Sanderson had before made a claim that a "secret committee" of Congress that helped write the Fourteenth Amendment had *meant* for it to equalize corporate persons and human persons. Delmas, if his performance before the Supreme Court was consistent with his later well-documented performances in criminal courtrooms, would have been trembling in righteous indignation as he said that the Fourteenth Amendment "is as broad as humanity itself":

> Wherever man is found within the confines of this Union, whatever his race, religion, or color, be he Caucasian, African, or Mongolian, be he Christian, infidel, or idolater, be he white, black, or copper-colored, he may take shelter under this great law as under a shield against individual oppression in any form, individual injustice in any shape. It is a protection to all men because they are men, members of the same great family, children of the same omnipotent Creator.
>
> In its comprehensive words I find written by the hand of a nation of sixty millions in the firmament of imperishable law the sentiment uttered more than a hundred years ago by the philosopher of Geneva, and re-echoed in this country by the authors of the Declaration of the Thirteen Colonies: Proclaim to the world the equality of man.

Speaking of the "object of the Fourteenth Amendment," Delmas said it straight out:

> Its mission was to raise the humble, the down-trodden, and the oppressed to the level of the most exalted upon the broad plain of humanity—to make man the equal of man; but not to make the creature of the State—the bodiless, soulless, and mystic creature called a corporation—the equal of the creature of God....

Therefore, I venture to repeat that the Fourteenth Amendment does not command equality between human beings and corporations...

In closing his argument, Delmas had to add a punctuation mark. This could be, he suggested, one of the most important Supreme Court cases in the history of the United States because if corporations were given the powerful cudgel of human rights secured by the Bill of Rights, their ability to amass wealth and power could lead to death, war, and the impoverishment of actual human beings on a massive scale.

"I have now done," he said. "Yet I cannot but think that the controversy now debated before your Honors is one of no ordinary importance."

A year and five months passed while the Supreme Court debated the issues in private. And then came the afternoon of May 10, 1886, the fateful moment for the fateful words of the Court, upon which hung much of the future of the United States and, later, much of the world.

Chief Justice Waite Rewrites the Constitution (or Does He?)

According to the record left to us, here's what seems to have happened. For reasons that were never recorded, moments before the Supreme Court was to render its decision in the now-infamous *Santa Clara County v. Southern Pacific Railroad* case, Chief Justice Waite turned his attention to Delmas and the other attorneys present.

As railroad attorney Sanderson and his two colleagues watched, Waite told Delmas and his two colleagues, "The court does not wish to hear argument on the question whether the provision in the Fourteenth Amendment to the Constitution, which forbids a state to deny to any person within its jurisdiction the equal protection of the laws, applies to these corporations. We are of the opinion that it does." He then turned to Justice John M. Harlan, who delivered the Court's opinion.

In the written record of the case, the court reporter noted, "The defendant corporations are persons within the intent of the clause in section 1 of the Fourteenth Amendment to the Constitution of the United States, which forbids a State to deny to any person within its jurisdiction the equal protection of the laws."

This written statement, that corporations were persons rather than artificial persons, with an equal footing under the Bill of Rights as humans, was not a formal ruling of the court but was reportedly a simple statement by its chief justice, recorded by the court reporter.

There was no Supreme Court decision to the effect that corporations are equal to natural persons and not artificial persons. There were no opinions issued to that effect and therefore no dissenting opinions on this immensely important constitutional issue.

The written record, as excerpted above, simply assumed corporate personhood without any explanation why. The only explanation provided was the court reporter's reference to something he says Waite said, which essentially says, "that's just our opinion" without providing legal argument.

In these two sentences (according to the conventional wisdom), Waite weakened the kind of democratic republic the original authors of the Constitution had envisioned, and he set the stage for the future worldwide damage of our environmental, governmental, and cultural commons. The plutocracy that had arisen with the East India Company in 1600 and had been fought back by America's Founders had gained a tool that was to allow it, in the coming decades, to once again gain control of most of North America and then the world.

Ironically, of the 307 Fourteenth Amendment cases brought before the Supreme Court in the years between Waite's proclamation and 1910, only 19 dealt with African Americans: 288 were suits brought by corporations seeking the rights of natural persons.

Supreme Court Justice Hugo Black pointed out fifty years later, "I do not believe the word 'person' in the Fourteenth Amendment includes corporations....Neither the history nor the language of the Fourteenth Amendment justifies the belief that corporations are included within its protection."[4]

Sixty years later Supreme Court Justice William O. Douglas made the same point, writing, "There was no history, logic or reason given to support that view [that corporations are legally 'persons']."[5]

There was no change in legislation, and then-president Grover Cleveland had not issued a proclamation that corporations should be considered the same as natural persons. To the contrary President Cleveland, the only Democrat to serve as president during the Robber Baron Era, in his December 3, 1888, State of the Union address, said,

> The gulf between employers and the employed is constantly widening, and
> classes are rapidly forming, one comprising the very rich and powerful, while

in another are found the toiling poor. As we view the achievements of aggregated capital, we discover the existence of trusts, combinations, and monopolies, while the citizen is struggling far in the rear or is trampled to death beneath an iron heel. Corporations, which should be the carefully restrained creatures of the law and the servants of the people, are fast becoming the people's masters.[6]

The U.S. Constitution does not even contain the word *corporation* and has never been amended to contain it because the Founders wanted corporations to be regulated as close to home as possible, by the states, so they could be kept on a short leash—presumably so nothing like the East India Company would ever again arise to threaten the entrepreneurs of America.

But as a result of this case, for the past one hundred–plus years corporate lawyers and politicians have claimed that Chief Justice Waite turned the law on its side and reinvented America's social hierarchy.

"But wait a minute," many legal scholars have said over the years. Why would Waite say, before arguments about corporations being persons, that the court had already decided the issue—and then allow Delmas and Sanderson to argue the point anyway? Alternatively, why would he say such a thing after arguments had already been made? By all accounts Waite was a rational and capable justice, so it wouldn't make sense that he would do either of those things.

Several theories have been advanced about what really happened. But first, let's look at what the Supreme Court decision actually said in the 1886 *Santa Clara* case.

What the Court Actually Said about Personhood

The Supreme Court generally tries to stay out of a fight. If a case can be thrown out or decided on simpler grounds, there's no need to complicate things by issuing a new decision. And in this case, the Court's decision specifically mentioned this: "These questions [regarding the constitutional amendment] *belong to a class which this court should not decide* unless their determination is essential to the disposal of the case..." (Italics added.)

It continued, saying that the question of "unless it is essential to the case" depended on how strong the other defenses were. "Whether the present cases require a decision of them depends upon the soundness of another proposition, upon which the court...in view of its conclusions upon other issues, did not deem it necessary to pass." In other words, because of other issues (who should assess the fences), the Court wasn't even going to consider whether to rule on the Fourteenth Amendment issue of corporate personhood.

The decision then identifies the fence issue and concludes that there's nothing left to decide because they're basing their ruling entirely on California law and the California Constitution. "If these positions are tenable, there will be no occasion to consider the grave questions of constitutional law upon which the case was determined...as the judgment can be sustained upon this ground, it is not necessary to consider any other questions raised by the pleadings..." So what actually happened? Why have people said, for all these years, that in 1886 the Waite Court in the *Santa Clara* case decided that corporations were persons under the Fourteenth Amendment? It turns out that the Court said no such thing, and it can't be found in the ruling.

It Was in the Headnote!

William Rehnquist, then the chief justice of the U.S. Supreme Court, was seriously irritated. It was April 1978, and the previous November a case had been argued before the Court in which the First National Bank of Boston asserted that, because it was a corporate "person," it had First Amendment free-speech rights with regard to political speech, that money was the same as speech (since a corporation doesn't have a mouth but it does have a checking account), and that therefore the laws that the good citizens of Massachusetts had passed to prevent corporations from throwing money around in political or advocacy campaigns should be thrown out.

Rehnquist and his clerks knew what every graduate of an American law school knew—that in 1886 the U.S. Supreme Court had ruled that the Fourteenth Amendment gave corporations the same, or very nearly the same, access to the Bill of Rights as human beings had.

The Court's majority had written their opinion on *First National Bank of Boston v. Bellotti,* delivered by Justice Lewis F. Powell and concurred to by Justices Warren Burger, Potter Stewart, Harry Blackmun, and John Paul Stevens. It opened with a quick summary of the issues:[7]

> Appellants, national banking associations and business corporations, wanted to spend money to publicize their views opposing a referendum proposal to amend the Massachusetts Constitution to authorize the legislature to enact a graduated personal income tax.

> They brought this action challenging the constitutionality of a Massachusetts criminal statute that prohibited them and other specified business corporations from making contributions or expenditures "for the purpose of...influencing or affecting the vote on any question submitted to the voters, other than one materially affecting any of the property, business or assets of the corporation.

The majority opinion then cut right to the chase: "The portion of the Massachusetts statute at issue violates the First Amendment as made applicable to the States by the Fourteenth."

Rehnquist, however, was both a curmudgeon and a conservative. In both cases, he believed that the protections from government power offered by the Bill of Rights should extend to only humans (particularly white humans; he had made much of his early career as a Republican partisan in Arizona, challenging the voting status of Blacks and Latinos at the polls from 1958 to 1964.)[8]

Thus, when the bank argued before the Court—and five Justices agreed with it—that the Massachusetts law in question "violates the First Amendment, the Due Process and Equal Protection Clauses of the Fourteenth Amendment," Rehnquist was offended, and his tone showed through in his choice of language for his solitary dissent, so provocative that the other dissenting justices did not even join in with it.

He started out by directly challenging his own understanding of *Santa Clara*:

> This Court decided at an early date, with neither argument nor discussion, that a business corporation is a "person" entitled to the protection of the Equal Protection Clause of the Fourteenth Amendment. *Santa Clara County v. Southern Pacific R. Co.,* (1886). Likewise, it soon became accepted that the property of a corporation was protected under the Due Process Clause of that same Amendment. *See, e.g., Smyth v. Ames,* (1898).

But that decision—as Rehnquist noted, made "with neither argument nor discussion" but merely proclaimed by the chief justice from the bench—was wrong, Rehnquist believed. "Early in our history [in 1819]," he wrote,

> Mr. Chief Justice Marshall described the status of a corporation in the eyes of federal law: "A corporation is an artificial being, invisible, intangible, and existing only in contemplation of law. Being the mere creature of law, it possesses only those properties which the charter of creation confers upon it, either expressly, or as incidental to its very existence. These are such as are supposed best calculated to effect the object for which it was created."

Restating that concept in his own words, Rehnquist continued in his dissent:

> It might reasonably be concluded that those properties, so beneficial in the economic sphere, pose special dangers in the political sphere.
>
> Furthermore, it might be argued that liberties of political expression are not at all necessary to effectuate the purposes for which States permit commercial corporations to exist. So long as the Judicial Branches of the State and Federal Governments remain open to protect the corporation's interest in its property, it has no need, though it may have the desire, to petition the political branches for similar protection. Indeed, the States might reasonably fear that the corporation would use its economic power to obtain further benefits beyond those already bestowed. I would think that any particular form of organization upon which the State confers special privileges or immunities different from those of natural persons would be subject to like regulation, whether the organization is a labor union, a partnership, a trade association, or a corporation....
>
> The free flow of information is in no way diminished by the Commonwealth's decision to permit the operation of business corporations with limited rights of political expression. All natural persons, who owe their existence to a higher sovereign than the Commonwealth, remain as free as before to engage in political activity.

But Rehnquist had lost. He quoted a fellow justice, Byron White, who also dissented from the ruling, saying,

> The interest of Massachusetts and the many other States which have restricted corporate political activity...is not one of equalizing the resources of opposing candidates or opposing positions, but rather of preventing institutions which have been permitted to amass wealth as a result of special advantages extended by the State for certain economic purposes from using that wealth to acquire an unfair advantage in the political process....

And then he turned to other matters. There were other cases to decide. The bank had won.

How We All Got It Wrong

Chief Justice Rehnquist was laboring under a misconception that was quite common over the past hundred years. In 2003, when the first edition of this book came out, I was invited to address about two hundred students and faculty at a New England law school. I asked for a show of hands "among those of you who know that in 1886 in the *Santa Clara County versus Southern Pacific Railroad* case, the U.S. Supreme Court declared that corporations were entitled to constitutional rights?" Every hand in the room went up. (And then they got an earful.)

When I first began research for this book, I read a lot of histories of America and commentaries on corporate power. Many referenced this 1886 case, and all said that the Supreme Court ruled in that case that corporations should get the same protections under the Constitution as do human beings.

In 1993 Richard L. Grossman and Frank T. Adams wrote, in *Taking Care of Business:*[9]

> Another blow to citizen constitutional authority came in 1886. The Supreme Court ruled in *Santa Clara County v. Southern Pacific Railroad* that a private corporation was a natural person under the U.S. Constitution, sheltered by the Bill of Rights and the 14th Amendment.

> "There was no history, logic or reason given to support that view," Supreme Court Justice William O. Douglas was to write sixty years later.

> But the Supreme Court had spoken. Using the 14th Amendment, which had been added to the Constitution to protect freed slaves, the justices struck down hundreds more local, state and federal laws enacted to protect people from corporate harms. The high court ruled that elected legislators had been taking corporate property "without due process of law."

David C. Korten, a dear friend, one of the smartest guys on the planet on these topics, and the author of the groundbreaking book *When Corporations Rule the World*, wrote in 1997, "The idea that corporations should enjoy the rights of flesh and blood persons—including the right of free speech—grew out of a U.S. Supreme Court decision in 1886 that designated corporations as legal persons entitled to all the rights and protections afforded by the Bill of Rights of the U.S. Constitution."

Even www.encyclopedia.com still, in 2010, says:

> Q. When did the Supreme Court hold that corporations were persons?

> A. In 1886, the Supreme Court held that corporations were "persons" for the purposes of constitutional protections, such as equal protection.

When I began writing this book, I was operating on the assumption that Justices Douglas and Rehnquist were right and that all the various histories I'd read—histories all the way back to the 1930s—which asserted that the Court had ruled in favor of corporate personhood in the *Santa Clara* case were right. And as I was finalizing work on the first draft of this book, I decided I probably should read the *Santa Clara* case in its original version.

At the time (2002), I lived just a few blocks from the Vermont state capitol complex and knew that that state had an old and very, very far-reaching law library. When Vermont joined the Union in 1791, it was already an independent republic (this was true of only Vermont and Texas). It issued its own coins and had its own legislature and constitution. It had its own capitol building and its own Supreme Court—and its own Supreme Court law library.

So, on a snowy winter day, I bundled up and walked the six blocks from my home to the Vermont Supreme Court building, in search of the original version of the decision that transformed this nation.

In the warmth of the granite block building, librarian Paul Donovan found for me Volume 118 of *United States Reports: Cases Adjudged in the Supreme Court at October Term 1885 and October Term 1886,* published in New York in 1888 by Banks & Brothers Publishers and written by J. C. Bancroft Davis, the Supreme Court's reporter.

What I found in the book, however, were two pages of text that are missing from the copies of the decision I could find online on the Supreme Court's Web site, which is the official version. They were not part of the decision. They weren't even written by the Supreme Court justices but were a quick summary-of-the-case commentary by Davis. He wrote commentaries like these for each case, "adding value" to the published book, from which he earned a royalty.

And there it was, in the notes.

The very first sentence of Davis's note reads, "The defendant Corporations are persons within the intent of the clause in section 1 of the Fourteenth

Court reporter J. C. Bancroft Davis
(December 22, 1822–December 27, 1907)

Amendment to the Constitution of the United States, which forbids a State to deny to any person within its jurisdiction the equal protection of the laws."

That sentence was followed by three paragraphs of small print that summarized the California tax issues of the case. In fact, the notes by Davis, farther down, say,

> The main—and almost only—questions discussed by counsel in the elaborate arguments related to the constitutionality of the taxes. This court, in its opinion *passed by these questions* [italics added], and decided the cases on the questions whether under the constitution and laws of California, the fences on the line of the railroads should have been valued and assessed, if at all, by the local officers, or by the State Board of Equalization...

In other words, the first sentence of "The defendant Corporations are persons..." has nothing to do with the case and wasn't the issue on which the Supreme Court decided.

Two paragraphs later, perhaps in an attempt to explain why he had started his notes with that emphatic statement, Davis remarks:

> One of the points made and discussed at length in the brief of counsel for defendants in error was that "Corporations are persons within the meaning of the Fourteenth Amendment to the Constitution of the United States." Before argument Mr. Chief Justice Waite said: "The court does not wish to hear argument on the question whether the provision in the Fourteenth Amendment to the Constitution, which forbids a State to deny to any person within its jurisdiction the equal protection of the laws, applies to these corporations. We are all of the opinion that it does."

A half-page later, the notes ended and the actual decision, delivered by Justice Harlan, begins—which, as noted earlier, explicitly says that the Supreme Court is *not,* in this case, ruling on the constitutional question of corporate personhood under the Fourteenth Amendment or any other amendment.

I paid my 70 cents for copies of the pages from the fragile and cracking book and walked down the street to the office of attorney Jim Ritvo, a friend and wise counselor. I showed him what I had found and said, "What does this mean?"

He looked it over and said, "It's just a headnote."

"Headnote? What's a headnote?"

He smiled and leaned back in his chair. "Lawyers are trained to beware of headnotes because they're not written by judges or justices but are usually put in by a commentator or by the book's publisher."

"Are they legal? I mean, are they the law or anything like that?"

"Headnotes don't have the value of the formal decision," Jim said. "They're not law. They're just a comment by somebody who doesn't have the power to make or determine or decide law."

"In other words, this headnote by court reporter J. C. Bancroft Davis, which says that Waite said corporations are persons, is meaningless?"

Jim nodded his head. "Legally, yes. It's meaningless. It's not the decision or a part of the decision."

"But it contradicts what the decision itself says," I said, probably sounding a bit hysterical.

"In that case," Jim said, "you've found one of those mistakes that so often creep into law books."

"But other cases have been based on the headnote's commentary in this case."

"A mistake compounding a mistake," Jim said. "But ask a lawyer who knows this kind of law. It's not my area of specialty."

So I called Deborah L. Markowitz, Vermont's secretary of state and one very bright attorney, and described what I had found. She pointed out that even if the decision had been wrongly cited down through the years, it's now "part of our law, even if there was a mistake."

I said I understood that (it was dawning on me by then) and that I was hoping to have some remedies for that mistake in my book, but, just out of curiosity, "What is the legal status of headnotes?"

She said, "Headnotes are not precedential," confirming what Jim Ritvo had told me. They are not the precedent. They are not the law. They're just a comment with no legal status.

In fact, I later learned that in the years since *Santa Clara* the Supreme Court has twice explicitly ruled that headnotes in cases have no legal standing whatsoever. The first was *United States v. Detroit Timber and Lumber Company* (1905), and the second was *Burbank v. Ernst* (1914). In the *Detroit Timber* case—in the Court's official decision and not in its headnote—the majority of the justices concurred that headnotes are "simply the work of the reporter...prepared for the convenience of the profession in the examination of the records."

So how did it come about that court reporter J. C. Bancroft Davis wrote that corporations are persons in his headnote? And why have one hundred years of American—and now worldwide—law been based on it? Here are the main theories that have been advanced regarding what happened.

The Republican Conspiracy Theory That Empowered FDR

In the early 1930s, the stock market had collapsed and the world was beginning a long and dark slide into the Great Depression and eventually to World War II. Millions were out of work in the United States, and the questions on many people's minds were *Why did this happen?* and *Who is responsible?*

The teetering towers of wealth created by American industrialists during the late 1800s and the early 1900s were largely thought to have contributed to or caused the stock market crash and the ensuing Depression. In less than one hundred years, corporations had gone from being a legal fiction used to establish colleges and trading companies to standing as the single most powerful force in American politics.

Many working people felt that corporations had seized control of the country's political agenda, capturing senators, representatives, the Supreme Court, and even recent presidents in the magnetic force of their great wealth. Proof of this takeover could be found in the Supreme Court decisions in the years between 1908 and 1914, when the Court, often citing corporate personhood, struck down minimum-wage laws, workers' compensation laws, utility regulation, and child labor laws—every kind of law that a people might institute to protect its citizenry from abuses.

Unions and union members were the victims of violence from private corporate armies and had been declared "criminal conspiracies" by both business leaders and politicians. It seemed that corporations had staged a coup, seizing the lives of American workers—the majority of voters—as well as the elected officials who were supposed to represent them. And this was in direct contradiction of the spirit expressed by the Founders of this country.

It was in this milieu that an American history book first published in 1927, but largely ignored, suddenly became a hot topic. In *The Rise of American Civilization,* Columbia University history professor Charles A. Beard and women's suffragist Mary Beard suggested that the rise of corporations on the American landscape was the result of a grand conspiracy that reached from the boardrooms of the nation's railroads all the way to the Supreme Court.[10]

They fingered two Republicans: former senator (and railroad lawyer) Roscoe Conkling and former congressman (and railroad lawyer) John A. Bingham. The theory, in short, was that Conkling, when he was part of the Senate committee that wrote the Fourteenth Amendment back in 1868, had intentionally inserted the word *person* instead of the correct legal phrase *natural*

Congressman (and railroad lawyer)
John A. Bingham (January 21, 1815–
March 19, 1900)

Senator (and railroad lawyer)
Roscoe Conkling (October 30, 1829–
April 18, 1888)

person to describe who would get the protections of the amendment. Bingham similarly worked in the House of Representatives to get the language passed.

Once that time bomb was put into place, Conkling and Bingham left elective office to join in litigating on behalf of the railroads, with the goal of exploding their carefully worded amendment in the face of the Supreme Court.

Thus "Republican lawmakers," the Beards said, conspired in advance to give full human constitutional rights to corporate legal fictions. "By a few words skillfully chosen," they wrote, "every act of every state and local government which touched adversely the rights of [corporate] persons and property was made subject to review and liable to annulment by the Supreme Court at Washington."

This conspiracy theory was widely accepted because the supposed conspirators themselves had said, very publicly, "We did it!" Earlier, in an 1882 case pitting the railroads against San Mateo County, California, Conkling testified (as a paid witness for the railroads) that he had slipped the "person" language into the amendment to ensure that corporations would one day receive the same civil rights Congress was giving to freed slaves. Bingham made similar assertions when appropriate during his turns as a paid witness for the railroads. As a result of these assertions, through the late years of the 1800s both were the well-off darlings of the railroads, basking in the light of their success-ful appropriation of human rights for corporations.

When the Beards' book was widely read in the early 1930s, it gave names and faces to the villains who had turned control of America over to what were then called the Robber Barons of industry. Conkling, Bingham, and Justice Waite were all dead by the time of the Great Depression, and all were judged guilty by the American public of pulling off the biggest con in the history of the republic.

The firestorm of indignation that swept the country helped set the stage for Franklin D. Roosevelt's New Deal, using legislative means and packing the Supreme Court to turn back the corporate takeover—at least in part—and returning to average working citizens some of the rights and the benefits they felt had been stolen from them in 1886.

It was widely accepted that Conkling and Bingham had pulled off this trick successfully—purposefully using *person* instead of *natural person* or *citizen* when they helped write the Fourteenth Amendment—and corpo-rate personhood was a fait accompli. It was done, and it couldn't be undone. Confronted with the reality of the language of the Fourteenth Amendment, the Supreme Court had been forced to recognize that corporations were per-sons under the U.S. Constitution because of the precedent of the 1886 *Santa Clara* case.

Senator Henry Cabot Lodge apparently ratified the coup on January 8, 1915, when he unwittingly promulgated Conkling's myth in a speech to the Senate about the 1882 *San Mateo* case:

> In the case of San Mateo County against Southern Pacific Railroad, Mr. Conk-ling introduced in his arguments excerpts from the Journal [of the Senate committee writing the Fourteenth Amendment], then unprinted, to show that the Fourteenth Amendment did not apply solely to Negroes, but applied to persons, real and artificial of any kind. It was owing to this, undoubtedly, that the [Supreme] Court extended it to corporations.

The journal Lodge referenced is the secret journal that never existed. Nonetheless, it was a done deal, conventional wisdom suggested, and the Supreme Court had been forced to acknowledge the reality of corporate per-sonhood—or, some suggested, had gone along with it because Waite and the other justices were corrupt stooges of the railroads but wielded the majority vote. In either case, it had been the intent of at least some of the legislators who drafted the Fourteenth Amendment (Conkling and Bingham) that corporations should have the constitutional rights of natural persons.

The Republican Conspiracy Theory Collapses

In the 1960s author, attorney, and legal historian Howard Jay Graham came across a previously unexamined treasure in the personal papers of Chief Justice Waite, which had been gathering dust at the Library of Congress.

In Waite's private correspondence with J. C. Bancroft Davis (his former recorder of the Court's decisions), Graham made a startling discovery: the entire thing had been a mistake.

What had vexed legal authorities for nearly eighty years was why Waite would say, "The Court does not wish to hear argument..." when the arguments were already finished. Further, why wasn't there any discussion of this explosive new doctrine of corporate personhood in the Court's ruling or in its dissents? It was as if they said it and then forgot they had said it. Complicating the situation further, if the Court had arrived at a huge constitutional decision with sweeping implications, why did the decision say it was based on a technicality about fences? It just didn't seem to add up.

Looking over Justice Waite's personal papers, Graham found a note from Davis to Waite. At one point in the arguments, Waite had apparently told railroad lawyer Sanderson to get beyond his arguments that corporations are persons and get to the point of the case. Court reporter Davis, apparently seeking to clarify that, wrote to Waite, "'In opening, the Court stated that it did not wish to hear argument on the question whether the Fourteenth Amendment applies to such corporations as are parties in these suits. All the judges were of opinion that it does.'

"Please let me know whether I correctly caught your words and oblige."

Waite wrote back, "I think your mem. in the California Rail Road Tax cases expresses with sufficient accuracy what was said before the argument began. I leave it with you to determine whether anything need be said about it in the report *inasmuch as we avoided meeting the constitutional question in the decision.*" (Italics added.)

With thanks to Michael Kinder, who found this in the J. C. Bancroft Davis collection of personal papers in the National Archives in Washington, D.C., where they had been sitting, largely unnoticed, for almost a century, the actual letters are reproduced on the following pages.

1621 H STREET,
WASHINGTON. 26 May
1886

Dear Chief Justice

I have a memorandum
in the California Cases
Santa Clara County
v
Southern Pacific &c &c
as follows.

"In opening the Court
stated that it did not
wish to hear argument
on the question whether
the Fourteenth Amendment

Court reporter J. C. Bancroft Davis's memo to Chief Justice Morrison Remick Waite applies to such corporations as are parties in these suits." All the judges were of opinion that it does".

Please let me know whether I correctly caught your words and oblige

Yours Truly

JCBDavis

Davis's memo to Chief Justice Waite (continued)

1415: J. Unit

May 31. 1886

My dear Davis,

    I think your mem.
on the California Rail
Road Tax cases expresses
with sufficient accuracy
what was said before the
arguments by all. I leave
it with you to determine
whether anything need be
said about it, on this
report inasmuch as we
avoided meeting the con —

8899

Chief Justice Waite's reply to Davis

stitutional question in
the decision—
Yrs. Very truly
M. R. Waite

Chief Justice Waite's reply to Davis (continued)

Graham notes in an article first published in the *Vanderbilt Law Review* that Waite explicitly pointed out to court reporter Davis that the constitutional question of corporate personhood was *not* included in their decision. According to Graham, Waite was instead saying,

> something to the effect of, "The Court does not wish to hear further argument on whether the Fourteenth Amendment applies to these corporations. That point was elaborately covered in 1882 [in the *San Mateo* case], and has been re-covered in your briefs. We all presently are clear enough there. Our doubts run rather to the substance [of the case...the fence issue]. Assume accordingly, as we do, that your clients are persons under the Equal Protection Clause. Take the cases on from there, clarifying the California statutes, the application thereof, and the merits."

In my opinion, Waite was saying something to the effect of, "Every judge and lawyer knows that corporations are persons of the artificial sort—corporations have historically been referred to as 'artificial persons,' and so to the extent that the Fourteenth Amendment covers them, it does so on a corporation-to-corporation basis. But we didn't rule on the railroad's claim that corporations should have rights equal to human persons under the Fourteenth Amendment, so I leave it up to you if you're going to mention the debates or not."

Another legal scholar and author, C. Peter Magrath, was going through Waite's papers at the same time as Graham for the biography he published in 1963 titled *Morrison R. Waite: Triumph of Character.* In his book he notes the above exchange and then says, "In other words, to the Reporter fell the decision which enshrined the declaration in the *United States Reports.* Had Davis left it out, *Santa Clara County v. Southern Pac. R. Co.* would have been lost to history among thousands of uninteresting tax cases."

It was all, at the very best, a mistake by a court reporter. There never was a decision on corporate personhood. "So here at last," writes Graham, "'now for then,' is that long-delayed birth certificate, the reason this seemingly momentous step never was justified by formal opinion." He adds, in a wry note for a legal scholar, "Think, in this instance too, what the United States might have been spared had events taken a slightly different turn."

Graham's Conspiracy Theory

In *Everyman's Constitution,* Howard Jay Graham suggests that if there was an error made on the part of court reporter J. C. Bancroft Davis—as the record

Supreme Court Justice Stephen J. Field
(November 4, 1816–April 9, 1899)

seems to show was clear—it was probably the result of efforts by Supreme
Court Justice Stephen J. Field.[11]

Field was very much an outsider on the Court and was despised by
Waite. As Graham notes,

> Field had repeatedly embarrassed Waite and the Court by close association
> with the Southern Pacific proprietors and by zeal and bias in their behalf. He
> had thought nothing of pressuring Waite for assignment of opinions in vari-
> ous railroad cases, of placing his friends as counsel for the railroad in upcom-
> ing cases, of hinting at times [of actions that] he and they should take, even of
> passing on to such counsel in the undecided *San Mateo* case "certain memo-
> randa which had been handed me by two of the Judges."

Field had presidential ambitions and was relying on the railroads to back
him. He had publicly announced on several occasions that if he were elected,
he would enlarge the size of the Supreme Court to twenty-two so that he could
pack it with "able and conservative men."

Field also thought poorly of Waite, calling him upon his appointment
"His Accidency" and "that experiment" of Ulysses Grant. Waite didn't have
the social graces of Field, who was often described as a "popinjay." And even
though Waite had been a lawyer for the railroads, the record appears to show
that he did his best to be a truly impartial chief justice during his tenure, eventually literally working himself to death from what was probably congestive
heart failure in 1888.

But Field was a grandstander who served on the Ninth Circuit Court of Appeals of California at the same time he was a justice of the Supreme Court of the United States. It was often his "corporations are persons" decisions in California cases that led them to reappear before the U.S. Supreme Court—no accident on Field's part—including the *San Mateo* case in 1882 and the *Santa Clara* case in 1886.

And when the justices decided (contrary to what court reporter Davis published months after the decision) that constitutional issues were *not* involved in *Santa Clara County v. Southern Pacific Railroad,* Justice Field was incensed.

In his concurring opinion to the *Santa Clara* case, even though he agreed with the finding that fenceposts should have a different tax rate than railroad land, he was clearly upset that the issue of corporate personhood was not addressed or answered in the case.

Field wrote:

> [The court had failed in] its duty to decide the important constitution questions involved, and particularly the one which was so fully considered in the Circuit Court [where Field was also the judge], and elaborately argued here, that in the assessment, upon which the taxes claimed were levied, an unlawful and unjust discrimination was made...and to that extent depriving it [the railroad "person"] of the equal protection of the laws.

> At the present day nearly all great enterprises are conducted by corporations... [a] vast portion of the wealth...is in their hands. It is, therefore, of the greatest interest to them whether their property is subject to the same rules of assessment and taxation as like property of natural persons...whether the State... may prescribe rules for the valuation of property for taxation which will vary according as it is held by individuals or by corporations.

> The question is of transcendent importance, and it will come here and continue to come until it is authoritatively decided in harmony with the great constitutional amendment (Fourteenth) which insures to every person, whatever his position or association, the equal protection of the laws; and that necessarily implies freedom from the imposition of unequal burdens under the same conditions.

In *Everyman's Constitution* Graham documents scores of additional attempts by Supreme Court Justice Field to influence or even suborn the legal process to the benefit of his open patrons, the railroad corporations. Field's personal letters, revealed nearly a century after his death, show that his motivations, in addition to wealth and fame, were presidential aspirations; he wrote about his hopes that in 1880 and 1888 the railroads would finance his rise to the presidency, which may explain his zeal to please his potential financiers in the 1882 *San Mateo* case and the 1886 *Santa Clara* case.

So, this conspiracy theory goes, after the case was decided—without reference to corporations being persons and without anybody on the court except Field agreeing with Sanderson's railroad arguments that they were persons under the Fourteenth Amendment—Justice Field took it upon himself to make sure the court's record was slightly revised: it wouldn't be published until J. C. Bancroft Davis submitted his manuscript of the Court's proceedings (titled *United States Reports*) to his publisher, Banks & Brothers in New York, in 1887 and not released until Waite's death in 1888 or later.

After all, Waite's comments to reporter Davis were a bit ambiguous—although he was explicit that no constitutional issue had been decided. Nonetheless, court reporter Davis, with his instruction from Waite that Davis himself should "determine whether anything need be said...in the report," may well have even welcomed the input of Field. And since Field, acting as the judge of the Ninth Circuit in California, had already and repeatedly ruled that corporations *were* persons under the Fourteenth Amendment, it doesn't take much imagination to guess that Field would have suggested that Davis include it in the transcript, perhaps even offering the language, curiously matching his own language in previous lower-court cases.

Graham and Magrath, two of the preeminent scholars of the twentieth century (Graham on this issue, and Magrath as Waite's biographer), both agree that this is the most likely scenario. At the suggestion of Justice Field, almost certainly unknown to Waite, "a few sentences" were inserted into Davis's final written record "to clarify" the decision. It wasn't until a year or more later, when Waite was fatally ill, that the lawyers for the railroads safely announced they had seized control of vital rights in the United States Constitution.

The Hartmann Theory

Court reporters had a very different role in the nineteenth century than they do today. It wasn't until 1913 that the stenograph machine was invented to automate the work of court reporters. Prior to that time, notes were kept in a variety of shorthand forms, both institutionalized and informal. Thus, the memory of the reporter and his (in the nineteenth century, nearly all were men) understanding of the case before him were essential to a clear and informed record being made for posterity.

Being a reporter for the Supreme Court was also not simply a stenographic or recording position. It was a job of high status and high pay. Although the chief justice in 1886 earned $10,500 a year, and the associate justices earned $10,000 per year, the reporter of the Court could expect an income of more than $12,000 per year, between his salary and his royalties from publishing *United States Reports.* And the status of the job was substantial, as Magrath notes in Waite's biography: "In those days the reportership was a coveted position, attracting men of public stature who associated as equals with the justices..."

Prior to his appointment to the Court, John Chandler Bancroft Davis was a politically active and ambitious man. A Harvard-educated attorney, Davis held a number of public service and political appointment jobs, ranging from assistant secretary of state for two presidents, to minister to the German Empire, to Court of Claims judge.

This was no ordinary court reporter, in the sense of today's professionals who do their jobs with clarity and precision but are completely uninvolved in the cases or with the associated parties. He was a political animal, well educated and traveled, and was well connected to the levers of power in his world, which in the 1880s were principally the railroads.

In 1875, while minister to Germany, Davis even took the time to visit Karl Marx, transcribing their conversations in what was considered one of the era's clearest commentaries about Marx. But Davis also left out part of what Marx said—Davis apparently viewed himself as both reporter and editor. In late 1878 a second reporter tracked down Marx and asked about Davis's omission. Here is an excerpt from that second article, as it appeared in the January 9, 1879, issue of the *Chicago Tribune:*

> During my visit to Dr. Marx, I alluded to the platform given by J. C. Bancroft Davis in his official report of 1877 as the clearest and most concise exposition of socialism that I had seen. He said it was taken from the report of the socialist reunion at Gotha, Germany, in May 1875. The translation was incorrect, he said, and he [Marx] volunteered correction, which I append as he dictated...

Marx then proceeds to give this second reporter an entire Twelfth Clause about state aid and credit for industrial societies and suggests that Davis had cooperated with Marx in producing a skewed record in recognition of the times and the place where the discussion was held.

I own twelve books written by Davis, which give an insight into the status and the role he held as reporter for the Supreme Court. My frayed, disintegrating copy of *Mr. Sumner, the Alabama Claims, and Their Settlement,* published in 1878 by Douglas Taylor in New York, is filled with Davis's personal thoughts and insights on a testimony before Congress.

The book, first published as an article by Davis in the *New York Herald* on January 4, 1878, says such things as,

> Like Mr. Sumner's speech in April 1869, this remarkable document would have shut the door to all settlement, had it been listened to. To a suggestion that we should negotiate for the settlement of our disputed boundary and of the fisheries, it proposed to answer that we would negotiate only on condition that Great Britain would first abandon the whole subject of the proposed negotiation. I well remember Mr. Fish's astonishment when he received this document.

Davis summarizes with extensive commentary, such as, "I add to the foregoing narrative that Mr. Motley's friends were (perhaps not unnaturally) indignant at his removal, and joined him in attributing it to Mr. Sumner's course toward the St. Domingo Treaty..."

He indirectly references his own time as envoy to Germany when he writes, "They apparently forgot that the more brilliant, the more distinguished, and the more attractive in social life an envoy is, the more dangerous he may be to his country when he breaks loose from his instructions and communicates socially to the world and officially..." As you can see, Davis was fond of flowery writing and thought well of himself.

And then I realized what I was reading. It related to the famous 1871 Geneva Arbitration case, led by attorney Morrison Remick Waite, which won more than $15 million for the U.S. government from England for its help of the Confederate army during the Civil War. Going to another book by Davis (which I had purchased while researching this book), published in 1903 and titled *A Chapter in Diplomatic History,* I discovered that Davis had been quite active in the Geneva Arbitration case.

During the negotiations with England, he writes:

> I answered that I was very sorry at the position of things, but that the difficulty was not of our making; that I would carry his message to Lord Tenterden, but could hold out little hope that he would adopt the suggestion; and that, in my opinion, the Arbitrators should take up the indirect claims and pass upon them while this motion was pending.

> That evening I saw Lord Tenterden and told him what had taken place between me and Mr. Adams and the Brazilian arbitrator....About midnight he came to me to say that he had told Sir Roundell Palmer what had passed between him and me, and that Sir Roundell had made a minute of some points which would have to be borne in mind, should the Arbitrators do as suggested. He was not at liberty to communicate these points to me officially; but, if I chose to write them down from his dictation, he would state them. I wrote them down from his dictation, and, early the next morning, convened a meeting of the counsel and laid the whole matter before them.

That Davis was playing more than just the role of a stenographer in this case was indisputable. And the case? It was, again, the Alabama Claims or Geneva Arbitration case, which had made Morrison Remick Waite's career. Checking the University of Virginia's law school library, I found the following notes on the Geneva Arbitration case: "The United States' case was argued by former Assistant Secretary of State Bancroft Davis, along with lawyers Caleb Cushing, William M. Evarts, and Morrison R. Waite, under the direction of Secretary of State Hamilton Fish and Secretary of Treasury George Boutwell."

Waite and Davis had worked side-by-side on one of the most famous cases in American history (at the time), both in Geneva, Switzerland, and before the U.S. Congress. And all this was a full fifteen years before Davis was to put his pen to his understanding of the *Santa Clara County v. Southern Pacific Railroad* case when it came before the Supreme Court of which Waite was now chief justice and for which Davis was the head court reporter.

Searching for traces of Davis on the Internet, I found an autograph for sale—it was a letter by President Ulysses Grant, signed by Grant, and also signed by Grant's acting secretary of state—J. C. Bancroft Davis. (Remember that Grant's own Republican Party refused to renominate him for the presidency because his administration was so wracked by railroad bribery and corruption scandals.)

Looking through the records of the City of Newburgh, New York, where Davis once lived, I found the *Orange County, New York, Directory of 1878–1879,* which lists the following note about one of that city's distinguished citizens. "The Newburgh and New York Railroad Company was organized December 14th, 1864, the road was completed September 1st, 1869. J. C. Bancroft Davis was elected President of the Board of Directors...[on] August 1st, 1868."

Given his distinguished background and his having worked with railroad tycoons James Taylor and Jay Cooke in the late 1860s, it's hard to imagine that Davis would insert "corporations are persons" into the record of a

Supreme Court proceeding without understanding full well its importance and consequences, even if he was encouraged to do so by Justice Field.

So here is the fourth and final possibility: J. C. Bancroft Davis undertook to rewrite that part of the U.S. Constitution himself, for reasons that to this day are still unknown but probably not inconsistent with his personal political worldview and affiliation with the railroads and that he did it with the encouragement of Field.

Waite was so ill that he missed the entire 1885 session of the Court, was very weak and sick in 1886 and 1887, and died in March 1888. In all probability, he never knew what Davis had written in his name.

Whether it was a simple error by Davis, or Davis was bending to pressure from Field, or Davis simply took it upon himself to use the voice of the Supreme Court to modify the U.S. Constitution—the fact is that an amendment to the Constitution which had been written by and passed in Congress, voted on and ratified by the states, and signed into law by the president, was radically altered in 1886 from the intent of its post–Civil War authors.

And the hand on the pen that did it was that of court reporter J. C. Bancroft Davis, aided and in all probability even persuaded or bought off by the same railroad barons who, through the money and the power of their railroad corporations, owned Justice Stephen J. Field.

CHAPTER 2

The Corporate Conquest of America

The legal rights of the...defendant, Loan Company, although it be a corporation, soulless and speechless, rise as high in the scales of law and justice as those of the most obscure and poverty-stricken subject of the state.

—Excerpt from the judge's ruling in
Brannan v. Schartzer, 25 Ohio Dec. 491 (1915)

WHILE CORPORATIONS CAN LIVE FOREVER, EXIST IN SEVERAL DIFFERENT places at the same time, change their identities at will, and even chop off parts of themselves or sprout new parts, the chief justice of the U.S. Supreme Court, according to its reporter, had said that they are "persons" under the Constitution, with constitutional rights and protections as accorded to human beings. Once given this key, corporations began to assert the powers that came with their newfound rights.

- **First Amendment.** Claiming the First Amendment right of all "persons" to free speech, corporate lawsuits against the government successfully struck down laws that prevented corporations from lobbying or giving money to politicians and political candidates.[1]

- **Fourth Amendment.** Earlier laws had said that a corporation had to open all its records and facilities to our governments as a condition of being chartered. But now, claiming the Fourth Amendment right of privacy, corporate lawsuits successfully struck down such laws. In later years they also sued to block Occupational Safety and Health Administration (OSHA) laws allowing for surprise safety inspections of the workplace and stopped Environmental Protection Agency (EPA) inspections of chemical factories.[2]

49

●   **Fourteenth Amendment:** Claiming Fourteenth Amendment protec-
     tion against discrimination (granting persons equal protection), the
     J. C. Penney chain store successfully sued the state of Florida, ending
     a law designed to help small, local business by charging chain stores
     a higher business license fee than that for locally owned stores.[3]

Women Ask, "Can I Be a 'Person,' Too?"

Interestingly, during the era of the *Santa Clara* decision granting corporations
the full protections of persons under the Constitution, two other groups also
brought cases to the Supreme Court, asking for similar protections. The first
group was women. This was a movement with a fascinating history, its roots in
the American Revolution itself.

In March 1776 thirty-two-year-old Abigail Adams sat at her writing table
in her home in Braintree, Massachusetts, a small town a few hours' ride south
of Boston. The war between the American colonists and their opponents—the
governors and the soldiers of the East India Company and its British protectors—had been going on for about a year. A small group of the colonists gathered in Philadelphia to edit Thomas Jefferson's Declaration of Independence
for the new nation they were certain was about to be born, and Abigail's husband, John Adams, was among the men editing that document.

Abigail had a specific concern. With pen in hand, she carefully considered her words. Assuring her husband of her love and concern for his well-
being, she then shifted to the topic of the documents being drafted, asking
John to be sure to "remember the Ladies, and be more generous and favour-
able to them than [were] your ancestors."[4]

Abigail knew that the men drafting the Declaration and other documents leading to a new republic would explicitly define and extol the rights
of men, but not of women, and she and several other well-bred women were
lobbying for the Constitution to refer instead to persons, people, humans,
or "men and women." Her words are well-preserved, and her husband later
became president of the United States, so her story is better known than those
of most of her peers.

By late April, Abigail had received a response from John, but it wasn't
what she was hoping for. "Depend upon it," the future president wrote to his
wife, "[that] we know better than to repeal our Masculine systems."

Furious, Abigail wrote back to her husband, saying, "If perticular [*sic*] care and attention is not paid to the Ladies, we are determined to foment a Rebellion..."

All of Abigail's efforts were ultimately for nothing. Richard Henry Lee of Virginia introduced on June 7, 1776, a resolution that the colonies be free and independent states governed solely by free *men,* based on a document written by Thomas Jefferson and edited by John Adams and Benjamin Franklin. Adams played a strong role in the heated debate over the following month, which concluded with a vote to adopt the gender-specific language of Lee's resolution on July 2, 1776. Congress formalized it two days later as the Declaration of Independence.

Adams, Jefferson, Hamilton, and the other men of the assembly explicitly demanded rights for male citizens—and not for female citizens—when they crafted the Declaration. "Men" was not a generic reference to humans; the authors meant humans of the male gender. They wrote: "We hold these Truths to be self-evident, that all Men are created equal, that they are endowed by their Creator with certain unalienable Rights, that among these are Life, Liberty and the Pursuit of Happiness—That to secure these Rights, Governments are instituted among Men, deriving their just Powers from the Consent of the Governed..."

The men had won. Among the earliest laws of the Colonies were several legislating that men had power over women:[5]

- A married woman was not allowed to make out a will because she was not allowed to own land or legally control anything else worthy of willing to another person.

- Any property a woman brought into the marriage became her husband's at the moment of marriage, and would revert to her only if he died and she did not remarry. But even then, she would get only one-third of her husband's property, and what third that was and how she could use it were determined by a male, court-appointed executor, who would supervise for the rest of her life (or until she remarried) how she used the third of her husband's estate she "inherited."

- When a widow died, the executor would either take the property for himself or decide to whom it would pass; the woman had no say in the matter because she had no right to sign a will. Women could not sue in a court of law except under the same weak procedures allowed for the mentally ill and children, supervised by men.

- If the man of a family household died, the executor would decide who would raise the wife's children and in what religion. She had no right to make those decisions and no say in such matters. If the woman was poor, it was a virtual certainty that her children would be taken from her.

- It was impossible in the new United States of America for a married woman to have legal responsibility for her children, control of her own property, own slaves, buy or sell land, or even obtain an ordinary license.

Women Work for, Then against, the Fourteenth Amendment

After the American Revolution, educated women picked up Abigail Adams's chant and began to quietly foment her "rebellion." They wrote poems and seemingly innocuous letters to the editors of newspapers, speaking indirectly about their demands for equal rights. Word spread. By the early 1800s, women's voices were getting louder, and many were demanding an amendment to the Constitution to give equal rights to women or prohibit discrimination against women.

But women didn't gain any legislative successes until 1868, and that turned out to be a Pyrrhic victory. It was the Fourteenth Amendment, passed after the Civil War, which guaranteed due process of law to all "persons." Oddly, when it was being drafted in 1866, suffragettes Susan B. Anthony and Elizabeth Cady Stanton had argued strongly against it because it was the first time the word *male* was used in the Constitution or any constitutional amendments.

The Fourteenth Amendment has two provisions, one guaranteeing due process of law to all persons and the other defining how lines would be drawn to decide how representation was to be apportioned in the House of Representatives. Section 2 includes the phrase "the proportion which the number of such male citizens shall bear to the whole number of male citizens."

Stanton wrote in 1866, "If the word 'male' be inserted [in this amendment] it will take a century to get it out again."[6]

Despite Stanton's objections to its sexually discriminatory language, the Fourteenth Amendment was passed and ratified by enough states to become law. And Stanton was off in her prediction by only two years: the Equal Pay Act of 1963 and the Civil Rights Act of 1964 required equal pay for women and men and prohibited discrimination against women by any company with more than twenty-four employees.

Women Test the Fourteenth Amendment

In an attempt to test the Fourteenth Amendment, Susan B. Anthony went to her local polling station and cast a vote on November 1, 1872. Justifying her vote on the grounds of the Fourteenth Amendment, on November 12 Anthony wrote, "All persons are citizens—and no state shall deny or abridge the citizen rights..."

Six days later, however, she was arrested for voting illegally. The judge, noting that she was female, refused to allow her to testify, dismissed the jury, and found her guilty. Lacking the resources available to huge corporations, she was unable to repeatedly carry her cause to the Supreme Court as the railroads customarily did, and that judge's decision stood.

One year later, in the 1873 *Bradwell v. Illinois* decision, the Supreme Court ruled that women were not entitled to the full protection of persons under the Fourteenth Amendment. Justice Joseph P. Bradley wrote the Court's concurring opinion, which minced no words: "The family institution is repugnant to the idea of a woman adopting a distinct and independent career from that of her husband. So firmly fixed was this sentiment in the founders of the common law that it became a maxim of that system of jurisprudence that a woman had no legal existence separate from her husband, who was regarded as her head and representative in the social state..."

Corporations had full legal existence and the constitutional rights of persons, but women could derive these rights only through their husbands. They didn't even exist as legal entities separate from their husbands. And the Supreme Court said that the Fourteenth Amendment didn't apply to them, even though the amendment explicitly said "persons."

Women didn't get the vote until 1920, and the Equal Rights Amendment that says, simply and entirely, "Equality of rights under the law shall not be denied or abridged by the United States or by any state on account of sex," has been introduced into Congress every year since 1923 but has never passed, blocked in every case by male legislators.

Freed Slaves Ask, "Can I Be a 'Person,' Too?"

The second group to petition the Supreme Court to be recognized as persons under the Fourteenth Amendment were the people for whom it was passed: freed slaves and their descendants. But ten years after giving corporations full rights of personhood, the Supreme Court ruled in *Plessy v. Ferguson* that any person more than "⅛th Negro" was not legally entitled to full interactions with white "persons."

Justice Henry B. Brown delivered the near-unanimous (one dissenter) opinion of the Court, which established nearly a century of Jim Crow laws, saying, "Gauged by this standard we cannot say that a law which authorizes or even requires the separation of the two races in public conveyances is unreasonable, or more obnoxious to the Fourteenth Amendment than the acts of Congress requiring separate schools for colored children in the District of Columbia, the constitutionality of which does not seem to have been questioned, or the corresponding acts of state legislatures."[7]

Court reporter J. C. Bancroft Davis, in the headnote he wrote as commentary to the *Plessy v. Ferguson* case, said that the case had come about when Plessy, "being a passenger between two stations within the State of Louisiana, was assigned by the officers of the [railroad] company to the coach used for the race to which he belonged, but he insisted upon going into a coach used by the race to which he did not belong."

Davis then quotes the Fourteenth Amendment and says afterward, "The object of the amendment was undoubtedly to enforce the absolute equality of the two races before the law, but in the nature of things it could not have been intended to abolish distinctions based upon color, or to enforce social, as distinguished from political equality, or a commingling of the two races upon terms unsatisfactory to either."

This institutionalization of segregation by the 1896 *Plessy* case prompted U.S. Supreme Court Justice Hugo Black to note in 1938, "Of the cases in this Court in which the Fourteenth Amendment was applied during the first fifty years after its adoption, less than one-half of one percent invoked it in protection of the Negro race, and more than fifty percent asked that its benefits be extended to corporations."[8]

PART II

From the Birth of American Democracy through the Birth of Corporate Personhood

I shall therefore conclude with a proposal that your watchmen be instructed, as they go on their rounds, to call out every night, half-past twelve, "Beware of the East India Company."

—Pamphlet signed by "Rusticus," 1773

CHAPTER 3

Banding Together for the Common Good

A corporation has no rights except those given it by law. It can exercise no power except that conferred upon it by the people through legislation, and the people should be as free to withhold as to give, public interest and not private advantage being the end in view.

—William Jennings Bryan, address to the Ohio
1912 Constitutional Convention

IN THE BEGINNING, THERE WERE PEOPLE.

For thousands of years, it was popular among philosophers, theologians, and social commentators to suggest that the first humans lived as disorganized, disheveled, terrified, cold, hungry, and brutal lone-wolf beasts. But both the anthropological and archeological records prove it a lie.

Even our cousins the apes live in organized societies, and evidence of cooperative and social living is as ancient as the oldest hominid remains. For four hundred thousand years or more, even before the origin of *Homo sapiens,* around the world we primates have made tools, art, and jewelry and organized ourselves into various social forms, ranging from families to clans to tribes. More recently, we've also organized ourselves as nations and empires.[1]

As psychologist Abraham Maslow and others have pointed out, the value system of humans is first based on survival. Humans must breathe air, eat food, drink water, keep warm, and sleep safely. Once the basic survival and safety needs are accounted for, we turn to our social needs—family, companionship, love, and intellectual stimulation. And when those are covered, we work to fulfill our spiritual or personal needs for growth.

Our institutions reflect this hierarchy of needs. Families, whether tribal nomads or suburban yuppies, first attend to food, water, clothing, and shelter. Then they consider transportation, social interaction, and livelihood. And when those basics are covered, our families turn to our intellectual and spiritual needs.

The Three Legal Entities

As populations grew, particularly in agriculture-based societies, humans recognized that some form of centralized coordination was needed to keep societies organized, defended, and well supplied. Thus government was born.

The value system of governments is always rooted in the survival and the well-being of humans (or, at the very least, the survival and the well-being of those who control the government). If big projects needed to be done, from building aqueducts to raising pyramids to conquering foreign lands, either the government undertook the task or it was financed and organized by wealthy individuals or churches made up of congregations functioning as a form of government. This was pretty much the way the world worked until the mid-1800s, with only a few exceptions.

Thus there were historically two distinctly different legal entities: humans and families, and the governments they created. (Religious institutions, until the past four centuries or so, operated either as governments or as families/clans. King David ruled a theocratic kingdom, and the popes and the mullahs and the gurus exercised political authority over their followers. Those who didn't rise to such power worked as a social collection of humans that was functionally an extended family or tribe.)

Some of our governments have been pretty tyrannical, but even they rarely behaved in ways that were openly and directly toxic to the survival of all humans. Even the most brutal, despotic regimes operated in a way to ensure that water continued to flow, food supplies were intact, and those in power had a place to sleep. There were often huge disparities in the quality of these commodities between the least and most powerful in the society, but at least the humans who controlled them kept in mind the full spectrum of human needs. When they failed to, they either collapsed or were overthrown, as we see in a long line of civilizations that have risen and then collapsed.

It's instructive to consider how various governments have come to power. For about the past six thousand years, it's happened in one of two ways: either someone claimed divine authority from the god or gods of those people, or a warlord seized power with brute force.

Ruled by the Gods

A good example of leadership by divine appointment is the Japanese Empire. The oldest Japanese history books, the Kojiki and the Nihon Shoki, explicitly say that the first emperor was crowned at least 2,660 years ago because he was a descendant of the sun goddess, Amaterasu Omikami, the greatest of the goddesses in the Japanese Shinto religion.[2] The lineage from that first emperor to today's Japanese emperor is believed to be unbroken, although during the intervening millennia the emperors have often shared power with warlords or shoguns.

Similarly, the Incan ruler Pachacuti organized the Inca into a huge empire in the early fifteenth century after claiming that he was a direct descendant of the sun god, Inti.[3]

While the Catholic line of popes couldn't claim a birth lineage back to the first person they recognized as a human descendant of God, they do claim direct lineage by appointment and blessing. Like the Japanese and Incan emperors, the popes used the powers that come with divine claims to rule much of Europe for millennia. Claiming divine inspiration, they started numerous wars and repeatedly mustered military forces and policelike agencies.

Similar scenarios have played out in nearly every part of the world where agriculture-based cultures have risen to power.

Ruled by Warlords

Taking power by military conquest is such a familiar story that it hardly seems necessary to recount it. But it's interesting to personally witness artifacts of the warlord days, before there were war machines and weapons of mass destruction. It makes real the fact that long ago, people came to power by expanding the area they controlled.

When my family and I lived in rural Germany in 1986 and 1987, a pleasant weekend walk through the forest took us to the ruins of an ancient castle called Nordeck. It's been a ruin for nearly a thousand years, surrounded now by a deep forest, on a steep hillside overlooking the Steinach River. But back in the tenth century, local warlords controlled commerce in that region of the Frankenwald by their control of the river.

From small starts like this, early in the history of modern Europe, local warlords took over increasingly large areas of land, building larger and larger armies and castles, conquering first villages and then states and then entire nations.

Similar scenarios played out in Asia as the Chinese emperors rose to power, and then the Huns attacked and were turned back by them. The Huns headed west to Europe and aided the Goths in defeating the Roman army, led by Emperor Valens, at Adrianople in AD 378. Warlords were on the march.

Ruled by Warlords from the Gods

Often when warlords took over an area, they would claim that their victory was the will of the local god or goddess. A few years ago, my wife, Louise, and I saw an ancient sign of this when we were walking through the temples at Luxor in Egypt; we came across a set of hieroglyphic inscriptions on one wall that were clearly of a different style and period than those surrounding them. We asked an archeologist friend, Ahmed Abdelmawgood Fayed, what the hieroglyphs meant, and he said that the Greek-born Alexander the Great had them carved into the wall after his conquest of the region.

"The hieroglyphics say that he was descended from the Egyptian god Amun, the greatest of the gods," Ahmed told us. Claiming lineage from Amun was Alexander's way of consolidating his local power among the Amun-worshiping Egyptians.

The warlord-blessed-by-divinity strategy played out in much of the world. To this day on British coins you will find the inscription *D.G. REG. F.D.* The *D.G.* stands for *Dei gratia,* Latin for "by the grace of God"; *REG* is short for *regina,* or queen, in Latin; and the *F.D.* represents *fidei defensor,* "defender of the faith."

As British attorney and author L. L. Blake notes in defense of the British system, "That is a good description of the natural order: First of all, there is God, and it is by His Grace that we have our system of Government; then there is the Queen, whose rule is utter service to the goodness which exists in men; finally there is the faith of the people, which needs to be maintained and defended."[4]

Democratic Governments and Republics

The first documented rise of democracy came in response to a warlord-governor, Peisistratus, who seized power in Athens three different times during the sixth century BCE (which stands for *before the common era,* a term equivalent to BC [*before Christ*]; BCE is increasingly preferred by historians). A hundred years after Greek poet and statesman Solon suggested a constitutional reform package with democratic aspects, in 508 BCE the Greek politician Cleisthenes successfully led a radical reform movement that brought about the first democratic constitution in Athens the following year.

Over the next fifty years, Ephialtes and Pericles presided over an increasingly democratic form of government that finally—for the first time in the history of what we call civilization—brought to power people from the poorest parts of Athenian society.

Most people today don't realize how brief that democratic experiment in Athens was. It came to an end in 322 BCE, when the warlord Alexander the Great conquered the nation. Later Greece fell under the rule of Rome.

The American Model

Democracy wouldn't return to Greece for more than two thousand years, in the Greek Revolution of 1821, which was largely inspired by and patterned after the American and French revolutions.

Those revolutions brought forth the idea that governments should overtly and explicitly be controlled by and operate to the benefit of their citizens. When the Declaration of Independence said, "Governments are instituted among Men, deriving their just Powers from the Consent of the Governed," it was quite a departure from the governments that maintained authority through raw power or "divine right" (backed up by force). The new model was what Abraham Lincoln described in his Gettysburg Address as "government of the people, by the people, for the people."

It's important to understand how different this was from all previous governments because it illustrates the priorities of the people who framed American government and set in place the beginnings of modern democracies worldwide.

Being learned men, they knew well the long history of popes, czars, kaisers, and kings who had claimed the divine right of rule, usually with one official state religion, and they were determined that such a specter would never arise in their part of North America. When the Bill of Rights was framed, the very first amendment guaranteed that individuals are free to practice the religion of their choice. And it doesn't stop there—it explicitly keeps government out of the religion business by declaring, "Congress shall make no law respecting an establishment of religion."

Clearly, the Founders were focused on protecting the freedom, rights, and liberty of the individual, in the model of Ephialtes and Pericles—the last elected officials to have explicitly governed in such a fashion.

The Third Entity Arises: Corporations

Meanwhile, back in the 1500s, European kingdoms had concluded that there were some human enterprises that were beyond the scope of government. These included organized religions, charities, international trade, and projects like discovering and administering distant lands.

The need for this started with problems like the ownership of land and other large assets, including buildings and ships. Governments could own things, and people could own things, but if a church or a business wanted land and buildings, historically it had been the property of either a local government (usually a town) or a family. This brought up problems of government involvement in religion and trade as well as issues of who in a family would inherit what.

A third type of entity was necessary to enable owning property independent of either the government or any one particular person or family. It was called the corporation, and it is today the third legal entity in the triad that begins with humans and continues with their two subordinate agents: governments and corporations. This new corporate entity was, of course, not something that was physically real; it was an agreement, a so-called legal fiction authorized by a government.

The first corporations were the Dutch trading companies, chartered in the 1500s. They came into being by declaration of the government but were owned and operated by wealthy and powerful individuals. The corporation had a status that allowed it to own land, to participate in the legal process, and to hold assets such as bank accounts. It could buy and sell things.

But while even sixteenth-century European kingdoms were acknowledging that humans had at least some "natural rights," corporations were explicitly limited to those rights granted by the governments that authorized them. In the early days, everybody knew that corporations weren't governments or humans. They were few and far between until the Industrial Revolution.

The U.S. Constitution doesn't mention the word *corporation*, leaving the power to authorize the creation of corporations to the states. The Founders were far more worried about governments' usurping human rights and privileges than they were about corporations taking over. They had put the East

India Company in its place with the Boston Tea Party, and that, they thought, was the end of that.

American revolutionaries Thomas Paine and Thomas Jefferson, and decades later even the French observer Alexis de Tocqueville, fretted about a return to America of a despotic government running roughshod over the rights of citizens. Few, however, seriously considered the possibility of corporations rising up to take over the people of the world and then to take control of the people's governments. It was only after he had left the presidency that Thomas Jefferson wrote in 1816 about the rise of power of the "moneyed corporations."

CHAPTER 4

The Boston Tea Party Revealed

*They [those who wrote and signed the Declaration of Independence]
meant to set up a standard maxim for free society, which would be
familiar to all, and revered by all; constantly looked to, constantly
labored for, and even though never perfectly attained, constantly
approximated, and thereby constantly spreading and deepening the
influence and augmenting the happiness and value of life to all people
of all colors everywhere. The assertion that "all men are created
equal" was of no practical use in effecting our separation from Great
Britain; and it was placed in the Declaration not for that, but for
future use. Its authors meant it to be—as, thank God, it is now proving
itself—a stumbling block to all those who in after times might seek to
turn a free people back into the hateful paths of despotism.*

—Abraham Lincoln, speech in Springfield,
June 26, 1857, commenting on the *Dred Scott*
decision of the U.S. Supreme Court

As Abraham Lincoln biographer Albert J. Beveridge noted in 1928:

> Facts when justly arranged interpret themselves. They tell the story. For this
> purpose a little fact is as important as what is called a big fact. The picture may
> be well-nigh finished, but it remains vague for want of one more fact. When
> that missing fact is discovered all others become clear and distinct; it is like
> turning a light, properly shaded, upon a painting which but a moment before
> was a blur in the dimness.[1]

There is such illumination in learning, for example, that in 1886 the
Supreme Court had not, in fact, granted corporations the rights of persons—
or in discovering that the battle between working people and what Grover
Cleveland called the "iron heel" of corporate power was actually at the core of
the American Revolution.

While the Pilgrims were early arrivers to America, and their deeds and experiences make outstanding folklore, they weren't the country's founders. This country was formally settled nineteen years before the pilgrims' arrival, when land from the Atlantic to the Mississippi was staked out by what was then the world's largest transnational corporation. The Pilgrims arrived in America in 1620 aboard a boat they chartered from that corporation. That boat, the *Mayflower,* had already made three trips to North America from England on behalf of the East India Company, the corporation that owned it. By the early-1600s colonization of North America, the British Empire was just starting to become a world empire.

A century or so before that, as western European nations extended their reach and rule across the world in the 1400s and 1500s, England was far from being a world power. Following a series of internal battles and wars with Scotland and Ireland, as well as power struggles within the royal family and with the Catholic Church, England at that time was considered by the Spanish, French, and Dutch to be an uncultured tribe of barbarians ruled by sadistic warlords.

Although Sir Francis Drake is touted in British history as a heroic explorer and battler of the Spanish Armada, as a treasure hunter and privateer he was in reality a de facto licensed pirate, and even in the late 1500s England lacked a coherent naval strategy or vision.

The British first got the idea about the importance of becoming a world power in the late 1400s when they observed the result of Christopher Columbus's voyage to America—he brought back slaves, gold, and other treasures. That got Europe's attention and threw Spain full-bore into a time of explosive boom. Then, in 1522, when Ferdinand Magellan sailed all the way around the world, he proved that the planet was a closed system, raising the possibility of tremendous financial opportunity for whatever company could seize control of international trade.

In many of the European countries, particularly Holland and France, consortia were put together to finance ships to sail the seas.

England got into the act a bit late, in 1580, with Queen Elizabeth I becoming the largest shareholder in *The Golden Hind,* a ship owned by Sir Francis Drake. She granted him "legal freedom from liability," an early archetype for modern corporations.[2]

The investment worked out very well for Queen Elizabeth. There's no record of exactly how much she made when Drake paid her her share of the *Hind*'s dividends, but it was undoubtedly vast, since Drake himself and the other minor shareholders all received a 5,000 percent return on their investment. Plus, the queen's placing a maximum loss to the initial investors of their investment amount only made it a low-risk investment to begin with. She also was endorsing an investment model that led to the modern limited-liability corporation.

The queen also often granted monopoly rights over particular industries or businesses in exchange for a fee. The 1624 Statute of Monopolies did away with this ability of the crown, although in the years thereafter the British government used tax laws to produce a similar result for the corporations favored by Parliament or the royal family.[3]

Limiting Risk by Incorporating

A business can operate at a profit, a break-even, or a loss. If the business is a sole proprietorship or a partnership (owned by one or a few people) and it loses more money than its assets are worth, the owners and the investors are personally responsible for the debts, which may exceed the amount they originally invested. A small-business owner could put up $10,000 of her own money to start a company, have it fail with $50,000 in debts, and be personally responsible for paying off that debt out of her own pocket.

But let's say you invest $10,000 in a limited-liability corporation, and the corporation runs up $50,000 in debts and then defaults on those debts. You would lose only your initial $10,000 investment. The remaining $40,000 wouldn't be your concern because the amount of your investment is the "limit of your liability," even if the corporation goes bankrupt, defaults in any other way, or causes millions of dollars in damage to the environment or even the deaths of people.

Who foots the bill? The creditors—the people to whom the corporation owes money—or the community that was devastated. The company took the goods or services from them, didn't pay, and leaves them with the bill, exactly as if you had put in a week's work and not gotten paid for it. Or it wreaks havoc and death and then simply shuts down, as so many asbestos companies have done recently.

And if the corporation declares bankruptcy and dissolves itself, there is nobody for the creditors to go after. That's the main thing that makes a corporation a corporation, and it's why in England the abbreviation for a corporation isn't *Inc.*, as in the United States, but *Ltd.*, which stands for *limited-liability corporation* (which is also used in the United States and other nations).

If you were a stockholder in a corporation that went under, it wouldn't even be reflected on your personal credit rating (unless you had volunteered to personally guarantee the corporation's debt). Your liability is limited to however much you invested.

Moreover, a corporation can outlast its founders. If you started a one-man glassblowing business, for example, when you die or can't work anymore, the income stops. But a glassblowing corporation is an entity unto itself and can continue on with new glassblowers and managers after the founders move on. The implication, of course, is that a corporation can pay profits as a dividend to its shareholders for centuries, theoretically forever.

This is what Queen Elizabeth had in mind. Incorporating *The Golden Hind* would limit her liability and that of the other noble and lesser noble investors and maximize their potential for profit. So after the big bucks she made on Drake's expeditions on *The Golden Hind,* she started pondering what could be done about the small role England played in world trade relative to Holland, France, Spain, and Portugal.

In part to remedy this situation and in part to exploit a relative vacuum of power, she authorized a group of 218 London merchants and noblemen to form a corporation that would take on the mostly Dutch control of the global spice trade. They formed what came to be the largest of England's corporations during that and the next century, the East India Company. Queen Elizabeth granted the company's corporate charter on December 31, 1600.[4]

The East India Company Builds England...and America

It went slowly at first. For several decades the East India Company struggled to establish a commercial beachhead among the many Spice Islands and distant lands where there were potential products, raw materials, or markets.

The Dutch had so sewn up the world at this point in the early 1600s, however, that the only island the company was able to secure on behalf of England was Puloroon (leading King James I, who commissioned the translation of the Bible into English, to declare himself "King of England, Scotland, Ireland, France, and Puloroon"). In addition, the company's hard-drinking captain, William Hawkins, managed to befriend the alcoholic ruler of India, the Mogul emperor Jehangir, building a powerful presence for the East India Company on the Indian subcontinent (which the company would take over and rule as a corporate-run state within two centuries).

During this time England had exported colonists to the Americas in large numbers, including many as prisoners (a practice they later moved to Australia, when it was no longer practical to send them to North America). There was also a steady and growing exodus from England of various types of malcontents who, on arrival in America, redefined themselves as explorers and pioneers or set up theocratic communities.

Much of this transportation was provided at a profitable price by the East India Company, which laid claim to parts of North America and created the first official colony in North America on company-owned land, deeded to the Virginia Company in 1606. (The companies had interlocking boards, as Sir Thomas Smythe administered the American operations of both from his house. Smythe was also the first North American governor of both the East India Company and the Virginia Company.)

The company called it Jamestown, after company patron and stockholder King James I (who took the throne and the royal share of the company's stock when Queen Elizabeth died in 1603), and placed Jamestown on the Chesapeake Bay in the company-owned Commonwealth of Virginia, named after the now-deceased "virgin queen," Elizabeth I, who had granted the company its original charter. On the maps from that time, the two companies' claim of Virginia extended from the Atlantic Ocean all the way to the Mississippi River.*

---

*Another corporation to claim America during that time was the Massachusetts Bay Colony. They weren't quite as successful, however, as the East India Company, and when the corporation wasn't performing up to the measure of King James, he threatened to revoke its charter. One of the documents in the possession of the University of Virginia, compiled as "Thomas Jefferson, Notes on the State of Virginia, Chapter 23" contains Jefferson's note to himself of his possessing "an order of council for issuing a quo warranto against the charter of the colony of the Massachuset's [sic] bay in New-England, with his majesty's declaration that in case the said corporation of Masschuset's [sic] bay shall before prosecution had upon the same quo warranto make a full submission and entire resignation to his royal pleasure, he will then regulate their charter in such a manner as shall be for his service and the good of that colony. 1683, July 26. 35. Car. 2." Much of America was then considered plantation land for British corporations. Another of Jefferson's documents in the same collection is titled "A proclamation for prohibiting the importation of commodities of Europe into any of his majesty's plantations in Africa, Asia, or America, which were not laden in England: and for putting all other laws relating to the trade of the plantations in effectual execution. 1675, Oct. 1. 27. Car. 2." The most powerful of the British corporations of the time, though, was the East India Company.

East India Company flag (ca. 1707)

America was one of the East India Company's major international bases of operations; and once the company figured out how to make a colony work, it grew rapidly. Through the 1600s and the early 1700s, the company and its affiliates largely took control of North America but also sent Captain James Cook on his explorations of Australia, Hawaii, and other Pacific islands. He was killed in Hawaii while on a company mission of exploration.

The company's influence was pervasive wherever it went. For example, one hundred years or more before Betsy Ross was born, the flag of the East India Company was made up of thirteen horizontal red and white alternating bars, with a blue field in the upper-left corner with the Union Jack in it. Although, according to the well-known legend, Ross reversed the order of the red and white bars, the American flag is startling similar to that of the East India Company in the 1700s.*

In its earliest years, the company began assembling its own private military and police forces. After a particularly bloody massacre of company employees by the Dutch at Amboina, Indonesia, in 1623, the company realized it needed to hire some new and uniquely competent people to ply the trade routes. To stop smugglers from competing with its trade to North America, the company authorized its governor of New York to hire Captain William Kidd to clean up its trade routes by killing colonial smugglers and sinking their ships. When Kidd began secretly competing with the company on the side (an activity the company called smuggling and piracy), it had him captured and executed in 1701.

---

*The East India Company designed its flag with thirteen red and white bars long before there were thirteen states. Many historians believe it was because most of the stockholders in the East India Company were initiates in the Masonic Order, and the Masons considered thirteen to be a metaphysically powerful number. Virtually every signer of the Constitution was also a Mason, which may be why they chose to limit the original colonies to thirteen. But that's all speculation; nobody knows for sure, or, if they do, they're not telling.

The company also approached the British Parliament and asked for authority and protection by British military forces.

Thus, many of the seemingly "political" appointees of England to the early Americas were first and foremost employees of the East India Company.

One of many examples of how the company and the British military were connected is General Charles Cornwallis. During the American Revolution, he lost the Battle of Yorktown in 1781 but later went on to "serve with great distinction in the company's service in India, and it was said of him that whilst he lost a colony in the West, he won one in the East."[5]

From India to Yale: The East India Company Influences

As its first century of existence was wrapping up, the company's worldwide reach had proven enormously profitable for its stockholders. For example, during these years Elihu and Thomas Yale grew up in the American colonies and, like many American colonists, went to work for the East India Company. Elihu became the company's governor of Madras, India, where he made a huge fortune for himself and the company, while his brother, Thomas, negotiated the company's first trade deals with China. Elihu returned home and made a large grant to the school that he and his brother had attended, which, in appreciation, renamed itself Yale College in 1718.

By the 1760s the East India Company's power had grown massive and global. It had taken control of much of the commerce of India, was aggressively importing opium into China to take control of that nation (which would lead to the Opium Wars of the mid-1800s, which China lost, ceding Hong Kong to Britain for ninety-nine years), and had largely taken control of all international commerce to and from North America. This very rapid expansion and attempt to keep ahead of the Dutch trading companies, however, was a mixed blessing, as the East India Company went deep in debt to support its growth and by 1770 found itself nearly bankrupt.

Among the company's biggest and most vexing problems were American colonial small businessmen and entrepreneurs, who ran their own small ships to bring tea and other goods directly into America without routing them through Britain or through the company. And there were many small-business tea retailers in North America who were buying their wholesale tea directly from Dutch trading companies instead of the East India Company. These two types of competition were very painful for the company.

The First Pro-corporate Tax Laws

The East India Company set a precedent that multinational corporations follow to this day: it lobbied for laws that would enable it to easily put its small-business competitors out of business. By 1681 most of the members of the British government and royalty were stockholders in the East India Company, so it was easy that year to pass "An Act for the restraining and punishing Privateers and Pirates." This law required a license to import anything into the Americas (among other British-controlled parts of the world), and the licenses were only rarely granted except to the East India Company and other large British corporations.*

As trade to the American colonies grew, and under pressure from the East India Company, the British government passed a series of laws that increased the company's power and influence and reduced its competition and barriers to international trade, including the Townshend Acts of 1767 and the Tea Act of 1773.

---

*The law was explicit about its purpose and the death penalty for operating without a license. It read, in part:

> It shall be felony for any Person, which now doth, or within four Years last past heretofore hath or here after shall Inhabit or belong to this Island, to serve in America in an hostile manner, under any Foreign Prince, state or Potentate in Amity with his Majesty of Great Britain, without special License for so doing, under the hand and seal of the Governour or Commander in chief of this Island for the time being, and that all and every such offender or offenders contrary to the true intent of this Act being thereof duly convicted in his Majesties supreme Court of Judicature within this Island to which court authority is hereby given to hear and to determine the same as other cases of Felony, shall suffer pains of Death without the benefit of Clergy.

> Be it further Enacted by the Authority aforesaid, that all and every Person or Persons that shall any way knowingly Entertain, Harbour, Conceal, Trade or hold any correspondence by Letter or otherwise with any Person or Persons, that shall be deemed or adjudged to be Privateers, Pirates or other offenders within the construction of this Act, and that shall not readily endeavour to the best of his or their Power to apprehend or cause to be apprehended, such Offender or Offenders, shall be liable to be prosecuted as accessories and Confederates, and to suffer such pains and penalties as in such case by law is Provided.

Source: http://www.quinnipiac.edu/other/ABL/etext/hinman-web/p149.html

The Tea Act was the most essential for the East India Company because the American colonies had become a huge market for tea—millions of pounds per month—which was largely being supplied at cheap prices by Dutch trading companies and American smugglers, also known as privateers because they operated privately instead of working for the company. (The company also often encouraged the British government to prosecute these entrepreneurial traders and smugglers as "pirates" under the 1681 law.)

Many people today think that the Tea Act—which led to the Boston Tea Party—was simply an increase in the taxes on tea paid by American colonists. Instead, the purpose of the Tea Act was to give the East India Company full and unlimited access to the American tea trade and to exempt the company from having to pay taxes to Britain on tea exported to the American colonies. It even gave the company a tax refund on millions of pounds of tea that it was unable to sell and holding in inventory.

One purpose of the Tea Act was to increase the profitability of the East India Company to its stockholders (which included the king) and to help the company drive its colonial small-business competitors out of business. Because the company temporarily no longer had to pay high taxes to England and held a monopoly on the tea it sold in the American colonies, it was able to lower its tea prices to undercut those of the local importers and the mom-and-pop tea merchants and teahouses in every town in America.

This infuriated the independence-minded colonists, who were, by and large, unappreciative of their colonies' being used as a profit center for the multinational East India Company corporation. They resented their small businesses still having to pay the higher, pre–Tea Act taxes without having any say or vote in the matter (thus the cry of "no taxation without representation!").

Even in the official British version of the history, the 1773 Tea Act was a "legislative maneuver by the British ministry of Lord North to make English tea marketable in America," with a goal of helping the East India Company quickly "sell 17 million pounds of tea stored in England..."[6]

A clue to the anti-globalization agenda of the American revolutionaries was found right on the Web site of the modern East India Company: "The infamous Boston Tea Party in 1773 was a direct result of the drawback of the government in London of duties on tea which enabled the East India Company to dump excess stocks on the American colonies, and acted as a rallying point for the discontented."[7]

The site also noted that American antipathy toward the corporation that had first founded, owned, ruled, and settled the original colonies continued even after the American Revolution. After the Revolutionary War, the company tried to resume trading with America, offering clothing, silks, coffee, earthenware, cocoa, and spices, but, "Even after Independence the East India Company remained a highly competitive importer of goods into the United States, resulting in occasional flare-ups such as the trade war between 1812 and 1814."[8]

America's First Entrepreneurs Protest

This economics-driven view of American history piqued my curiosity when I first discovered it. So when I came upon an original first edition of one of this nation's earliest history books, I made a sizable investment to buy it to read the thoughts of somebody who had actually been alive and participated in the Boston Tea Party and the subsequent American Revolution. I purchased from an antiquarian bookseller an original copy of *A Retrospect of the Boston Tea-Party with a Memoir of George R. T. Hewes, a Survivor of the Little Band of Patriots Who Drowned the Tea in Boston Harbour in 1773*, published in New York by S. S. Bliss in 1834.

Because the identities of the Boston Tea Party participants were hidden (other than Samuel Adams) and all were sworn to secrecy for the next fifty years, this account (published sixty-one years later) is singularly rare and important, as it's the only actual first-person account of the event by a participant that exists, so far as I can find. Turning its brittle, age-colored pages and looking at printing on unevenly sized sheets, typeset by hand and printed on a small hand press almost two hundred years ago, was both fascinating and exciting. Even more interesting was the perspective of the anonymous ("by a citizen of New York") author and of George Robert Twelvetrees Hewes, whom the author interviewed extensively for the book.

Although Hewes's name is today largely lost to history, he was apparently well known in colonial times and during the nineteenth century.

Esther Forbes's classic 1942 biography of Paul Revere, which depended heavily on Revere's "many volumes of papers" and numerous late-eighteenth- and early-nineteenth-century sources, mentions Hewes repeatedly. For example, when young Paul Revere went off to join the British army in the spring of 1756, he took Hewes along with him.

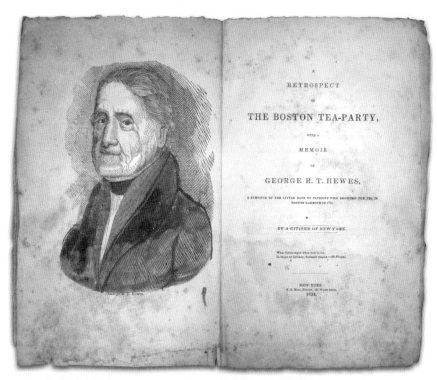

Frontispiece and title page of *A Retrospect of the Boston Tea-Party with a Memoir of George R. T. Hewes, a Survivor of the Little Band of Patriots Who Drowned the Tea in Boston Harbour in 1773* (New York: S. S. Bliss, 1834)

"Paul Revere served in Richard Gridley's regiment," Forbes writes, noting Revere's recollection that the army had certain requirements for its recruits. "All must be able-bodied and between seventeen and forty-five, and must measure to a certain height. George Robert Twelvetrees Hewes could not go. He was too short, and in vain did he get a shoemaker to build up the inside of his shoes; but Paul Revere 'passed muster' and 'mounted the cockade.'"[9]

Hewes wasn't of noble birth, according to Forbes.

> George was of poor family. He had started out apprenticed to a shoemaker, ran away to sea and fished on the Grand Banks. At the time of the great inoculation, he was of age, back in Boston, and completing his apprenticeship to a shoemaker. In spite of his diminutive size and the dignity of his name, he was mixed up in every street fight, massacre, or tea party that occurred in the Boston of his day.

Even the wealthy John Hancock, who kept careful records of his philanthropy, knew Hewes. According to Forbes, "He [Hancock] called that young scamp, George Robert Twelvetrees Hewes, 'my lad' and 'put his hand into his breeches-pocket and pulled out a crown piece, which he placed softly in his hand.'"

Hewes was present for the Boston Massacre, one of the early events that led to the Tea Party. "George Robert Twelvetrees Hewes, of course, was in the middle of it," writes Forbes. "He was a little fellow, but 'stood up straight... and spoke up sharp and quick on all occasions.' Recently he had married Sally Sumner, a young washerwoman. When Captain Preston and his men shoved their way across King Street, they had bumped smack into Hewes."

And when it came to the Boston Tea Party, Forbes notes, "No one invited George Robert Twelvetrees Hewes, but no one could have kept him home." She quotes him as to the size of the raiding party, noting, "Hewes says there were one hundred to a hundred and fifty 'indians'" that night.

Hewes apparently came to Boston, writes Forbes, through the good graces of America's first president:

> George Robert Twelvetrees Hewes fished nine weeks for the British fleet until he saw his chance [to escape] and took it. Landing in Lynn, he was immediately taken to [George] Washington at Cambridge. The General enjoyed the story of his escape—"he didn't laugh to be sure but looked amazing good natured, you may depend." He asked him to dine with him, and Hewes says that "Madam Washington waited upon them at table at dinner-time and was remarkably social." Hewes was one of the many Boston refugees who never went back there to live. Having served as a privateersman and soldier during the war, he settled outside of the state.

And there, outside the state, was where Hewes lived into his old age, finally telling his story to those who would listen, including S. S. Bliss, who published the little book I found. While Forbes doesn't list my volume among her bibliography, she does note that George R. T. Hewes was holding young listeners spellbound out in Oswego County, New York, in his old age, and references Peleg W. Chandler's *American Criminal Trials,* published in 1841, as a source that "gives what seems to me the most careful analysis of the [Boston] Massacre and I have used this book as my primary source, adding to it various contemporary accounts, especially George Robert Twelvetrees Hewes."

Reading Hewes's account, I learned that the Boston Tea Party resembled in many ways the growing modern-day protests against transnational corporations and small-town efforts to protect themselves from chain-store retailers or factory farms. With few exceptions the Tea Party's participants thought of themselves as protesters against the actions of the multinational East India Company and the government that "unfairly" represented, supported, and served the company while not representing or serving the residents.

Hewes said that many American colonists either boycotted the purchase of tea or were smuggling tea or purchasing smuggled tea to avoid supporting the East India Company's profits and the British taxes on tea, which, according to Hewes's account of 1773,

> rendered the smuggling of [tea] an object and was frequently practiced, and their resolutions against using it, although observed by many with little fidelity, had greatly diminished the importation into the colonies of this commodity. Meanwhile, an immense quantity of it was accumulated in the warehouses of the East India Company in England. This company petitioned the king to suppress the duty of three pence per pound upon its introduction into America...[10]

That petition was successful and produced the Tea Act of 1773. The result was a boon for the transnational East India Company corporation and a big problem for the entrepreneurial American "smugglers."

According to Hewes, "The [East India] Company, however, received permission to transport tea, free of all duty, from Great Britain to America," allowing it to wipe out its small competitors and take over the tea business in all of America. "Hence," he wrote,

> it was no longer the small vessels of private merchants, who went to vend tea for their own account in the ports of the colonies, but, on the contrary, ships of an enormous burthen, that transported immense quantities of this commodity, which by the aid of the public authority, might, as they supposed, easily be landed, and amassed in suitable magazines. Accordingly, the company sent its agents at Boston, New York, and Philadelphia, six hundred chests of tea, and a proportionate number to Charleston, and other maritime cities of the American continent. The colonies were now arrived at the decisive moment when they must cast the dye [*sic*], and determine their course...

Interestingly, Hewes notes that it wasn't just American small businesses and citizens who objected to the new monopoly powers granted the East India Company by the English Parliament. The company was also putting out of business many smaller tea exporters in England, who had been doing business with American family-owned retail stores for decades, and those companies began a protest in England that was simultaneous with the American protests against transnational corporate bullying and the East India Company's buying of influence with the British Parliament. Hewes continues:

> Even in England individuals were not wanting, who fanned this fire; some from a desire to baffle the government, others from motives of private interest, says the historian of the event, and jealousy at the opportunity offered the East India Company, to make immense profits to their prejudice.

> These opposers [sic] of the measure in England [the Tea Act of 1773] wrote therefore to America, encouraging a strenuous resistance. They represented to the colonists that this would prove their last trial, and that if they should triumph now, their liberty was secured forever; but if they should yield, they must bow their necks to the yoke of slavery. The materials were so prepared and disposed that they could easily kindle.

The battle between the small businessmen of America and the huge multinational East India Company actually began in Pennsylvania, according to Hewes. "At Philadelphia," he writes,

> those to whom the teas of the [East India] Company were intended to be consigned, were induced by persuasion, or constrained by menaces, to promise, on no terms, to accept the proffered consignment.

> At New-York, Captain Sears and McDougal, daring and enterprising men, effected a concert of will [against the East India Company], between the smugglers, the merchants, and the sons of liberty [who had all joined forces and in most cases were the same people]. Pamphlets suited to the conjecture, were daily distributed, and nothing was left unattempted by popular leaders, to obtain their purpose.

Resistance was organizing and growing, and the Tea Act was the final straw. The citizens of the colonies were preparing to throw off one of the corporations that for almost two hundred years had determined nearly every aspect of their lives through its economic and political power. They were planning to destroy the goods of the world's largest multinational corporation, intimidate its employees, and face down the guns of the government that supported it.

A newsletter called *The Alarm* circulated through the colonies; the May 27, 1773, issue, signed by an enigmatic "Rusticus,"[11] made clear the feelings of colonial Americans about England's largest transnational corporation and its behavior around the world:

Are we in like Manner to be given up to the Disposal of the East India Company, who have now the Assurance, to step forth in Aid of the Minister, to execute his Plan, of enslaving America? Their Conduct in Asia, for some Years past, has given simple Proof, how little they regard the Laws of Nations, the Rights, Liberties, or Lives of Men. They have levied War, excited Rebellions, dethroned lawful Princes, and sacrificed Millions for the Sake of Gain. The Revenues of Mighty Kingdoms have centered in their Coffers. And these not being sufficient to glut their Avarice, they have, by the most unparalleled Barbarities, Extortions, and Monopolies, stripped the miserable Inhabitants of their Property, and reduced whole Provinces to Indigence and Ruin. Fifteen hundred Thousands, it is said, perished by Famine in one Year, not because the Earth denied its Fruits; but [because] this Company and their Servants engulfed all the Necessaries of Life, and set them at so high a Rate that the poor could not purchase them.

The Pamphleteering Worked

After turning back the company's ships in Philadelphia and New York, Hewes writes, "In Boston the general voice declared the time was come to face the storm."

Hewes writes about the sentiment among the colonists who opposed the naked power and wealth of the East India Company and the British government that supported it:

Why do we wait? they exclaimed; soon or late we must engage in conflict with England. Hundreds of years may roll away before the ministers[*] can have perpetrated as many violations of our rights, as they have committed within a few years. The opposition is formed; it is general; it remains for us to seize the occasion. The more we delay the more strength is acquired by the ministers. Now is the time to prove our courage, or be disgraced with our brethren of the other colonies, who have their eyes fixed upon us, and will be prompt in their succor if we show ourselves faithful and firm.

This was the voice of the Bostonians in 1773. The factors who were to be the consignees of the tea, were urged to renounce their agency, but they refused and took refuge in the fortress. A guard was placed on Griffin's wharf, near where the tea ships were moored. It was agreed that a strict watch should be

---

*Hewes refers to the local East India Company employees who doubled as agents of Britain as the "ministers" and their local claim at governance in cooperation with and to the profit of the East India Company as the "ministerial enterprises."

kept; that if any insult should be offered, the bell should be immediately rung; and some persons always ready to bear intelligence of what might happen, to the neighbouring towns, and to call in the assistance of the country people.

Rusticus added his voice in the May 1773 pamphlet, saying, "Resolve therefore, nobly resolve, and publish to the World your Resolutions, that no Man will receive the Tea, no Man will let his Stores, or suffer the Vessel that brings it to moor at his Wharf, and that if any Person assists at unloading, landing, or storing it, he shall ever after be deemed an Enemy to his Country, and never be employed by his Fellow Citizens."[12]

Colonial voices were getting louder and louder about their outrage at the giant corporation's behavior. Another issue of *The Alarm,* signed Hampden and dated October 27, 1773, said, "It hath now been proved to you, That the East India Company, obtained the monopoly of that trade by bribery, and corruption. That the power thus obtained they have prostituted to extortion, and other the most cruel and horrible purposes, the Sun ever beheld."[13]

The People Challenge the Corporation

And then, Hewes says, on a cold November evening, the first of the East India Company's ships of reduced-tax tea arrived:

> On the 28th of November, 1773, the ship Dartmouth with 112 chests arrived; and the next morning after, the following notice was widely circulated.
>
> Friends, Brethren, Countrymen! That worst of plagues, the detested TEA, has arrived in this harbour. The hour of destruction, a manly opposition to the machinations of tyranny, stares you in the face. Every friend to his country, to himself, and to posterity, is now called upon to meet in Faneuil Hall, at nine o'clock, this day, at which time the bells will ring, to make a united and successful resistance to this last, worst, and most destructive measure of administration.

The reaction to the pamphlet—back then one part of what was truly a "free press" in America—was emphatic. Hewes's account was that, "Things thus appeared to be hastening to a disastrous issue. The people of the country arrived in great numbers, the inhabitants of the town assembled. This assembly which was on the 16th of December, 1773, was the most numerous ever known, there being more than 2,000 from the country present."

Hewes continues,

This notification brought together a vast concourse of the people of Boston and the neighbouring towns, at the time and place appointed. Then it was resolved that the tea should be returned to the place from whence it came in all events, and no duty paid thereon. The arrival of other cargoes of tea soon after, increased the agitation of the public mind, already wrought up to a degree of desperation, and ready to break out into acts of violence, on every trivial occasion of offence....

Finding no measures were likely to be taken, either by the governor, or the commanders, or owners of the ships, to return their cargoes or prevent the landing of them, at 5 o'clock a vote was called for the dissolution of the meeting and obtained. But some of the more moderate and judicious members, fearing what might be the consequences, asked for a reconsideration of the vote, offering no other reason, than that they ought to do every thing in their power to send the tea back, according to their previous resolves. This, says the historian of that event,[*] touched the pride of the assembly, and they agreed to remain together one hour.

The people assembled in Boston at that moment faced the same issue that citizens who oppose combined corporate and co-opted government power all over the world confront today: Should they take on a well-financed and heavily armed opponent when such resistance could lead to their own imprisonment or death? Even worse, what if they lose the struggle, leading to the imposition on them and their children of an even more repressive regime to support the profits of the corporation?

There Are Corporate Spies among Us!

There was a debate late that afternoon in Boston, Hewes notes, but it was short because a man named Josiah Quiney pointed out that some of the people in the group worked directly or indirectly for the East India Company or held loyalty to Britain or both. Quiney suggested that if they took the first step of confronting the East India Company, it would inevitably mean they would have to take on the army of England. He pointed out that they were really discussing the possibility of going to war against England to stop England from enforcing the East India Company's right to run its "ministerial enterprise"

---

*Presumably Hewes is referring to himself in the third person, a form considered good manners in the eighteenth century, or this is the voice of the narrator who interviewed him.

and that some who profited from that enterprise were right there in the room with them.

Hewes goes on to say,

> In this conjuncture, Josiah Quiney, a man of great influence in the colony, of a vigorous and cultivated genius, and strenuously opposed to ministerial enterprises, wishing to apprise his fellow-citizens of the importance of the crisis, and direct their attention to probable results which might follow, after demanding silence said, "This ardour and this impetuosity, which are mani-fested within these walls, are not those that are requisite to conduct us to the object we have in view; these may cool, may abate, may vanish like a flittering shade. Quite other spirits, quite other efforts are essential to our salvation.

> "Greatly will he deceive himself, who shall think, that with cries, with excla-mations, with popular resolutions, we can hope to triumph in the conflict, and vanquish our inveterate foes. Their malignity is implacable, their thirst for vengeance insatiable. They have their allies, their accomplices, even in the midst of us—even in the bosom of this innocent country; and who is igno-rant of the power of those who have conspired our ruin? Who knows not their artifices? Imagine not therefore, that you can bring this controversy to a happy conclusion without the most strenuous, the most arduous, the most terrible conflict; consider attentively the difficulty of the enterprise, and the uncertainty of the issue. Reflict [*sic*] and ponder, even ponder well, before you embrace the measures, which are to involve this country in the most perilous enterprise the world has witnessed."

Most Americans today believe that the colonists were upset only because they didn't have a legislature they had elected that would pass the laws under which they were taxed: "taxation without representation" was their rallying cry. And while that was true, Hewes points out, the thorn in their side, the pin-prick that was really driving their rage, was that England was passing tax laws solely for the benefit of the transnational East India Company at the expense of the average American worker and America's small-business owners.

Thus "taxation without representation" also meant hitting the average person and small business with taxes while letting the richest and most pow-erful corporation in the world off the hook for its taxes. It was government sponsorship of one corporation over all competitors, plain and simple.

And the more the colonists resisted the predations of the East India Company and its British protectors, the more reactive and repressive the Brit-ish government became, arresting American entrepreneurs as smugglers and defending the trade interests of the East India Company.

Among the reasons cited in the 1776 Declaration of Independence for separating America from Britain are, "For cutting off our Trade with all parts of the world: For imposing Taxes on us without our Consent." The British had used tax and anti-smuggling laws to make it nearly impossible for American small businesses to compete against the huge multinational East India Company, and the Tea Act of 1773 was the final straw.

Thus the group assembled in Boston responded to Josiah Quiney's comment by calling for a vote. The next paragraph in Hewes's book says:

> The question was then immediately put whether the landing of the tea should be opposed and carried in the affirmative unanimously. Rotch [a local tea seller], to whom the cargo of tea had been consigned, was then requested to demand of the governor to permit to pass the castle [return the ships to England]. The latter answered haughtily, that for the honor of the laws, and from duty towards the king, he could not grant the permit, until the vessel was regularly cleared. A violent commotion immediately ensued; and it is related by one historian of that scene, that a person disguised after the manner of the Indians, who was in the gallery, shouted at this juncture, the cry of war; and that the meeting dissolved in the twinkling of an eye, and the multitude rushed in a mass to Griffin's wharf.

A First-person Account of the Tea Party

On what happened next, Hewes is quite specific in pointing out that not only were the protesters registering their anger and upset over domination by England and the East India Company but they were willing to commit a million-dollar act of vandalism to make their point. Hewes says:

> It was now evening, and I immediately dressed myself in the costume of an Indian, equipped with a small hatchet, which I and my associates denominated the tomahawk, with which, and a club, after having painted my face and hands with coal dust in the shop of a blacksmith, I repaired to Griffin's wharf, where the ships lay that contained the tea. When I first appeared in the street after being thus disguised, I fell in with many who were dressed, equipped and painted as I was, and who fell in with me and marched in order to the place of our destination.
>
> When we arrived at the wharf, there were three of our number who assumed an authority to direct our operations, to which we readily submitted. They divided us into three parties, for the purpose of boarding the three ships which contained the tea at the same time. The name of him who commanded

the division to which I was assigned was Leonard Pitt. The names of the other commanders I never knew.

We were immediately ordered by the respective commanders to board all the ships at the same time, which we promptly obeyed. The commander of the division to which I belonged, as soon as we were on board the ship appointed me boatswain, and ordered me to go to the captain and demand of him the keys to the hatches and a dozen candles. I made the demand accordingly, and the captain promptly replied, and delivered the articles; but requested me at the same time to do no damage to the ship or rigging.

We then were ordered by our commander to open the hatches and take out all the chests of tea and throw them overboard, and we immediately proceeded to execute his orders, first cutting and splitting the chests with our tomahawks, so as thoroughly to expose them to the effects of the water.

In about three hours from the time we went on board, we had thus broken and thrown overboard every tea chest to be found in the ship, while those in the other ships were disposing of the tea in the same way, at the same time. We were surrounded by British armed ships, but no attempt was made to resist us.

We then quietly retired to our several places of residence, without having any conversation with each other, or taking any measures to discover who were our associates; nor do I recollect of our having had the knowledge of the name of a single individual concerned in that affair, except that of Leonard Pitt, the commander of my division, whom I have mentioned. There appeared to be an understanding that each individual should volunteer his services, keep his own secret, and risk the consequence for himself. No disorder took place during that transaction, and it was observed at that time that the stillest night ensued that Boston had enjoyed for many months.

The participants were absolutely committed that none of the East India Company's tea would ever again be consumed on American shores. Hewes continues:

During the time we were throwing the tea overboard, there were several attempts made by some of the citizens of Boston and its vicinity to carry off small quantities of it for their family use. To effect that object, they would watch their opportunity to snatch up a handful from the deck, where it became plentifully scattered, and put it into their pockets.

One Captain O'Connor, whom I well knew, came on board for that purpose, and when he supposed he was not noticed, filled his pockets, and also the lining of his coat. But I had detected him and gave information to the captain of what he was doing. We were ordered to take him into custody, and just as he was stepping from the vessel, I seized him by the skirt of his coat, and in attempting to pull him back, I tore it off; but, springing forward, by a rapid effort he made his escape. He had, however, to run a gauntlet through the crowd upon the wharf; each one, as he passed, giving him a kick or a stroke.

Another attempt was made to save a little tea from the ruins of the cargo by a tall, aged man who wore a large cocked hat and white wig, which was fashionable at that time. He had slightly slipped a little into his pocket, but being detected, they seized him and, taking his hat and wig from his head, threw them, together with the tea, of which they had emptied his pockets, into the water. In consideration of his advanced age, he was permitted to escape, with now and then a slight kick.

The next morning, after we had cleared the ships of the tea, it was discovered that very considerable quantities of it were floating upon the surface of the water; and to prevent the possibility of any of its being saved for use, a number of small boats were manned by sailors and citizens, who rowed them into those parts of the harbor wherever the tea was visible, and by beating it with oars and paddles so thoroughly drenched it as to render its entire destruction inevitable. In all, the 342 chests of tea—more than ninety thousand pounds— thrown overboard that night were enough to make 24 million cups of tea and were valued by the East India Company at 9,659 pounds sterling or, in today's U.S. currency, just over $1 million.[14]

In response to the Boston Tea Party, the British Parliament immediately passed the Boston Port Act, stating that the port of Boston would be closed until the citizens of Boston reimbursed the East India Company for the tea they had destroyed. The colonists refused. A year and a half later, the colonists would again openly state their defiance of the East India Company and Great Britain by taking on British troops in an armed conflict at Lexington and Concord ("the shots heard 'round the world") on April 19, 1775.

That war—finally triggered by a transnational corporation and its government patrons trying to deny American colonists a fair and competitive local marketplace—would last until 1783.

CHAPTER 5

Jefferson versus the Corporate Aristocracy

Let monopolies and all kinds and degrees of oppression be carefully guarded against.

—Samuel Webster, 1777

ALTHOUGH THE FIRST SHOTS WERE FIRED IN 1775 AND THE DECLARATION was signed in 1776, the war against a transnational corporation and the nation that used it to extract wealth from its colonies had just begun. These colonists, facing the biggest empire and military force in the world, fought for five more years—the war didn't end until General Charles Cornwallis surrendered in October 1781. Even then some resistance remained; the last loyalists and the British left New York starting in April 1782, and the treaty that formally ended the war was signed in Paris in September 1783.

The first form of government, the Articles of Confederation, was written in 1777 and endorsed by the states in 1781. It was subsequently replaced by our current Constitution, as has been documented in many books. In this chapter we take a look at the visions that motivated what Alexis de Tocqueville would later call America's experiment with democracy in a republic. One of its most conspicuous features was the lack of vast wealth or any sort of corporation that resembled the East India Company—until the early 1800s.

The First Glimpses of a Powerful American Company

Very few people are aware that Thomas Jefferson considered freedom from monopolies to be one of the fundamental human rights. But it was very much a part of his thinking during the time when the Bill of Rights was born.

In fact, most of the Founders never imagined a huge commercial empire sweeping over their land, reminiscent of George R. T. Hewes's "ships of an enormous burthen" with "immense quantities" of goods. Rather, most of them saw an America made up of people like themselves: farmers.

In a speech before the House of Representatives on April 9, 1789, James Madison referred to agriculture as the great staple of America. He added, "I think [agriculture] may justly be styled the staple of the United States; from the spontaneous productions which nature furnishes, and the manifest preference it has over every other object of emolument in this country."[1]

In a *National Gazette* article on March 3, 1792, Madison wrote,

> The class of citizens who provide at once their own food and their own raiment, may be viewed as the most truly independent and happy. They are more: they are the best basis of public liberty, and the strongest bulwark of public safety. It follows, that the greater the proportion of this class to the whole society, the more free, the more independent, and the more happy must be the society itself.[2]

The first large privately owned corporation to rise up in the new United States during the presidential terms of Jefferson (1801 to 1809) and Madison (1809 to 1817) was the Second Bank of the United States. By 1830 the bank was one of the largest and most powerful private corporations and, to extend its own power, was even sponsoring its directors and agents as candidates for political office.

In President Andrew Jackson's annual message to Congress on December 3, 1833, he explicitly demanded that the bank cease its political activities or receive a corporate death sentence—revocation of its corporate charter. He said, "In this point of the case the question is distinctly presented whether the people of the United States are to govern through representatives chosen by their unbiased suffrages or whether the money and power of a great corporation are to be secretly exerted to influence their judgment and control their decisions."[3]

Jackson succeeded in forcing a withdrawal of all federal funds from the bank that year, putting it out of business. Its federal charter expired in 1836 and was revived only as a state bank authorized by the State of Pennsylvania. It went bankrupt in 1841.

Although thousands of federal, state, county, city, and community laws of the time restrained corporations vastly more than they are today, the presidents who followed Jackson continued to worry out loud about the implications if corporations expanded their power.

In the middle of the thirty-year struggle, on March 10, 1827, James Madison wrote a letter to his friend James K. Paulding about the issue:

> With regard to Banks, they have taken too deep and too wide a root in social transactions, to be got rid of altogether, if that were desirable....they have a hold on public opinion, which alone would make it expedient to aim rather at the improvement, than the suppression of them. As now generally constituted, their advantages whatever they be, are outweighed by the excesses of their paper emissions, and the partialities and corruption with which they are administered.[4]

Thus, while Madison saw the rise of corporate power and its dangers during and after his presidency, the issues weren't obvious to him when he was helping write the U.S. Constitution decades earlier. And that may have been significant when the Bill of Rights was being put together.

The Federalists versus the Democratic Republicans

Shortly after George Washington became the first president of the United States in 1789, his secretary of the treasury, Alexander Hamilton, proposed that the federal government incorporate a national bank and assume state debts left over from the Revolutionary War. Congressman James Madison and Secretary of State Thomas Jefferson saw this as an inappropriate role for the federal government, representing the potential concentration of too much money and power. (The Bill of Rights, with its Tenth Amendment reserving powers to the states, wouldn't be ratified for two more years.)

The disagreement over the bank and assuming the states' debt nearly tore apart the new government and led to the creation—by Hamilton, Washington, and Vice President John Adams (among others, including Thomas and Charles Pinckney, Rufus King, DeWitt Clinton, and John Jay)—of the Federalist Party.

Several factions arose in opposition to the Federalists, broadly referred to as the Anti-Federalists, including two groups who called themselves Democrats and Republicans. Jefferson pulled them together by 1794 into the Democratic Republican Party (which dropped the word *Republican* from its name in the early 1830s, today known as the Democratic Party, the world's oldest and longest-lived political party), united in their opposition to the Federalists' ideas of a strong central government that could grant the power to incorporate a national bank and bestow benefits to favored businesses through the use of tariffs and trade regulation.

During the Washington and Adams presidencies, however, the Federalists reigned, and Hamilton was successful in pushing through his programs for assuming state debts, creating a United States Bank and a network of bounties and tariffs to benefit emerging industries and businesses.

In 1794 independent whiskey distillers in Pennsylvania revolted against Hamilton's federal taxes on their product, calling them "unjust, dangerous to liberty, oppressive to the poor, and particularly oppressive to the Western country, where grain could only be disposed of by distilling it."[5]

The whiskey distillers tarred and feathered a tax collector and pulled together a local militia of seven thousand men. But President Washington issued two federal orders and sent in General Henry Lee, commanding militias from Pennsylvania, Maryland, New Jersey, and Virginia. To demonstrate his authority as commander in chief, Washington rode at the head of the soldiers in their initial attack.

The Whiskey Rebellion was put down, and the power of the Federalists wasn't questioned again until the election of 1800, which Jefferson's Democratic Republican Party won, in a contest referred to as the Second American Revolution or the Revolution of 1800.

In the election of 1804, the Federalists carried only Delaware, Connecticut, and part of Maryland against Jefferson's Democratic Republicans; and by 1832, as the Industrial Revolution was taking hold of America, the Federalists were so marginalized that they ceased to exist as an organized party, being largely replaced by the short-lived Whigs, who were themselves replaced by today's Republican Party, organized in the 1850s.

Jefferson and Natural Rights

Back in the earliest days of the United States, Jefferson didn't anticipate the scope, meaning, and consequences of the Industrial Revolution that was just starting to gather steam in Europe about the time he was entering politics in the Virginia House of Burgesses. He distrusted letting companies have too much power, but he was focusing on the concept of "natural rights," an idea that was at the core of the writings and the speeches of most of the Revolutionary-era generation, from Thomas Paine to Patrick Henry to Benjamin Franklin.

In Jefferson's mind "the natural rights of man" were enjoyed by Jefferson's ancient tribal ancestors of Europe, were lived out during Jefferson's life by some of the tribal peoples of North America, and were written about most explicitly sixty years before Jefferson's birth by John Locke, whose writings were widely known and often referenced in pre-revolutionary America.

Natural rights, Locke said, are things that people are born with simply by virtue of their being human and born into the world. In 1690, in his *Second Treatise of Government,* Locke put forth one of the most well-known definitions of the natural rights that all people are heirs to by virtue of their common humanity. He wrote, "All men by nature are equal...in that equal right that every man hath to his natural freedom, without being subjected to the will or authority of any other man...being all equal and independent, no one ought to harm another in his life, health, liberty or possessions..."

As to the role of government, Locke wrote, "Men being...by nature all free, equal and independent, no one can be put out of his estate and subjected to the political power of another without his own consent which is done by agreeing with other men, to join and unite into a community for their comfortable, safe, and peaceable living...in a secure enjoyment of their properties..."

This natural right was asserted by Jefferson first in his *Summary View of the Rights of British America,* published in 1774, in which he wrote, "The God who gave us life gave us liberty at the same time; the hand of force may destroy, but cannot disjoin them." His first draft of the Declaration of Independence similarly declared, "We hold these truths to be sacred and undeniable; that all Men are created equal and independent, that from that equal creation they derive rights inherent and unalienable, among which are the preservation of life, and liberty, and the pursuit of happiness."[6]

Individuals asserted those natural rights in the form of a representative government that they controlled, and that same government also protected their natural rights from all the forces that in previous lands had dominated, enslaved, and taken advantage of them.

The Three Threats

Thomas Jefferson's vision of America was quite straightforward. In its simplest form, he saw a society where people were first and institutions were second. In his day Jefferson saw three agencies that were threats to humans' natural rights:

- Governments (particularly in the form of kingdoms and elite groups like the Federalists)

- Organized religions* (he rewrote the New Testament to take out all the "miracles" so that in *The Jefferson Bible*—which is still in print—Jesus became a proponent of natural rights and peace)

- Commercial monopolies and the "pseudo aristoi," or pseudo aristocracy (in the form of extremely wealthy individuals and overly powerful corporations)

Instead he believed it was possible for people to live by self-government in a nation in which nobody controlled the people except the people themselves. He found evidence for this belief both in the cultures of Native Americans such as the Cherokee and the Iroquois Confederation, which he studied extensively; in the political experiments of the Greeks; and in histories that documented the lives of his own tribal ancestors in England and Wales.

Jefferson Considers Freedom against Monopolies a Basic Right

Once the Revolutionary War was over and the Constitution had been worked out and presented to the states for ratification, Jefferson turned his attention to what he and Madison felt was a terrible inadequacy in the new Constitution: it didn't explicitly stipulate the natural rights of the new nation's citizens, and it didn't protect against the rise of new commercial monopolies like the East India Company.

On December 20, 1787, Jefferson wrote to James Madison about his concerns regarding the Constitution. He said bluntly that it was deficient in several areas:

> I will now tell you what I do not like. First, the omission of a bill of rights, providing clearly, and without the aid of sophism, for freedom of religion, freedom of the press, protection against standing armies, restriction of monopolies, the eternal and unremitting force of the habeas corpus laws, and

---

*The First Amendment protected citizens from the predations of churches by guaranteeing freedom of religion in a new nation that still had states and cities that demanded obedience to and weekly participation in state-recognized churches or religious doctrine. The Ninth Amendment was a direct and clear acknowledgement of Jefferson's concept of the natural right of humans to hold all personal powers that they haven't specifically and intentionally given to their government of their own free will. It reads, in its entirety, "The enumeration in the Constitution, of certain rights, shall not be construed to deny or disparage others retained by the people."

trials by jury in all matters of fact triable by the laws of the land, and not by the laws of nations.[7]

Such a bill protecting natural persons from out-of-control governments or commercial monopolies shouldn't be limited to America, Jefferson believed. "Let me add," he summarized, "that a bill of rights is what the people are entitled to against every government on earth, general or particular; and what no just government should refuse, or rest on inference."

In 1788 Jefferson wrote about his concerns to several people. In a letter to Alexander Donald, on February 7, he defined the items that should be in a bill of rights. "By a declaration of rights, I mean one which shall stipulate freedom of religion, freedom of the press, freedom of commerce against monopolies, trial by juries in all cases, no suspensions of the habeas corpus, no standing armies. These are fetters against doing evil, which no honest government should decline."[8]

Jefferson kept pushing for a law, written into the Constitution as an amendment, which would prevent companies from growing so large that they could dominate entire industries or have the power to influence the people's government.

On February 12, 1788, he wrote to Mr. Dumas about his pleasure that the U.S. Constitution was about to be ratified, but he also expressed his concerns about what was missing from the Constitution. He was pushing hard for his own state to reject the Constitution if it didn't protect people from the dangers he foresaw:

With respect to the new Government, nine or ten States will probably have accepted by the end of this month. The others may oppose it. Virginia, I think, will be of this number. Besides other objections of less moment, she [Virginia] will insist on annexing a bill of rights to the new Constitution, i.e. a bill wherein the Government shall declare that, 1. Religion shall be free; 2. Printing presses free; 3. Trials by jury preserved in all cases; 4. No monopolies in commerce; 5. No standing army. Upon receiving this bill of rights, she will probably depart from her other objections; and this bill is so much to the interest of all the States, that I presume they will offer it, and thus our Constitution be amended, and our Union closed by the end of the present year.[9]

By midsummer of 1788, things were moving along, and Jefferson was helping his close friend James Madison write the Bill of Rights. On the last day of July, he wrote to Madison,

> I sincerely rejoice at the acceptance of our new constitution by nine States. It is a good canvass, on which some strokes only want retouching. What these are, I think are sufficiently manifested by the general voice from north to south, which calls for a bill of rights. It seems pretty generally understood, that this should go to juries, habeas corpus, standing armies, printing, religion, and monopolies.[10]

The following year, on March 13, he wrote to Francis Hopkinson about continuing objection to monopolies:

> You say that I have been dished up to you as an anti-federalist, and ask me if it be just. My opinion was never worthy enough of notice to merit citing; but since you ask it, I will tell it to you. I am not a federalist....What I disapproved from the first moment also, was the want of a bill of rights, to guard liberty against the legislative as well as the executive branches of the government; that is to say, to secure freedom in religion, freedom of the press, freedom from monopolies, freedom from unlawful imprisonment, freedom from a permanent military, and a trial by jury, in all cases determinable by the laws of the land.[11]

All of Jefferson's wishes, except two, would soon come true. But not all of his views were shared universally.

The Rise of an American Corporate Aristocracy

Years later, on October 28, 1813, Jefferson would write to John Adams about their earlier disagreements over whether a government should be run by the wealthy and powerful few (the pseudo-aristoi) or a group of the most wise and capable people (the "natural aristocracy"), elected from the larger class of all Americans, including working people:

> The artificial aristocracy is a mischievous ingredient in government, and provision should be made to prevent its ascendancy. On the question, what is the best provision, you and I differ; but we differ as rational friends, using the free exercise of our own reason, and mutually indulging its errors. You think it best to put the pseudo-aristoi into a separate chamber of legislation [the Senate], where they may be hindered from doing mischief by their coordinate branches, and where, also, they may be a protection to wealth against the agrarian and plundering enterprises of the majority of the people. I think that to give them power in order to prevent them from doing mischief, is arming them for it, and increasing instead of remedying the evil.[12]

Adams and the Federalists were wary of the common person (who Adams referred to as "the rabble"), and many subscribed to the Calvinist notion that wealth was a sign of certification or blessing from above and a certain minimum level of morality. Because the Senate of the United States was appointed by the states (not elected by the voters, until 1913) and made up entirely of wealthy men, it was mostly on the Federalist side. Jefferson and the Democratic Republicans disagreed strongly with the notion of a Senate composed of the wealthy and powerful.

"Mischief may be done negatively as well as positively," Jefferson wrote to Adams in the next paragraph of that 1813 letter, still arguing for a directly elected Senate: .

> Of this, a cabal in the Senate of the United States has furnished many proofs. Nor do I believe them necessary to protect the wealthy; because enough of these will find their way into every branch of the legislation, to protect themselves....I think the best remedy is exactly that provided by all our constitutions, to leave to the citizens the free election and separation of the aristoi from the pseudo-aristoi, of the wheat from the chaff. In general they will elect the really good and wise. In some instances, wealth may corrupt, and birth blind them; but not in sufficient degree to endanger the society.

Jefferson's vision of a more egalitarian Senate—directly elected by the people instead of by state legislators—finally became law in 1913 with the passage of the Seventeenth Amendment, promoted by the Populist Movement and passed on a wave of public disgust with the corruption of the political process by giant corporations.

Almost all of Jefferson's visions for a Bill of Rights—all except "freedom from monopolies in commerce" and his concern about a permanent army— were incorporated into the actual Bill of Rights, which James Madison shepherded through Congress and was ratified on December 15, 1791.

But the Federalists fought hard to keep "freedom from monopolies" out of the Constitution. And they won. The result was a boon for very large businesses in America in the nineteenth and twentieth centuries, which arguably brought our nation and much of the world many blessings.

But as we'll see in the way things have unfolded, some of those same principles have also given unexpected influence to the very monopolies Jefferson had argued must be constrained from the beginning. The result has sometimes been the same kind of problem the Tea Party rebels had risked their lives to fight: a situation in which the government protects one competitor against all others and against the will of the people whose money is at stake—along with their freedom of choice.

As the country progressed through the early 1800s, corporations were generally constrained to act within reasonable civic boundaries. In the next chapter, we examine how Americans and their government viewed the role of corporations, up to the time of the Civil War and its subsequent amendments.

CHAPTER 6

The Early Role of Corporations in America

*An effort is being made to build a railroad from Springfield to Alton.
A [corporate] charter has been granted by the legislature, and books
are now open for subscriptions to the stock. The chief reliance for taking
the stock must be on the eastern capitalists; yet, as an inducement
to them, we, here must do something. We must stake something
of our own in the enterprise, to convince them that we believe it
will succeed, and to place ourselves between them and subsequent
unfavorable legislation, which, it is supposed, they very much dread.*

—Illinois Congressman Abraham Lincoln, addressing the
leaders of Sangamon County, Illinois, June 30, 1847

JANE ANNE MORRIS IS A CORPORATE ANTHROPOLOGIST AND WRITER IN
Madison, Wisconsin, and she is affiliated with the Program on Corporations,
Law, and Democracy (POCLAD), one of the leading organizations doing
research and work in illuminating the story of corporate personhood.

Morris discovered that on the eve of his becoming chief justice of Wisconsin's Supreme Court, Edward G. Ryan said ominously in his 1873 address to
the graduating class of the University of Wisconsin Law School,

> [There] is looming up a new and dark power...the enterprises of the country
> are aggregating vast corporate combinations of unexampled capital, boldly
> marching, not for economical conquests only, but for political power....The
> question will arise and arise in your day, though perhaps not fully in mine,
> which shall rule—wealth or man [*sic*]; which shall lead—money or intellect;
> who shall fill public stations—educated and patriotic freemen, or the feudal
> serfs of corporate capital....[1]

In researching nineteenth-century laws regulating corporations, Morris found that in Wisconsin, as in most other states at that time:

- Corporations were required to have a clear purpose, to be fulfilled but not exceeded.[2]

- Corporations' licenses to do business were revocable by the state legislature if they exceeded or did not fulfill their chartered purpose(s).[3]

- The state legislature could revoke a corporation's charter if it misbehaved.[4]

- The act of incorporation did not relieve corporate management or stockholders/owners of responsibility or liability for corporate acts.[5]

- As a matter of course, corporation officers, directors, or agents couldn't break the law and avoid punishment by claiming they were "just doing their job" when committing crimes but instead could be held criminally liable for violating the law.[6]

- State (not federal) courts heard cases where corporations or their agents were accused of breaking the law or harming the public.[7]

- Directors of the corporation were required to come from among stockholders.[8]

- Corporations had to have their headquarters and meetings in the state where their principal place of business was located.[9]

- Corporation charters were granted for a specific period of time, such as twenty or thirty years (instead of being granted "in perpetuity," as is now the practice).[10]

- Corporations were prohibited from owning stock in other corporations, to prevent them from extending their power inappropriately.[11]

- Corporations' real estate holdings were limited to what was necessary to carry out their specific purpose(s).[12]

- Corporations were prohibited from making any political contributions, direct or indirect.[13]

- Corporations were prohibited from making charitable or civic donations outside of their specific purposes.[14]

- State legislatures could set the rates that some monopoly corporations could charge for their products or services.[15]

- All corporation records and documents were open to the legislature or the state attorney general.[16]

Similar laws existed in most other states. It is important to understand that tens of thousands of entrepreneurs did business in the early colonies and continue to do so today without being incorporated—the proverbial butcher, baker, and candlestick maker. To do business in America or most of the world does not require a corporate structure—people can run partnerships, individual proprietorships, or simply manufacture and sell products or offer services without any business structure whatsoever other than keeping track of the money for the Internal Revenue Service.

It's only when a group of people get together and put capital (cash) at risk and want to seek from the government legal limits on their liability, and to legally limit their possible losses, that a corporate form becomes necessary. In exchange for these limitations on liability, governments demand certain responsibilities from corporations. The oldest historic one was that corporations "operate in the public interest" or "to the public benefit." After all, if the people, through their elected representatives, are going to authorize a legal limitation of liability for a group of people engaged in the game of business, it's quite reasonable to ask that the game be played in a way that throws off some benefit to the government's citizens or at least doesn't operate counter to the public welfare.

But the bigger they got, the less America's corporations (or their investors) seemed to like regulation and the more they started to seek more flexibility. Railroads, in particular, were finding themselves increasingly subject to local and state taxes, regulations, and tariff and passenger fare limits, which were specifically designed to keep prices affordable for the people and to limit the profits of the railroads to what the people's governments considered fair for state-authorized monopolies.

So, starting in the 1870s, the railroads and their owners began directing massive legal attacks against the power of governments to regulate them.

Corporations under Control

From the 1500s until the 1880s, corporations were considered the artificial creations of their owners and the state legislatures that authorized them. Because they were artificial legal entities, created only and exclusively by the states and referred to in the law as "artificial persons," they were subject to control by the people of the state in which they were incorporated, who asserted their will through representative government. In American republican democracy, government's role is to serve the people and protect them from the predations of both foreign and domestic threats to their life, liberty, and pursuit of happiness. This has historically included control of corporate behavior.

Although until 1886 corporations operated in many of the same ways as today's corporations do, the local, state, and federal legislatures had what the owners of America's largest corporations considered a distressing tendency to limit their behaviors. Many states had laws on the books similar to this old Wisconsin statute:

> **Political contributions by corporations.** No corporation doing business in this state shall pay or contribute, or offer consent or agree to pay or contribute, directly or indirectly, *any* money, property, free service of its officers or employees or thing of value to *any* political party, organization, committee or individual for *any* political purpose whatsoever, or for the purpose of influencing legislation of *any* kind, or to promote or defeat the candidacy of *any* person for nomination, appointment or election to any political office.

> **Penalty.** *Any officer, employee, agent or attorney or other representative* of any corporation, acting for and in behalf of such corporation, who shall violate this act, shall be punished upon conviction by a fine of not less than one hundred nor more than five thousand dollars, or by *imprisonment in the state prison for a period of not less than one nor more than five years,* or by both such fine and imprisonment in the discretion of the court or judge before whom such conviction is had and if the corporation shall be subject to a penalty then by forfeiture in double the amount of any fine and *if a domestic corporation it may be dissolved,* if after a proper proceeding upon quo warranto, in either the circuit or supreme court of the state to be prosecuted by the attorney general of the state, the court shall find and give judgment that section 1 of this act has been violated as charged, and if a foreign or non-resident corporation *its right to do business in this state may be declared forfeited.* [Italics added.][17]

Pennsylvania corporate charters were required to carry revocation clauses starting in 1784; and in 1815 Massachusetts Justice Joseph Story said explicitly that corporations existed only because they were authorized by state legislatures. In his ruling in the *Terrett v. Taylor* case, he said, "A private corporation created by the legislature may lose its franchises by a misuser or nonuser of them....This is the common law of the land, and is a tacit condition annexed to the creation of every such corporation."[18]

The Supreme Court Takes Over

But the states, as Charles and Mary Beard write in *The Rise of American Civilization,* "had to reckon with the Federalist interpretation of the Constitution by John Marshall, who, as Chief Justice of the Supreme Court of the United States from 1801 to 1835, never failed to exalt the [pro-business] doctrines of Hamilton above the claims of the states."[19]

Marshall, appointed to the Court by Federalist John Adams (who had appointed—for life—only Federalists to all federal judgeships), was what would today be called a judicial activist. As the Beards wrote, "By historic irony, he [Marshall] administered the oath of office to his bitterest enemy, Thomas Jefferson; and for a quarter of a century after the author of the Declaration of Independence retired to private life, the stern Chief Justice continued to announce old Federalist rulings from the Supreme Bench."

In 1803, during the second year of Jefferson's presidency, Marshall took on a power for himself and future Supreme Courts that made President Jefferson apoplectic. In the *Marbury v. Madison* case, as the Beards relate it,

> Marshall had been in his high post only two years when he laid down for the first time in the name of the entire Court the doctrine that the judges have the power to declare an act of Congress null and void when in their opinion it violates the Constitution. This power was not expressly conferred on the Court [by the Constitution]. Though many able men had held that the judicial branch of the government enjoyed it, the principle was not positively established until 1803 [by Marshall's ruling in this case]...

Jefferson, shocked, bluntly expressed his concern to his old friend Judge Spencer Roane, the son-in-law of Patrick Henry and a justice of the Virginia Supreme Court:

> If this opinion be sound," Jefferson wrote, "then indeed is our Constitution a complete *felo de se* [legally, a suicide]. For intending to establish three departments, co-ordinate and independent, that they might check and balance one another, it has given, according to this opinion, to one of them alone, the right to prescribe rules for the government of the others, and to that one too, which is unelected by, and independent of the nation....

Jefferson continued in full fury,

The Constitution, on this hypothesis, is a mere thing of wax in the hands of the judiciary, which they may twist and shape into any form they please. It should be remembered, as an axiom of eternal truth in politics, that whatever power in any government is independent, is absolute also; in theory only, at first, while the spirit of the people is up, but in practice, as fast as that relaxes. Independence can be trusted nowhere but with the people in mass. They are inherently independent of all but moral law. My construction of the Constitution is very different from that you quote. It is that each department is truly independent of the others, and has an equal right to decide for itself what is the meaning of the Constitution in the cases submitted to its action; and especially, where it is to act ultimately and without appeal....

A judiciary independent of a king or executive alone is a good thing; but independent of the will of the nation is a solecism [an error or blunder], at least in a republican government.[20]

In his decision putting the Supreme Court above the elected officials (the legislature and the president), Marshall was echoing Hamilton's Federalist mistrust of any form of government constrained solely by those elected by the people. Kings had faced challenges, the Federalists argued, and fought back because as kings they could force decisions without having to wait for a consensus by the people. This powerful federal judiciary, only partially answerable to the people, the Federalists believed, was essential to the survival of the nation.

As Hamilton wrote in the Federalist Papers (No. 23), about whether there should be constraints in the Constitution that would prevent the U.S. government from operating outside the will of its people,

These [constitutional] powers ought to exist without limitation, BECAUSE IT IS IMPOSSIBLE TO FORSEE OR DEFINE THE EXTENT AND VARIETY OF NATIONAL EXIGENCIES, OR THE CORRESPONDENT EXTENT AND VARIETY OF THE MEANS WHICH MAY BE NECESSARY TO SATISFY THEM [capitals Hamilton's]. The circumstances that endanger the safety of nations are infinite, and for this reason no constitutional shackles can wisely be imposed on the power to which the care of it is committed.[21]

(Hamilton's argument is essentially what was said by the Bush administration lawyers who argued in their legal briefs for massive increases in presidential power post-9/11.)

Madison, an ally of Jefferson, rebutted Hamilton's worldview perhaps most eloquently in the Federalist Papers (No. 39) when he wrote: "It is ESSENTIAL [capitals Madison's] to such a government that it be derived from the great body of the society, not from an inconsiderable proportion, or a favored class of it; otherwise a handful of tyrannical nobles, exercising their oppressions by a delegation of their powers, might aspire to the rank of republicans, and claim for their government the honorable title of republic."[22]

Jefferson further elaborated his arguments for three independent and equal-in-power branches of government as well in numerous writings during the 1780s as the Constitution was being formed.

But that was then and this was 1803: The deed was done by Marshall, and the Federalists had won. That said, there is also no doubt that Marshall, like Hamilton, believed he was doing the best thing for the nation that he had served as a soldier during the Revolutionary War. In the 1819 *McCulloch v. Maryland* decision, for example, he referenced government's deriving all its power from and "by the people" no fewer than eleven times in his majority opinion.[23] It was just that his notion of who "the people" were was more in line with Hamilton's and Adams's than with Jefferson's and Madison's.

Rulings and Laws on Revoking Corporate Charters

In a sense, a corporate charter is like a driver's license: It is permission to operate in a particular way, granted by the government. (The comparison is imperfect in technical details, but this point doesn't depend on those details.) Like a driver's license, a charter can be revoked if the privilege is abused.

In 1819 Chief Justice John Marshall used the power he had given himself and the Supreme Court to alter the states' power to regulate or dissolve corporations.

King George III had chartered Dartmouth College in 1769 as a private college, but one part of Jefferson's agenda was to make a college education available to any citizen regardless of the ability to pay. In keeping with Jefferson's Democratic Republican philosophy of free public education, the state of New Hampshire dissolved Dartmouth's corporate charter and rechartered it as a public state school. Dartmouth sued to retain its private corporate charter status, claiming that the corporate charter granted by King George before the Revolution was still valid, and the case went to the Supreme Court.

Chief Justice Marshall, in an opinion clearly reflective of Federalist thought and opposed to Jefferson's plans, ruled that because the original corporate charter of Dartmouth College didn't contain a clause that would allow for its own revocation, and the charter "was a contract between the state and the College, which under the federal Constitution no legislature could impair," the state of New Hampshire had no authority to revoke the college's charter.[24]

Even at this, Marshall was explicit about the need for restrictions on corporations, including that they are not citizens.

As corporate historian and law professor James Willard Hurst notes, "The Dartmouth College case put states on warning that regulation of their corporate creatures must be compatible with the contract clause of the federal Constitution. Concerned to respect state control of corporate activity, the Court took pains to deny that a corporation was a 'citizen' of the chartering state so that it might claim in other states the benefits of the Constitution's privileges and immunities clause."[25]

Even with this qualification, the response from the states—feeling that the Marshall Court had usurped their power to control or dissolve corporations—was furious. Newspapers wrote scathing editorials about the decision, citizens were outraged, and over the following years numerous state legislators took action.

In response to the *Dartmouth* decision, Pennsylvania's legislature passed a law in 1825 that declared the legislature had the power to "revoke, alter or annul the charter" of corporations. New York State passed a similar law in 1828, including "Section 320," which said that any acts by a corporation not specifically authorized in their charter were *ultra vires* (Latin for "beyond the power"; it basically means "you can't do that because you lack the legal authority") and grounds for revocation of the corporation's charter. Michigan, Louisiana, and Delaware all passed laws in 1831 limiting the time of corporate charters.[26]

In the following decade, Michigan, Delaware, Florida, and New York all passed laws that corporate charters could be created or renewed only by a two-thirds vote of the legislature. Altogether during the nineteenth century, nineteen states passed laws in response to Marshall's ruling in the Dartmouth case, each specifying they had the authority to control corporations. Rhode Island's 1857 law is characteristic: "The charter or acts of association of every corporation hereafter created may be amendable or repealed at the will of the general assembly."

In 1855 the U.S. Supreme Court went along with the trend, ruling in *Dodge v. Woolsey* that the states have not "released their powers over the artificial bodies which originate under the legislation of their representatives." The Court added, "combinations of classes in society...united by the bond of a corporate spirit...unquestionably desire limitations upon the sovereignty of the people....But the framers of the Constitution were imbued with no desire to call into existence such combinations."

Early Presidents Wary of Corporations

The Founders knew that without business there would be little progress in the new nation they had helped birth. Yet on commerce, Madison and many of the Founders were of mixed minds. They had seen firsthand the abuses of large monopolistic trusts and corporations like the East India Company, yet they also knew that the future of America was based in part on people's pursuing entrepreneurial, mercantile dreams. In a letter to Edmund Randolph on September 30, 1783, Madison wrote, "Wherever Commerce prevails there will be an inequality of wealth, and wherever [an inequality of wealth prevails] a simplicity of manners must decline."[27]

On the other hand, given the widespread nature of trade in his day, Madison knew it was foolish to try to restrain it, at least unless it got as big as the ill-fated Second Bank of the United States. For example, in a speech to the House of Representatives on April 9, 1789, Madison said,

> I own myself the friend to a very free system of commerce, and hold it as a truth, that commercial shackles are generally unjust, oppressive and impolitic—it is also a truth, that if industry and labour are left to take their own course, they will generally be directed to those objects which are the most productive, and this in a more certain and direct manner than the wisdom of the most enlightened legislature could point out.[28]

When commerce was taken over by large corporate or religious enterprises, however, Madison knew exactly where he stood. In 1817 he wrote, "There is an evil which ought to be guarded against in the indefinite accumulation of property from the capacity of holding it in perpetuity by...corporations. The power of all corporations ought to be limited in this respect. The growing wealth acquired by them never fails to be a source of abuses."[29]

And in a letter to James K. Paulding on March 10, 1827, Madison made absolutely explicit a lifetime of thought on the matter:

> Incorporated Companies, with proper limitations and guards, may in particular cases, be useful, but they are at best a necessary evil only. Monopolies and perpetuities are objects of just abhorrence. The former are unjust to the existing, the latter usurpations on the rights of future generations. Is it not strange that the Law which will not permit an individual to bequeath his property to the descendants of his own loins for more than a short and strictly defined term, should authorize an associated few, to entail perpetual and indefeasible appropriations..."[30]

Because the Founders of America tended to agree with Thomas Hobbes that corporations had the potential to be "worms in the body politic,"[31] governments at all levels—municipal, county, state, and federal—had laws carefully circumscribing the behaviors of corporations.

After the American Revolution, it was a basic principle of democratic government to protect the people it represented from unrestrained corporate power. Thus during the first few decades of the existence of the new United States of America, there were only a handful of corporations, most formed for international trade or banking.

Seeing in even these few corporations the possible reincarnation of an East India Company type of corporate plutocracy, in 1816 Thomas Jefferson wrote, "I hope we shall crush in its birth the aristocracy of our moneyed corporations which dare already to challenge our government in a trial of strength, and bid defiance to the laws of our country."[32]

Those "moneyed corporations" grew in power and influence through Jefferson's lifetime and after his death in 1826. As mentioned earlier, the rise of the Second Bank of the United States caused considerable consternation. Legislators railed against it for decades, particularly when the bank started involving itself in politics, and they tried to terminate its corporate charter, an effort that finally succeeded when the bank went under in 1841.

President Martin Van Buren, in his first annual message to Congress in December 1837, said, "I am more than ever convinced of the dangers to which the free and unbiased exercise of political opinion—the only sure foundation and safeguard of republican government—would be exposed by any further increase of the already overgrown influence of corporate authorities."[33]

Early Growth of the Railroads—and Their Legal Tactics

During the middle of the nineteenth century—roughly from the late 1820s to the early 1870s—the first incarnations of our modern economy evolved out of a previously agrarian and local small-business economy. Other than the Second Bank of the United States, which was out of business by 1841, the dominant industries in America were the plantations, largely staffed by slaves, and the textile mills of the northeast, largely staffed by indentured immigrants from Europe.

Cheap coal, the cheap steel it made possible, and the telegraph brought dramatic changes to America between 1820 and 1850. During this time the railroads grew from obscurity to dominate the corporate and political landscape of the nation. Just twenty-six years after the steam locomotive was invented in England, the first public railway in the world opened in England in 1823. Four years later, with subsidies from the city of Baltimore, the first railroad in America—the Baltimore & Ohio, or B&O Railroad—was incorporated. In 1830 the first scheduled passenger train began operation, using the first U.S.-built steam locomotive, "The Best Friend of Charleston." In 1833 there were only 380 miles of track laid in the United States, and that year President Andrew Jackson became the first sitting president to ride a railroad, creating a new mass-transport sensation.

By 1840 more than 2,700 miles of track were in use in the United States, serving seven states, and by 1850 the total had exploded to more than 9,000 miles of track. By 1860, largely through government subsidies to the new rail companies, more than 30,000 miles of track were in regular use in the United States, and the railroads were the largest and most powerful corporations the nation had ever seen. By 1890 more than 180 million acres of taxpayer-owned land had been deeded to the owners of the nation's largest railroads by various federal, state, and county governments.

Abe Lincoln Reluctantly Joins the Railroads

As the railroads grew in size, they also grew in political power. And they hired some of the nation's best lawyers. For example, in May 1853 the Illinois Central Railroad Company chose not to pay its property taxes to McLean County, Illinois, and sued the county in the Circuit Court to prevent collection. James F. Joy of Detroit, the head lawyer for the railroad, contacted a former Illinois state representative, now an attorney in private practice in the McLean County city of Bloomington, with an offer of employment.

But a young lawyer, who had already gained quite a reputation as an attorney and from his days in the legislature, felt that his personal loyalties in the case were with the county and not the railroad. So the attorney—young Abraham Lincoln—wrote a letter to T. R. Webber, the Champaign County clerk of court, asking for the job of defending the county against the railroad:

> An effort is about to be made to get the question of the right to so tax the [Railroad] Co. before the court and ultimately before the Supreme Court, and the [Railroad] Co. are offering to engage me for them....
>
> I am...feeling that you have the first right to my services, if you choose to secure me a fee something near such as I can get from the other side.[34]

Lincoln knew that the case would be big and the issues important, and the fee an attorney could earn from it would be a big help to his family. "The question in its magnitude to the [Railroad] Co. on the one hand and the counties in which the Co. has land on the other is the largest law question that can now be got up in the State," he wrote to the county's clerk, "and therefore in justice to myself, I can not afford, if I can help it, to miss a fee altogether."[35]

The county didn't answer his letter, so Lincoln wrote to the railroad's attorney, Mason Brayman, saying, "Neither the County of McLean nor anyone on its behalf has yet made any engagement with me in relation to its suit with the Illinois Central Railroad on the subject of taxation, so I am now free to make an engagement for the [rail]road, and if you think of it you may 'count me in.'"[36]

Brayman immediately sent Lincoln a $200 check as a retainer, and Lincoln went to work for the railroad along with James Joy.

Lincoln's Case Foreshadows a Corporate Claim of Personhood

The case sailed through the Circuit Court and immediately went to the Illinois Supreme Court. In the May 1854 term of the court, Brayman and Lincoln represented the Illinois Central Railroad.

A brief written by Lincoln noted that Section Two, Article Nine of the Illinois State Constitution of 1847 required "uniform taxation" of all "persons using and exercising franchises and privileges." Arguing for the railroad, Lincoln claimed that it was a "person" and thus the nonuniform taxation of different railroad properties at different tax rates was unfair and unconstitutional under the Illinois State Constitution.

Lincoln both lost and won the case. The Illinois Supreme Court ruled unanimously that, on the one hand, the state legislature could "make exceptions from the rule of uniformity" with regard to corporations it had chartered, thus losing him the corporate personhood argument.

On the other hand, the Supreme Court ruled that the railroad's charter—which functioned also as a sort of contract between it and the state, since early railroad charters were more similar to modern-day state-subsidized public utilities than traditional private corporations—allowed for direct taxation of the railroad by the state based on its revenues, and therefore the county didn't have the authority to tax the railroad and the railroad didn't have to pay the tax bill.[37]

Lincoln Sues the Railroad

Lincoln sent the Illinois Central Railroad—whose directors all lived in New York and thus had its headquarters there—a bill for his services in the case: he asked for $5,000. James F. Joy refused to pay him that much, suggesting that Lincoln was asking for more than he was worth. (Joy's fee had been only $1,200 for his work on the case.) "The simple truth is that the whole trouble was with Mr. James F. Joy...whom Mr. Lincoln afterward despised," a company memo later noted.[38]

To resolve the issue, the railroad's president, William H. Osborne, suggested that Lincoln simply sue the railroad and let a judge decide how much he should be paid. Lincoln preferred not to sue his client, and almost three years later, in March 1857, he traveled by railroad to New York but was unsuccessful in prying his fee out of the railroad. With no other option, Lincoln filed a lawsuit against the railroad in McLean County Circuit Court, asking for his $5,000 legal fee.

The case opened on Thursday, June 18, 1857, then was postponed to the following Tuesday when it was well attended, as Lincoln was a rising star and there was a huge curiosity factor. In the courtroom that day was a young law student, Adlai E. Stevenson, who, when he was later vice president of the United States (1893 to 1897) would recall that, "It appeared to me in the nature of an amicable suit."[39] In a process that took only a few minutes, the railroad agreed to pay Lincoln's $5,000 fee except that he had to reduce it by $200, as the client had already advanced him that amount as a retainer. Lincoln admitted that he had forgotten about the $200 and agreed to the terms.

The Great Corporate Crash

Lincoln left the courtroom having won the judgment but without any money. The railroad procrastinated in paying him, and on August 1, 1857, Lincoln had the sheriff issue a writ. On August 12 he was paid his $4,800 in a check, which he deposited and then converted to cash on August 31, 1857.

It was a fortunate date for Lincoln to get his cash because just over a month later, in the Great Panic of October 1857, both the bank on which the check was drawn and the railroad itself were "forced to suspend payment."[40]

Of the sixty-six banks in Illinois, the *Central Illinois Gazette* (Champaign) reported that by the following April, "27 have gone into liquidation"[41] in a recession/depression. The *Chicago Democratic Press* had declared on September 30, 1857, "The financial pressure now prevailing in the country has no parallel in our business history."

The Railroad's President and His Generals

Attesting to the power of the railroads as an employer is that Lincoln, throughout the entire time he was negotiating with and suing the railroad, continued to work as its attorney. One of the railroad's other attorneys noted, "We had a contract that Lincoln was to take no case against us and that I could call on him to help me when he was there; and when my clients [the railroads] wanted help I always got Lincoln."[42]

Lincoln enjoyed, as did all the railroad's lawyers, a free pass for unlimited travel, which no doubt helped when he was floating his candidacy for president—he served as a railroad lawyer up until the day of his nomination.

On March 19, 1860, just two weeks before the opening of the Republican Convention in Chicago, where he was nominated as a candidate for president (on May 18), Lincoln defended the railroad in court in that same city and won the case, helping cement his credentials as a candidate for the Republicans.

Perhaps most interesting, and demonstrative of how tightly knit the railroads of the day were with the present and future leaders of the nation, is that while working for the railroad in Illinois, Lincoln met and befriended three men: George B. McClellan was, when Lincoln was first suing the railroad, the vice president and chief engineer of the Illinois Central Railroad. Ambrose E. Burnside was treasurer of the railroad. And a veteran of the Mexican war, Ulysses Grant, "was without success trying to win a livelihood at Galena, Illinois" and had apparently approached the railroad for employment.[43]

Lincoln's biographer, Albert J. Beveridge, noted, "Within five years Lincoln was to make each of these [three] men a general in the Union army."[44]

As the *History of the Illinois Central Railroad* notes, "Stephen A. Douglas, Abraham Lincoln, George B. McClellan, Ulysses S. Grant and Edward Harriman all played a major or minor role in the [railroad] line's development."[45]

The Emergency of the Civil War

The Civil War was a huge boon for the largest corporations in America because government spending exploded for just about every conceivable commodity that was needed by the troops. By the time the war was over, several corporations that supplied war materials and transportation, particularly the railroads, were operating in multistate and monopolistic ways that were raising alarm bells among citizens and in legislatures across the nation.

On July 1, 1862, President Lincoln signed into law under "military necessity" the Pacific Railway Bill, which granted to the Union Pacific and the Central Pacific railroads ten sections of land along a right-of-way from Iowa to San Francisco. The bill also included government loans for building rail lines of $16,000 per mile for level ground, $32,000 per mile for railways crossing deserts, and $48,000 per mile for rails crossing mountains. The national railroad-building campaign became a frenzied activity, sloshing with money and manpower.[46]

But the money was everywhere, and it spawned rampant corruption. As Attorney General Edward Bates wrote in his diary on March 9, 1863, "The demoralizing effect of this civil war is plainly visible in every department of life. The abuse of official powers and the thirst for dishonest gain are now so common that they cease to shock."[47]

In his classic biography of Lincoln, Carl Sandburg wrote, "A procession of mouthpieces and fixers twined in and out of Lincoln's office from week to week..."[48]

Sandburg notes that General James Grant Wilson wrote to Lincoln, "Every contractor has to be watched" because "some of the most competent and most energetic contractors were the most dishonest, [and] could not be content with a fair profit." He quotes *Blackwood Magazine* of England as noting, "A great war always creates more scoundrels than it kills."

Between just June 1863 and June 1864, the War Department paid out more than $250 million. A letter attributed to Lincoln by many historians over the years but not verifiably his (it was probably written by one of the progressives or populists of the late nineteenth century, and just sounded so Lincoln-esque that it stuck) has him saying:

> We may congratulate ourselves that this cruel war is nearing its end. It has cost a vast amount of treasure and blood. The best blood of the flower of American youth has been freely offered upon our country's altar that the nation might live. It has indeed been a trying hour for the Republic; but I see in the near future a crisis approaching that unnerves me and causes me to tremble for the safety of my country.
>
> As a result of the war, corporations have been enthroned and an era of corruption in high places will follow, and the money power of the country will endeavor to prolong its reign by working upon the prejudices of the people until all wealth is aggregated in a few hands and the Republic is destroyed. I feel at this moment more anxiety than ever before, even in the midst of war. God grant that my suspicions may prove groundless.[49]

Whether or not Lincoln said it (the letter first appeared in the 1880s, and its veracity was denied by the head of the Republican Party, Perry Heath, in the *New York Times* on October 3, 1896, although by that time the Republican Party was virtually a wholly owned appendage of the Robber Barons and their corporations and no longer shared the worldview of Lincoln's Radical Republicans), it reflected a widespread sentiment in the United States at the time.

The Railroads Rise to Power

During the Civil War, the railroads rose to become the most powerful of the American corporations. Lincoln mentioned both their "great enterprise" and the conflicts that they were causing across the nation by defying state and federal attempts to regulate them. Because most of the railroads were essentially monopolies (except where they met in large cities), as "the only game in town" they could charge whatever prices they wanted for the transportation of goods and people.

The resulting expenses caused by this domination of the transportation industry by a few very large railroad corporations were increasingly passed along to consumers, government, and smaller companies who received their workers or materials by rail. The unrestrained price increases that drove their profits were also driving a general inflation, even as they helped interconnect and build the nation.

"The great enterprise of connecting the Atlantic with the Pacific states by railways and telegraph lines has been entered upon with a vigor that gives assurance of success," Lincoln noted in his fourth annual message to the nation on December 6, 1864, "notwithstanding the embarrassments arising from the prevailing high prices of materials and labor."[50]

At the same time, under the growing influence of railroad money and power, courts and legislatures were making business more risk-free for the railroad corporations. In 1864 Congress passed the Contract Labor Law, which allowed employers to exchange a year's low-cost or free labor for passage and immigration from a foreign nation to the United States. The main effect—and one of the main goals—of this legislation was to break up strikes and lower labor costs by increasing the labor pool and thus introducing greater competition among workers for jobs.

While the courts ruled that if a corporation broke a contract with another corporation, the aggrieved company would still have to pay for what it had already received, they also ruled that if a human broke a Contract Labor Law contract with a railroad corporation, that corporation wasn't obligated to pay the worker anything. As historian Howard Zinn points out, "The pretense of the law was that a worker and a railroad made a contract with equal bargaining power,"[51] the same as if two powerful corporations had entered into a contract with each other with equal legal resources. Thus the railroads always won.

The first transcontinental railroad line, proposed by Lincoln during his campaign and started during his presidency, was completed on May 10, 1869. By 1871 more than 45,000 miles of track crisscrossed the nation. John D. Rockefeller was eleven years away from forming the Standard Oil Trust, and Andrew Carnegie's steel monopoly and John Pierpont Morgan's banking monopoly were rising in power and influence but not yet dominant forces in American business.* At that time railroads were king; they were the first truly

---

*The most wealthy and powerful of the railroad barons were famous names in the nineteenth century: Leland Stanford, Colis Huntington, Jay Gould, and James J. Hill.

huge American corporations, with the power to transport people and goods and crops from place to place and state to state, energizing the American economy and driving the westward expansion of the new nation.

The growth of the railroads, while supported in part by government grants of millions of acres of free land and millions of dollars of subsidies and tax abatements, also drew expressions of concern from the president and the state legislatures. Transportation is a fundamental need, and people quickly became dependent on the railroads for fast long-distance transport, so the public became prey to predatory pricing practices.

On December 4, 1882, President Chester Arthur said in his annual address to Congress and the nation,

> One of the incidents of the marvelous extension of the railway system of the country has been the adoption of such measures by the corporations which own or control the [rail]roads as have tended to impair the advantages of healthful competition and to make hurtful discriminations in the adjustment of freightage [prices]. These inequalities have been corrected in several of the States by appropriate legislation, the effect of which is necessarily restricted to the limits of their own territory.[52]

As President Arthur noted, the states considered the railroad's ability to charge whatever they pleased as unfair, and by the mid-1880s virtually all states had passed laws setting maximum fees and prices for fares (for people) and tariffs (for freight) or otherwise regulating the railroads. There was nationwide sentiment in favor of continuing to regulate the behavior of the country's largest and most aggressive corporations, particularly the railroads.

How Freeing the Slaves Became the Railroads' Secret Weapon

On July 9, 1868, just after the Civil War, three-quarters of the states ratified the Fourteenth Amendment to the U.S. Constitution as part of a set of laws to end slavery. The intent of Congress and the states was clear: to provide full constitutional protections and due process of law to the now-emancipated former slaves of the United States. The Fourteenth Amendment's first article says, in its entirety:

> All persons born or naturalized in the United States, and subject to the jurisdiction thereof, are citizens of the United States and of the state wherein they

reside. No state shall make or enforce any law which shall abridge the privileges or immunities of citizens of the United States; nor shall any state deprive any person of life, liberty, or property, without due process of law; nor deny to any person within its jurisdiction the equal protection of the laws.

Along with the Thirteenth Amendment ("Neither slavery nor involuntary servitude...shall exist within the United States") and the Fifteenth Amendment ("The right of citizens of the United States to vote shall not be denied or abridged by the United States or by any State on account of race, color, or previous condition of servitude"), the Fourteenth Amendment guaranteed that freed slaves would have full access to legal due process within the United States.

Acting on behalf of the railroad barons, attorneys for the railroads repeatedly filed suits against local and state governments that had passed laws regulating railroad corporations. The main tool the railroads' lawyers tried to use was the fact that corporations had historically been referred to under law not as corporations but as "artificial persons."* Based on this, they argued, corporations should be considered persons under the free-the-slaves Fourteenth Amendment and enjoy the protections of the Constitution just like living, breathing, human persons.

Using this argument for their base, the railroads (in particular, but a few other corporations got into the act) repeatedly sued various states, counties, and towns, claiming that they shouldn't have to pay local taxes because different railroad properties were taxed in different ways in different places and this constituted the creation of different "classes of persons" and was thus illegal discrimination. For almost twenty years, these arguments did not succeed.

In 1873 one of the first Supreme Court rulings on the Fourteenth Amendment, which had been passed only five years earlier, involved not slaves but corporations. Writing in the lead opinion, Justice Samuel F. Miller minced no words in chastising corporations for trying to claim the rights of human beings.

---

*This usage began in sixteenth-century England, when lawyers for the East India Company argued that their corporation could not be convicted of a crime because the corporation was not a person and English laws regulating criminal behavior always began with, "No person shall..." In response to this, legislators from that time on began passing laws to specifically regulate the "artificial persons" of corporations. While they wanted to regulate corporations, they also wanted to acknowledge that corporations shared some things with humans: they were taxed, were subject to laws, and could be parties to lawsuits.

The Fourteenth Amendment's "one pervading purpose," he wrote in the majority opinion, "was the freedom of the slave race, the security and firm establishment of that freedom, and the protection of the newly-made freeman and citizen from the oppression of those who had formerly exercised unlimited dominion over him."[53]

The railroads, however, had a lot of money to pay for lawyers, and railroad lawyer S. W. Sanderson had the reputation of a pit bull. Undeterred, the railroads again and again argued their corporations-are-persons position all the way to the Supreme Court. The peak year for their legal assault was 1877, with four different cases reaching the Supreme Court in which the railroads argued that governments could not regulate their fees or activities or tax them in differing ways because governments can't interfere to such an extent in the lives of "persons" and because different laws and taxes in different states and counties represented illegal discrimination against the persons of the railroads under the Fourteenth Amendment.[54]

By then the Supreme Court was under the supervision of Chief Justice Morrison Remick Waite, himself a former railroad attorney. Associate Justice Stephen J. Field, who was so openly on the side of the railroads in case after case that he annoyed his colleagues, also heavily influenced the Court. In each of the previous four cases, the Court ruled that the Fourteenth Amendment was not intended to regulate interstate commerce and therefore was not applicable. But in none of those cases did Waite or any other justice muster a majority opinion on the issue of whether railroad corporations were persons under the Constitution, and so Miller's "one pervading purpose" of the Fourteenth Amendment as being to free slaves prevailed.

Having lost four cases in one year took a bit of the wind out of the sails of the railroads, and there followed a few years of relative calm. The railroads continued to assert that they were persons, but states and localities continued to call them artificial persons and pass laws regulating their activities.

Throughout the 1870s and 1880s, the issue of corporate personhood was frequently debated in newspapers and political speeches, with a handful of the nation's largest corporations arguing "for" and most of the voters, newspaper editorialists, and politicians arguing "against." Across America politicians were elected repeatedly on platforms that included the regulation of corporations, particularly the railroads. And yet the legal fight continued.

The Railroads Claim There Was a "Secret Journal"

In 1882 the railroads' attorneys floated the claim in a Supreme Court pleading that when the Fourteenth Amendment was drafted, "a journal of the joint
Congressional Committee which framed the amendment, secret and undis-
closed up to that date, indicated the committee's desire to protect corporations
by the use of the word 'person.'"[55]

It was a complete fabrication, and they lost the 1882 case: nobody took
the "secret journal theory" seriously except Justice Field, who had ruled in the
railroad's favor in the Ninth Circuit Court, where he was a judge at the same
time he was on the Supreme Court and which brought the case before the
Supreme Court.

In future cases the railroad attorneys were unable to produce or even
prove legislative reference to the secret journal of the congressional committee.

Years later Supreme Court Justice Hugo Black wrote, in a dissenting
opinion in the *Connecticut General Life Insurance Company v. Johnson* case,

> Certainly, when the Fourteenth Amendment was submitted for approval, the
> people were not told that the states of the South were to be denied their normal
> relationship with the Federal Government unless they ratified an amendment
> granting new and revolutionary rights to corporations. This Court, when the
> Slaughter House Cases were decided in 1873, had apparently discovered no
> such purpose. The records of the time can be searched in vain for evidence
> that this amendment was adopted for the benefit of corporations.

> It is true [303 U.S. 77, 87] that in 1882, twelve years after its adoption, and
> ten years after the Slaughter House Cases, an argument was made in this
> Court that a journal of the joint Congressional Committee which framed the
> amendment, secret and undisclosed up to that date, indicated the committee's
> desire to protect corporations by the use of the word "person."

> A secret purpose on the part of the members of the committee, even if such
> be the fact, however, would not be sufficient to justify any such construction.
> The history of the amendment proves that the people were told that its pur-
> pose was to protect weak and helpless human beings and were not told that
> it was intended to remove corporations in any fashion from the control of
> state governments. The Fourteenth Amendment followed the freedom of a
> race from slavery.

> Justice Swayne said in the Slaughter Houses Cases, supra, [ruled] that: "By 'any
> person' was meant all persons within the jurisdiction of the State. No distinc-
> tion is intimated on account of race or color." Corporations have neither race

nor color. He knew the amendment was intended to protect the life, liberty, and property of human beings. The language of the amendment itself does not support the theory that it was passed for the benefit of corporations.[56]

The 1882 case, however, would not be the last time attorneys for the railroads would try to use this fabricated story in their attempts to change the meaning of the Constitution.

There's an important lesson here about the relative ability of different parties to use the legal system for their protection or to gain advantage. A human individual might try to advance a ludicrous claim such as "There was a secret journal" without the slightest evidence. Indeed, from time to time we hear of defendants trying such things. But it's highly unlikely that an actual person would have the ability to carry claims to the Supreme Court year after year after year with so little to go on.

This is directly relevant to the issue of a level playing field: when one party has dramatically more power, property, and wealth than another, it makes no sense to assert that both require equal protection.

Indeed, one aspect of the concentration of wealth that worried Jefferson and most American legislatures in our nation's earliest decades was that with enough wealth, a corporation can keep trying in the courts for centuries (literally centuries, because a corporation doesn't die), no matter how much it costs, until it gets what it wants.

And, ultimately, that's what happened.

CHAPTER 7

The People's Masters

*Private capital tends to become concentrated in few hands, partly
because of competition among the capitalists, and partly because
technological development and the increasing division of labor
encourage the formation of larger units of production at the expense
of the smaller ones. The result of these developments is an oligarchy
of private capital the enormous power of which cannot be effectively
checked even by a democratically organized political society.*

*This is true since the members of legislative bodies are selected by
political parties, largely financed or otherwise influenced by private
capitalists who, for all practical purposes, separate the electorate from
the legislature. The consequence is that the representatives of the people
do not in fact sufficiently protect the interests of the underprivileged
sections of the population.*

*Moreover, under existing conditions, private capitalists inevitably
control, directly or indirectly, the main sources of information (press,
radio, education). It is thus extremely difficult, and indeed in most
cases quite impossible, for the individual citizen to come to objective
conclusions and to make intelligent use of his political rights.*

—Albert Einstein, *Monthly Review,* May 1949[1]

Fast on the heels of the passage and then Supreme Court interpreta-
tions of the Fourteenth Amendment, a new type of feudalism emerged in
America with the Industrial Revolution; it included women, people of color,
and first-generation immigrants. The explosion of factories in the East and the
Midwest was so great and so rapid that millions of workers emigrated from
Europe to the United States, many of them arriving deeply in debt and indentured to their new employers.

My wife, Louise, and I once bought a truckload of slate from a local quarry to pave an area in front of our home in Vermont. The quarry owner who delivered the stone told us, "This is from a huge pile of seconds that were mined over 150 years ago by indentured Welshmen." Looking into the history of the quarry industry in New England, I discovered that the incredibly difficult and often deadly job of quarryman was filled for more than a hundred years almost exclusively by indentured men freshly arrived from Wales, Scotland, and Ireland.

It turns out, according to author Peter Kellman, "Roughly half the immigrants to the English colonies were indentured servants. At the time of the War of Independence, three out of four persons in Pennsylvania, Maryland, and Virginia were or had been indentured servants, people who had exchanged a certain number of years of bonded work (usually 4 to 25) for passage to America and/or to reduce family debts or avoid prison back in Europe."[2] Increasing the labor pool with immigrants so that more people were forced to compete for the same jobs reduced the problems of strikes and of workers demanding a living wage.

Eliminating Competition

More than two thousand corporations had been chartered between 1790 and 1860. They helped protect themselves from economic disasters by keeping tight control over the economy and the markets within which they operated. In this they echoed the Federalist ideas of Alexander Hamilton and John Adams.

Many companies deal with competition by working hard to earn our business, just as Adam Smith—whose 1776 book *The Wealth of Nations* summarized many economic principles for the founders of this nation—envisioned. But others don't; they feel that the best way to deal with competition is to eliminate it. And, as the East India Company had shown, two ways to do so were by getting the government to grant a monopoly or special tax favors or by crushing or buying out one's competition.

Railroads were the leaders in the movement of monopoly grants, convincing lawmakers to use the government's power of eminent domain to seize land from farmers and settlers and grant it, free, to the railroads, to provide convenient and financially low-risk rights-of-way. In just seven years after 1850, more than 25 million acres of land were given to railroads, and often it was alleged to be the consequence of bribes. For example, the LaCrosse and Milwaukee Railroad in Wisconsin passed out $900,000 worth of stocks and bonds to the governor, thirteen senators, and fifty-nine assemblymen...and soon after received a million acres in free land and freedom from competition.[3]

Another way of limiting the risk of competition was for large corporations to become even larger. Some did this by buying their competitors, although many states had outlawed such practices in the nineteenth century. An easier method was to form consortia, trade associations, and what were later called trusts, to muscle upstart entrepreneurs out of the marketplace.

By the time of *Santa Clara,* the generation that knew the East India Company was dead, and the corporate excesses that would eventually bring about the Great Depression hadn't yet happened. So most of these associations were quite open and free in declaring their intent to control prices, markets, and competition.

The American Brass Association, for example, came right out and said that its purpose in organizing was "to meet ruinous competition." Similar language was found in the charters, articles, and publications of trade groups that organized to protect large companies, in business categories as diverse as selling cotton, manufacturing matches, and distributing steel.[4]

On December 3, 1888, President Grover Cleveland delivered his annual address to Congress. Over the previous twenty years, the equivalent of hundreds of billions of today's dollars in both cash and land had been given to the railroads, a process initially accelerated by Abraham Lincoln during the Civil War, so that he could more efficiently move around war material, and which continued after the war on the excuse of improving transportation infrastructure to enhance commerce.

The result was that, for the first time in its hundred-year history, the United States of America had seen arise among its citizens individuals whose wealth rivaled that of the "landed gentry" controlling the East India Company against whom the Revolutionary War had been fought. We had our first billionaires (in today's dollars). Their names were well known to the people of the time: Jay Gould, Edward Harriman, Leland Stanford, and Charles Crocker. Over the next few decades, their numbers would grow to include John Jacob Astor, Andrew Carnegie, Henry Flagler, Cornelius Vanderbilt, and John D. Rockefeller.

With their enormous fortunes—made always through the use of the corporation—came enormous power. The only Democrat to be elected president during the Gilded Age was Grover Cleveland, and in that 1888 State of the Union address[5] he noted,

The Government itself is under bond to the American People...that no condition in life shall give rise to discrimination in the treatment of the people by their Government.

The citizen of our Republic in its early days rigidly insisted upon full compliance with the letter of this bond...[and therefore] combinations, monopolies, and aggregations of capital were either avoided or sternly regulated and restrained. But no longer. That bond between government and its people had become frayed as the result of the sudden rise of a new wealthy aristocracy.

"A century has passed," Cleveland noted in the same speech, on the ninety-ninth anniversary of the ratification of the U.S. Constitution, and "our business men are madly striving in the race for riches, and immense aggregations of capital outrun the imagination in the magnitude of their undertakings."

And it wasn't that these men were getting rich because they were good or smart businessmen. Instead they were buying politicians, corrupting the Constitution, and brazenly destroying their smaller business competitors.

President Cleveland continued:

We discover that the fortunes realized by our manufacturers are no longer solely the reward of sturdy industry and enlightened foresight, but that they result from the discriminating favor of the Government and are largely based on undue exactions from the masses of our people. The gulf between employers and the employed is constantly widening, and classes are rapidly forming, one comprising the very rich and powerful, while in another are found the toiling poor.

As we view the achievements of aggregated capital, we discover the existence of trusts, combinations, and monopolies, while the citizen is struggling far in the rear or is trampled to death beneath an iron heel. Corporations, which should be the carefully restrained creatures of the law and the servants of the people, are fast becoming the people's masters.

Somebody had finally said it out loud. In particular, and—for the time—shockingly, a *president* had finally said it out loud. The newspapers and the early union movements were both loudly protesting the "iron heel" of the corporate behemoths and the wealthy men who ran them. Equal protection under the law had become vastly unequal over a period of just a few short decades.

"This flagrant injustice and this breach of faith and obligation...," the president told Congress, "is not equality before the law. The existing situation

is injurious to the health of our entire body politic. It stifles in those for whose
benefit it is permitted all patriotic love of country, and substitutes in its place
selfish greed and grasping avarice."

And the men who had amassed these fortunes through creating mega-
corporations were shameless in their brazenness (back then they weren't
"mergers and acquisitions" but instead were called "combinations" when one
corporation bought dozens or hundreds of others to control entire markets).
They dictated terms to politicians, bought off Supreme Court justices like
Field, exploited the working class to the point that much of America was experiencing riots and strikes, and flaunted their wealth.

"The arrogance of this assumption is unconcealed," President Cleveland
said in that 1888 State of the Union address.

> It appears in the sordid disregard of all but personal interests, in the refusal to
> abate for the benefit of others one iota of selfish advantage, and in combina-
> tions to perpetuate such advantages through efforts to control legislation and
> improperly influence the suffrages of the people....
>
> Our workingmen, enfranchised from all delusions and no longer frightened...
> [were getting restive and] will reasonably demand through such revision
> steadier employment, cheaper means of living in their homes, freedom for
> themselves and their children from the doom of perpetual servitude, and an
> open door to their advancement beyond the limits of a laboring class.

A new danger was arising in America, as the writings of Karl Marx were
becoming widespread—they would soon lead to a revolution in Russia—and
were viewed by many Americans as a way to challenge the Robber Barons.

"Communism is a hateful thing and a menace to peace and organized
government," Cleveland noted, "but the communism of combined wealth and
capital, the outgrowth of overweening cupidity and selfishness, which insidi-
ously undermines the justice and integrity of free institutions, is not less dangerous than the communism of oppressed poverty and toil, which, exasperated
by injustice and discontent, attacks with wild disorder the citadel of rule."

One of the arguments put forward by the Robber Barons for their continued riches was that if the wealthy weren't protected in their wealth, they
wouldn't create jobs for laborers, and that with their spending benefits would
not trickle down to the working poor.

Cleveland wasn't buying it: "He mocks the people who proposes that the
Government shall protect the rich and that they in turn will care for the labor-

ing poor," he told Congress bluntly. Trickle-down economics was, he said, "a glittering delusion."

He complained about how agents of the wealthy were writing appropriation bills themselves, giving themselves more and more of the government's money and protections. It had become an open secret that the very wealthy had brought under their control Congress itself.

"Appropriation bills for the support of the Government are defaced by items and provisions to meet private ends," Cleveland said, "and it is freely asserted by responsible and experienced parties that a bill appropriating money for public internal improvement would fail to meet with favor unless it contained items more for local and private advantage than for public benefit."

Cleveland said that he now carried "the sacred trust they [the people] have confided to my charge; to heal the wounds of the Constitution and to preserve it from further violation" inflicted on it "by powerful monopolies and aristocratical establishments..."

It was a nice speech, and a year later Congress would actually take on the "combinations and trusts" Cleveland saw as a threat to democracy.

The Earliest "Private Equity" Firms

The railroads made possible the rapid growth of other industries that previously had been hampered by an inability to quickly and easily transport their raw materials or finished goods. After the Civil War, this growth took on explosive proportions. Entrepreneurs of every stripe were starting and building companies, and the competition was cutthroat.

To deal with this excessive competition, companies joined together within industries to fix prices and control markets.

By 1889 there were at least fifty of these consortia operating in the United States; most were called trusts. They were essentially the same as what are today called corporate mergers, with each participating company selling its company to the trust in exchange for stock in the larger entity. This method would allow 8, 10, or 20 companies to become a single company, with the attendant benefits of larger economies of scale, joint purchasing, and the ability to control a large market while crushing smaller competitors.

A committee of the New York State Senate noted on March 6, 1888, "That combination [anticompetitive collusion] is the natural result of excessive competition there can be no doubt. The history of the Copper Trust, the Sugar Trust, the Standard Oil Trust, the American Cotton Oil Trust, the combination of railroads to fix the rates of freight and passenger transportation, all prove beyond question or dispute that combination grows out of and is a natural development of competition..."[6]

When that New York Senate committee pursued their investigation in 1888, they called witnesses from trusts representing meat, milk, oil, sugar, cottonseed oil, oilcloth, and glass, among others. They learned that in just the six years since its creation in 1882, John D. Rockefeller's Standard Oil Trust increased the value of its holdings to the point where dividends paid out to trustees in 1888 were more than $50 million (more than $100 billion in today's dollars). Simultaneously, the trust drove thousands of small oil and kerosene dealers out of business. The Sugar Trust had caused the price of sugar to soar nationally, and the Bagging Trust had doubled the price of bags in the previous decade. The Copper Trust had succeeded in raising the cost of copper from 12 to 17 cents per pound, making all the copper companies profitable but hitting small businesses and consumers hard.[7]

The revelations of the trusts' wild profits hit the newspapers as a big story, and the U.S. House of Representatives began its own investigation of trusts in April 1888, under the leadership of Representative Henry Bacon of New York.

Testimony before Congress showed that the trusts played hardball with entrepreneurs and small businesses that tried to compete with them. Unrelated trusts even cooperated with one another to wipe out small businesses in each other's markets.

A small businessman named Harlan Dow testified before Congress that when he tried to market kerosene in West Virginia in competition with Rockefeller's Standard Oil Trust, the railroads raised their prices to him for transporting his product. He tried to survive by shipping his kerosene in his own horse-drawn wagon, but in response to this the Standard Oil Trust cut its price to consumers for kerosene in the areas where Dow was trying to sell it. "I stopped the wagon and it has been idle in the stable ever since," Dow told the investigating committee.[8]

One of Standard's distributors, a man named F. D. Carley, even corroborated Dow's testimony, bragging about how he had been able to destroy every small competitor who tried to enter the marketplace or stay in business. "For instance," Carley said, "a man named Pettit got on some [oil] tanks at New Orleans...I dropped the price on him pretty lively."[9] In the absence of competition and free choice, giant corporations have the power to do this, and consumers have nowhere else to go.

As newspapers nationwide screamed headlines about how the fat cats of industry were raking in millions while wiping out small businesses and fixing prices, the states got into the act. Although most states already had laws or constitutional prohibitions against restraint of trade, the years from 1887 to 1896 saw dozens of new laws enacted. The first were in 1887 in Texas, then 1889 in Idaho, Kansas, Tennessee, and Michigan; by 1892 virtually every state had passed some sort of legislation, with one of the most powerful being passed in New York that year. The corporate charters of the Standard Oil Trust in California and the Sugar Trust in New York were both revoked in this early wave of reaction.

Senator Sherman Tries to Protect Small Businesses and Entrepreneurs

Both of the major political parties denounced trusts in the 1888 Cleveland-Harrison presidential campaigns, and on December 4, 1889, Senator John Sherman of Ohio submitted Senate Bill No. 1, "A bill to declare unlawful, trusts and combinations in restraint of trade and production." In promoting his bill, Sherman said that the people "are feeling the power and grasp of these combinations, and are demanding from every legislature and of Congress a remedy for this evil....Society is now disturbed by forces never felt before."[10]

The bill was championed by Senators James Z. George of Mississippi, George F. Edmunds of Vermont, and George F. Hoar of Massachusetts. It passed by an almost unanimous vote and was signed into law by President Benjamin Harrison in 1890. The Sherman Antitrust Act of 1890, in its entirety, says:

> **Section 1.** Every contract, combination in the form of trust or otherwise, or conspiracy, in restraint of trade or commerce among the several States, or with foreign nations, is declared to be illegal. Every person who shall make any contract or engage in any combination or conspiracy hereby declared to be illegal shall be deemed guilty of a felony, and, on conviction thereof, shall be punished by fine not exceeding ten million dollars if a corporation, or, if any other person, three hundred and fifty thousand dollars, or by imprisonment not exceeding three years, or by both said punishments, in the discretion of the court.

> **Section 2.** Every person who shall monopolize, or attempt to monopolize, or combine or conspire with any other person or persons, to monopolize any part of the trade or commerce among the several States, or with foreign nations, shall be deemed guilty of a felony, and, on conviction thereof, shall be

punished by fine not exceeding ten million dollars if a corporation, or, if any other person, three hundred and fifty thousand dollars or by imprisonment not exceeding three years, or by both said punishments, in the discretion of the court.

The Standard Oil Trust was clearly in violation of the new law and of state laws that mirrored it. Six days after the state of Ohio ruled his trust an anti-competitive monopoly that violated the law, John D. Rockefeller announced on March 10, 1892, that his Standard Oil Trust would be dissolved into separate companies. By then federal and state prosecutions of trusts were under way nationwide.

But They're Still Persons

But although the trusts were now under attack, one of the ways they fought back was by making "contributions" to politicians and their campaigns. In response, Republican President Theodore Roosevelt proposed campaign finance reform legislation in his annual address to Congress on December 3, 1906, saying, "I again recommend a law prohibiting all corporations from contributing to the campaign expenses of any party....Let individuals contribute as they desire; but let us prohibit in effective fashion all corporations from making contributions for any political purpose, directly or indirectly."[11]

Teddy Roosevelt made another run at trying to rein in the new corporate "persons" a year later, when in December 1907 he addressed Congress and said,

> The fortunes amassed through corporate organization are now so large, and vest such power in those that wield them, as to make it a matter of necessity to give to the sovereign—that is, to the Government, which represents the people as a whole—some effective power of supervision over their corporate use. In order to ensure a healthy social and industrial life, every big corporation should be held responsible by, and be accountable to, some sovereign strong enough to control its conduct.[12]

The result was the Tillman Act of 1907, the first law to bar (in a very limited fashion) corporate money from political campaigns. The Tillman Act (still on the books but highly modified over the years) says, unambiguously:

> That it shall be unlawful for any national bank, or any corporation organized by authority of any laws of Congress, to make a money contribution in connection with any election to any political office. It shall also be unlawful for

any corporation whatever to make a money contribution in connection with any election at which Presidential and Vice-Presidential electors or a Representative in Congress...or any election...of a United States Senator.

The Tillman Act also said that "every officer or director of any corporation who shall consent to any contribution by the corporation" shall be fined or punished "by imprisonment for a term of not more than one year, or both fine and imprisonment at the discretion of the court."

The Republican Roosevelt followed this by building a popular reputation as "the trustbuster" through his aggressive enforcement of the Sherman Antitrust Act, using it to break up more than forty large corporations during his presidency.

From 1909 to 1913, President William Howard Taft continued Teddy Roosevelt's tradition by further breaking up John D. Rockefeller's Standard Oil Trust into thirty-three separate companies as well as breaking up American Tobacco. Working people loved him for it, as did entrepreneurs who again had opportunities in the newly freed marketplace.

But in the first year of the administration of President Woodrow Wilson, the corporations reacted by trying to use the same law—the Sherman Antitrust Act—to get unions outlawed. They essentially argued that if it was illegal for corporate persons to conspire or form monopolies for their own benefit, it should be equally illegal for human persons to do the same in the form of unions.

When corporations started using the Sherman Act against unions, going against the spirit of a law that was passed to protect the average person from excessive corporate power, the U.S. Congress passed the Clayton Antitrust Act of 1914 at the urging of President Wilson. It specifically outlawed tying together multiple products, price discrimination, corporate mergers, and interlocking boards of directors. The Clayton Act also mandated the creation of the Federal Trade Commission (FTC). The FTC's original job was to control corporate wrongdoing, and it still carries that mission.

Through the Roaring Twenties, little was done to enforce these various acts by the corporate-friendly administrations of Warren Harding, Calvin Coolidge ("the business of America is business"), and Herbert Hoover. Seven years after the onset of the Republican Great Depression, however, Franklin D. Roosevelt again began to enforce the Sherman Act, and it was pretty much the law of the land from that time until Ronald Reagan was elected president, and he stopped enforcing it in 1981.

Other Attempts to Put Humans First Fail

On the one hand, legislation was being pushed through state legislatures right and left, granting corporations human and superhuman powers. In the state of Ohio, for example, Senate Bill No. 8 "became effective on March 8, 1927, amending over 70 statutes and enacting more than 50 others." It repealed the "single purpose" requirement of incorporation, streamlined the processes, insulated corporate owners and managers from personal liability for corporate wrongdoing, and, in a sweepingly phrased provision, enabled Ohio corporations to "perform all acts," both within and outside the state, that could be performed by a natural person.[13]

In 1936 the Robinson-Patman Act was passed, which made price discrimination illegal in an attempt to revive the Sherman Antitrust Act;* it is still law, yet it is largely ignored today. And in 1950 the Celler-Kefauver Antimerger Act (another attempt to update and re-empower the Sherman Antitrust Act) was passed; it too is still law, yet since Reagan it is now largely ignored.

Since 1950 no legislation of any consequence has passed that would put corporate power or personhood under the control of the people and their democratically elected governments, and most of the earlier laws have been watered down substantially.

For example, the Hart-Scott-Rodino Antitrust Improvements Act of 1976, itself a watering down of the Sherman Antitrust Act, was amended during the 2000 term of Congress through passage of the Commerce-State-Justice appropriations bill, to reduce by about half the number of corporate mergers that would come under FTC review. Other mergers could proceed without such regulation—and have.

---

*This is how the FTC defines *price discrimination:*

> A seller charging competing buyers different prices for the same "commodity" or discriminating in the provision of "allowances"—compensation for advertising and other services—may be violating the Robinson-Patman Act. This kind of price discrimination may hurt competition by giving favored customers an edge in the market that has nothing to do with the superior efficiency of those customers....Price discrimination also might be used as a predatory pricing tactic—setting prices below cost to certain customers—to harm competition at the supplier's level.

Source: www.ftc.gov

The Working Class Tests the Fourteenth Amendment

Between the Civil War and the Great Depression, workers tried many times to gain equal rights with corporations and thus bargain on a level playing field for fair wages and decent working conditions. Carl Sandburg, in his biography of Lincoln, points out that the word *strike* was so new during the Civil War era that newspapers put it in quotes in their headlines. And, Sandburg notes, Lincoln was the first U.S. president to explicitly defend the rights of strikers, intervening in several situations where local governments were planning to use police or militia to break strikes and preventing the local governments from cooperating with the local corporate powers.[14]

Nonetheless, from the time of Lincoln's death to the era of the Great Depression and Franklin D. Roosevelt, strikes were most often brutally put down, and corporations sometimes used intimidation, violence, and even murder to keep their workers in line. Probably the biggest turning point in the union movement, however, happened on February 11, 1937, when striking workers at General Motors won recognition for their union in the Great Sit-down Strike in Flint, Michigan.

After the Great Depression, in the three years between 1937 and 1940, union membership more than tripled in the United States and the American working class became, for the first time since the Jefferson-Madison-Monroe era, a class with some powers of self-determination. Along with it, however, came the exploitation of some workers by their own union bosses. All forms of organized business activity where there is money or power at stake, it seems, are equally susceptible to these corrupting forces, although unions never achieved as much power as corporations because more laws were passed to limit union behaviors—and they never achieved personhood status under the Fourteenth Amendment.

Chartermongering and the Race to the Bottom, ca. 1900

As we've seen, throughout most of the eighteenth and nineteenth centuries, states were moving to restrict corporate activities by placing limits on the term, activities, and powers a corporation could take in its charter. When Ohio broke up the Standard Oil Trust in 1892, Rockefeller and other corporate giants with similar problems began looking for states in which they could recharter their corporations without all of the restrictions that Ohio and most other states had placed on them.

New Jersey was the first state to engage in what was then called "charter-mongering"—changing its corporate charter rules to satisfy the desires of the nation's largest businesses. In 1875 its legislature abolished maximum capitalization limits, and in 1888 the New Jersey legislature took a huge and dramatic step by authorizing—for the first time in the history of the United States—companies to hold stock in other companies.

In 1912 New Jersey Governor Woodrow Wilson was alarmed by the behavior of corporations in his state, and "pressed through changes [that took effect in 1913] intended to make New Jersey's corporations less favorable to concentrated financial power."[15]

As New Jersey began to pull back from chartermongering, Delaware stepped into the fray by passing in 1915 laws similar to but even more liberal for corporations than New Jersey's. Delaware continued that liberal stance to corporations, and thus, as the state of Delaware says today, "More than 850,000 business entities have their legal home in Delaware including more than 50% of all U.S. publicly-traded companies and 63% of the Fortune 500. Businesses choose Delaware because we provide a complete package of incorporation services including modern and flexible corporate laws, our highly-respected Court of Chancery, a business-friendly State Government, and the customer service oriented Staff of the Delaware Division of Corporations."[16]

As New Jersey and then Delaware threw out old restrictions on corporate behavior, allowing corporations to have interlocking boards, to live forever, to define themselves for "any legal purpose," to own stock in other corporations, and so on, corporations began to move both their corporate charters and, in some cases, their headquarters to the chartermongering states. By 1900 trusts for everything from ribbons to bread to cement to alcohol had moved to Delaware or New Jersey, leaving twenty-six corporate trusts controlling, from those states, more than 80 percent of production in their markets.[17]

Chartermongering Goes National, Then International

To remain competitive, between 1900 and 1970 nearly all U.S. states rolled back their constitutions or laws to make it easier for large corporations to do business in their states without having to answer to the citizens for what they do or how they do it. At the same time, America's largest corporations—including the burgeoning defense industry—began to look overseas and see a whole new frontier of minerals and wood and raw materials owned by poor or powerless people; they saw great new places to build factories because the people would work for extremely low wages compared with workers in the United States, who were trying to maintain a middle-class lifestyle. Not to mention all those potential customers for their products.

The race to the bottom of costs, regulation, taxes, and prices was under way and would bring with it a race to the top in wealth for a few hundred multinational corporations and the politicians and media commentators they supported.

And soon that race would turn worldwide.

CHAPTER 8

Corporations Go Global

Curtin, what do you think of those fellows in Wall Street who are gambling in gold at such a time as this?...For my part, I wish every one of them had his devilish head shot off.

—President Abraham Lincoln, personal letter to
Pennsylvania Governor Andrew Curtin, April 25, 1864

PEOPLE, AT THE TIME, GENERALLY WEREN'T ALL THAT CONCERNED ABOUT the fate of the world's dolphins.

It was the last week of June 1944, and the war wasn't going well for Adolf Hitler. The killing machines of his death camps were running full out, straining his resources and creating consternation as word leaked out across Europe. His forces were falling back before the Soviets, and his generals openly worried about an Allied invasion on the French coast. On Thursday, June 29, almost all of the eighteen hundred Jews of Corfu were murdered upon their arrival at Auschwitz, while twenty thousand Jewish women were relocated to the concentration camp at Stutthof. On Friday, June 30, more than a thousand Parisian Jews arrived at Auschwitz.

This same weekend that opened July 1944, a three-week meeting was convened in an isolated hotel in New Hampshire's White Mountains near the town of Bretton Woods. Bankers, economists, and representatives of the governments of forty-four nations arrived for the meeting, which was convened as the International Monetary and Financial Conference of the United and Associated Nations.

The official history of the meeting suggests it was a group of nations getting together to work out a new international economic world order that would prevent a repeat of the Great Depressions and the European inflations that had occurred in the 1930s and driven Hitler to prominence and power with his promises to "restore Germany to greatness."

Four years earlier, in November 1940, the German minister of finance, Walther Funk, had suggested a "New Order" for the world's finances and banking that would be dominated by Germany. Partly in response to this, in 1942 John Maynard Keynes had begun to create a plan for an International Clearing Union, which formed part of the eventual basis of the Bretton Woods discussions.

According to Raymond F. Mikesell, who was present at the meetings, on the night of December 13, 1941, the U.S. secretary of the treasury, Henry Morganthau, "dreamed about an international currency" and the next morning called his undersecretary, Harry Dexter White, to ask him to write up a paper on how it could be brought to pass.[1]

"Two weeks later," Mikesell wrote, "White responded with a general outline of an International Stabilization Fund (ISF) and a (World) Bank."

During these three weeks and in subsequent meetings, the attendees hammered out the Bretton Woods Agreement, which created the International Monetary Fund (IMF) and the World Bank and laid early foundations for the General Agreement on Tariffs and Trade (GATT), which gave birth to the World Trade Organization (WTO). The group selected as the first U.S. executive director of the IMF the lead U.S. representative to the meeting and then–U.S. undersecretary of the treasury, Harry Dexter White.

The Bretton Woods Agreement wasn't ratified in whole by the United States until Bill Clinton's administration roughly fifty years later. And the near-immediate result of that would be hundreds of thousands of dead dolphins—along with the loss of as many as 20 million American manufacturing jobs.

The Fear of the Worldwide Communist Conspiracy

To understand what saved—and then re-endangered—the dolphins and threw the American manufacturing worker under the train, it's necessary to first have a bit of background.

The main obstacle to full ratification of all parts of the Bretton Woods Agreement was conservative conspiracy theorists—both in and outside the U.S. government but particularly in the U.S. Congress—who suspected that the Bretton Woods meeting was an early attempt to use the United Nations to impose a "one-world government" on the United States, perhaps even in collaboration with what they saw as an international communist conspiracy. That the meetings began more than a year before the war ended was evidence, in the minds of some of those suspicious of the agreement, that there was something up the sleeves of those who met to hammer out an accord. That at that time the Soviets were our World War II allies made it all the more suspicious to the American hard-right wing.

Although GATT's predecessors were worked out before the end of World War II as part of Bretton Woods, the Eisenhower, Kennedy, Johnson, Nixon, Ford, Carter, and Reagan administrations couldn't or didn't work to get anything like it ratified by the U.S. Congress. As far as I could find, the first president to overtly push for full ratification of GATT was George H. W. Bush, as part of his "New World Order" agenda.

In the early years after World War II, members of both parties in the U.S. Congress were wary of one-world government and an internationalist agenda. They not only refused to ratify all parts of the Bretton Woods Agreement but also went after Harry Dexter White, the IMF's first U.S. executive director.

In 1948 conservatives dragged White and Alger Hiss before a federal grand jury in New York City and accused them of "advocating the overthrow of the U.S. government by force" as agents of the Soviet Union, which in the three years since the end of the war had gone from anti-Nazi ally to Communist enemy.*

While White himself ultimately wasn't charged, his name was dragged through the newspapers along with that of Alger Hiss, who was indicted along with twelve others under the Smith Act. White, looking back on that time and the anti-Soviet hysteria in Congress, later noted that none of the organizers of Bretton Woods thought there would one day be such enmity on the part of the United States toward the Soviet Union or that fear of the Soviets would sabotage their attempts to create a single worldwide banking and trading network.

White wrote, "It was expected that the early post-war world would witness a degree of unity and good-will in international political relationships among the victorious allies [including Russia] never before reached in peacetime. It was expected that the world would move rapidly...toward 'One World'... No influential person, as far as I can remember, expressed the expectation or the fear that international relations would worsen during those years."[2]

---

*The Smith Act of 1940 made it a criminal offense for anyone to knowingly or willfully advocate, abet, advise, or teach the duty, necessity, desirability, or propriety of overthrowing the government of the United States or of any state by force or violence; or for anyone to organize any association that teaches, advises, or encourages such an overthrow; or for anyone to become a member of or to affiliate with any such association.

Source: http://caselaw.lp.findlaw.com

Mikesell, in his memoir of the Bretton Woods meetings, mentioned a private meeting he had with White the evening of April 19, 1947, just a few weeks before White was scheduled to testify before Joseph McCarthy's House Committee on Un-American Activities. "Some say he committed suicide to avoid testifying before the House Committee," wrote Mikesell about White's self-inflicted death shortly after their meeting. "I do not believe it," he added, although he offered no other explanation for White's death.[3]

Joe McCarthy's concern about any sort of "one-world agenda" persisted: GATT wasn't ratified until roughly a half century later.

The Worrisome Power of Treaties

Congress was reluctant to accept all the provisions of the Bretton Woods Agreement for an important reason: international treaties almost always supersede national laws. If the United States signed a treaty with, for example, Saudi Arabia that said, "In exchange for a cheap oil deal, all American gas stations must display a picture of the King of Saudi Arabia out front," that would become the binding law of the United States from coast to coast, even though neither Congress nor the American citizens had ever voted on it. If you didn't put a picture of the king on your gas station, you could be subject to fines or imprisonment.

As former Secretary of State John Foster Dulles said on April 11, 1952, before a Louisville, Kentucky, American Bar Association meeting, "Treaties make international law and also they make domestic law. Under our Constitution, treaties become the supreme law of the land...."[4]

The language that provides for this is in the Constitution. Clause 2 of Article VI of the U.S. Constitution says, "This Constitution and the laws of the United States which shall be made in pursuance thereof, and all treaties made, or which shall be made, under the authority of the United States, shall be the supreme law of the land; and the judges in every state shall be bound thereby, anything in the constitution or laws of any state to the contrary notwithstanding." In other words, treaties and some agreements can supersede federal, state, or local law, or court decisions, with the single exception of constitutionally defined rights or explicit state laws.

That's why the Founders were so wary of treaties. Knowing how draconian this treaty power was, the Framers of the Constitution made it difficult for treaties to be ratified, by requiring a full two-thirds vote of the Senate instead of just a simple majority as with normal legislation. Such concerns kept the GATT from being ratified for years.

Reagan, Bush, and Clinton Make a Fast Track around the Constitution

The Reagan administration ushered in an era of mergers and acquisitions that in many ways resembled the trusts of the Gilded Age of the late 1800s and the Roaring Twenties. Corporations were well represented in the corridors of power, and their power to combine into market behemoths was again blessed by an American president.

Time magazine reported on August 3, 1981,

> President [Reagan] appointed William Baxter, a Stanford law professor who firmly believes in the virtues of large-scale enterprises unfettered by excessive Government regulation, to be his antitrust chief in the Justice Department. Baxter's boss, Attorney General William French Smith, succinctly stated the new Administration's philosophy in an oft-quoted speech before the District of Columbia Bar. Said Smith: "Bigness in business is not necessarily badness. Efficient firms should not be hobbled under the guise of antitrust enforcement."[5]

According to supply-side booster George Gilder, during the Reagan era there were "42,621 merger and acquisition deals worth $3.1 trillion, $89.9 billion in shareholder gains, [and] the doubling of stock market value in real terms..."[6]

In addition to merging into giants that could keep out small competitors and largely control entire marketplaces, multinational corporations wanted the government to ease up on restrictions on their activities overseas. The U.S. Constitution specifically states that the president "shall have Power, by and with the Advice and Consent of the Senate, to make Treaties, provided two thirds of the Senators present concur."

That two-thirds-of-the-senators requirement, however, made for a slow and contentious process, particularly when it came to issues that could affect American jobs. During the Gerald Ford era, the administration proposed that the Senate go around the Constitution and turn its power to negotiate and define the details of treaties over to the sole person of the president. The Senate did this by using an obscure provision of the 1974 Trade Act that gave the president the right to negotiate trade treaties and then let him submit them to

Congress for a straight up-or-down vote with no amendments allowed. Under these rules debate is limited to forty-five days in committee and fifteen days on the floor of the House or Senate.

Each president from Richard Nixon to Bush Sr. pushed to get this "fast-track authority" for himself. Bush Sr. pushed for ratification of the GATT agreement but was unsuccessful.

But Bill Clinton, in the final days of his first four-year term, joined with Senate leader Bob Dole to use political pressure, fast-track procedures, and careful timing (just before the Christmas recess) to bring the GATT agreement to pass.

Thus, after much lobbying and giving out of substantial campaign contributions by multinational business interests and a Senate vote to invoke cloture—a procedure that allowed only thirty hours of congressional debate and forbade amendments—the final parts of the Bretton Woods Agreement and its offspring were ratified in November 1994, just as Congress was hurrying to head home for the holidays. Most of the members of Congress didn't read the document they voted on, but it became the law of the land in any case. One month later the now-fully-empowered GATT gave birth to the World Trade Organization.

Somebody Read the Agreement

Of course, the legislation had been around for years, but the record at the time, based on statements by at least one member of Congress, is that only one senator, Hank Brown of Colorado, actually read the agreement. He was a supporter of the trade agreements when he first decided to read their nearly thirty thousand pages. By the time Brown finished reading it, however, he had changed his mind. On December 9, 1994, he wrote,

> The GATT, which cleared Congress December 1, creates a form of world government limited to trade matters without fair representation for the United States, and an international court system without due process. The details of this new government called the World Trade Organization (WTO) are buried in the thousands of pages of the Agreement.
>
> Fifty new committees, boards, panels and organizations will be created by the WTO making it an international bureaucracy of unprecedented size. The United States could be responsible for up to 23 percent of the cost of running the WTO, yet will have less than 1 percent of the control of how the money

is spent. The WTO courts' (Dispute Settlement Body Panels) proceedings will be secret and decisions will be rendered anonymously by unaccountable bureaucrats. No conflict of interest rules exist to ensure impartial panelists.... Unfortunately, efforts which I supported to block the passage of the GATT implementing legislation (H.R. 5110/S. 2467) failed. The final measure, which I voted against, passed the Senate by a margin vote of 76-24.[7]

Senator Brown resigned after his one term and became a director of a multibillion-dollar corporation. Both the World Bank and the WTO were now reality.

Bretton Woods biographer Mikesell, looking back on the Bretton Woods Agreement, wrote in 1994, "There is little resemblance between the present functions and operations of the Fund and Bank and the way they were conceived at Bretton Woods." He noted that over a period as long as fifty years, most organizations either change or disappear. The IMF and the World Bank changed but didn't die. "They had too much money to fail," Mikesell remarked, "and they have increased their assets, and their staff, at a rate that rivals the postwar growth of the largest international behemoths."[8]

GATT/WTO/NAFTA Become the Law of the Land

The result of the fast-track implementation of these trade agreements was both swift and dramatic.

For example, back in 1972, in response to consumer outcries and twenty-five years of lobbying by the Humane Society, Congress passed the Marine Mammal Protection Act, which required U.S. tuna fishermen to reduce dolphin mortality in tuna nets that killed hundreds of thousands of dolphins each year. (Dolphins often swim above schools of tuna.) In 1990, with the support of the U.S. tuna industry, after extensive lobbying by American voters concerned about imported tuna, the law was strengthened with a provision banning the importation into the United States of canned tuna caught by chasing and netting dolphins from anywhere in the world and allowing for a "Dolphin Safe" label on tuna. The U.S. "Dolphin Safe" standards mean no dolphins were chased by tuna boats or caught in nets cast to catch tuna.

In 1991 Mexico challenged the United States under the rules of the GATT, claiming that the Marine Mammal Protection Act and subsequent laws that strengthened it were illegal violations of "free trade." Although a GATT panel ruled in Mexico's favor, the decision was never ratified by the full GATT tribunal.

The Clinton administration took Mexico's side in 1995 (it was actually the transnational corporate food industry's side), and Mexico prevailed: it is now legal to catch and import into the United States tuna from anywhere in the world whether it is "Dolphin Safe" or not.

Due to lawsuits filed by Earth Island Institute and the Dolphin Safe/Fair Trade Coalition, however, the "Dolphin Safe" label cannot be used on canned tuna that was caught by methods that chase and net dolphins. Resulting dolphin deaths have been reduced from an estimated 80,000 to 100,000 dolphins per year in the late 1980s to less than 2,000 dolphins, mostly by tuna purse seiners in Mexico, Colombia, and Venezuela.[9]

The GATT ruling was a problem for American packagers of imported and domestic tuna because consumers loved the "Dolphin Safe" labeling; so they lobbied Congress and U.S. regulatory agencies to get rules passed that upheld the "Dolphin Safe" standards of not netting dolphins, but Mexico's position, backed by the Clinton and George W. Bush administrations, was supported in Congress.

Fortunately, a combination of amendments to the legislation (passed in 1997) and the Earth Island federal lawsuits, have maintained the strong "Dolphin Safe" tuna label standards in the United States. Dolphin-deadly tuna can still be imported into the United States from Mexico and other countries (as of 2010), but it cannot carry a "Dolphin Safe" label. Mexico is now back before the World Trade Organization (which replaced the GATT), protesting the "Dolphin Safe" label standards.

According to Noreena Hertz, PhD, of Cambridge University, in every environmental or species dispute that had come before the WTO, "the WTO has ruled in favor of corporate interests against the wishes of democratically elected governments."[10]

It remains to be seen, as of this writing in 2010, if Mexico can prevail against the "Dolphin Safe" label standards for canned tuna, which have been voluntarily adopted by 90 percent of the world's tuna companies.

The Role of NAFTA and GATT/WTO

The biggest hit on the average family in the developed world has been the result of changes in how international trade is regulated. While Ross Perot stepped up to the podium during the presidential campaign and warned about "giant sucking sounds" from the south, both Bill Clinton and George Bush Sr.

supported the U.S. ratification of the North American Free Trade Agreement (NAFTA), both saying that it would produce at least 170,000 new jobs.

NAFTA did, in fact, create that many new jobs and more—in Mexico. But in the United States, more than 420,000 jobs vanished by 1996 as a result of NAFTA, and over $28 billion in business was lost to U.S.-based workers. When job losses because of other international trade deals and the resultant U.S. trade deficit are factored in, more than 20 million U.S. manufacturing jobs have disappeared since the 1970s, most of them year-round and full-time, although many have been replaced by part-time or low-pay service-sector jobs, thus the "net loss" of "only" 420,000 jobs.*

Speaking in opposition to giving George W. Bush new fast-track authority, Congressman Bernie Sanders of Vermont wrote in the December 14, 2001, *Burlington Free Press,*

> Our current trade policy has resulted in a record-breaking trade deficit in goods of more than $400 billion in 2000, including a trade deficit with China of more than $80 billion. Anyone with even a modest understanding of economics has to realize that a net [out]flow of $400 billion a year is a disaster. And it is.
>
> The result has been the loss of millions of decent-paying jobs as companies go abroad in search of cheap labor, or are forced to shut down because they can't compete against companies who set up shop in developing countries so they can pay starvation wages....
>
> Today, the average American worker is working longer hours for lower wages than was the case 28 years ago—before the explosion of "free trade." This wage crisis is especially acute for entry-level workers without a college education. For men with less than six years in the work force and no college education, average real wages fell about 28 percent between 1979 and 1997.[11]

Congressman Sanders noted and then refuted the argument that the WTO free-trade agreements "would benefit the poorest people in the developing world. Really? Since the passage of NAFTA, more than 1 million more

---

*www.lights.com summarizes an analysis of NAFTA's impact by Public Citizen's Global Tradewatch and the Institute for Policy Studies. Interestingly, in 1996 the U.S. government stopped including "inputs of imported goods and services" in its calculations of "U.S. Jobs Supported by Goods and Services Exports." See John R. MacArthur, *The Selling of Free Trade* (Hill & Wang, 2000).

Mexicans work for less than the minimum wage of $3.40 per day, and 8 million Mexicans have fallen from the middle class into poverty."

An earlier editorial in the Gannett-owned *Burlington Free Press* in favor of fast track and free trade had noted how many people in Pakistan are now employed making clothing for Americans.*

Congressman Sanders replied,

> The *Free Press* mentions that fabric and apparel factories employ 60 percent of the industrial work force in Pakistan. True. But the *Free Press* forgets to mention that while the apparel industry in America has been decimated, and tens of thousands of jobs have been lost here, the average Pakistani worker is paid 25 cents an hour. The *Free Press* may think that the Tommy Hilfiger company is producing shirts in Pakistan because they want to help the poor people there. I think they're there because they can pay slave wages and increase their profit margin.[12]

The bottom line is that neither the average working people of rich nations nor those of poor nations have benefited from free trade or its corollaries: the gains have gone to a few hundred corporations that are each larger, economically, than most nations. These treaties and agreements, Sanders concluded, "simply encourage a 'race to the bottom,' pushing wages down here and exploiting poor people abroad so that multinational corporations can expand their profits."

And now Americans are discovering that the WTO can bite back when it comes to internal domestic tax policy. On January 15, 2002, the Associated Press reported that the WTO had concluded that American tax laws that let American-based transnational corporations exempt themselves from paying American taxes on income they earned abroad were illegal.

"The WTO appeals panel in Geneva ruled against a U.S. law granting multibillion-dollar tax breaks to Microsoft, Boeing, and thousands of other American companies operating overseas," the article said, indicating, "the EU [European Union] could ask the WTO for permission to start imposing up to $4 billion in sanctions almost immediately." The trade representative for the United States, Robert Zoellick, said, "We are disappointed with the outcome."[13]

---

*Gannett, a $6 billion corporation, also owns *USA Today* as well as ninety-seven newspapers and twenty-two television stations across the United States and the United Kingdom as of this writing.

The New "Harmonization": Leveling to the Lowest Common Denominator

Since 1995 virtually every area of consumer and industrial product has been affected by the new WTO or NAFTA regulations, which have the force of law in those countries where they're ratified. Thousands of U.S., Canadian, European, and other safety and consumer protection laws and regulations have been overturned or, through a process called harmonization, weakened to the point of irrelevance.

Harmonizing is a term that refers to bringing the laws of different nations into alignment. The effect is usually to force all nations to accept the most corporate-friendly and least restrictive laws of any of the member nations. Anti-globalization folks have referred to the process as leveling all nations to the standards of the lowest common denominator. Supporters point out that harmonization increases profits for corporations that participate, and assert that that has a positive social benefit.

These trade agreements use tribunals and Dispute Resolution Panels (DRPs) to review complaints. Their largest effect has been to put corporations on a level ground with national governments. Corporations can sue countries under NAFTA, and many have successfully won tens of millions of dollars for "unfair restraint of trade" because of laws designed to protect the environment or workers. So far no countries have sued a corporation.

If a DRP decides a law is obstructing corporations from their right to engage in free trade across national borders, fines are assessed unless all of the WTO members vote within sixty days to dispute the DRP's decision. As of this writing, this has rarely happened. If a nation continues to try to enforce laws ruled antitrade by a DRP, it suffers huge ongoing fines, must pay reparations, and can be branded a renegade nation and suffer massive trade penalties.

Thus the DRPs are among the most powerful groups in the world—they can pressure governments to repeal or change laws that were legally passed by the people of those nations, and they can enforce their judgments with penalties, sanctions, and fines. Even with all this worldwide power, the DRPs are not democratic, not elected by the people, and not controllable by the voters of any nation, and they don't meet in public.

The Dispute Resolution Panels meet in private in Geneva, Switzerland. The panels comprise three to five members in total. The public is forbidden to watch, listen, or participate in the meetings; the experts on whom the panels rely for testimony are never publicly named or identified; and the documents resulting from the meetings are forever sealed from public view.

NAFTA actually allows corporations to sue countries, although its scope is limited to the United States, Canada, and Mexico. It operates similar programs and offices out of its headquarters in Dallas, Texas, and its decisions are equally binding on the nations they affect. (NAFTA's Chapter 11 processes are even more draconian than are similar rules of the WTO.)

Here are a few examples of laws in the United States or Europe that were passed by elected legislatures and supported by citizens but were overturned because of the unelected, secret Dispute Resolution Panels of NAFTA or the WTO:

- The state of Massachusetts and thirty other local governments in the United States had passed laws that banned imports of products that were manufactured with slave or child labor from the repressive dictatorship of Myanmar, formerly known as Burma. Facing a WTO challenge from Japan and the European Union, the U.S. Supreme Court struck down these laws, making now illegal the kind of boycott that led to the freedom of Nelson Mandela and the end of apartheid in South Africa.

- Laws in England and France restricting the use of asbestos in construction were challenged by Canada, which exports asbestos.

- Asian laws that barred the marketing of tobacco products were overturned.

- The Venezuelan government successfully challenged the 1990 U.S. Clean Air Act's provisions banning the import of "dirty gasoline" reformulated in refineries of Venezuela.

- Laws in several European countries restricting the import of lumber cut from old-growth forests or by environmentally destructive clear-cutting were successfully challenged by Canada's Department of Foreign Affairs and International Trade.

- Japanese laws proposed to reduce automobile emissions by cars sold in that country were successfully challenged by the United States.

- U.S. laws banning the import of shrimp taken from regions where the shrimp industry is destroying habitats of endangered sea turtles were successfully challenged by several nations and corporations.

- European laws banning the importation of genetically modified organisms (GMOs) were successfully challenged by the United States.

- A Canadian ban on the gasoline additive MMT (methylcyclopentadienyl manganese tricarbonyl), which can cause disabling neurological impairments in movement and speech, was struck down, and the Canadian government paid millions to MMT's American manufacturer for the "economic harm to that corporation" caused by Canada's law to protect its citizens.*

- A California ban on the gasoline additive MTBE (methyl tertiary butyl ether) that the EPA has found to be a "known animal carcinogen and probable human carcinogen" was challenged.[14] MTBE is manufactured by a Canadian corporation, which sued the United States for $75 million to make up for their loss of profits in California because they cannot now sell their product in that state.

- European laws, passed by elected legislatures, that banned beef laced with hormones, regulated cosmetic testing on animals, and banned the import of furs caught with steel-jaw leg holds were all thrown out.

Under NAFTA a corporation can sue a foreign government and can also force the taxpayers of the defendant nation to pay the corporation for any profits it *might have earned* if the nation had not passed laws that "restricted free trade." The effect of the treaties has been to not only validate the *Santa Clara* contention that corporations have human rights but also expand those rights and powers to the point where multinational corporations have greater powers even than sovereign governments.

For example, a Canadian multinational corporation lost a court case in Mississippi when a jury ruled that the corporation had engaged in fraudulent and predatory trade practices; the corporation paid $175 million to settle the case after losing in the jury trial. Rather than appeal the jury's ruling to a higher court and eventually to the U.S. Supreme Court, however, the Canadian corporation went over the Supreme Court by appealing directly to a NAFTA-authorized tribunal, demanding $725 million in damages. The NAFTA tribunal, like the WTO's DRPs, meets in secret, does not allow in the public or

---

*Just a week after Canada paid $10 million to the American corporation for lost revenues during that ban, another American company slapped Canada with a similar lawsuit under NAFTA's multilateral agreement on investment (MAI) provision, which allows corporations to sue sovereign states. That case is pending as of this writing.

report their discussions to the public, and is accountable to no democratically elected government.* The government being sued by the corporation, in fact, does not even have the right to be present at the deliberations, and there is no possibility of an appeal to any nation's Supreme Court.

Reactions to these and other changes in the international trade landscape brought about by the International Monetary Fund and the World Bank have been mixed. The news media owned by multinational corporations have tended to either ignore such events or report them as victories for "free trade."

At the citizen level across the world, the response has also been mixed. When the World Bank demanded that Argentina cut social programs and services to its citizens so that it could speed up payments of its debt to the World Bank, the resulting loss of much of Argentina's social safety net led to riots, martial law, and the resignation of that nation's president the week before Christmas 2001. Similar scenes have been repeated around the world, as more than a hundred nations are now required by the World Bank to adopt "budgetary austerity, trade liberalization and privatization." Local liberation movements are demanding that their governments stop privatizing their commons by selling natural resources to transnational corporations.[15]

Jock Gill was director of White House Special Projects in the Clinton administration and, as such, had occasion to work with many people in governments around the world both during and after his time in the White House. He reports a chilling effect of WTO regulations on the rights of government to oversee the commons of its people.

Recalling the benefits that FDR's Rural Electrification Administration (REA) and Truman's telephony program had on rural America, Gill related a conversation he had after leaving the White House. "When I asked some representatives of the Mexican Telephone Company if they could institute a program in Mexico modeled after the REA and Truman's solution to rural telephony and electrification," Gill said, "they said, 'Absolutely not.' Why? Because the WTO treated such plans as outlaw solutions requiring drastic penalties."[16]

Imagine if the WTO had been in power in the time of Teddy Roosevelt, who said,

> This country, as Lincoln said, belongs to the people. So do the natural
> resources which make it rich. They supply the basis of our prosperity now and
> hereafter. In preserving them, which is a national duty, we must not forget that

---

*The World Bank provides NAFTA with a private court system called the International Center for Settlement of Investment Disputes.

monopoly is based on the control of natural resources and natural advantages, and that it will help the people little to conserve our natural wealth unless the benefits which it can yield are secured to the people.[17]

The Problem of International Poverty—and Why More Corporate Power Is *Not* the Solution

The United Nations Millennium Report[18] submitted to member nations and the world by then Secretary General Kofi Annan pointed out that as of the year 2000:

- More than 2.8 billion people, close to half the world's population, lived on less than the equivalent of $2 per day. More than 1.2 billion people, or about 20 percent of the world's population, lived on less than the equivalent of $1 per day.

- More than 1 billion people did not have access to clean water; some 840 million people went hungry or faced food insecurity.

- About one-third of all children under the age of five suffered from malnutrition.

- The top fifth (20 percent) of the world's people who live in the highest-income countries had access to 86 percent of world gross domestic product (GDP). The bottom fifth, in the poorest countries, had about 1 percent.

- The assets of the world's three richest men exceeded the combined GDPs of the world's forty-eight poorest countries.

- In 1998, for every $1 that the developing world received in grants, it spent $13 on debt repayment.

Since that report—the result of years of research leading up to the transition from the twentieth to the twenty-first century—although the United Nations has not issued a new and comprehensive similar world overview, it has kept track of many of the developing world's problems. With the exception of industrializing China, in virtually every other respect all of these problems continue to move in the wrong direction.

The need (and the moral imperative) for developed-world citizens to help bring people up out of poverty in most of the world is very real. But how?

The advocates of corporatism suggest that the way to bring this about is to unleash corporations and let them roam freely from nation to nation to "create jobs" and "recover resources" (to use phrases common in modern corporate marketing). And it's important to acknowledge that when corporations do this—moving manufacturing from high-labor-cost nations to low-labor-cost nations, or mining/drilling/cutting in nations with lax environmental regulations—they are doing so not for humanly immoral reasons but for reasons that are at the very core of corporate morality: profits.

Yet this profit-driven behavior does, over the short term, create jobs in and extract resources from the developing world, although at the same time it is placing the very nations that are trying to emerge from poverty at high risk of social upheaval because of the natural tension between democratic social stability and corporatism.

Many of those same corporations that are now providing jobs for wage earners in low-wage nations also explicitly warn those countries that if their workers begin to demand higher standards of living and their wages go too high, the corporations will simply move elsewhere—as has already happened to the United States, Japan, the developed European nations, Korea, Taiwan, and Thailand. Each struggles with the social crises brought about by this form of unconstrained global free trade that allows the unrestricted movement of corporations in constant search of cheaper resources, including human labor.

The result is that most of the workers of the developed world experience a continuous decline in their standard of living, while developing nations find themselves in a competitive battle against one another for corporate largesse, which is also socially destabilizing and anti-democratic. In this competition these nations essentially have only two things they can use to raise their standard of living in the direction demanded by their citizens who watch American-produced television and movies: sell off their natural resources to the highest bidders and do whatever they can to suppress labor movements and other efforts within their nations to raise living standards to the point where they'll no longer be "competitive" with poorer nations. This, in part, is why more than twenty-five hundred union members and organizers have been murdered just in the country of Colombia since 1985 (some put the number much, much higher).[19]

The end result is that the nations are strip-mined of their natural resources, corporations "play the spread" between labor costs among nations to skim off the cream, and the developed-world countries (where the corporations are based) play the role England once did for the East India Company—building a huge military with worldwide reach so that it can act as the suppressor of local independence movements all around the world where "our" corporations are mining local resources or labor. And often those suppressed movements for local culture bite back: When the United States did it in 1776, we called our citizen-soldiers "patriots." Today, however, when other nations' peoples do it against us, we most often call them "terrorists."

How to Respond to Poverty

So what can we do about this? On the one hand, there is the very real problem of poverty around the world and the reality that in many ways industrialization helps that problem in the short term. On the other hand, there is the very real problem of how such development becomes anti-democratic (both in the developing and developed worlds) and eventually leads to political crises in emerging nations.

The corporate position is clear: let the "invisible hand of the marketplace" work things out, while the corporations pry as many of the natural resources of the commons as possible out of the hands of democratically elected governments and put them into the invisible hands of the corporations.

But both Adam Smith and history tell us that such privatization schemes and the invisible hand work only to place more and more wealth into the pockets of the corporations and their stockholders. Citizens and their elected officials must intelligently constrain that invisible hand, or it will end up holding those officials and the resources of the citizens by the throat, as we can so clearly see in the entanglement of Enron and governments around the world.

The response the Founders of America came up with when they faced this same sort of problem was to encourage business but at the same time place controls and limits on what corporations could do both domestically and abroad. Developed and developing nations both need essential economic stability, but when corporations operate in what they call a free environment (creaming off labor and natural resources then moving on to greener pastures when it's profitable to do so), stability is threatened worldwide, indigenous peoples' cultures are destroyed, and the natural world is spoiled.

The suggestion I'm putting forth in this book is to try democracy—government of, by, and for We the People—and to encourage it in nations all around the world once it is reinstated in the United States and other developed nations.

Because raw or free-trade corporatism is essentially undemocratic—it answers to stockholders instead of citizens, and it drives to the moral imperative of profit, thus ignoring future generations and long-term consequences to environments, cultures, and governments—there is a natural and dynamic antagonism between corporatism and democracy.

The Founders of the United States faced this in the Boston Tea Party and the Revolutionary War, and they solved the problem in early America with the passage of thousands of laws—all put into place by citizens or officials elected by citizens—to control and constrain corporate behavior. Since the era of the *Santa Clara* mistake, however, corporatism has steadily been overwhelming democracy, both in the developed and developing worlds.

Globalism Drives a Permanent Defense Industry

In the novel *1984* by George Orwell, the way a seemingly democratic president kept his nation in a continual state of repression was by having a continuous war. That lesson wasn't lost on Richard Nixon, who, history suggests, extended the Vietnam War specifically so it would run over an election cycle, knowing that a wartime president's party is more likely to be reelected and has more power than a president in peacetime.

Similarly, the first ghostwriter hired by George W. Bush's campaign advisers (presumably Karl Rove) in 1998 to write Bush Jr.'s autobiography (*A Charge to Keep*), was a Texas author and Bush family friend named Mickey Herskowitz. In an interview with investigative reporter Russ Baker, Herskowitz laid out how two years before George W. Bush was handed the presidency by a corrupted Supreme Court, he was already planning to invade Iraq. And it was not to "protect" America but purely to get "political capital" so that he could accomplish things like his lifelong goal of privatizing Social Security.

In 2004 Baker wrote:

> "He was thinking about invading Iraq in 1999," said author and journalist Mickey Herskowitz. "It was on his mind. He [Bush] said to me: 'One of the keys to being seen as a great leader is to be seen as a commander-in-chief.' And he said, 'My father had all this political capital built up when he

drove the Iraqis out of Kuwait and he wasted it.' He said, 'If I have a chance to invade, if I had that much capital, I'm not going to waste it. I'm going to get everything passed that I want to get passed and I'm going to have a successful presidency.'"[20]

An earlier president had considered the idea of war as a way to increase presidential power. On April 20, 1795, James Madison, who had just helped shepherd through the Constitution and the Bill of Rights and would become president of the United States in the following decade, wrote:

Of all the enemies to public liberty war is, perhaps, the most to be dreaded because it comprises and develops the germ of every other. War is the parent of armies; from these proceed debts and taxes. And armies, and debts, and taxes are the known instruments for bringing the many under the domination of the few.

Reflecting on the ability of a president to use war as an excuse to become a virtual dictator, Madison continued his letter:

In war, too, the discretionary power of the Executive [President] is extended. Its influence in dealing out offices, honors, and emoluments is multiplied; and all the means of seducing the minds, are added to those of subduing the force of the people. The same malignant aspect in republicanism may be traced in the inequality of fortunes, and the opportunities of fraud, growing out of a state of war...and in the degeneracy of manners and morals, engendered by both.

"No nation," our fourth president and the father of the Constitution concluded, "could preserve its freedom in the midst of continual warfare."[21]

Since Madison's warning, "continual warfare" has been used repeatedly in the real world.

Adolf Hitler used the 1933 burning of the Reichstag (Parliament) building in Berlin by a deranged Dutchman to declare a "war on terrorism" and establish his legitimacy as a leader (even though he hadn't won a majority in the previous election).

"You are now witnessing the beginning of a great epoch in history," he proclaimed, standing in front of the burned-out building, surrounded by national media. "This fire," he said, his voice trembling with emotion, "is the beginning." He used the occasion—"a sign from God" he called it—to declare an all-out war on terrorism and its ideological sponsors, a people, he said, who traced their origins to the Middle East and found motivation for their "evil" deeds in their religion.

Two weeks later the first prison for terrorists was built in Oranienburg, holding the first suspected allies of the infamous terrorist.

Within four weeks of the terrorist attack, the nation's now-popular leader had pushed through legislation, in the name of combating terrorism and fighting the philosophy he said spawned it, that suspended constitutional guarantees of free speech, privacy, and habeas corpus. Police could now intercept mail and wiretap phones without warrants; suspected terrorists could be imprisoned without specific charges and without access to their lawyers; and police could sneak into people's homes without warrants if the cases involved terrorism.

To get his patriotic "Decree on the Protection of People and State" passed over the objections of concerned legislators and civil libertarians, he agreed to put a four-year sunset provision on it: if the national emergency provoked by the terrorist attack on the Reichstag building was over by then, the freedoms and the rights would be returned to the people, and the police agencies would be re-restrained.

As he was leaving office, the old warrior president Dwight D. Eisenhower looked back over his years as president and as a general and supreme commander of the Allied Forces in France during World War II and noted that the Cold War had brought a new, Orwellian type of war to the American landscape—a perpetual war supported by a perpetual war industry.

He first pointed out that before World War II, "the United States had no armaments industry." But by 1961, "We annually spend on military security more than the net income of all United States corporations."

Eisenhower added, "This conjunction of an immense military establishment and a large arms industry is new in the American experience. The total influence—economic, political, even spiritual—is felt in every city, every State house, every office of the Federal government."

And while he felt it important to have a strong military, he noted:

> We must not fail to comprehend its grave implications. Our toil, resources, and livelihood are all involved; so is the very structure of our society. In the councils of government, we must guard against the acquisition of unwarranted influence, whether sought or unsought, by the military-industrial complex. The potential for the disastrous rise of misplaced power exists and will persist.

We must never let the weight of this combination endanger our liberties or democratic processes. We should take nothing for granted. Only an alert and knowledgeable citizenry can compel the proper meshing of the huge industrial and military machinery of defense with our peaceful methods and goals, so that security and liberty may prosper together.[22]

Unfortunately, Eisenhower's warning was a bit too late by the time it was given.

War Profits for the Largest Transnational Corporations

War has become big business in America, and now not only are we a big user of military equipment but we sell it to the world: we're the world's largest exporter of weapons of virtually all sizes and types. While some consider the U.S. defense budget excessive, others argue that we live in a dangerous world and that a strong military is necessary. After all, there are sociopaths and psychopaths out there, and sometimes they rise to the highest levels of power and threaten life and liberty around the world.

But in a nation where the political process is more strongly influenced by the profit value than by human and life-based values—where corporations have human rights but not human vulnerabilities—Eisenhower's warning becomes more of a concern.

Military spending is the least effective way to help, stimulate, or sustain an economy for a very simple reason: military products are used once and destroyed.

When a government uses taxpayer money to build a bridge or highway or hospital, that investment will be used for decades, perhaps centuries, and will continue to fuel economic activity throughout its lifetime. But when taxpayer dollars are used to build a bomb or a bullet, that military hardware will be used once and then vanish. As it vanishes, so does the wealth it represented, never to be recovered.

As Eisenhower said in an April 1953 speech, "Every gun that is made, every warship launched, every rocket fired, signifies, in the final sense, a theft from those who hunger and are not fed, those who are cold and are not clothed. The world in arms is not spending money alone. It is spending the sweat of its laborers, the genius of its scientists, the hopes of its children."[23]

It was a brilliant articulation of human needs in a world increasingly dominated by nonbreathing entities whose values were not human values. But it was a call unheeded, and today it is nearly totally forgotten.

Meanwhile the ruling elites of the developing world, aligned with transnational corporations, generally become richer and better armed as their people become poorer. The world, in part as a result of the notion contained in the *Santa Clara* ruling's corrupt headnote—that corporations have the rights of persons—is becoming more unsafe and unequal day by day.

CHAPTER 9

The Court Takes the Presidency

"The election is over. We won."

Reporter's voice: "How do you know that?"

"It's all over but the counting. And we'll take care of the counting."

> —Republican Congressman Peter King on July 4,
> 2003, speaking of the 2004 presidential election,
> interviewed by filmmaker Alexandra Pelosi for the
> HBO documentary *Diary of a Political Tourist*[1]

ON DECEMBER 12, 2000, THE U.S. SUPREME COURT GRANTED YET ANOTHER gift to corporate power—and hammered yet another nail into the coffin of democracy in America. They did it in a strikingly dramatic fashion: by stealing the presidency.

In the process five members of the unelected third branch of government made sure that its majority character and nature probably wouldn't change for a long enough time that the Court could cast a hugely conservative shadow over the American electoral process, guaranteeing that people like themselves and their patrons—wealthy, powerful, and corporate-connected—would continue to have a disproportionate impact on future elections.

Here's how they did it and what their actions mean for the future of the battle between corporations and citizens for the soul of the nation.

Sandra Day O'Connor (R)

Supreme Court Justice Sandra Day O'Connor was no stranger to Republican politics. She'd served three terms as a Republican state senator in Arizona, her last term as majority leader—the ultimate political insider's job. Appointed to the U.S. Supreme Court in 1981 by President Ronald Reagan, nineteen years later she had decided she wanted out. The workload was intense, and her husband was starting to display some of the same early symptoms of Alzheimer's that she had observed in Reagan during his second term as president. And she missed Arizona terribly.

So on the evening of November 7, 2000, when O'Connor and her husband were guests at an election-eve party watching the CBS election reporting and Dan Rather came on to call Florida for Al Gore, making Gore president, she was horrified.

"This is terrible," *Newsweek* reporters Evan Thomas and Michael Isikoff quote two different witnesses as saying she "exclaimed." O'Connor was so troubled that she got up "with an obvious look of disgust" and left the room.

The puzzled guests turned to her husband, John O'Connor, who with the candor that often accompanies early dementia, explained that she wanted to retire to Arizona but wasn't willing to do so if her successor would be appointed by a Democratic president.[2]

On the first day of December, however, she would do something about her concern, voting to block the state of Florida from conducting a recount that had just been ordered by the Florida Supreme Court. That vote froze in place the "win" of George W. Bush, as the constitutional clock was running out on when the election had to be decided.

Clarence Thomas (R)

George H. W. Bush Court appointee Justice Clarence Thomas—as is usually the case—wasn't in a public setting on election eve, but it's not hard to guess his concern. His wife, Virginia, worked for the Heritage Foundation, a far-right think tank in Washington, D.C., as the director of executive branch relations. As such she was organizing résumés for loyal right-wingers who could become appointees to a Bush White House. The week her husband's Court accepted the *Bush v. Gore* case and before it was decided, she sent out e-mails soliciting potential appointments for the Bush administration.

The *New York Times* noted in a December 12, 2000, article ("Job of Thomas' Wife Raises Conflict-of-interest Questions"):

> A federal appellate judge, Gilbert S. Merritt of the U.S. Court of Appeals for the Sixth Circuit, said he saw a serious conflict of interest for Justice Thomas in deciding a case that could throw the election to Governor Bush.

"The spouse has obviously got a substantial interest that could be affected by the outcome," he said in an interview from his home in Nashville. "You should disqualify yourself. I think he'd be subject to some kind of investigation in the Senate...."

But he urged Justice Thomas to remove himself from the case in order to prevent any violation of a federal law—he cited Section 455 of Title 28 of the U.S. Code, "Disqualification of Justices, Judges or Magistrates"—that requires court officers to excuse themselves if a spouse has "an interest that could be substantially affected by the outcome of the proceeding."[3]

And Thomas himself, as the former legislative assistant to Republican Senator John Danforth (who championed his appointment to the Supreme Court), was no stranger to Republican politics and, after a bruising confirmation hearing (Anita Hill), bore no goodwill for Democrats.

Antonin Scalia (R)

Reagan appointee Justice Antonin Scalia, on December 1, looked down from his leather chair in the Supreme Court chambers to see Ted Olson, a senior partner—the lawfirm equivalent of a senior executive or director—of the law firm Gibson, Dunn & Crutcher. As a senior partner at GD&C, Olson was among the management—the boss—of Scalia's son Eugene Scalia, who was merely a partner in the firm.

Scalia chose not to mention his son's association with Olson and didn't recuse himself.[4] Later he would famously and sarcastically tell a student at a law forum, of the *Bush v. Gore* ruling, "Get over it!"

William Rehnquist (R)

Nixon appointee William Rehnquist had made a name for himself in Arizona Republican politics in the 1960s, leading what a U.S. Senate investigation termed a "ballot security" effort to challenge the votes of American Indians and African Americans, who were more likely to vote Democratic. The Senate investigation further noted that Rehnquist, back in the day in Arizona, had "publicly opposed a Phoenix public accommodations ordinance, and he publicly challenged a plan to end school segregation in Phoenix..."[5]

And by 2000, seventy-six years old and in unreliable health, Rehnquist had discussed with more than one friend his concern about retiring or even dying on the bench and who would replace him.[6]

Anthony Kennedy (R)

Reagan appointee Anthony Kennedy had been a close friend of Ronald Reagan, helping draft for him tax cuts when Reagan was governor of California, and got his appointment to the federal bench on Reagan's suggestion to then-president Gerald Ford. Reagan then appointed him to the Supreme Court after first trying unsuccessfully (this was back in the days when Democrats would say no to a Republican president) to put Robert Bork and Douglas Ginsburg in that slot.

An affable man, Kennedy was far more follower than leader: during the years Rehnquist was alive and Kennedy was on the bench (1992 to 2005), Kennedy voted identically with Rehnquist 92 percent of the time, more than any other justice.[7]

The Future of the Court

In the *Bush v. Gore* case, these five Republican justices were faced with the opportunity to shape the very Court itself for the next generation. They, and they alone, had the power to make sure that a Republican, regardless of their personal opinions of George W. Bush, would appoint at least one and possibly more justices, thus keeping the majority of the Court on their side.

Al Gore had won the presidency by 543,895 votes nationally; no candidate in the history of the republic had ever had such a large popular vote win and lost the presidency. He also, it turned out, had won the vote in Florida. (Although his initial legal strategy of only recounting three counties wouldn't have proven it; it took a recount of the entire state.)

President Gore?

Almost a year after the election, a consortium of news organizations actually physically counted *all* the Florida ballots, as the Florida Supreme Court had ordered. What they found—just a few weeks after the 9/11 attacks—so horrified them that they chose to report the story in an intentionally confusing way so as not to diminish President Bush's authority during a time of crisis.

The *New York Times,* on November 12, 2001, published the results of the statewide recount that, it said, "could have produced enough votes to tilt the election his [Gore's] way, *no matter what standard was chosen to judge voter intent.*"[8] [Italics added.]

The *Times* article went on to document how Al Gore won Florida in 2000:

> If all the ballots had been reviewed under any of seven single standards [all the ones that were used by either party], and combined with the results of an examination of overvotes, Mr. Gore would have won, by a very narrow margin. For example, using the most permissive "dimpled chad" standard, nearly 25,000 additional votes would have been reaped, yielding 644 net new votes for Mr. Gore and giving him a 107-vote victory margin....

> Using the most restrictive standard—the fully punched ballot card—5,252 new votes would have been added to the Florida total, producing a net gain of 652 votes for Mr. Gore, and a 115-vote victory margin.

> All the other combinations likewise produced additional votes for Mr. Gore, giving him a slight margin over Mr. Bush, when at least two of the three coders agreed.

And yet all of this information was buried well after the seventeenth paragraph of the story, which carried the baffling headline "Study of Disputed Florida Ballots Finds Justices Did Not Cast the Deciding Vote."

The *Times* analysis further showed that had "spoiled" ballots—ballots normally punched but "spoiled" because the voter also wrote onto the ballot the name of the candidate—been counted, the results were even more spectacular.

While 35,176 voters wrote in Bush's name after punching the hole for him, 80,775 wrote in Gore's name while punching the hole for Gore. Katherine Harris decided that these were "spoiled" ballots because they were both punched and written upon and ordered that *none* of them should be counted. Many were from African American districts, where older and often broken machines were distributed, causing voters to write onto their ballots so their intent would be unambiguous. The *New York Times* added this information in a sidebar article with a self-explanatory title by Ford Fessenden: "Ballots Cast by Blacks and Older Voters Were Tossed in Far Greater Numbers."[9]

Although it took a year for these findings to become public, even at the time of the election reports were leaking into Washington, D.C.—and thus to the five Republican appointees on the Court—that there were huge irregularities in Florida. The Florida secretary of state, Katherine Harris, was also in charge of the Bush campaign in that state, and African-American groups like the NAACP were protesting that as many as eighty thousand Blacks had been purged from the voter rolls because a Republican-affiliated Texas corporation Harris had hired to "clean" the Florida list found that those Florida residents had names "similar" to the names of Texas felons.

Absentee ballots were also problematic: those from Americans overseas tend to swing Democratic, whereas military ballots tend to swing Republican. As the *New York Times* noted a year later, when the ballots had finally been opened and counted:

> A statistical analysis conducted for *The Times* determined that if all counties had followed state law in reviewing the absentee ballots, Mr. Gore would have picked up as many as 290 additional votes, enough to tip the election in Mr. Gore's favor in some of the situations studied in the statewide ballot review.[10]

The Court Acts

On November 17, 2000, the Florida Supreme Court blocked Katherine Harris from certifying the election. On November 21 it ruled that *all* the ballots in the entire state must be recounted (which, we now know, would have led to an indisputable Gore win).

The Bush campaign brought in hired gun James Baker and attorney Ted Olson to take over. Congressman Tom DeLay, aka "The Hammer," flew nearly his entire congressional staff (along with a few others) down to Florida to stage a moblike stunt, posing as Floridians and banging on windows where votes were being counted, shouting "Stop the count!" Republicans organized protesters to stand, 24/7, around the Gore's Washington, D.C., home (the Naval Observatory is what it's called), shouting through bullhorns throughout the night, "Get out of Dick Cheney's house!" Gore later recounted to me how terrified his children were by the ongoing and angry display.

Baker and Olson turned to Rehnquist's former clerk, a millionaire Washington, D.C., corporate attorney named John Roberts, to come down to Florida to plan strategy with them to take a case to the Supreme Court that would stop the statewide recount. Roberts, who had become a friend of Rehnquist as well as his clerk, had argued many times before the Rehnquist Court and had an impressive record of wins.

As *Miami Herald* reporter Marc Caputo documented in an article for that paper ("Roberts Had Larger 2000 Recount Role"), Roberts "was a member of a tight-knit circle of former clerks for the court's chief justice, William Rehnquist—a group jokingly referred to as 'the cabal.'" Roberts also helped run a "dress rehearsal to prepare the Bush legal team for the U.S. Supreme Court," as well as meeting with the candidate's brother, Florida Governor Jeb Bush.[11]

Prepped by Roberts, Olson and his team flew to Washington, D.C., and argued that, among other things, because the Fourteenth Amendment demands equal protection under the law, and different Florida counties used different voting systems and different criteria for determining the intent of the voter, the state was in violation of the Fourteenth Amendment.

It was just what the Republican Five on the Supreme Court needed. Although logically if they were to rule that this was true, it would mean that every state in the union was in violation of the Constitution and that national standards would have to be immediately implemented, they used the argument nonetheless, but said that it counted *only* for this *one* case, *only* in Florida for the 2000 presidential election, and did *not* constitute a precedent.

To put an icing on the cake, the Republican Five on the Court ruled that they *had* to rule because if they didn't stop the count of the vote in Florida, it would result in "irreparable harm" to the man bringing the lawsuit, George W. Bush.

Stevens Dissents

The four minority justices on the Court were incensed. Justice John P. Stevens (with Ruth Bader Ginsburg and Stephen Breyer joining) wrote in his dissent of *Bush v. Gore,* "When questions arise about the meaning of state laws, including election laws, it is our settled practice to accept the opinions of the highest courts of the States as providing the final answers." Although there may be "rare occasions" where the Supreme Court should intervene, "This is not such an occasion."[12]

Stevens wrote that the Court had no business inserting itself into Florida's election: "The federal questions that ultimately emerged in this case are not substantial." He went on to quote several previous cases where the Court had left state voting problems to the states, as provided for by Article II of the Constitution:

> Lest there be any doubt, we stated over 100 years ago in *McPherson v. Blacker* that "what is forbidden or required to be done by a State" in the Article II context "is forbidden or required of the legislative power under state constitutions as they exist." In the same vein, we also observed that "the [State's] legislative power is the supreme authority except as limited by the constitution of the State."

Stevens added that the only basis on which it would be reasonable for the Rehnquist Court to accept Bush's lawsuit against Al Gore's campaign was if the Florida Supreme Court's justices—who had already ruled on the case—were totally corrupt. In fact, Stevens said, by overturning the Florida Court's decision, the Supreme Court was nakedly suggesting that:

> The endorsement of that position by the majority of this Court can only lend credence to the most cynical appraisal of the work of judges throughout the land. It is confidence in the men and women who administer the judicial system that is the true backbone of the rule of law. Time will one day heal the wound to that confidence that will be inflicted by today's decision. One thing, however, is certain.

> Although we may never know with complete certainty the identity of the winner of this year's Presidential election, the identity of the loser is perfectly clear. It is the Nation's confidence in the judge as an impartial guardian of the rule of law.

Ginsburg Dissents

Justice Ruth Bader Ginsburg's dissent was even more scathing than that of Justice Stevens, particularly with regard to the Fourteenth Amendment.

"I agree with JUSTICE STEVENS that petitioners have not presented a substantial equal protection claim," she wrote; she then endorsed the Florida Supreme Court's decision to recount the vote. She concluded her dissent by saying, "In sum, the Court's conclusion that a constitutionally adequate recount is impractical is a prophecy the Court's own judgment will not allow to be tested. Such an untested prophecy should not decide the Presidency of the United States."

Breyer Dissents

The dissent of Justice Breyer (which even David Souter joined, along with Ginsburg and Stevens) was perhaps the most direct and eloquent. It started in the first paragraph by stating: "The Court was wrong to take this case. It was wrong to grant a stay. It should now vacate that stay and permit the Florida Supreme Court to decide whether the recount should resume."

He went on to ridicule the Fourteenth Amendment arguments, noting that "the majority raises three Equal Protection problems," which he then describes and knocks down, saying, "there is no justification for the majority's remedy, which is simply to reverse the lower court and halt the recount entirely."

Justice Breyer continued to bluntly say out loud that this was a political, and not a legal, decision:

> By halting the manual recount, and thus ensuring that the uncounted legal votes will not be counted under any standard, this Court crafts a remedy out of proportion to the asserted harm. And that remedy harms the very fairness interests the Court is attempting to protect....

> Despite the reminder that this case involves "an election for the President of the United States," no preeminent legal concern, or practical concern related to legal questions, required this Court to hear this case, let alone to issue a stay that stopped Florida's recount process in its tracks.

He hits home this point, saying that if there is to be a debate about who won the presidency (as there was in 1876), that debate should be resolved by Congress (as it was in 1876, later ratified in law by Congress in 1886). The Court, Breyer notes, echoing Jefferson, is the unelected of the three branches of government and as such should stay as far away from politics as possible:

> The decision by both the Constitution's Framers and the 1886 Congress to minimize this Court's role in resolving close federal presidential elections is as wise as it is clear. However awkward or difficult it may be for Congress to resolve difficult electoral disputes, Congress, being a political body, expresses the people's will far more accurately than does an unelected Court. And the people's will is what elections are about.

This is about an election, not the Constitution, said Breyer. As such, for the Court to involve itself would bring disrepute on it and cause the public to lose confidence in it, thus wounding both the Court and the nation itself:

> At the same time, as I have said, the Court is not acting to vindicate a fundamental constitutional principle, such as the need to protect a basic human liberty. No other strong reason to act is present. Congressional statutes tend to obviate the need. And, above all, in this highly politicized matter, the appearance of a split decision runs the risk of undermining the public's confidence in the Court itself.

> That confidence is a public treasure. It has been built slowly over many years, some of which were marked by a Civil War and the tragedy of segregation. It is a vitally necessary ingredient of any successful effort to protect basic liberty and, indeed, the rule of law itself.

We run no risk of returning to the days when a President (responding to this Court's efforts to protect the Cherokee Indians) might have said, "John Marshall has made his decision; now let him enforce it!" But we do risk a self-inflicted wound—a wound that may harm not just the Court, but the Nation.

The Court Gets What It Wants

But the majority decided, in large part using the unequal protection argument.

In the first application for the stay, Bush's lawyers had argued that if the statewide vote count continued in Florida, the petitioners—the people bringing the lawsuit (Bush and Cheney)—would suffer "irreparable harm." Justice Scalia, probably considering the future makeup of his own Court, agreed: "The counting of votes that are of questionable legality," Scalia wrote, "does in my view threaten irreparable harm to petitioner [Bush], and to the country, by casting a cloud upon what he claims to be the legitimacy of his election."

Apparently, for the guy who'd won the most votes, Al Gore, being frozen out of an election that he'd actually won, did not, in Scalia's world, constitute an "irreparable harm" that was the consequence of "unequal protection" by the highest court in the land.

By freezing the Florida recount, the Rehnquist Court handed the election to a Republican president, who would go on to replace both O'Connor and Rehnquist with corporate-friendly conservative stalwarts who had each either endorsed or associated themselves with organizations that endorsed corporate personhood. Roberts's reward was particularly spectacular—the man he helped make president, George W. Bush, would eventually appoint him chief justice of the Supreme Court.

But first the Court had to deal with the issue of the corporate "right to lie."

CHAPTER 10

Protecting Corporate Liars

With yearly revenues of over $9 billion, NIKE has the resources to spread their corporate message far and wide. Do they also have the Constitutionally protected right to distort or misrepresent the truth for commercial gain?

Corporations are not people, and the First Amendment should account for their unique motivation: sales.

—Congressman Dennis Kucinich, writing about the Supreme Court case *Kasky v. Nike*[1]

THE FIRST DIRECT SHOT ACROSS THE BOW OF THE DOCTRINE OF A CORPORATION's "right to lie" by using its "personhood" to claim First Amendment "free speech" rights came in April 1998, when Mark Kasky, a California political activist, noticed that Nike was engaged in what he considered to be a deceptive greenwashing campaign. Kasky had long been a runner and wore Nike shoes, so he was particularly distressed when he saw Nike's communications director, Lee Weinstein, publish a letter in the *San Francisco Examiner* in December 1997 that said, in part, "Consider that Nike established the sporting goods industry's first code of conduct to ensure our workers know and can exercise their rights."[2]

This letter was just a small part, it turned out, of a national campaign by Nike to convince the American public that it was making sure that its contractors and subcontractors were treating their employees in Asia well. The year before, Steve Miller, Nike's sports marketing director, pledged in a letter to athletic program directors and presidents of U.S. universities that Nike's manufacturers complied with "government regulations regarding minimum wage and overtime as well as occupational health and safety, environmental regulations, workers' insurance, and equal opportunity provisions."[3]

What Nike wasn't mentioning, but which was leaked to the press in 1997, was a 1996 audit of one of the company's overseas factories (this one in Vietnam) by Ernst & Young. The audit, which Nike had commissioned but then tried to keep secret, documented how workers in the Vietnamese factory were exposed to cancer-causing solvents like acetone and toluene in ways that would have been flatly illegal in the United States and were not protected from deafening levels of noise; it also raised a series of questions on other workplace issues. As *Mother Jones* documented in a February 2001 article ("Greenwashing on Trial" by Josh Richman), "another Nike-funded study found evidence of physical and verbal abuse and sexual harassment at nine of its contract factories in Indonesia."[4]

Kasky was outraged that Nike held itself out as the model corporate citizen. He told filmmaker Lori Cheatle (for her movie *This Land Is Your Land*, which also features Naomi Klein, Thomas Frank, Jim Hightower, and me, along with seven others): "The Nike code of conduct stated that they maintained the highest standards of health, worker safety, and compensation, and they used that to market their products. So I felt very upset when I realized that a lot of the representations they were making might not be true."

He and a lot of people in California were buying Nike products under false assumptions or misrepresentations, so he called an attorney and decided to take the company to court.

Kasky went to attorney Alan Caplan (of the "Joe Camel" cigarette lawsuit fame), and together they invoked a rather unique California law that allowed individuals to behave as if they were the state's attorney general and sue companies for fraudulent or other illegal practices, producing what would ultimately become the Supreme Court case *Kasky v. Nike*.

In 1999 the case was dismissed by San Francisco Superior Court Judge David Garcia, who suggested that Nike's right to lie—to "free speech"—was protected by the First Amendment of the U.S. Constitution. Kasky and Caplan appealed to the U.S. Court of Appeals, where, in March 2000, that court ruled against Kasky again, with Justice Douglas Swager arguing that Nike was only promoting its products, as any company would, could, and should be able to do in a world of corporate "persons" endowed with free-speech rights.

His comment specifically noted that Nike's use of inaccurate letters to the editors in newspapers across America, letters telling untruths to university presidents, and other false statements to the press were "within the core area of expression protected by the First Amendment."

Undeterred, Kasky carried his suit to the California Supreme Court, which ruled in May 2002 (by one vote, 4 to 3) that Nike had violated the California laws against unfair competition and false advertising. The Supreme Court justices didn't, however, challenge the notion that First Amendment protections didn't extend to commercial "speech" by corporations; instead they suggested that such rights should be limited to the commercial interests of the corporation and that the action of Nike in this case "bears only a tangential relation to commercial transactions."

At that point Nike decided that, rather than pay the fine and change its business practices, it would take the case all the way to the U.S. Supreme Court, where a very curious thing happened.

The Supreme Court typically gets more than ten thousand requests every year to hear cases. It has a small army of clerks and lawyers (usually including clerks for the justices—Samuel Alito chooses not to have his clerks participate—known as the "cert pool") who filter through them to find the ones that have reasonable merit and which the justices may be interested in hearing. The Court as a whole then considers the thousand or so that survive the culling process, further reducing the caseload for the year to a number typically around one hundred total cases (it takes the votes of four justices to grant certiorari, allowing the case to be argued before the Court).

After the Court has gone through all this work to whittle down its caseload, each case comes before the justices in two ways. First, both parties to the case file their own legal briefs or arguments in writing. Second, interested parties—"friends" of either side (by virtue of association or concern for the issue behind the case)—file Friend of the Court, or amicus curiae, briefs, adding their voices to the arguments. Then the justices hear oral arguments, which these days are limited to thirty minutes for each side, after which each justice and his or her staff retire to their offices to consider the arguments, more carefully look over the amicus briefs, and correspond with other justices about each case.

Eventually—typically over a period of a few months—a consensus emerges or a vote is taken, and on each case the Court decides who wins or loses. The justices then write agreements or dissents with or from the majority opinion, and when all is ready for the public they announce their decision.

Except in the Kasky case.

The Court did agree to hear the case, in the 2003 session. The justices heard the oral arguments on June 26. They accepted the amicus briefs—including filings from companies that included ABC, Inc.; the American Society of

Newspaper Editors; the Associated Press; Forbes, Inc.; Fox Entertainment Group; Gannett Company; the Hearst Corporation; the McClatchy Company; the National Association of Broadcasters; the National Broadcasting Company (NBC); National Public Radio, Inc.; the New York Times Company; Newsweek, Inc.; PR Newswire; the Seattle Times Company; Time, Inc.; Tribune Company; *U.S. News & World Report;* and the Washington Post Company—all agreeing with Nike.

ExxonMobil, Bank of America, and Microsoft filed their own three-company brief on behalf of Nike, and similar separate filings came from the National Association of Manufacturers, Pfizer, and the U.S. Chamber of Commerce, among others.

Even the American Civil Liberties Union (ACLU) filed a brief defending Nike's right to "free speech" as a "person" in America. The legal department of the AFL-CIO (American Federation of Labor and Congress of Industrial Organizations) filed a brief defending Nike's "right to lie" (it is true that as persons we have a "right to lie" except in particular cases such as when under oath). Even the very liberal *New York Times* columnist Bob Herbert wrote an impassioned op-ed supporting Nike's right to deceive the public. All three mistakenly believed that corporations had had First Amendment rights since 1886, and all three were strong advocates of the First Amendment. And the AFL-CIO, of course, was a corporation itself, albeit a unique nonprofit form of incorporation.

There was also a loud public debate on the issue. Citizen activist groups picketed the Supreme Court, decrying corporate personhood and the entire idea that constitutional protections like free speech should be granted to corporations instead of being the exclusive province of humans, while the *New York Times,* the *Wall Street Journal,* and the *Washington Post* (among others) ran shrill editorials warning of dire consequences for the future of capitalism and democracy if corporations weren't finally and fully granted the constitutional right of free speech.

The Court then heard the oral arguments, in which Kasky's lawyers, Alan Caplan and Philip Neumark, revisited the series of very specific lies that they asserted Nike had told the American public in their original lawsuit. They said that Nike:

> In order to maintain and/or increase its sales, made misrepresentations by the use of false statements and/or material omissions of fact, including but not limited to the following:

(a) claims that workers who make NIKE products are protected from and not subjected to corporal punishment and/or sexual abuse;

(b) claims that NIKE products are made in accordance with applicable governmental laws and regulations governing wages and hours;

(c) claims that NIKE products are made in accordance with applicable laws and regulations governing health and safety conditions;

(d) claims that NIKE pays average line-workers double-the-minimum wage in Southeast Asia;

(e) claims that workers who produce NIKE products receive free meals and health care;

(f) claims that the GoodWorks International (Andrew Young) report proves that NIKE is doing a good job and "operating morally"; and

(g) claims that NIKE guarantees a "living wage" for all workers who make NIKE products.[5]

Nike, for its part, argued that when it hired former UN ambassador and Atlanta mayor Andrew Young to check them out, he found that everything was hunky dory: "Although some news organizations concluded that some allegations against Nike had merit, former United Nations Ambassador Andrew Young concluded in an independent review commissioned by Nike that the charges were largely false."[6]

Further, Nike's lawyers said that when the California Supreme Court concluded that it was okay for Marc Kasky to use the consumer protection laws to hold Nike accountable for what it said to the public, it was way too broad a use of the laws against fraud or deception in commerce. Nike's lawyers wrote: "The California court's conclusion that government may regulate all statements of fact by commercial entities that could influence consumers sweeps far too broadly..."

Nike's lawyers also didn't like the law in California that let an individual act as if he were the attorney general: "The private attorney general provisions of the UCL and FAL thus violate the First Amendment because they omit not only any requirement that the plaintiff have suffered harm, but also any other meaningful constraint on the ability of private plaintiffs to bring lawsuits..." which could impose a "crushing burden" on a multibillion-dollar corporation like Nike.

And, finally, calling implicitly on the doctrine that a corporation is a person protected by the Bill of Rights, Nike argued: "Even if petitioner's [Nike's] statements could be characterized as 'commercial speech,' the legal regime approved by the California Supreme Court violates the First Amendment." In other words, "We're a company, which is the same as a person, and so we have the First Amendment right to say whatever we want, just like anybody else. To say that we have to only say things that are accurate violates our First Amendment right of free speech."

All of this was laid before the Court. There were multiple dimensions to the case, but at its heart was the issue of whether a corporate "person" had the same "right to lie," guaranteed by the First Amendment to the U.S. Constitution, as you and me. If I can tell my wife that she looks great in a dress that I really think is ugly (but know she loves), Nike had the right to tell Americans that it was treating its workers well (even though it wasn't and knew it).

But something caught in the Court's throat. Chief Justice William Rehnquist, with six of his colleagues, decided that the Court had made a big mistake when it granted a writ of certiorari, the declaration that the case was legitimate and appropriate for the Court to hear.

Remember that it was Rehnquist who, in the earlier *First National Bank of Boston v. Bellotti* case (mentioned in chapter 1), had said that he disagreed with what he believed was the decision of the Supreme Court in 1886, that corporations were persons. And, interestingly, the attorneys who crafted the amicus brief on behalf of Marc Kasky took special pains to point out—with the hope that Rhenquist would read it and have a "EUREKA!" moment—that the Court had actually *never created corporate personhood* in 1886.

Quoting from the first edition of this very book, Kasky's attorneys wrote directly to Rehnquist in their brief:

> Indeed, the initial grant of "personhood" under the Fourteenth Amendment to corporations was, to a certain extent, a judicial mistake. Corporate personhood is generally attributed to the Court's decision in *Santa Clara County v. Southern Pacific Railroad Co.,* 118 U.S. 394 (1886), although the Court in that case specifically declined to address the issue. In *Santa Clara County,* Santa Clara County sued the Southern Pacific Railroad Company for failure to pay taxes, and the railroad presented the Court with six defenses, including the argument that corporations were persons under the Equal Protection Clause of the Fourteenth Amendment. Because one of the other five defenses was

successful, the Court had no occasion to decide the question of corporate personhood and specifically declined to do so:

> If these [other] positions are tenable, there will be no occasion to consider the grave questions of constitutional law upon which the case was determined below; for, in that event, the judgment can be affirmed upon the ground that the assessment cannot properly be the basis of a judgment against the defendant.

> As the judgment can be sustained upon this [other] ground, it is not necessary to consider any other questions raised by the pleadings and the facts found by the court.

Id. at 411, 416. Indeed, in a companion case, Justice Field in a concurring opinion lamented that the "tax cases from California" did not "decide the important constitutional questions involved." *County of San Bernardino v. Southern Pac. R. Co.,* 118 U.S. 417, 422 (1886) (Field, J., concurring).

Nevertheless, it appears that the court reporter, J.C. Bancroft Davis, included a headnote stating, "The defendant Corporations are persons within the intent of the clause in section 1 of the Fourteenth Amendment to the Constitution of the United States, which forbids a State to deny to any person within its jurisdiction the equal protection of the laws." *See* Thom Hartmann, *Unequal Protection: The Rise of Corporate Dominance and the Theft of Human Rights* 107 (2002) (*quoting* J.C. Bancroft Davis, 118 *United States Reports: Cases Adjudged in the Supreme Court at October Term 1885 and October Term 1886* 394 (Banks & Brothers Publishers).[7]

In other places in the brief, its authors took special pains to point out how *Santa Clara* had been misinterpreted over the years. (One sentence, for example, begins, "Notwithstanding the mistaken 'personification' of corporations in *Santa Clara,* the Court's subsequent rulings reveal that this Court has not consistently applied the implications...")

Every step along the way helped telegraph to Rehnquist that his dislike of what he *thought* had been decided in 1886 in *Santa Clara* was a good gut instinct because he *was right*. Corporations aren't persons, and the Court had *not* said they were in 1886!

Nobody knows what happened when this bombshell hit Rehnquist's desk, as the Court is notoriously secretive. But something big happened because Rehnquist leapt into action—and that action was to decide *not* to decide the Kasky case. Inexplicably, astoundingly, and virtually without precedent, Rehnquist and most of his colleagues issued a very, very terse statement.

The single sentence the Court issued said only: "The writ of certiorari is dismissed as improvidently granted."

In other words, "When we decided to listen to these arguments and look over this case, granting it legal certification before us, we screwed up. Therefore we're tossing out the certification and going to pretend we never even heard this case or read its briefs."

While this dismissal represented the thinking of the majority of the Court, Justices Sandra Day O'Connor and Stephen Breyer were incensed. Breyer wrote: "In my view...the questions presented directly concern the freedom of Americans to speak about public matters in public debate, no jurisdictional rule prevents us from deciding those questions now, and delay itself may inhibit the exercise of constitutionally protected rights of free speech without making the issue significantly easier to decide later on."

But regardless of Breyer's or O'Connor's concern that the Court was kicking the can down the road, the case came to a halt, and Kasky and Nike settled out of court almost immediately when the California courts granted Kasky the legal right to access Nike's internal files (known as a grant of discovery). The amount of money Nike paid Kasky's lawyers to stop at that point and not pursue discovery, rather than legally riffle through Nike's internal papers, was never disclosed, and Kasky, for his part, agreed with the decision to stop discovery when Nike made a seven-figure gift to an organization that worked to help sweatshop workers around the world.

The world was safe for corporate liars (although California's citizens were still free to go after them in a limited fashion). Corporate personhood hadn't been challenged. And the weird coalition of liberals (Bob Herbert and the ACLU) and conservatives (NBC, ABC, the Chamber of Commerce, and others) who worried that ending a corporation's right to call on the First Amendment would be a disaster for America all breathed a sigh of relief.

Until 2010.

CHAPTER 11

Corporate Control of Politics

The government silences a corporate objector, and those corporations may have the most knowledge of this on the subject. Corporations have lots of knowledge about environment, transportation issues, and you are [proposing] silencing them during the election?

> —U.S. Supreme Court Justice Anthony Kennedy, speaking from the bench during September 9, 2009, oral arguments in the case *Citizens United v. Federal Election Commission*

DURING THE BRUISING PRIMARY ELECTION SEASON OF 2008, A RIGHT-WING group put together a ninety-minute hit-job on Hillary Clinton and wanted to run it on TV stations in strategic states. The Federal Election Commission (FEC) ruled that advertisements for the "documentary" were actually "campaign ads" and thus fell under the restrictions on campaign spending of the McCain-Feingold Act and thus stopped them from airing. (Corporate contributions to campaigns have been banned repeatedly and in various ways since 1907 when Republican President Teddy Roosevelt pushed through the Tillman Act.)

Citizens United, the right-wing group, sued to the Supreme Court, with right-wing hit man and former Reagan solicitor general Ted Olson—the man who argued Bush's side of *Bush v. Gore*—as their lead lawyer.

This new case, *Citizens United v. Federal Election Commission,* presented the best opportunity for the Roberts Court to use its five-vote majority to totally rewrite the face of politics in America, rolling us back to the pre-1907 Era of the Robber Barons. And if there was a man to do it, it was John Roberts.

Although he was handsome, with a nice smile and photogenic young children, Roberts was no friend to average working Americans. If anything, he was the most radical judicial activist appointed to the Court in more than a century. He had worked most of his life in the interest of the rich and powerful and was chomping at the bit for a chance to turn more of America over to his friends.

As Jeffrey Toobin wrote in the *New Yorker* ("No More Mr. Nice Guy"):

> In every major case since he became the nation's seventeenth Chief Justice, Roberts has sided with the prosecution over the defendant, the state over the condemned, the executive branch over the legislative, and the corporate defendant over the individual plaintiff. Even more than Scalia, who has embodied judicial conservatism during a generation of service on the Supreme Court, Roberts has served the interests, and reflected the values, of the contemporary Republican Party.[1]

And the fastest way the modern Republican Party could recover its power over the next decade was to immediately clear away all impediments to unrestrained corporate participation in electoral politics. If a corporation likes a politician, it can ensure that he is elected every time; if it becomes upset with a politician, it can carpet-bomb her district with a few million dollars' worth of ads and politically destroy her.

In the *Citizens United* case, the Roberts Court listened to arguments and took briefs and even discussed it among themselves as if they were going to make a decision. But instead of deciding the case on the relatively narrow grounds on which it had originally been argued—whether a single part of a single piece of legislation (McCain-Feingold) was unconstitutional—the Court asked for it to be reargued in September 2009 and asked that the breadth of the arguments be expanded to reexamine the rationales for Congress to have *any* power to regulate corporate "free speech."

In this they were going along with a request from Theodore B. Olson, who argued *Bush v. Gore,* and would now not just look at this narrow case but go back nearly twenty years to reexamine and perhaps overturn their own ruling in the *Austin v. Michigan Chamber of Commerce* case, where the Court had held that it was constitutional for Congress to pass limits on corporate political activities, as well as its decision in 2003 to uphold McCain-Feingold as constitutional."[2]

The Background of *Citizens United*

The setup for this 2010 decision came in June 2007 in the *Federal Election Commission v. Wisconsin Right to Life* case,[3] in which the Roberts Court ruled that the FEC couldn't prevent Wisconsin Right to Life from running ads just because it was a corporation.

"A Moroccan cartoonist," Justice Scalia opened his opinion in *FEC v. WRTL* with his usual dramatic flair,

> once defended his criticism of the Moroccan monarch (lèse majesté being a serious crime in Morocco) as follows: "I'm not a revolutionary, I'm just defending freedom of speech. I never said we had to change the king—no, no, no, no! But I said that some things the king is doing, I do not like. Is that a crime?" Well, in the United States (making due allowance for the fact that we have elected representatives instead of a king) it is a crime, at least if the speaker is a union or a corporation (including not-for-profit public-interest corporations)... That is the import of §203 of the Bipartisan Campaign Reform Act of 2002 (BCRA)...

The idea of Congress passing laws that limited corporate "free speech" was clearly horrifying to Scalia. He went after the 1990 *Austin v. Michigan Chamber of Commerce* case, in which the then-Rehnquist Court had ruled that the Michigan Chamber of Commerce was limited in its "free speech" in a political campaign because it was a corporation.

"This [*Austin*] was the only pre-*McConnell* case in which this Court had ever permitted the Government to restrict political speech based on the corporate identity of the speaker," Scalia complained. "*Austin* upheld state restrictions on corporate independent expenditures," and, God forbid, "The statute had been modeled after the federal statute that BCRA §203 amended..."

The *Austin* case, Scalia concluded, with four others nodding, "was a significant departure from ancient First Amendment principles. In my view, it was wrongly decided."

Scalia also quoted at length from opinions in the *Grosjean v. American Press Co.* 1936 case, in Scalia's words, "holding that corporations are guaranteed the 'freedom of speech and of the press, safeguarded by the due process of law clause of the Fourteenth Amendment'"; he also quoted from the 1986 *Pacific Gas & Elec. Co. v. Public Util. Comm'n of California* case: "The identity of the speaker is not decisive in determining whether speech is protected"; "corporations and other associations, like individuals, contribute to the 'discussion, debate, and the dissemination of information and ideas' that the First Amendment seeks to foster."

The bottom line, for Scalia, was, "The principle that such advocacy is 'at the heart of the First Amendment's protection' and is 'indispensable to decision making in a democracy' is 'no less true because the speech comes from a corporation rather than an individual.'"

Continuing to quote from a plurality opinion in *Pacific Gas,* Scalia "rejected the arguments that corporate participation 'would exert an undue influence on the outcome of a referendum vote'; that corporations would 'drown out other points of view' and 'destroy the confidence of the people in the democratic process...'"

As Scalia himself wrote in his earlier opinion in *FEC v. Wisconsin Right to Life*: "FECA was directed to expenditures not just by 'individuals,' but by 'persons,' with *'persons' specifically defined to include 'corporation[s].'*" (Italics added.)

Chief Justice Roberts weighed in, too, in the main decision.[4] It's a fascinating decision to read—and search for occurrences of the word *corporation.* Here is one of Roberts's more convoluted observations in defense of corporate free-speech rights:

> Accepting the notion that a ban on campaign speech could also embrace issue advocacy would call into question our holding in *Bellotti* that the corporate identity of a speaker does not strip corporations of all free speech rights. It would be a constitutional "bait and switch" to conclude that corporate campaign speech may be banned in part because corporate issue advocacy is not, and then assert that corporate issue advocacy may be banned as well, pursuant to the same asserted compelling interest, through a broad conception of what constitutes the functional equivalent of campaign speech, or by relying on the inability to distinguish campaign speech from issue advocacy.

Bottom line: corporate free-speech rights are *real rights that must be respected.*

Justice Souter wrote a rather frightening dissent[5] (this was a 5-to-4 decision, with the usual right-wing suspects in the majority) in the *FEC v. WRTL* case. In it he worried out loud that the unelected Court's knocking down restrictions on corporate or union funding of elections would be destructive of the core values of democracy and the electoral process on which it rests:

> Finally, it goes without saying that nothing has changed about the facts. In Justice Frankfurter's words, they demonstrate a threat to "the integrity of our electoral process," which for a century now Congress has repeatedly found to be imperiled by corporate, and later union, money: witness the Tillman Act, Taft-Hartley, FECA, and BCRA.
>
> *McConnell* was our latest decision vindicating clear and reasonable boundaries that Congress has drawn to limit "the corrosive and distorting effects of immense aggregations of wealth," and the decision could claim the

justification of ongoing fact as well as decisional history in recognizing Congress's authority to protect the integrity of elections from the distortion of corporate and union funds.

After today, the ban on contributions by corporations and unions and the limitation on their corrosive spending when they enter the political arena are open to easy circumvention, and the possibilities for regulating corporate and union campaign money are unclear.

The ban on contributions will mean nothing much, now that companies and unions can save candidates the expense of advertising directly, simply by running "issue ads" without express advocacy, or by funneling the money through an independent corporation like Wisconsin Right to Life.

Sounding almost depressed, Souter closed his dissent with these words: "I cannot tell what the future will force upon us, but I respectfully dissent from this judgment today."

Attempts by corporations (and their lawyers, like Roberts was before ascending to a federal court) to usurp American democracy are nothing new, as David Souter well knew. Corporatism has always been a threat to democracy. The problem was that corporations were gaining increasing traction in what had become a dire conflict with democracy itself. The rights of "natural" persons were losing ground at an accelerating pace, and in 2010 things got a whole lot worse very, very fast.

Citizens United: The Roberts Court Overturns a Century of Law

On January 21, 2010, in another 5-to-4 decision with the Republican five justices on the winning side, the Supreme Court ruled that it is unconstitutional for Congress to pass or the president to sign into law any restrictions on the "right" of a corporation to pour money into political campaigns, so long as the money isn't directly given to the politicians, their campaigns, or their parties.

The majority decision, written by Justice Kennedy, was quite explicit in saying that the government has no right to limit corporate power or corporate "free speech."[6]

Kennedy began this line of reasoning by positing, "Premised on mistrust of governmental power, the First Amendment stands against attempts to disfavor certain subjects or viewpoints."

It sounds reasonable. He even noted, sounding almost like something from a Martin Luther King Jr or JFK speech, that:

> By taking the right to speak from some and giving it to others, the Government deprives the disadvantaged person or class of the right to use speech to strive to establish worth, standing, and respect for the speaker's voice. The Government may not by these means deprive the public of the right and privilege to determine for itself what speech and speakers are worthy of consideration.

But who is that "disadvantaged person or class" of whom Kennedy was speaking? He lays it out bluntly (the parts in single quotation marks are where he is quoting from previous Supreme Court decisions): "The Court has recognized that First Amendment protection extends to corporations....Under that rationale of these precedents, political speech does not lose First Amendment protection 'simply because its source is a corporation.'"

Two sentences later he nails it home: "The Court has thus rejected the argument that political speech of corporations or other associations should be treated differently under the First Amendment simply because such associations are not 'natural persons.'"

Bemoaning how badly corporations and their trade associations had been treated by the Congress of the United States for more than a hundred years in passing laws all the way back to the 1907 Tillman Act (which forbade corporations from giving money to politicians), Kennedy stuck up for the "disadvantaged" corporate "persons" the Roberts Court was seeking in this decision to protect:

> The censorship we now confront is vast in its reach. The Government has "muffled the voices that best represent the most significant segments of the economy." And "the electorate has been deprived of information, knowledge, and opinion vital to its function." By suppressing the speech of manifold corporations, both for-profit and non-profit, the Government prevents their voices and viewpoints from reaching the public and advising voters on which persons or entities are hostile to their interests.

Paraphrasing James Madison's plea in Federalist No. 10 that Americans resist the human tendency to form political factions but instead work together for the common good, Kennedy added at the end of that paragraph, "Factions should be checked by permitting them all to speak, and by entrusting the people to judge what is true and what is false."

In other words, if a single corporation spends $700 million in television advertising to tell you that, for example, Senator Bernie Sanders is a "bad person" because he sponsored legislation it doesn't like or that limits its profitability, and Sanders can raise only $3 million to defend himself with a few local

TV spots, you as the TV viewer and voting citizen can easily decide which is true and which is not.

Justices Kennedy, Alito, Roberts, Thomas, and Scalia were writing as if they had never seen a political—or, for that matter, a consumer product—advertisement. The whole point of such campaigns is not to present the "truth" but to present an emotional (and often misleading) argument that will change people's minds to conform to the message of the advertiser. But you won't find a word of that simple reality of advertising and marketing anywhere in the *Citizens United* decision.

Corporate executives and their lobbyists saw the value to them of this Supreme Court decision immediately. On February 7, 2010, the *New York Times* published an article by David D. Kirkpatrick titled "In a Message to Democrats, Wall St. Sends Cash to G.O.P." The article explicitly quoted banking industry sources who said that now that they could use their considerable financial power politically, they were experiencing "buyer's remorse" over having given Obama's presidential campaign $89 million in 2008: "Republicans are rushing to capitalize on what they call Wall Street's 'buyer's remorse' with the Democrats. And industry executives and lobbyists are warning Democrats that if Mr. Obama keeps attacking Wall Street 'fat cats,' they may fight back by withholding their cash."[7]

The article quoted several banking sources as saying they were outraged that the president had criticized their industry for the financial meltdown of 2008 or their big bonuses. It wrapped up with a quote from Texas Republican John Cornyn, the senator tasked with raising money for the National Republican Senatorial Committee, noting that he was now making regular visits to Wall Street in New York City because: "I just don't know how long you can expect people to contribute money to a political party whose main plank of their platform is to punish you."

It was a loud shot across Obama's bow, and within two weeks he had changed his tune on a wide variety of initiatives, ranging from taxes on the wealthy to banking, insurance, and pharmaceutical industry reforms.

The simple fact is that about $5 billion was spent in *all* the political campaigns from coast to coast in the elections of 2008, a bit less than $2 billion of that on the presidential race. Compare that with January 2010, when a small cadre of senior executives and employees of the nation's top banks on Wall Street split up among themselves over $145 billion in *personal bonus* money.

If just those few thousand people had decided to take just 3 percent of their bonus and redirect it into a political campaign, no politician in America could stand against them. And now none do. And that's just the banksters! Profits in the tens and hundreds of billions of dollars were reported in 2009 by oil, pharmaceutical, insurance, agriculture, and retailing industries—all now considering how to use part of their profits to influence political races.

Justice John Paul Stevens, with the concurrence of Justices Ruth Bader Ginsburg, Stephen Breyer, and Sonia Sotomayor, wrote the main dissent in the *Citizens United* case. Calling the decision "misguided" in the first paragraph of his ninety-page dissent, Stevens (and colleagues) pointed out that the majority on the Court had just handed our country over to any foreign interest willing to incorporate here and spend money on political TV ads.

> If taken seriously, our colleagues' assumption that the identity of a speaker has no relevance to the Government's ability to regulate political speech would lead to some remarkable conclusions. Such an assumption would have accorded the propaganda broadcasts to our troops by "Tokyo Rose" during World War II the same protection as speech by Allied commanders. More pertinently, it would appear to afford the same protection to multinational corporations controlled by foreigners as to individual Americans: To do otherwise, after all, could "'enhance the relative voice'" of some (i.e., humans) over others (i.e., corporations).

Speaking directly to that issue, on the day of the decision British Broadcasting Corporation (BBC) investigative journalist Greg Palast wrote an article whose headline is self-explanatory: "Supreme Court to OK Al Qaeda Donation for Sarah Palin?"[8]

Palast laid it out explicitly and, according to four of the most senior members of the U.S. Supreme Court, correctly when he wrote, "Think: Manchurian Candidate." He pointed out that our elections could now be decided not just by money-bombs from American corporations but "from ARAMCO, the Saudi Oil corporation's US unit...or the Chinese People's Liberation Army. Or from Bin Laden Construction corporation. Or Bin Laden Destruction Corporation."

Ted Olson, the lawyer who argued the winning *Citizens United* side before the Court, lost his wife on the plane hijacked on 9/11 and flown into the Pentagon. "Maybe it was a bit crude of me," Palast said, "but I contacted Olson's office to ask how much 'Al Qaeda, Inc.' should be allowed to donate to support the election of his local congressman." As of this writing, Palast tells me, Olson has not replied to his question.

In the same paragraph of the dissent just quoted about foreign corporations, Justice Stevens further points out the absurdity of granting corporations what are essentially citizenship rights under the Constitution, suggesting that perhaps the next SCOTUS decision will be to give corporations the right to vote: "Under the majority's view, I suppose it may be a First Amendment problem that corporations are not permitted to vote, given that voting is, among other things, a form of speech."

(Ironically, ten years earlier in the *Alexander v. Mineta* case, where citizens of Washington, D.C., were asking for the right to vote for a real member of Congress, just a few months before the *Bush v. Gore* case the Rehnquist Court had explicitly ruled that the Constitution does *not* guarantee the right of U.S. citizens to vote for president.)

Stevens recounted the history of the evolution of corporations in America, noting, "Corporations were created, supervised, and conceptualized as quasi-public entities, 'designed to serve a social function for the state.' It was 'assumed that [they] were legally privileged organizations that had to be closely scrutinized by the legislature because their purposes had to be made consistent with public welfare.'"

Quoting earlier Supreme Court cases and the Founders, Stevens wrote: "The word 'soulless' constantly recurs in debates over corporations...Corporations, it was feared could concentrate the worst urges of whole groups of men." Stevens was right: Thomas Jefferson famously fretted that corporations would subvert the Republic.

And, Stevens continued, the Founders could not have possibly meant to confer First Amendment rights of free speech on corporations when they wrote the Constitution in 1787 and the Bill of Rights in 1789 because, "All general business corporation statues appear to date from well after 1800":

> The Framers thus took it as a given that corporations could be comprehensively regulated in the service of the public welfare. Unlike our colleagues, they had little trouble distinguishing corporations from human beings, and when they constitutionalized the right to free speech in the First Amendment, it was the free speech of individual Americans they had in mind.

In an incredible irony, Stevens even quoted Chief Justice John Marshall, the man who had first, in the 1803 *Marbury* case, given the Court itself the power to overrule laws like McCain-Feingold passed by Congress: "A corporation is an artificial being, invisible, intangible, and existing only in contemplation of law. Being a mere creature of law, it posses only those properties which the charter of its creation confers upon it."

Stevens's dissent called out Roberts, Alito, Scalia, Thomas, and Kennedy for their behavior in this case, which he said was "the height of recklessness to dismiss Congress' years of bipartisan deliberation and its reasoned judgment...":

> The fact that corporations are different from human beings might seem to need no elaboration, except that the majority opinion almost completely elides it....Unlike natural persons, corporations have "limited liability" for their owners and managers, "perpetual life," separation of ownership and control, "and favorable treatment of the accumulation of assets...that enhance their ability to attract capital and to deploy their resources in ways that maximize the return on their shareholders' investments." Unlike voters in U.S. elections, corporations may be foreign controlled.

Noting that "they inescapably structure the life of every citizen," Stevens continued: "It might be added that corporations have no consciences, no beliefs, no feelings, no thoughts, no desires. Corporations help structure and facilitate the activities of human beings, to be sure, and their 'personhood' often serves as a useful legal fiction. But they are not themselves members of 'We the People' by whom and for whom our Constitution was established."

In this very eloquent and pointed dissent, Stevens even waxed philosophical, asking a series of questions for which there couldn't possibly be any clear or obvious answers given the Roberts court's decision:

> It is an interesting question "who" is even speaking when a business corporation places an advertisement that endorses or attacks a particular candidate. Presumably it is not the customers or employees, who typically have no say in such matters. It cannot realistically be said to be the shareholders, who tend to be far removed from the day-to-day decisions of the firm and whose political preferences may be opaque to management. Perhaps the officers or directors of the corporation have the best claim to be the ones speaking, except their fiduciary duties generally prohibit them from using corporate funds for personal ends. Some individuals associated with the corporation must make the decision to place the ad, but the idea that these individuals are thereby fostering their self-expression or cultivating their critical faculties is fanciful.

Stevens noted further, "The majority seems oblivious to the simple truth" that they are, with this decision, setting up a situation that "does not merely pit the anticorruption interest against the First Amendment, but also pit[s] competing First Amendment values against each other." And it becomes particularly problematic "when the speakers in question are not real people" but corporations.

This decision wasn't merely wrong—both in a contemporary and a historical sense—the Stevens minority argued in their dissent; it was dangerous. The four-judge dissent was explicit, clear, and shocking in how bluntly the three seniormost members of the Court (plus the newbie, Sotomayor) called out their colleagues, two of whom were just recently appointed to the Court by George W. Bush.

They started by pointing out that the American people weren't clamoring for corporations to have personhood and free-speech rights—that call was coming only from the Republican Five justices themselves: "The distinctive threat to democratic integrity posed by corporate domination of politics was recognized at 'the inception of the republic' and 'has been a persistent theme in American political life' ever since. It is only certain Members of this Court, not the listeners themselves, who have agitated for more corporate electioneering."*

They continued, noting that even if we citizens—"the listeners" to corporate speech—were clamoring to hear more of it, it wouldn't work to our interest because corporate interests are inherently different from human interests:

> *Austin* recognized that there are substantial reasons why a legislature might conclude that unregulated general treasury expenditures will give corporations "unfair influence" in the electoral process, and distort public debate in ways that undermine rather than advance the interests of listeners. The legal structure of corporations allows them to amass and deploy financial resources on a scale few natural persons can match. The structure of a business corporation, furthermore, draws a line between the corporation's economic interests and the political preferences of the individuals associated with the corporation; the corporation must engage the electoral process with the aim "to enhance the profitability of the company, no matter how persuasive the arguments for a broader or conflicting set of priorities."

---

*Again, the words in single quotation marks are where, in the dissent, the justices themselves are quoting from previous SCOTUS rulings. I've removed all the reference citations, as they make it hard to read; anybody wanting to dive deeper into this ninety-page dissent can read it online at www.supremecourtus.gov/opinions/09pdf/08-205.pdf.

In point of fact, they continued, corporations have a legal obligation to work toward an interest (profits) that is often at odds with the needs of humans and, particularly, local communities. Regardless of how sweet or touchy-feely their Madison Avenue–produced commercials may be, at their core they are machines to make money, not living things and not citizens of a democratic republic. By having free-speech rights equal with people, they argued, corporations will actually harm the "competition among ideas" that the Framers envisioned when they wrote the First Amendment:

> "[A] corporation...should have as its objective the conduct of business activities with a view to enhancing corporate profit and shareholder gain." In a state election such as the one at issue in *Austin,* the interests of nonresident corporations may be fundamentally adverse to the interests of local voters. Consequently, when corporations grab up the prime broadcasting slots on the eve of an election, they can flood the market with advocacy that bears "little or no correlation" to the ideas of natural persons or to any broader notion of the public good. The opinions of real people may be marginalized. "The expenditure restrictions of [2 U.S.C.] §441b are thus meant to ensure that competition among actors in the political arena is truly competition among ideas."

Even worse than the short-term effect of a corporation's dominating an election or a ballot initiative, just the fact that it can participate on an unlimited basis as an actor in the political process will, inevitably, cause average working Americans—the 95 percent who make less than $100,000 a year—to conclude that their "democracy" is now rigged. The result will be that more and more people will simply stop participating in politics (it's interesting to note how many politicians announced within weeks of this decision that they would not run for reelection), stop being informed about politics, and stop voting. Our democracy will wither and could die.

> In addition to this immediate drowning out of noncorporate voices, there may be deleterious effects that follow soon thereafter. Corporate "domination" of electioneering can generate the impression that corporations dominate our democracy. When citizens turn on their televisions and radios before an election and hear only corporate electioneering, they may lose faith in their capacity, as citizens, to influence public policy. A Government captured by corporate interests, they may come to believe, will be neither responsive to their needs nor willing to give their views a fair hearing.
>
> The predictable result is cynicism and disenchantment: an increased perception that large spenders "call the tune" and a reduced "willingness of voters

to take part in democratic governance." To the extent that corporations are allowed to exert undue influence in electoral races, the speech of the eventual winners of those races may also be chilled. Politicians who fear that a certain corporation can make or break their reelection chances may be cowed into silence about that corporation. On a variety of levels, unregulated corporate electioneering might diminish the ability of citizens to "hold officials account-able to the people," and disserve the goal of a public debate that is "uninhib-ited, robust, and wide-open." At the least, I stress again, a legislature is entitled to credit these concerns and to take tailored measures in response.

And even if humans were willing to try to take on corporations (maybe a billionaire or two with good ethics would run for office?), virtually every single person who tries to run for office will have to dance to the corporate tune or risk being totally destroyed by the huge and now-unlimited amounts of cash that corporations can rain down on our heads.

The majority's unwillingness to distinguish between corporations and humans similarly blinds it to the possibility that corporations' "war chests" and their special "advantages" in the legal realm may translate into special advantages in the market for legislation. When large numbers of citizens have a common stake in a measure that is under consideration, it may be very difficult for them to coordinate resources on behalf of their position. The corporate form, by contrast, "provides a simple way to channel rents to only those who have paid their dues, as it were."

Anyone concerned with the integrity of the political system should note that this decision affects the legitimacy of elections not only of the legisla-tive and executive branches but also of judges. As Bill Moyers and Michael Winship wrote in the *Huffington Post* in February 2010,

Ninety-eight percent of all the lawsuits in this country take place in the state courts. In 39 states, judges have to run for election—that's more than 80 per-cent of the state judges in America.

The *Citizens United* decision made those judges who are elected even more susceptible to the corrupting influence of cash, for many of their decisions in civil cases directly affect corporate America, and a significant amount of the money judges raise for their campaigns comes from lobbyists and lawyers.[9]

Those inclined to underestimate the influence of cash on judicial elec-tions should be reminded that during the 1990s, candidates for high court judgeships in states around the country and the parties that supported them raised $85 million dollars for their campaigns. Since the year 2000, the numbers have more than doubled to over $200 million.

The nine justices currently serving on the Texas Supreme Court have raised nearly $12 million in campaign contributions. The race for a seat on the Pennsylvania Supreme Court last year was the most expensive judicial race in the country, with more than four and a half million dollars spent by the Democrats and Republicans. With the Supreme Court's *Citizens United* decision, corporate money's muscle got a big hypodermic needle full of steroids.[10]

This decision was a naked handoff of raw political power to corporate forces by five unelected judges, and the other four members of the Court (as you just read) said so in the plainest and most blunt terms. Horrified by the dissent and of being called "misguided," "dangerous," and "reckless" by his colleagues, Justice Scalia wrote a short concurring opinion with his four conservative peers, trying to push back against the Stevens/Ginsburg/Sotomayor/Breyer dissent:

> The dissent embarks on a detailed exploration of the Framers' views about "the role of corporations in society." The Framers didn't like corporations, the dissent concludes, and therefore it follows (as night the day) that corporations had no rights of free speech....
>
> Despite the corporation-hating quotations the dissent has dredged up, it is far from clear that by the end of the 18th century corporations were despised. If so, how came there to be so many of them?...Indeed, to exclude or impede corporate speech is to muzzle the principal agents of the modern free economy. We should celebrate rather than condemn the addition of this [corporate] speech to the public debate.

Justice Roberts offered his own short concurring opinion, in self-defense. "The government urges us in this case to uphold a direct prohibition on [corporate] political speech," he wrote. And, of course:

> First Amendment rights could be confined to individuals, subverting the vibrant public discourse that is at the foundation of our democracy.
>
> The Court properly rejects that theory, and I join its opinion in full. The first Amendment protects more than just the individual on a soapbox and the lonely pamphleteer.

Indeed, with this decision in place and the law of the land, the First Amendment now protects the "free speech" rights of the presidents of Russia and China and Iran to form corporations in the United States and pour millions of dollars toward supporting or defeating the politicians of their choice.

It protects the "right" of the largest polluting corporations on earth to politically destroy any politician who wants to give any more authority to the Environmental Protection Agency. It protects their "right" to elevate to elected status any politician who is willing to dismantle the EPA—or any other government agency that protects or defends the people of America from corporate predation.

Corporatism or Fascism?

In the 1930s and the 1940s, the kind of corporatism that the Roberts Court created in America with the *Citizens United* ruling had a different name. As the 1983 *American Heritage Dictionary* noted, *fascism* is "a system of government that exercises a dictatorship of the extreme right, typically *through the merging of state and business leadership,* together with belligerent nationalism." [Italics added.]

Today, knowing the horrors of what Hitler committed in the name of fascism, it's difficult to use the word in contemporary writing because so many people think the discussion is about Nazism or genocide. But fascism is something the generation that grew up in the 1930s knew well—it was even a popular and widespread movement in the United States during that decade—and it wasn't until after the world saw the horrors of World War II that the word fell into popular disuse other than as an epithet.

But before the war ended and the word's popular meaning became contaminated with Hitler's death camps, Americans used it to describe the authoritarian corporatism of its founder, Benito Mussolini, his fascist follower and ally Franco (Francisco Franco Bahamonde) in Spain, and, of course, in Germany, where German corporations had come to play such a large role in the administration of the government.

Thus in early 1944 the *New York Times* asked Vice President Henry Agard Wallace to, as Wallace noted, "write a piece answering the following questions: What is a fascist? How many fascists have we? How dangerous are they?"

Vice President Wallace's answers to those questions were published in the *Times* on April 9, 1944, at the height of the war against the Axis powers of Germany and Japan:[11]

> The really dangerous American fascists are not those who are hooked up directly or indirectly with the Axis. The FBI has its finger on those...With a fascist the problem is never how best to present the truth to the public but how best to use the news to deceive the public into giving the fascist and his group more money or more power....

> American fascism will not be really dangerous until there is a purposeful coalition among the cartelists, the deliberate poisoners of public information...

Noting that, "Fascism is a worldwide disease," Wallace further suggested that fascism's "greatest threat to the United States will come after the war" and will manifest "within the United States itself."

In his strongest indictment of the tide of fascism, the vice president of the United States saw rising in America, he added:

> They claim to be super-patriots, but they would destroy every liberty guaranteed by the Constitution. They demand free enterprise, but are the spokesmen for monopoly and vested interest. Their final objective toward which all their deceit is directed is to capture political power so that, using the power of the state and the power of the market simultaneously, they may keep the common man in eternal subjection.

Finally, Wallace said,

> The myth of fascist efficiency has deluded many people....Democracy to crush fascism internally must...develop the ability to keep people fully employed and at the same time balance the budget. It must put human beings first and dollars second. It must appeal to reason and decency and not to violence and deceit. We must not tolerate oppressive government or industrial oligarchy in the form of monopolies and cartels.

Wallace's president, Franklin D. Roosevelt, also called out corporate power when he accepted his party's renomination in 1936 in Philadelphia:[12]

> Out of this modern civilization economic royalists [have] carved new dynasties....It was natural and perhaps human that the privileged princes of these new economic dynasties, thirsting for power, reached out for control over government itself. They created a new despotism and wrapped it in the robes

of legal sanction....And as a result the average man once more confronts the problem that faced the Minute Man.

Speaking indirectly of the fascists that Wallace would directly name almost a decade later, Roosevelt brought the issue to its core:

> These economic royalists complain that we seek to overthrow the institutions of America. What they really complain of is that we seek to take away their power.
>
> And our allegiance to American institutions requires the overthrow of this kind of power!

Fascism is rising in America, this time calling itself "compassionate conservatism," and "the free market" in a "flat" world. The point of its spear is "corporate personhood" and "corporate free-speech rights."

The behavior of the Roberts Court in *Citizens United* eerily parallels the day in 1936 when Roosevelt said: "In vain they seek to hide behind the flag and the Constitution. In their blindness they forget what the flag and the Constitution stand for."[13]

Even before the *Citizens United* case blew open the doors to a corporate takeover of American politics, the corrosive influence of corporations' having "rights" was already evident. Now these "unequal consequences" have been put on steroids.

PART III

Unequal Consequences

In our every deliberation, we must consider the impact of our decisions on the next seven generations.

—From the Great Law (or Constitution)
of the Iroquois Confederacy

CHAPTER 12

Unequal Uses for the Bill of Rights

Of the cases in this court in which the Fourteenth Amendment was applied during its first fifty years after its adoption, less than one half of one percent invoked it in protection of the Negro race, and more than fifty percent asked that its benefits be extended to corporations.

—Justice Hugo Black, 1938

THE STATISTIC IN THIS CHAPTER'S EPIGRAPH IS SOBERING INDEED. IT SAYS corporations sought protection under the Fourteenth Amendment a hundred times more often than did the people it was intended to protect. And this is not a victimless shift—there have been real and substantial consequences. In the years following the *Santa Clara* decision and the cases that referred to it, companies have used their personhood rights in an amazing variety of ways. What follows in this chapter is a small selection.

First Amendment

Supreme Court Justice Oliver Wendell Holmes Jr. noted in the landmark 1919 *Shenck v. United States* case that shouting "Fire!" in a crowded theater does not constitute free speech; the Bill of Rights guarantees that a person's opinion can be expressed, not that there are no limits on what one can do. But consider how this fundamental freedom has been bent by corporations since *Santa Clara*.

By claiming the same right as humans to express themselves, companies won approval to spend whatever they want on lobbyists in Washington. At one point there was a full-time tobacco lobbyist for every two legislators on Capitol Hill. As of 2005 there were roughly 64 registered lobbyists for every member of Congress, and 138 of them are former members of Congress. Include state lobbyists, and there are more than 60,000 (because of variations in state laws on what is or isn't a lobbyist, and who and how they should register, this may well be a significant underestimate: nobody really knows the true number).[1]

As Jeffrey H. Birnbaum noted in the *Washington Post* in June 2005, "The number of registered lobbyists in Washington has more than doubled since 2000 to more than 34,750 while the amount that lobbyists charge their new clients has increased by as much as 100 percent. Only a few other businesses have enjoyed greater prosperity in an otherwise fitful economy."[2]

He added that "lobbying firms can't hire people fast enough" and that salaries *started* at $300,000 a year. "Big bucks lobbying is luring nearly half of all lawmakers who return to the private sector when they leave Congress," Birnbaum noted, citing a study by Public Citizen's Congress Watch. The situation has only gotten worse since then.

And in a bizarre twist, during the administration of George W. Bush more than a hundred very well-paid lobbyists decided to forsake their big paychecks for, relatively speaking, paltry Civil Service paychecks for a year or two to become the actual regulators for the agencies they used to lobby.

J. Steven Griles, for example, moved from a $585,000-per-year paycheck as a lobbyist for oil and gas interests to become the number two person in the Department of the Interior, right under Interior Secretary Gale Norton. The Department then opened 8 million acres of western lands for oil and gas exploration and gave $2 million in no-bid contracts to one of Griles's former clients—and Griles continued to receive a four-year $284,000-per-year bonus from his former employer.

Charles Lambert, a fifteen-year lobbyist for the meat industry in its effort to block labeling and mad cow disease investigations, went to work for the U.S. Department of Agriculture (USDA), where he officially determined that mad cow disease wasn't a threat and shouldn't be investigated and that meat shouldn't be labeled with regard to its safety.

Daniel E. Troy worked for a lobbying firm representing Pfizer, Eli Lilly, and others. In 2001 he left the lobbying firm and became the top lawyer (chief counsel) for the Food and Drug Administration (FDA). Mysteriously, the FDA's position on regulating the drug companies became that it wants "to discourage frivolous lawsuits, which drive up costs," making it harder for consumers damaged by prescription drug side effects to sue Troy's former employers.

Lobbyist Thomas A. Scully represented HCA, a huge hospital corporation originally started by Bill Frist's family; HCA was embroiled in a fraud investigation by the Federal Centers for Medicare and Medicaid Services, started by a whistleblower, that looked like it was going to cost HCA $250 million. In 2001 Scully left his job to head the Federal Centers for Medicare and Medicaid Services. By coincidence, the agency worked out a settlement that kept the feds from looking further into HCA's books and kept the Justice Department away. Scully then left the Centers for Medicare and Medicaid and is working again as a lobbyist for Medicare providers.

Lobbyist Jeffrey Holmstead had represented big utility companies and as a lawyer for them had proposed twelve paragraphs of changes in EPA regulations affecting those utilities. Holmstead then went to work for the EPA as a regulator, and soon thereafter those twelve paragraphs—which gave a pollution exemption to 168 of 232 western-based power plants—appeared in proposed EPA rules changes. The case was so blatant that forty-five U.S. senators—including three Republicans—and ten states' attorneys general wrote a letter asking the EPA to void the proposed rule because of "undue industry influence." Their complaints were largely ignored by the Bush administration.[3]

The American Academy of Pediatrics has proposed that the federal government initiate controls on advertising directed at children and has recommended that parents educate their children about how advertising can manipulate them. Corporations, using their First Amendment rights to freedom of expression, have instead increased their spending on ads to children.[4]

The California Public Utilities Commission ordered a public utility to include a statement-stuffer in its bills, informing consumers of a key point. In a move that was startlingly reminiscent of the *Santa Clara* case, the utility (a corporate monopoly) sued the state and took the case all the way to the U.S. Supreme Court—and won. The utility asserted that it didn't have to comply because it had a First Amendment right "not to speak" and so could avoid informing its customers about issues as it chose. The Supreme Court, extending the logic of the *Santa Clara* case, agreed.[5]

Lawyers at a 1988 judicial conference recommended that corporations "use the First Amendment to invalidate a range of Federal regulations, including Securities and Exchange Commission disclosure requirements that govern corporate takeovers, and rules affecting stock offerings."[6] Since that time, this has become a routine claim made by corporations.

Fourth Amendment

The Fourth Amendment, instituted to prevent government agents from bursting into homes and unreasonably searching and seizing property, has been used by corporations to avoid government regulators as if they were British dragoons.

Supreme Court cases in 1967 and 1978 affirmed that corporations do not have to submit to random inspections because, as persons, they are entitled to privacy and freedom from unreasonable searches.[7] Corporations have pursued this logic for many years. Referencing the 1886 *Santa Clara* decision, the Supreme Court granted Fourth Amendment privacy rights to a corporation in 1906, just sixteen years after the Sherman Act had been passed.[8] As William Meyers notes in *The Santa Clara Blues: Corporate Personhood versus Democracy*, "This ruling made it difficult to enforce the Sherman anti-monopoly act, which naturally required the papers of corporations in order to determine if there existed grounds for an indictment."[9]

An electrical and plumbing corporation in Idaho cited the Fourth Amendment and deterred a health and safety investigation.[10]

In a 1986 Supreme Court case, a corporation sued the Environmental Protection Agency because the EPA hired a professional photographer to fly over the plant with a camera after the corporation had turned down a request by the EPA for an on-site inspection. The Court acknowledged the corporation's right to privacy from inspections by the EPA within its buildings.[11] Meyers says that, "Without random inspections it is virtually impossible to enforce meaningful anti-pollution, health, and safety laws."[12]

Fifth Amendment

Like the Fourth Amendment, the Fifth Amendment was written to prevent a recurrence of government abuses from colonial days. Among other things, it says that a person cannot be compelled to testify against himself (as often happened under English royal rule) or be tried twice for the same crime. This was in a time when the balance of power was definitely in favor of the government, which could and routinely did execute people.

Today the shoe is on the other foot: business, the more powerful party, is claiming protection, again to avoid government investigation of alleged misdoings. Convicted once of criminal misdoing in an anti-trust case, a textile supply company used Fifth Amendment protections and barred retrial.

In a Democracy...

The constitutional rights of free speech, privacy, and protection from overzealous prosecution all were the results of the Founders' of the United States having lost these rights to a multinational corporation and the government that supported its right to so-called free trade. They and the Fourteenth Amendment that was part of the post–Civil War legislation necessary to free slaves in the United States were all put in place specifically to benefit and protect humans.

The core concept of American democracy, as established in the writings of the Founders, is that all institutions, from churches that claim to be created by gods to businesses created by the wealthy or ambitious to the very government itself—all institutions—are authorized by the people to exist and are answerable to the people for their existence. And, as the Declaration of Independence notes, when an institution's behavior "becomes destructive of these ends, it is the Right of the People to alter or to abolish it...as to them shall seem most likely to effect their Safety and Happiness."

CHAPTER 13

Unequal Regulation

There can be no effective control of corporations while their political activity remains.

—Theodore Roosevelt, speech, August 31, 1910

THERE'S A SIDE TO REGULATION THAT MOST PEOPLE DON'T THINK ABOUT, and it has far-reaching effects if representatives of corporations are writing the rules. Once a regulation is passed saying, "you can emit no more than 10 ppm [parts per million] of mercury," you can legally emit up to 10 ppm. Before that rule was passed, any amount you emitted might subject you to potential lawsuits from nearby humans made ill by your emissions, by other states, or even by the federal government. The regulatory rule essentially legalizes what a corporation is doing. In the best of worlds, this wouldn't be a problem. But in practice it means that business interests are often directly involved in writing the regulations that they themselves will have to obey.

Regulations Can Legalize Activity That Causes Public Harm

During the Reagan administration, Robert Monks and Nell Minow worked with the Presidential Task Force on Regulatory Relief. Monks says, "We found that business representatives continually sought more rather than less regulation, particularly when [the new regulations] would limit their liability or protect them from competition."

Monks and Minow became disenchanted with the process. In their 1991 book *Power and Accountability,* they say, "The ultimate commercial accomplishment is to achieve regulation under law that is purported to be comprehensive and preempting and is administered by an agency that is in fact captive to the industry."[1] In this way corporations find an actual government shield for their actions. For example:

- Tobacco companies point to the government-mandated warnings on their labels, saying that the labels relieve them of responsibility for tobacco-related deaths because they're obeying government rules.

- Producers of toxic wastes can't be sued or attacked if they are releasing their toxins within guidelines defined by a government agency.

- Telemarketing companies push for laws and regulations that define their practice, thus legalizing it.

- Manufacturers of genetically modified products can bring them to market without labeling, so long as the products are made within the guidelines of the regulations.[2]

The Fox Guarding the Chicken Coop

Before there was a single genetically modified food product on the market, Monsanto, a leading provider of agricultural products to farmers, including Roundup, the world's best-selling herbicide, and a pioneer in genetically altered crops, sent lobbyists to the White House in late 1986 to meet with Vice President George H. W. Bush.

"There were no products at the time," Leonard Guarraia, one of the Monsanto executives at the meeting, told the *New York Times* in 2001. "But we bugged him for regulation. We told him that we have to be regulated."[3]

And so, the *Times* reports, "the White House complied," and Monsanto got the regulations it wanted from the EPA, FDA, and USDA.

Those regulations evolved throughout the Reagan and Bush administrations into a regulatory policy, announced by Vice President Dan Quayle on May 26, 1992, when he said, "We will ensure that biotech products will receive the same oversight as other products, instead of being hampered by unnecessary regulation."

Certainly there would be no unnecessary regulation, but the regulations that were now in place were necessary for the industry. Said the *New York Times,* "The new policy strictly limited the regulatory reach of the FDA."[4]

Under the regulations shepherded through government agencies by the White House, the dangers of genetically modified foods would be determined by the manufacturers, not the government, and testing would occur only when the companies wanted it to. And consumers were not to be notified if their food contained genetically modified organisms (as does now a substantial percentage of the American food supply).

"Labeling was ruled out as potentially misleading to the consumer, since it might suggest that there was reason for concern," notes *Times* reporter Kurt Eichenwald.[5] In the meantime, gene-altered corn accounted for about 32 percent of the 1998 U.S. crop, 38 percent for soybeans, and 58 percent for Canadian canola oil.[6]

In the summer of 2000, the Clinton administration had to select an American representative to the World Trade Organization talks on genetically modified foods. Ignoring the nomination of a scientist from the Consumers Union, the administration instead chose a former lobbyist for one of the largest companies in the business of genetically modified foods.

And in one of the most notorious cases, a multinational chemical and agricultural-products company's attorney quit his job with the company's law firm; went to work for the FDA, where he wrote a regulation that allowed that company's product into the food supply; quit the FDA and went to work for the USDA, where he participated in writing regulations eliminating labeling of the product for consumers; and then quit the USDA and went back to work for the law firm representing the multinational.[7]

Unfortunately, because of "veggie libel laws" passed in numerous states after much lobbying by pesticide manufacturers and others in the agricultural products industry (under which Oprah Winfrey was sued for her hamburger remarks), it would be a crime in at least fourteen states (where, hopefully, this book will be for sale) for me (or any reporter) to give you the details of this episode.*

The GMO (genetically modified organism) regulations followed a pattern set out years before by the chemical industry. As Paul Hawken pointed out in 1994 in *The Ecology of Commerce,* the industry launched such a huge lobbying effort to fight regulations on toxic chemicals after the passage of the 1970 Clean Air Act that by 1990 "the agency has been able to muster regulations for exactly 7 of the 191 toxins that fell under the original legislation."[8]

A decade later things are still problematic, with profit driving the equation at every turn. The last year for which EPA statistics are available on the

---

*Even Ben & Jerry's must, by law, say something nice about the outcome of this incident on their labels, although you can read the entire story on the wall of their Waterbury, Vermont, manufacturing facility, as Vermont has not yet passed a law making it illegal to question the safety of the American food supply.

release of toxic chemicals into the environment by industry is 1999, and in that year 7.7 billion pounds of toxins were released directly into our air and water, most with unknown short- or long-term effects.[9] And as huge as that statistic may sound, it's actually only the tip of the iceberg:

- Lobbyists defined EPA regulations so that now only 650 of the more than 80,000 chemicals being used in industry have to be reported—which means that the 7.7-billion-pound total represents only 1 percent of the possible chemicals in use.

- Only America's largest chemical manufacturers are required to report their figures.

- Those figures include only accidents and spills. As the Worldwatch Institute's Anne Platt McGinn noted in a commentary titled "Detoxifying Terrorism" on November 16, 2001, "Releases during routine use are not included" in that 7.7-billion-pound figure. Platt added that we don't yet even know how dangerous or carcinogenic are more than "71 percent of the most widely used chemicals in the United States today" because the data simply doesn't exist or hasn't been released by the industry.[10]

The Impact on Small Business

Small businesses rarely lobby Congress, the White House, or regulatory agencies for more regulations. But because large businesses have an infrastructure to deal with regulations, the burden of regulations on small businesses sometimes wipes them out. Many regulations come along with benefits. Farm subsidies represent a huge transfer of tax money to corporations, but only a very small portion goes to family farmers.

In the agriculture industry, four multinational corporations control 82 percent of the beef cattle market; five companies control 55 percent of the hog-packing marketplace. Although large agricultural corporations numerically own only 6 percent of U.S. farms, that 6 percent accounts for almost two-thirds of all farm income.[11]

In a growing trend known as contract farming, farmers are forced (because they can't compete against large-scale multinational purchasing) to sell their farms to agribiz companies and then work on the land they once owned. The United States lost 300,000 family-owned farms between 1979 and

1998. As agriculture writer Julie Brussell notes, "This agrarian 'genocide' mirrors the descent of much of America's rural country into economic serfdom."[12] The result, as documented by the Community Environmental Legal Defense Fund's (CELDF) Thomas Linzey, is that, "Suicides have replaced equipment-related deaths as the number one cause of farmer deaths."[13]

CHAPTER 14

Unequal Protection from Risk

Corporations are neither physical nor metaphysical phenomena. They are socioeconomic ploys—legally enacted game-playing—agreed upon only between overwhelmingly powerful socioeconomic individuals and by them imposed upon human society and its all unwitting members.

—R. Buckminster Fuller, *Grunch of Giants*

WHEN CORPORATIONS GAINED THE PROTECTIONS THAT HAD BEEN WRITTEN for persons in the United States, a substantial shift began in who bears what risk, resulting in an imbalance that now affects virtually all parts of the world. Most companies handle risk responsibly, but many corporations are legally allowed to avoid responsibility in ways that would never be permitted for an individual.

Risk is a matter of who suffers when something goes wrong. Corporations and their shareholders may risk loss of income or even loss of their investment, but that pales in comparison with the risks that humans share as a result of a corporate activity—such as degradation of the environment, higher rates of cancer and other diseases, job-related disfigurement or death, community and family breakdown after a factory is closed and jobs are shipped overseas, and even a life with no income or health insurance if we choose not to affiliate with a corporation.

Large companies rarely risk anything nearly that serious. They rarely undergo corporate death (charter revocation) or disfigurement. The burden of risk is unequal, and one source of this inequality is the changes in laws and regulations that happened after companies gained access to the law-making process when they were declared to share the same rights as persons.

The Nature of Risk

Risk means different things to different people, and it has meaning only in context. Sometimes creating a risk to humans—manufacturing cancer-causing chemicals or designing risky gas tanks—is a source of profit to a company. If regulations are imposed or scandals erupt from human deaths, our current system of accounting and measuring risk does not allow us to factor in the value of human life or the loss of quality of life from pollution or other consequences of corporate activity.

We have strayed far indeed from America's founding laws in the 1700s, under which corporate behavior was suspect and tightly controlled, and the 1800s, when states exercised control of corporate behavior and could revoke a corporation's "driver's license" if it harmed people.

In a classic Darwinian sense, corporations have learned how to manage risks by anticipating them and doing what they can to eliminate them. There's nothing inherently wrong with that, per se, but as William Jennings Bryan said at the 1912 Ohio Constitutional Convention, when one group is vastly larger than another so it has far more ability to bend events in its favor, the result is unfair and unequal.

Unequal Accountability

Humans are responsible for the effects of their actions. If they violate laws, they can be fined or imprisoned; if they violate the rights of another person, they can be sued. They can even be sued or prosecuted for failing to anticipate the effects of their actions. Companies too can be sued (though big corporations are rarely if ever driven out of business that way). But one group bears no responsibility whatsoever for the effects of its actions: investors have no liability for the actions they enable through their investments.

Of course, few investors, if any, mean any harm when they invest. When the United States was founded, the concept of limiting the financial liability of corporate stockholders was defined by the states in which the corporations were chartered. So too was liability for the behavior of the corporation, or of the people making decisions for the corporation. As the Supreme Court said, "The individual liability of stockholders in a corporation is always a creature of statute. It does not exist at common law."[1]

It wasn't until 1811 that New York was the first state to pass a law that put a barrier (sometimes called the corporate veil) between the behavior of corporations and the responsibilities for that behavior that may otherwise have fallen to the corporation's stockholders.[2] During the chartermongering period of the late 1800s, this became more common, although many states still reserved the right to hold stockholders, officers, directors, or managers responsible for the behaviors and the impacts of the corporations that they owned or controlled.

Different states have different laws about what corporations must and must not do to continue to exist in their states. To remedy this situation, the American Bar Association, Section of Business Law, Committee on Corporate Laws, has proposed a new set of state laws regulating corporations, called the Model Business Corporation Act (MBCA). Today seven states have laws based on the 1969 version of this, and variations on the updated version had been adopted by an additional twenty-four states as of 2009.

This proposal gives corporate shareholders no responsibility whatsoever for the acts or debts of the corporation that they own. They can invest without legal risk, only financial risk. They might lose the money itself, but if their money is used to commit crimes or to support business decisions that knowingly lead to deaths, the shareholders are considered to have nothing to do with it legally. Some question the logic of a doctrine that somebody who funds an operation should be allowed to share in its profits if it succeeds but have no responsibility for what it does or whether it harms others while getting those profits.

Under this setup it's little wonder that shareholders rarely tell executives to behave themselves. In contrast, if shareholders carried even a small liability for the consequences of what they sponsor, it stands to reason that in their hiring and firing decisions the shareholders and the board members might take into account the ethics and the legal tendencies of the executives. But Section 6.22 of the MBCA concerns shareholder liability and explicitly says, "(b) Unless otherwise provided in the articles of incorporation, a shareholder of a corporation is not personally liable for the acts or debts of the corporation except that he may become personally liable by reason of his own acts or conduct."[3]

Where Does This Immunity Come From?

Interestingly, not all states have adopted these laws. And the Constitution does not limit shareholder liability for debt, crimes, or other acts of corporations.

Nor is there such a provision in English common law. So what happens in those other states?

In the 1965 case *Fields v. Synthetic Ropes, Inc.,* the Delaware Supreme Court said, "A stockholder of a corporation is not personally liable for the corporate debts."[4] When attorney Dan Brannen Jr. researched this, he noted that, "The court, however, cited no statute for this proposition, and I find none in Delaware's current corporate code."[5]

Apparently, the Delaware Supreme Court isn't the only one to have such notions. In a CERCLA (Comprehensive Environmental Response, Compensation, and Liability Act, usually referred to as the EPA's Superfund) case before the U.S. Supreme Court in 1998, Justice David Souter said on behalf of the unanimous Court:

> It is a general principle of corporate law deeply ingrained in our economic and legal systems that a parent corporation...is not liable for the acts of its subsidiaries....Thus it is hornbook law that the exercise of the control which stock ownership gives to the stockholders...will not create liability beyond the assets of the subsidiary....Although this respect for corporate distinctions when the subsidiary is a polluter has been severely criticized in the literature...nothing in CERCLA purports to reject this bedrock principle, and against this venerable common law backdrop, the congressional silence is audible.[6]

In other words, the U.S. Supreme Court unanimously said in this decision:

- In practice, parent companies have not been held responsible for the illegal polluting acts of their subsidiaries.

- Many people have said it's wrong (Souter said, "severely criticized in the literature") to pretend that the subsidiary is not part of the parent company ("this respect for corporate distinctions").

- But Congress has conspicuously done nothing about it.

- So the Court says it's not illegal. A company can form a subsidiary that it knows is a notorious polluter, and not only are the executives legally blameless, even the parent company is completely blameless. Or the subsidiary could even be a killer, like with Halliburton subsidiary KBR in Iraq; there is no liability to Halliburton stockholders like Dick Cheney.

Reading this, I wondered what would happen if Congress were to break its silence. Certainly, the congresses of virtually every state in the union have done so at various and numerous times before 1886. Attorney Brannen's thoughts were more blunt. He wrote to me, citing the above, "This is scary. At our country's birth, corporations were state creations, with stockholder liability subject to state control. Today, American jurisprudence has given corporations life under the Fourteenth Amendment and [then, since that time] declared their distinctiveness to be a matter of American corporate law too basic and obvious to challenge."

That's especially ironic, considering that the Supreme Court did not actually give corporations such rights to life. It was an 1886 court reporter's mistake that's been institutionalized into law to the point where we have become accustomed to it.

Let's look at a practical, real-world effect of this principle in today's world, using as an example who is accountable for the risks of newly developed chemicals, in the United States and elsewhere, and what it means to our children.

The Benefits of Marketing Untested Chemicals Outweigh the Risk?

In America newly developed chemicals are usually released into the environment before there has been time to do studies on their long-term low-dose human toxicity. But what are we doing to our children and our grandchildren? Where did we get the idea that anyone (corporate or real person) has every right to market what they developed, whether or not we know what effect it has? And where did we get the idea that we can't change that rule?

In effect, we and our children are the lab animals for modern new chemicals, as were our parents for DDT, PCBs, and lead in gasoline.* The product is put on the market, and if it turns out to be carcinogenic, everyone finds out the hard way. And the developer isn't responsible because it was a company "regulated" by a government agency.

---

*DDT, or dichlorodiphenyltrichloroethane, is toxic to human beings and animals when swallowed or absorbed through the skin. It was widely used in the mid-twentieth century and has been banned in the United States for most uses since 1972. PCBs, or polychlorinated biphenyls, are a class of organic compounds and an environmental pollutant associated with birth defects and cancer. The 1975 Toxic Substances Control Act required that the production of PCBs be phased out within three years.

It wasn't that way in the past. Whole books have been written on this subject. Here is one current example and some statistics to indicate how big the issue is:

- PCE (perchloroethylene) is an industrial solvent used for a variety of purposes ranging from dry cleaning to plastics and electronics fabrication. In 1968 it was used in pipes and glues for 650 miles of a plastic-lined concrete water main on Cape Cod, Massachusetts. Decades later clusters of cancer were discovered where the chemical had leached into the water supply. By the time the possible link was discovered, "people had been drinking contaminated water, some for as long as 10 years," Boston University's lead researcher Ann Aschengrau said in an interview with the *Cape Cod Times*.[7]

- The EPA classifies 3,800 chemicals as "high production volume chemicals." A study by the Environmental Defense Fund in the late 1990s found that fewer than half of them had ever been tested for the possibility of toxic effects on humans.[8]

- It's even more rare (fewer than 10 percent of those 3,800 chemicals) that we test chemicals for their impact on developing children.[9]

There's Another Way: The Precautionary Principle

The alternative system—used widely in Europe—is known as the precautionary principle. It was written into the 1992 Treaty of the European Union. It moves risks from human persons to the manufacturer: a substance is considered potentially dangerous until proven beyond any reasonable doubt that it is safe, and the burden of proving its safety is with the corporation that would profit from its release, whether it's a new chemical or a genetically modified organism. In other words, just as was the intention of our country's Founders, a company is welcome to do business so long as the welfare of the community is respected.

Interestingly, although American business often portrays this as a fanatical idea, it's the principle we already use in America to approve new drugs and medical devices. It was even invoked by former New Jersey governor Christine Todd Whitman, who is usually reviled by environmentalists, when in October 2000 she told the National Academy of Sciences in Washington, D.C., that "policymakers need to take a precautionary approach to environmental protection....We must acknowledge that uncertainty is inherent in managing natural resources, recognize it is usually easier to prevent environmental damage than to repair it later, and shift the burden of proof away from those advocating protection toward those proposing an action that may be harmful."[10] (Unfortunately, her actions in office rarely reflected this perspective.)

But the precautionary principle is not law in the United States. In the United States, a company is entitled to calculate risks, assess the economic risk of potential casualties without considering any impact on humans, and decide solely on that basis.

Unequal Risk of Lawsuit

The Fourteenth Amendment was written to ensure equal protection under the law for people, including the ability to sue for these protections. In practice, however, it has turned out to give humans very little protection against wealthy corporations that wish to shut them up.

SLAPP suits are defined in *Black's Law Dictionary* as: "abbr. A strategic lawsuit against public participation—that is, a suit brought by a developer, corporate executive, or elected official to stifle those who protest against some type of high-dollar initiative or who take an adverse position on a public-interest issue (often involving the environment)."[11]

SLAPP suits started out as suits by polluters, toxic-waste sites, nuclear facilities, and the like, against people who get up in public venues like town meetings or public hearings and offer anti-pollution or anti-nuclear opinions. The next thing they know, they're SLAPPed—having to spend thousands of dollars in legal fees to defend themselves for having exercised what they thought was their First Amendment right of free speech—and it often shuts people up in a hurry.

This variety of lawsuit has expanded over the years beyond just public hearings, and the suing corporations usually charge slander, libel, harassment, or interference with contract. Now that the Patriot Act has defined "interfering with commerce" as a criterion for a "terrorist act," corporations have even used the force of criminal law to assert that public-interest groups like Greenpeace and PETA are "terrorists."

The bottom line is that the corporation initiating the lawsuit is usually not suing to win in court; they're just working to shut people up or wipe them out by forcing them to pay huge legal bills to defend themselves. In the eyes of the law, since 1886, a corporate person with billions of dollars and a human person who works for a living are entitled to equal protection under the law. But the people across America who have been SLAPPed certainly could not intimidate a corporation by threatening to drive it bankrupt with legal bills.

Further irony is that under the most recent tax laws, the corporation could deduct from its income taxes the cost of its lawyer to SLAPP-sue an individual, counting it as an ordinary cost of doing business. A working person, however, though legally equal, cannot deduct the costs of defending himself. As Delphin M. Delmas so eloquently pointed out in his pleadings before the Supreme Court in the 1886 *Santa Clara* case, the law has come to "a position ridiculous to the extreme."

In a Democracy...

So we see that there are some very unequal risks here. Corporations risk profits but rarely anything else, while humans risk much more.

At the moment the world's largest corporations are able to influence—and, in most cases today, even write—legislation that benefits them because their personhood gives them the constitutionally protected right of free speech, assembly, and to meet with "their" elected representatives.

If we were to return to the idea that only humans are persons, perhaps our human legislators would drift back to supporting the communities they represent. It would be a first step toward equaling the now very unequal risks between corporations and humans.

CHAPTER 15

Unequal Taxes

You must pay the price if you wish to secure the blessings.

—President Andrew Jackson

IT COSTS MONEY TO RUN A GOVERNMENT, AND THE MORE YOU WANT THE GOVernment to do, the more it usually costs. One point to consider is how much do we want our government to do? Another is, who should pay for it? Tax policy is how government funds its services and also one way it fulfills the will of the people who elect it by providing tax incentives or disincentives for particular types of behaviors. Consider how home mortgage interest deductibility has fueled home buying, for example.

As we have seen, starting well before *Santa Clara,* some companies have worked hard to get out of paying for anything, including taxes. Some even spent years resisting paying taxes on land the government had given them for free; they then worked the issue to a ludicrous extent. The *Santa Clara* case involved going to the Supreme Court to fight a tax of one-tenth of 1 percent.

You and I could never afford to do such a thing, but economies of scale mean that for huge property owners such efforts can have very big paybacks. Motivated to pursue the subject, with the means to do so, and in the absence of regulations preventing it, they do the obvious thing, as Adam Smith predicted anyone would: they act in their own self-interest.

The result has been an additional inequity that could not possibly have been intended by the framers of the Fourteenth Amendment. After *Santa Clara* (and subsequent cases continuing well into the twentieth century), increased corporate access to lawmakers has resulted in a shift in the tax burden that rivals the shift in risk from corporate to individual shoulders. In this chapter we cover four aspects of this issue:

- A shift in income-tax burden from corporations to workers

- A shift in property-tax burden from corporations to residents

- The use of federal tax breaks and subsidies to help large corporations

- The use of tax breaks at state and regional levels to lure businesses

There is an appropriate concern about not overtaxing corporations; to do so could endanger the survival of business. But as you will see, this particular pendulum has swung very far away from that risk. To the contrary, the additional shift in tax burden being proposed today is financially crushing individuals who can least afford it.

The Start of Income Taxes

The main purpose of a business corporation is as an instrument for the accumulation of wealth, and it has worked well in that respect. In the Robber Baron Era of the late 1800s and the early 1900s, wealth was being concentrated at an amazing rate among the owners of the trusts. If you've ever had a chance to visit Newport, Rhode Island, to see the mansions of the rich from those days, you know how much wealth there was. For example, The Breakers is the seventy-room Italian Renaissance–style villa of Cornelius Vanderbilt II, president and chairman of the New York Central Railroad. The Elms is the French-style chateau of Edward Julius Berwind, who made his millions providing coal to the railroads.[1]

And these were their summer homes—cottages, as they called them. In New York City, Vanderbilt's "real" home filled the length of a city block along Fifth Avenue from 57th to 58th Street. Illustrating that the Newport house was truly just a cottage, the Victorian mansion in New York City had 137 rooms. "I have been insane on the subject of moneymaking all my life," he told the *New York Daily Tribune*.[2]

The working poor, however, who at that time constituted the vast majority of people in America and Europe, were truly poor: a middle class was largely unknown, outside of self-sufficient farming communities. At the turn of the century, more than half a worker's wage went to cover rent—often in slum tenements—and the remainder barely covered food and clothing. Children worked to supplement the family income because, as Annie S. Daniel documented in 1905, four-year-old boys "can sew on buttons and pull basting threads" and a girl "from 8 to 12 can finish trousers as well as her mother."[3] The Supreme Court declared a minimum wage unconstitutional and illegal, and it wasn't unusual for people to work fourteen-hour days, with two half-hour meal breaks, six days a week for $1 a day.[4] As is always the case in situations of poverty, infant mortality in these communities was high.

Nobody filed income-tax returns because nobody paid income taxes. From the founding of the republic, all the costs of the federal government were paid by taxes on imported goods and on alcohol and tobacco. The taxes on imported goods served the beneficial effect of making domestically produced goods cheaper, which stimulated business in America. But financing government entirely by duties and what were in effect sales taxes (as they were usually passed on to the consumer) also had the effect of virtually all the tax falling on those people who spend all of their paychecks on goods (the working poor), with people who simply saved or invested their earnings paying very little tax. In 1913, during the Progressive Movement, a constitutional amendment initiated the federal income tax, which allowed spreading the cost of government over a much wider base—not just what was spent but what was earned. Thus, the wealthy could no longer pocket almost all of their income. They shared the burden, which laid the foundation for the middle class.

By 1922 tariffs on tobacco and alcohol represented only 8 and 9 percent of federal government tax revenue respectively, whereas income taxes on wealthy individuals produced 13 percent of government revenue and taxes on corporations paid 19 percent of the cost of running the governments that authorized their existence.[5] This sharing has been increasingly reversed in recent years, however.

- Corporate taxes as a share of the nation's tax revenues plunged from 28 percent in 1956 to only 11.8 percent in 1996 and to below 10 percent in the early 2000s.[6]

- In the past three decades, after-tax income of the middle class, which had been rising, has collapsed to inflation-adjusted 1969 levels, and, according to statistics compiled by the AFL-CIO, "average hourly wage of production and nonsupervisory workers in the U.S. economy was $12.77 last year—down 9 percent compared with 1973."[7]

- The share of all property taxes paid by corporations has dropped from 45 percent in 1957 to 16 percent in 1995 (more recent figures are hard to find, as most states have changed their accounting rules to not break out corporate from personal tax payments, in response to lobbying pressures from corporations).[8]

- During the first year of the Reagan administration's "tax reforms," General Electric actually received a tax refund—an omen of things to come.[9]

- *Austin Chronicle* columnist Jim Hightower pointed out, "Forty-one of America's largest corporations earned $25.8 billion in profits between 1996 and 1999, yet not only did they avoid paying their fair share of taxes—they got $3.2 billion in rebate checks from taxpayers. Among these tax dodgers are such brand-names as Chevron, PepsiCo, Pfizer, J. P. Morgan, Saks, Goodyear, Ryder, Enron, Colgate-Palmolive, MCI, Weyerhaeuser, GM, and Northrop Grumman."[10]

- By setting up almost nine hundred subsidiaries in tax havens such as the Cayman Islands and through exploiting the tax-deductibility of stock options given to senior executives, Enron Corporation was able to pay no federal taxes in four of the five years prior to its implosion in 2002. As the *Washington Post* pointed out, in 2000 the corporation was successful in converting a $112 million potential tax bill into a $278 million tax refund.[11]

- According to the U.S. General Accounting Office (GAO), almost one-third of all "large" corporations (assets of at least a quarter-billion dollars) in the United States paid no income tax whatsoever between 1989 and 1995, and more than 60 percent of such companies paid less than $1 million in taxes. By 2005, according to the GAO, more than two-thirds of American corporations, accounting for more than $2.5 trillion in revenue, paid no corporate income taxes whatsoever (the same was true of 28 percent of foreign-owned corporations).[12]

- Looking at all U.S. corporations, the GAO concluded, "In each year between 1989 and 1995, a majority of corporations, both foreign- and U.S.-controlled, paid no U.S. income tax." The situation since then has only deteriorated.[13]

A similar shift has occurred within the human domain, with the wealthy carrying less of the burden than the middle class. The decline in corporate income taxes has been paralleled by a decline in the income taxes paid by the CEOs and the senior executives of those corporations.

- The wealthiest 1 percent of Americans paid $46,726 less in taxes in 1996 than they would have paid had there been no changes in the tax laws since 1977. But among those earning less than $80,000, those "tax reductions" were worth an average of only $115.[14]

- In the 1980s the Reagan administration pushed through several massive tax cuts for millionaires and billionaires, including the Economic Recovery Tax Act, which, added to a Johnson-era tax cut, slashed the income tax for America's top 1 percent of families by more than 50 percent.[15]

- The George W. Bush administration drove the top income bracket's taxes even lower—from a high averaging around 80 percent between 1935 and 1986 to a current low of 33 percent. Those wealthy families who "earn" their livings by waiting for dividend or interest checks to arrive in the mail from their investments pay a maximum 15 percent income tax.[16]

This may not be financially healthy, even for the wealthy. The following figures for the period leading up to the crash of 1929 are startlingly similar to those above:

- The 1926 tax cut reduced income taxes for millionaires from 60 percent to 20 percent just three years after the minimum wage was repealed in 1923.

- America's top 1 percent of families reaped a 75 percent increase in after-tax income during the 1920s.

- From 1920 to 1929, corporate profits rose 62 percent and dividends rose 65 percent.[17]

What Happens When Corporate Insiders Run the Government

In May 2001 the idea of taxation without representation came full circle when a government leader proposed that we shift all tax burdens back onto the people, lowering the corporate income tax to zero. Paul H. O'Neill is a multimillionaire who has been a top executive at Alcoa and International Paper, two of the world's largest multinational corporations. When I was writing the first edition of this book, O'Neill was secretary of the U.S. Treasury, appointed by the Bush administration and approved by the Senate.

In May 2001 O'Neill suggested that corporations should be totally exempt from all income tax. He said that the roughly 10 percent of federal funds they currently pay in corporate income taxes to provide for and administer our commons is too much; corporations should be just as tax-exempt as churches and synagogues.

O'Neill also called for the abolition of Social Security, Medicaid, and Medicare for working people because, he told a reporter for London's *Financial Times,* "Able-bodied adults should save enough on a regular basis so that they can provide for their own retirement, and, for that matter, health and medical needs." In O'Neill's opinion, corporations should pay no taxes and individuals should pay all costs of the federal government while also saving to pay for their retirement and all of their own medical costs.[18]

Yes, He Really Said It

While O'Neill's proposal was widely reported in England's business press, the media of the United States chose to ignore it, with the single exception of the suburban New York tabloid *Newsday.* When Newsday columnist Paul Vitello called the Treasury Department, he reported the following conversation:

> *Vitello:* "The secretary didn't really mean to say that no matter how old, no person who has paid into the Social Security system all his or her life would be entitled to benefits until he or she is physically no longer able to work? He didn't really mean to say that ExxonMobil and Time Warner should be treated as we treat the church—as tax exempt?"
>
> *Treasury Department Spokesman:* "Yes, that is our position. The quotes were all accurate."[19]

Checking Vitello's work (and somewhat incredulous myself), I called O'Neill's Washington, D.C., office on June 20, 2001.[20] I was eventually connected to a friendly and helpful woman at the Public Liaison Office. She confirmed that, yes, that's what the secretary said. She added, "We were surprised we didn't hear anything back about this [from the American media]. We were waiting for it, but nothing came."

Unequal Tax Breaks

In the early 1990s, Paul Hawken, author of *The Ecology of Commerce,* found data indicating that the nation's corporations were net consumers, rather than producers, of tax monies. Several recent books on corporate welfare point to similar trends and conclusions, although hard data are difficult to come by because the necessary statistics are spread across literally thousands of separate local, state, and federal government agencies and their reports. "It was almost certainly the case, when I did my initial research in 1992," Hawken told me, "that the nation's corporations took more out of the economy in tax dollars than they pay in."[21]

Around the same time as Secretary O'Neill's modest proposal, a major aerospace corporation illustrated how much power it has in the economy. It announced that it would relocate its corporate headquarters from Seattle and then played the offers of three cities against one another. By the time the decision was announced on May 10, 2001, the *New York Times* announced that the winning destination had "promised tax breaks and incentives that could total $60 million over 20 years" to seal the deal.[22]

This is far from rare. According to a 1996 report from the Cato Institute, businesses in America receive direct tax subsidies of more than $75 billion annually.[23] That equates to every household in America paying a $750 annual subsidy to corporations, according to author and former faculty member of the Harvard Graduate School of Business Dr. David C. Korten.[24]

The way that this happens clearly illustrates the consequences of unrestrained "freedom of expression" in the halls of a government that was designed to serve the public good. In a situation that is reminiscent of the chartermongering era, companies can once again be aggressive in getting local governments to offer tax breaks that are never offered for humans. All of the following have the effect of cash taken out of human pockets and put into corporate ones:

- In Louisiana a multinational chemical company was given a $15 million tax break.[25]

- In Ohio $2.1 billion worth of business property was taken off the tax rolls, leaving public schools struggling to find resources because they depend most on the now-eviscerated property-tax revenues.*

- New York State companies had, from just 1991 to 1992, "earned" $242 million in tax credits and held $938 million in "unused" tax credits they could "use" in future years.[26]

---

*Noreena Hertz notes in *The Silent Takeover* (London: Heinemann, 2001) that, "beneficiaries of Ohio's 'corporate welfare' included Spiegel, Wal-Mart, and Consolidated Stores Corporation, all of which were absolved from property taxes....As one school treasurer put it, 'Kids get hurt and stockholders get rich.'"

- Alabama offered $153 million to a German automobile company to build a factory there, an amount equal to about $200,000 per job created.[27]

- Illinois gave a national retail chain $240 million in land and tax breaks to keep it from moving out of state.[28]

- The state of Indiana borrowed millions from its citizens by a bond issue and gave that money as an "upfront cash subsidy," along with other grants and tax breaks that totaled $451 million, to an airline to build a maintenance facility.[29]

- Pennsylvania gave a Norwegian transnational corporation $235 million in economic incentives to build a shipyard, an amount that cost the state, according to *Time* magazine, $323,000 per job.[30]

- New York City gave tax breaks of $235 million, $98 million, and $97 million to three corporations to keep them from moving to New Jersey, and $25 million to a media corporation to keep it in town. (Few of these breaks created any new jobs anywhere.) Says the *New York Times,* "Since Mr. Giuliani took office in 1994, he has provided 34 companies with tax breaks and other incentives totaling $666.7 million."[31]

- Kentucky gave nearly $140 million to two steel manufacturers—more than $350,000 per job created.[32]

- In Louisiana over a ten-year period, just the top ten corporations getting breaks (there were others) received $836 million to "create jobs." *Time* magazine did the math and found that the cost to the state's taxpayers *per job created* among those ten ranged from $900,000 to $29 million.[33]

- The state of Michigan created the Michigan Economic Growth Authority (MEGA), which as of 1999 had awarded over $900 million in tax breaks and grants to corporations, costing Michigan taxpayers, according to the Mackinac Center for Public Policy, $40,000 per job created or moved from other states into Michigan.[34]

In almost every case, benefits to one community were subtracted from another. "No new jobs are created in the process" of most of these sorts of tax breaks, according to former U.S. Secretary of Labor Robert B. Reich, quoted in the *New York Times.* "They're merely moved around. Meanwhile, the public spends a fortune subsidizing these companies. But there's no way that mayors or governors can withstand the heat once a major company announces it is thinking about leaving."[35]

Senator Bernie Sanders (I-VT) suggested a simple solution on my radio show in 2008: "Just pass a law denying federal highway matching funds to any state that participates" in these efforts by corporations to play one state off against another. Great idea, but because our federal legislature is now so completely owned by corporate interests, it'll never pass.

And the list of tax legislation corrupted by corporate influence over legislators could easily go on for pages and extends from the local to the national. Indeed, entire books and Web sites are devoted to "corporate welfare."

On November 6, 2001, the *Barre-Montpelier Times Argus* ran a syndicated article from the Knight Ridder News Service by Micah L. Sifry about proposals put before Congress within days and weeks of the September 11 terrorist attacks. The title speaks for itself: "At a Time of Sacrifice, Corporations Are Picking Our Pockets."[36]After the attacks, corporations began lobbying hard for a Bush administration proposal to repeal retroactively the alternative minimum tax passed in 1986. The result:

- $250 million for Enron

- $572 million for Chevron Texaco Inc.

- $671 million for General Electric

- $184 million for American Airlines

- $833 million for General Motors

- $608 million for TXU Corporation

- $241 million for Phillips Petroleum Company

- $600 million for DaimlerChrysler Corporation

- $1.424 billion for IBM[37]

The consumer advocacy group Common Cause estimated that there may be a relationship between the $4.6 million given by ten of America's largest corporations to the Democrats, the $10-plus million they gave the Republicans, and the $6.305 *billion* in tax rebates just those ten corporations would receive as result of the "economic stimulus package" lobbyists were promoting after the September 11 tragedy.[38]

With or without such legislation, 7 of America's 82 largest corporations paid "less than zero" in federal income taxes in 1998 (they got rebates instead), and 44 of the 82 didn't pay the standard federal corporate income tax rate of 35 percent.[39]

The Trend Goes International

Trends of business influencing government are becoming more uniform worldwide. In a famous recent case, a coalition of Deutsche Bank, Dresdner Bank, Allianz, Daimler-Benz, BMW, and the German energy group RWE all threatened to leave Germany if they didn't get tax breaks and subsidies from the government. (In the past twenty years, corporate profits in Germany had gone up more than 90 percent and corporate tax revenues had actually fallen by half, but this wasn't enough.) Finance Minister Oskar Lafontaine tried to fight them, but in the end he himself was crushed. When he quit his job over the issue in 1999, Lafontaine said, "The heart isn't traded on the stock market yet."

As the *Washington Post* pointed out on March 15, 1999, Lafontaine's experience "shows the limits of any single politician, or any single country, to stem the tide of global capitalism."[40]

The next voice from the German government, Chancellor Gerhard Schröder's top aide, Bobo Hombach, apparently got the message and said, "Things will be different now. We have to move in a different direction." The companies got their money and stayed in Germany: human taxpayers and family-owned businesses will make up the difference.

Often, however, corporations don't have to make threats to get their cash from the government: they make "investments."

In the late 1980s and early 1990s, the tobacco companies donated more than $30 million to various politicians and their parties. In 1997 Trent Lott (Senate) and Newt Gingrich (House of Representatives) inserted a single and mostly unnoticed forty-six-word sentence into that year's massive tax law. The sentence granted the tobacco industry a $50 billion tax break and was passed with bipartisan support. Yes, *billion* with a *b*.[41]

As Charles Lewis documented in his book *The Buying of the President*, a large national bank gave the Democratic National Committee a $3.5 million line of credit at an attractive interest rate two weeks after Democrats helped push through the 1994 Fair Trade in Financial Services Act, which netted that same bank $50 million a year in savings.[42]

The final irony is that while all of this fiscal benefit has accrued to companies through their personhood privileges and while they shift the tax burden to humans, they continue to claim exemptions from liability. Additionally, because the structure and the culture of corporations is driven to maximize quarterly profits, otherwise well-intentioned people working in company boardrooms find themselves pushed to make decisions that may not be in the best interest of the long term, of the commons, or even of the company's employees.

In a Democracy...

In a democracy the citizens—the voters—would decide these issues without pressure or influence from corporate or other special interest groups.

CHAPTER 16

Unequal Responsibility for Crime

A wicked big interest is necessarily more dangerous to the community than a wicked little interest.

—Teddy Roosevelt, Ohio Constitutional Convention, 1912

CONSIDER THIS AUGUST 3, 2001, WHITE HOUSE PRESS BRIEFING, IN WHICH the editor of *Corporate Crime Reporter,* Russell Mokhiber, asked a question of White House Press Secretary Ari Fleischer:

> Mokhiber: Ari, the Federal Communications Commission requires that if you're going to have a broadcast license you have to be of sound moral character. So when you make the application, you have to answer whether you've ever been convicted of a felony. They are now going after a gentleman in Missouri who's been convicted of a felony—
>
> Fleischer: Be careful, there are many broadcasters in this room.
>
> Mokhiber: I understand, that's why I'm raising the question. This gentleman was convicted of a felony, child molestation, and they're trying to strip him of five radio licenses. On the other hand, General Electric, which owns NBC, has been convicted of felonies, and they're not being stripped of their license. Why the double standard?
>
> Fleischer: I think you need to talk to the FCC about their standards. That's their jurisdiction to deal with licensing. [Looks around the room at another reporter] Ron?
>
> Mokhiber: I understand, but generally, does the president have a position on—?

At that point, Fleischer cut off Mokhiber and moved on.

The case Mokhiber cited is not unique. In 1982 a study of America's five hundred largest corporations reported that "23 percent of them had been convicted of a major crime or had paid more than $50,000 in penalties for serious misbehavior during the previous decade."[1]

If Corporations Are Persons, Why Aren't Their Crimes in the Statistics?

Every year the Federal Bureau of Investigation (FBI) issues a press release on its Uniform Crime Reporting Program, which determines the "Nation's Crime Index." It reports crimes by persons—but it excludes corporate persons, even when the corporations have been convicted of felonies. In its entire history, the FBI has never issued an annual report on crimes by corporate persons, although its reports on crimes by human persons are well researched and well publicized. The upshot of this is that when you ask people how most money and property are stolen, or how most people are killed, they think of burglars and muggers and bank robbers and crimes of passion. They think of human persons.

The reality, though, is that more money and property are stolen by or lost to corporate criminals than to human criminals. Mokhiber's *Corporate Crime Reporter* notes that in 1998, when the FBI estimated robberies and burglaries at almost $4 billion, the cost of corporate crimes was in the hundreds of billions... as it is every year. These include:

- Securities scams that ran around $15 billion that year

- Car-repair fraud that hit around $40 billion

- Insurance swindles and corporate fraud found on your health insurance/HMO/hospital billings that runs between $100 billion and $400 billion a year...a hundred times greater than all the burglaries in the country combined.[2]

Then there are the occasional "really big crimes," like Neil Bush's savings and loan scandal that then–Attorney General Dick Thornburgh called the biggest white-collar swindle in history, or the actions of banksters and defense "contractors" that got no investigations whatsoever from either the Bush or Obama administrations.

Deaths from Corporate Actions Are Not Included

More people die as a result of corporate activity than because of the actions of deranged killers or overwrought spouses. According to *Corporate Crime Reporter,* the FBI reported that 1998 saw about nineteen thousand Americans murdered at the hands of other people. But that same year fifty-six thousand people died from work-related diseases like black lung and asbestosis—that were unreported by the FBI—and many times that number died from "the silent violence of pollution, contaminated food, hazardous consumer products, and hospital malpractice."[3]

Much of the human death caused by corporate activity has arguable benefits—for example, the many cancers caused by compounds associated with plastics or pesticides. But the cost of these deaths isn't factored into the unit cost of the products, so there's no financial incentive for industry to develop toxin-free or toxin-reduced alternatives, or to use the more expensive but less toxic alternatives that already exist.

This is a process known as "internalizing profits and externalizing costs." The corporation profits from the toxins, and the public pays for the cancers both in health-care costs and lost productivity from sick and dying workers. It's been standard operating procedure for centuries and was pushed back against for only a few decades in the 1960s and 1970s after the publication of Rachel Carson's book *Silent Spring.*

Since the Reagan administration, however, dumping externalities on the public has become a common and accepted practice. One of the easiest ways to do it is to simply move the toxin-producing or toxin-using factory or process to a country with lax environmental and labor laws, like China or Vietnam, so not only are labor costs lowered but, more importantly, the cost of dealing with externalities like workers' compensation for injury/exposure and toxic emissions drops to zero or close to it.

And Then There Are the Big Mistakes

In 1998 one of America's largest meatpacking companies replaced a refrigeration unit on one of its processing lines. Shortly thereafter the detectors it had in place on the line to look for deadly cold-loving bacteria like *Listeria monocytogenes* started to react, indicating high levels of bacterial contamination.[4]

The company's response was immediate. Caroline Smith DeWaal of the Center for Science in the Public Interest told reporters Russell Mokhiber and Robert Weissman, "Then their tests started coming up positive, so they stopped testing." This company's Fourth Amendment right to privacy blocked surprise inspections by the government.

The detectors were apparently turned off for a full month before the Centers for Disease Control, frantically trying to find the source of the bacteria that was killing people—mostly children—all over the United States, used DNA fingerprinting to track the bacteria that was causing a national outbreak of *Listeria* back to the plant, provoking a nationwide recall of a million pounds of product.

But during that month, hundreds of people consuming this company's products were sickened by *Listeria,* and twenty-one humans died from it.

The U.S. Attorney's office, according to Mokhiber and Weissman, "said there was insufficient evidence to bring a felony charge" against the company. Instead the company paid a $200,000 fine and issued an unprecedented joint press release with the Bush administration's USDA that managed to say that the company had paid the fine without ever mentioning the brand name of the product that had been contaminated and caused the deaths.

Mokhiber and Weissman raised the case at the White House with Press Secretary Ari Fleischer. Here's the transcript of the interaction:

> Question: Ari, has the president expressed a view on the death penalty for corporate criminals—that is, revoking the charter of a corporation that has been convicted of a crime that resulted in death?
>
> Fleischer: The president does not weigh in on those matters of justice. They should not be dictated by decisions made at the White House.
>
> Question: No, Ari, wait a second. Ari, Ari, wait a second. He's in favor of the death penalty for individuals generally. Is he in favor of the death penalty for corporations convicted of crimes that result in death?
>
> Fleischer: These are questions that are handled by officials of the Justice Department—not by people at the White House.[5]

The Bush White House never commented further, and the Obama White House's position seems to mirror that of the Bush administration. And because the FBI doesn't report on such deaths, or on workplace deaths, it's hard to know how many deaths every year could have been prevented.

In a Democracy...

The risk to a person who kills another is high: prison and, in some states, execution. But the risk to a corporation of killing people is relatively low, and industry lobbies to keep it that way. For instance, when Congress considered putting criminal penalties into the National Traffic and Motor Vehicle Safety Act, the auto industry lobbied hard against it and won.

As a result, today if a person working as a part-time mechanic in his backyard were to knowingly and willfully repair or build a car for somebody that killed them, he could go to prison for manslaughter or even murder. But if a corporation knowingly and willfully were to repair or build a car that killed a human, it now has a legal exemption. It would face only civil penalties and fines under the act, and none of its human decision-makers would ever be held responsible.

Many human deaths are a result of corporate activities that are permitted by the government—but even deaths that result from corporate felony convictions are not included in FBI crime statistics. In a democracy we can do better.

CHAPTER 17

Unequal Privacy

The right of the people to be secure in their persons, houses, papers, and effects, against unreasonable searches and seizures, shall not be violated...

—Fourth Amendment to the Constitution of the United
States, guaranteeing privacy from snooping

W<small>HO READS YOUR MAIL? NOBODY? IT DEPENDS WHAT SYSTEM YOU USE FOR</small> communication.

Paper mail that is delivered by the government-run U.S. Postal Service carries legal protections for the privacy of our communications. Nobody, at least without a court order, can read our letters or track what we send and receive.

But if you send an e-mail, the corporation that provides your Internet access can keep track of who you correspond with, what Web sites you visit, and everything you write, read, and view. Even after the terrorist attacks on the World Trade Center and the Pentagon in September 2001, the FBI needed an act of Congress to get that kind of power, even in limited form. But the corporations who transmit our e-mail have had it from day one.

And not only can multinational media corporations track our individual Internet activity, they do. If I walk around in my local bookstore, Bear Pond Books, nobody is following me and noting every book I pick up and look over. But when I browse the Web, both my Internet provider and the owners of the Web sites I visit may know who I am and what I've looked at. In fact, unless we intentionally install or activate security software, it's highly likely that they do know where we've been. That's because when I click on a Web site, it sends a coded signal through my Internet company and to the Web site host. Both of them can easily record my clicks—at practically no cost to themselves.

In our increasingly electronic age, there's more: the corporation that sells me telephone service keeps complete records of whom I call, where, and when. If I had digital interactive cable television, the cable corporation could keep a list of every program I watch and when.

Microsoft got a lot of publicity because, according to the online journal PCWorld.com, "It was unaware that a feature in its Windows 98 operating system was transmitting a hardware serial number to a Microsoft server, even if the user had requested that the number not be sent." Microsoft said it would take two months to make it stop sending the information. In a similar glitch, Microsoft said its Office software was accidentally inserting a unique ID code into documents that could be used to track where a document originated.[1] "Unaware"? "Accidentally"?

One thing Americans value very highly is their Fourth Amendment right to privacy, and polls have shown that it's one of the few issues that will get Americans out of their seats on Election Day. That fact should be even more persuasive to legislators than campaign contributions, although in 2008 while on the campaign trail, Senator Barack Obama went back to Washington, D.C., to vote for a Foreign Intelligence Surveillance Act (FISA) bill that gave protections to AT&T and other companies accused of illegally violating our privacy at the illegal request of the Bush administration (which was also protected by that vote).

While the names of only a few of the participants in the Boston Tea Party are known today, more than 220 years later such anonymity is impossible. And without anonymity, the skeptics argue, anybody who would try to shift power away from corporations and back to the people can be neutralized before they have a chance to be effective. Access to the media is denied, whistleblowers often find themselves unemployable and without resources, and, in a worst-case scenario, they may suffer the fate of Karen Silkwood, who was murdered on her way to share corporate inside information with a reporter.

Corporations Want Privacy—for Themselves but Not for Humans

Although corporations keep all their constitutional rights as a person intact throughout the business day and night, seven days a week, 365 days a year, the Supreme Court has ruled that when a human steps onto the corporate-owned property of his or her employer, that human is voluntarily giving up his constitutional rights to privacy, freedom from search, and free speech.

Your employer can read your e-mails, monitor your computer use, secretly photograph you, listen in on your telephone calls, fire you if you say things it doesn't like (even unrelated to work), and even demand that you provide samples of your bodily fluids or subject you to external and internal physical examinations.

At the same time, however, the corporation you work for continues to assert its full constitutional rights against these same types of "interference" by the representative of humans—the government. The EPA can't inspect a chemical factory without the permission of the corporation that owns it, but that same corporation can inspect its employees in the minutest detail without their permission.

Additionally, information about U.S.-based multinational corporations is not available in the following areas because those corporations are entitled, as persons with privacy rights, to keep secret:

- How much they pay overseas workers

- How many overseas employees they have, or where

- Levels of toxic emissions from their plants overseas, or of those of their contractors

- Where they have overseas plants or contractors[2]

In a Democracy...

Not only was it not always this way in America, but it's the opposite of what the Founders of this nation intended. In a democracy this can change.

CHAPTER 18

Unequal Citizenship and Access to the Commons

fas-cism *(fâsh'iz'em) n. A system of government that exercises a dictatorship of the extreme right, typically through the merging of state and business leadership, together with belligerent nationalism. [Ital. fascio, group.] -fas'cist n. -fas-cis'tic (fa-shis'tik) adj.*

—American Heritage Dictionary, 1983

THERE ARE RESOURCES AND THERE ARE RESOURCES. FOR CORPORATIONS, resources include raw materials, labor, the property and the equipment they use, the talents of the people they employ, and cash. For humans, resources include air, water, food, shelter, clothing, health care, and the means of exchange to ensure these.

I remember growing up fifty-plus years ago in an America where an employer's responsibilities to their community were so well understood that bosses who laid off people were considered either evil or failures. There was a dramatic recalibration of this during the 1980s, as the word *layoff* was replaced with the more politically tolerable euphemism *downsizing* and then further euphemized to *rightsizing*. In England the same event is described much more directly: "I was made redundant."

This chapter is about what has happened to humans as their protections have been given to entities (corporations) that have entirely different values from those of living beings. Ironically, the bigger companies get, the more ability they have to influence people's lives for better or worse—but the bigger they get, the fewer choices are available to workers and customers. And in recent years, health researchers have identified that the inability to do anything about one's problems is a key contributing factor to stress.

Stress Kills

For many Americans a lengthening workweek, increasing debt, and dwindling job security are now part of life. Not surprisingly, this triad produces stress. Debt carries risk. A longer workweek reduces options for enjoying life and for escaping from debt. The decline of job security increases the risk of complete economic disaster—a scenario that corporations rarely have to confront.

The Clinton administration's ratification of NAFTA and GATT/WTO (as well as numerous other "trade agreements" since then) made it possible to shift manufacturing and production jobs from the United States to the developing world. The American situation is mirrored throughout the world, as industrialized nations lose manufacturing jobs and developing countries become spotted with sweatshops like a child with measles. Humans require passports and visas to travel from nation to nation, but corporations can now move anywhere with virtually no restrictions.

- The U.S. Centers for Disease Control notes, "From 1952 to 1995, the incidence of suicide among adolescents and young adults nearly tripled. From 1980 to 1997, the rate of suicide among persons aged 15 to 19 years increased by 11 percent and among persons aged 10 to 14 years by 109 percent."[1]

- Between 1972 and 1994, the number of Americans living below the poverty line almost doubled from roughly 23 million to about 40 million. By 2009 poverty had become so widespread and systemic in America that 58.8 percent of all Americans have or will spend at least a year of their lives in poverty.[2]

- Across Latin America, Africa, and Asia, the United Nation's International Labor Organization catalogs more than 250 million children between the ages of five and fourteen who are working in hazardous industries and slave labor.[3]

- The World Health Organization lists unemployment as one of its risk factors for child abuse.[4]

Elizabeth Warren, Harvard law professor and chair of the Congressional Oversight Panel for the so-called TARP funds used to bail out the banks in 2008 and 2009, noted bluntly in a posting on the *Huffington Post* on December 3, 2009:

Today, one in five Americans is unemployed, underemployed or just plain out of work. One in nine families can't make the minimum payment on their credit cards. One in eight mortgages is in default or foreclosure. One in eight Americans is on food stamps. More than 120,000 families are filing for bankruptcy every month. The economic crisis has wiped more than $5 trillion from pensions and savings, has left family balance sheets upside down, and threatens to put 10 million homeowners out on the street.[5]

While this has been tragic for the people who are affected, a cynical view is that an increase in the number of desperate people can be beneficial to business: wages drop when more people are out of work and competing for available jobs. In fact, wages are lowest when the worker literally has no choice.

The Prisoner as Employee

Under the new WTO and NAFTA rules, an importing country *cannot* consider the conditions under which a product was produced. So, some corporations have discovered that they can profit by using prison labor to manufacture export products or perform services for offshore clients.

Although corporations can't be put in prison, they find it very profitable to put humans there: corporations in nations like Myanmar (Burma), China, and the United States have opened manufacturing or service facilities in prisons, paying their laborers anywhere from a few cents an hour down to nothing at all.

It's an enormously profitable enterprise, and some nations have moved to capitalize on it by passing laws that are easy to violate (so that people end up in prison who would not otherwise have been there), increasing the severity of penalties for existing crimes, more heavily criminalizing health problems (such as drug use), or criminalizing "anti-state" behaviors (such as practicing religion in China).

Although China and Myanmar don't publish their figures, in the United States (the nation with the world's highest incarceration rate), the "correctional population" in 2006 was 7.2 million adults, resulting in one in every thirty-one Americans (3.2 percent of the U.S. adult population) in jail, on parole, or on probation. The consequence was a substantial pool of potential prison labor—about one in every one hundred Americans.[6]

Since the 1985 passage of new laws increasing criminal penalties for drug use and sale, drug convictions accounted for more than 80 percent of the increase in the federal prison population, driving up the budget of the Federal

Bureau of Prisons by 1,954 percent.[7] Prison populations in the United States were relatively stable compared with population growth from the early years of the twentieth century until the election of Ronald Reagan, whose administration blessed the private prison industry in the United States.

We were at a quarter-million prisoners in 1930, a number that slowly rose with population growth to a half-million in 1980. During Reagan's decade of the 1980s, prison populations in the United States doubled to more than 1 million people in 1990. The next decade they doubled again, hitting 2 million in 2000.[8]

From its birth in the 1980s, the American private prison industry has grown to be worth more than $1 billion today and is now moving international, with the two largest players having moved into direct construction or alliance partnerships in more than sixty nations.[9]

The percentage of American prisoners in private prisons who are now working for multinational corporations more than doubled between 1993 and 1998, according to www.prisonactivist.org. (Detailed and more recent statistics are hard to come by because the industry is not required to release such information and therefore chooses not to.) At the same time, American corporate prisons carry the highest rates of tuberculosis and HIV infection (and new infections) in the nation, and have a suicide rate twenty times higher than the country as a whole.[10]

But they can be very profitable: On February 8, 2002, America's largest private prison corporation "reported record high annual revenues for fiscal year 2001 of $2.8 billion, a 12.1 percent increase over its 2000 revenues of $2.5 billion" and that the security part of its business was doing well. The company's president said, "The North American security operations had a very strong quarter and year with a margin increase of 20 basis points for the fourth quarter, and a margin increase of 80 basis points for the year."[11]

Privatizing the Commons

Privatization is the idea of taking commons functions or resources out of the hands of elected governments responsible to their voters and handing their management or ownership over to private enterprise answerable to shareholders. Many arguments have been advanced about privatization; those in favor argue that corporations run for a profit can be more efficient than government, and those opposed usually argue that the resources of the commons should always be held in the hands of institutions that are answerable only to the people who use them—the citizens—and thus must be managed by elected and responsive governments.

Opponents of privatization of the commons also usually point out that whatever increases in efficiency a corporation may bring to a utility, the savings produced by those increases in efficiency rarely make their way to the consumer but instead are raked off the top by the corporation and distributed to shareholders. One of the more high-profile examples is Enron and its role in the privatization of electricity worldwide, with particular focus on how Enron's privatization of electricity in California worked to the detriment of California's citizens but produced millions in profits for a small group of Texas stockholders; another example is an Enron subsidiary's meetings in 1999 with Governor Jeb Bush of Florida in which it proposed to privatize and take over much of the state's water supply.[12]

Supporters of privatization point to the creative ways corporations can extract profits from things governments previously just supervised in a boring and methodical fashion. For example, an article in the *Houston Chronicle* in January 2001 titled "Enron Is Blazing New Business Trail" noted the "extraordinary year" the Houston-based company was having, with most of the company's revenues coming "from buying and selling contracts in natural gas and electricity."

The article quoted Kenneth Lay, who, the newspaper said, "has a doctorate in economics," as extolling the virtues of profiting from trading in previously regulated or government-run commodities. "The company's emphasis on trading to hedge against risk has been emulated by other firms in energy," the article said, including "Duke Energy, Dynegy, Williams Energy—and increasingly in other industries."[13]

Who Owns the World's Water?

While Enron started the discussion in Florida in 1999 about privatizing that state's water supplies and the Everglades, the process was already a done deal in Bolivia. In 1998 the Bolivian government requested a $25 million loan guarantee to refinance its water services in the community of Cochabamba. The World Bank told the Bolivian government that it would guarantee the loan only if Bolivia privatized the water supply, so it was handed over to Aguas del Tunari, a subsidiary of several large transnationals, including an American corporation that is one of the world's largest private construction companies.

The next year Aguas del Tunari, in an effort to squeeze profits out of Bolivia's water, announced that water prices were doubling. For minimum wage or unemployed Bolivians, this meant water would now take half their monthly income, costing more than food. The Bolivian government, acting on suggestions from the World Bank and Aguas del Tunari, declared all water corporate property, so even to draw water from community wells or to gather rainwater on their own properties, peasants and small farmers had to first pay for and obtain permits from the corporation.

The price of water was pegged to the U.S. dollar to protect the corporation, and the Bolivian government announced that none of the World Bank loan could go to poor people to help with their water bills.

With more than 90 percent of the Bolivian people opposing this move, a people's rebellion rose up to deprivatize the water system. A former machinist and union activist, Oscar Olivera, built a broad-based coalition of peasants, workers, and farmers to create La Coordinadora de Defensa del Agua y de la Vida, or La Coordinadora. Hundreds of thousands of Bolivians went on a general strike, brought transportation in Cochabamba to a standstill, and evoked violent police response in defense of the Aguas del Tunari corporation's "right" to continue to control the local water supply and sell it for a profit. Victor Hugo Danza, one of the marchers, was shot through the face and killed: he was seventeen.

The government declared martial law, and members of La Coordinadora were arrested and beaten in the middle of an early April night. The government seized control of the radio and television stations to prevent anti-corporate messages from being broadcast. But the uprising continued and grew.

The situation became so tense that the directors of the American corporation and Aguas del Tunari abandoned Bolivia on April 10, 2000. They took with them key files, documents, computers, and the assets of the company— leaving a legal shell with tremendous debt.

The Bolivian government handed the debts and the water company, SEMAPA, to La Coordinadora. The new company is now run by the activist group—essentially a local government itself now—and its first action was to restore water to the poorest southern neighborhoods, more than four hundred communities, which had been cut off by the for-profit company because the residents didn't have the money to pay profitable rates for water. Throughout the summer of 2000, La Coordinadora held hearings through the hundreds of neighborhoods it now served.

In the meantime the American corporation moved its holding company for Aguas del Tunari from the Cayman Islands to Holland so that it could legally sue the government of Bolivia (South America's poorest country) under WTO and Bilateral Investment Treaty (BIT) rules that Bolivia had signed with Holland.

On January 19, 2006, a settlement was reached between the government of Bolivia and Aguas del Tunari, and it was agreed that "the concession was terminated only because of the civil unrest and the state of emergency in Cochabamba and not because of any act done or not done by the international shareholders of Aguas del Tunari." With this statement both parties agreed to drop any financial claims against the other.[14]

Why take such extraordinary steps against such a poor country? There's more at stake than the immediate situation. If this citizens' group is successful in turning a water supply back from private to government hands, and thus improving water service and making it more egalitarian and less expensive in this poverty-stricken country, it could threaten water-privatizing plans of huge corporations around the world.

The stakes are high, even as cities across India, Africa, and other South American countries hand their local water systems to for-profit corporations. Nonetheless politicians around the world are stepping up the rate at which they're pushing for a transfer of the commons to the hands of for-profit corporations. Checking voting records and lists of corporate contributors, it's hard not to conclude that there is a relationship between this political activity and the generous contributions these corporations give to pro-privatization politicians.

"Private Equity" Can Erase a Firm's Values

In today's business environment, when corporations are run in ways that benefit the environment or their workers as much as their stockholders, they're at risk. When good salaries and pension plans are cut, it's referred to as "unnecessary fat" that can be trimmed. (Note that such cuts are made much more feasible when wages are forced down by exporting jobs from the local economy.) Similarly, behaving in a more expensive but environmentally friendly way is "not efficient."

In an article in *Yes!* magazine, economist and author David C. Korten pointed out that for many years the Pacific Lumber Company was, in many regards, a model corporate citizen. It paid good salaries, fully funded its pension fund, offered an excellent benefit package to employees, and even had an explicit no-layoffs policy during soft times in the lumber economy. Perhaps most important to local residents who weren't employed by the company, Pacific Lumber "for years pioneered the development of sustainable logging practices on its substantial holdings of ancient redwood timber stands in California."[15]

In a nation where such employee- and nature-friendly values were both valued and defended, Pacific Lumber Company would have a bright future. But in a world where profit is the prime value, and humans and ancient trees are merely excess fat, Pacific Lumber was a sitting duck.

As Korten documents in his article, a corporate raider

> gained control in a hostile takeover. He immediately doubled the cutting rate of the company's holding of thousand-year-old trees, reaming a mile-and-a-half corridor into the middle of the forest that he jeeringly named 'Our wildlife-biologist study trail.' He then drained $55 million from the company's $93 million pension fund and invested the remaining $38 million in annuities of the life insurance company which had financed the junk bonds used to make the purchase and subsequently failed. The remaining redwoods were the subject of a last-ditch effort by environmentalists to save from clear-cutting.[16]

In the end the government stepped in to save some of the old-growth forests, but the business and its employees were already screwed, and the private equity artist had already taken his cut.

Once upon a time, America had laws that corporations couldn't own other corporations. If that were still true, situations like that chronicled by Korten would become illegal rather than the norm. (And people who become multimillionaires by employing such predatory leveraged-buyout and private equity techniques, from Mitt Romney to T. Boone Pickens, would actually have to work for a living.)

The reason Madison and Jefferson—and even Hamilton and Adams— worried so loudly about "associations and monopolies" growing too large and powerful is that they would begin to usurp the very lives and liberties of the humans who created them. It becomes particularly problematic when companies are bought and stripped of their assets by other companies that aren't even in their industry but are simply asset hunting.

In the realm of government, the Founders kept power close to the people with the Tenth Amendment and other constitutional references to the powers of states over the federal government. A similar principle could apply to corporations.

The breakup of AT&T between 1974 and 1984 led to vigorous growth in the telecommunications industry, although that industry is once again reconsolidating in the absence of Sherman Act enforcement.

Seizing Other Nations' Commons via Patent

Because international courts have recently held that life forms and their by-products are patentable, multinational corporations in wealthy nations have been busily patenting the living products of poorer nations.

For example, people in India have been using the oil of the neem tree as a medicine for millennia: but now more than seventy patents have now been granted on the tree and its by-products in various nations. One European patent on its use as a fungicide was recently thrown out, but others stand.[17]

In similar fashion, Maggie McDonald notes in the British magazine *New Scientist* that "a botanical cure for hepatitis traditionally used in India can be patented in the U.S." She notes that Vandana Shiva documents how this is not a process that is driving innovation or competition, as multinationals often claim, but instead, "a survey in the U.S. showed that 80 percent of patents are taken out to block competitors."[18]

Ironically, that same issue of *New Scientist* has a feature on recruitment news that extols the wonders of becoming a patent agent. In the new world of international biotechnology, the article says, "Wealth is measured not in gold mines, but in the new currency of 'intellectual property.'" Eerily echoing Shiva's claim, the very upbeat article on getting a job in the patent business says, "The aim is to lock away these prize assets [for your company] so they can't be plundered by commercial rivals."[19]

And the business of locking up these assets pays very well. Ted Blake of Britain's Chartered Institute of Patent Agents is quoted as saying, "You're looking at six-figure salaries for those who make it as partners in an agents' firm." Not only is the pay good but the work is also very chic. Reiner Osterwalder of the European Patent Office told the magazine, "Patents are no longer stuck in a dusty corner. They're sexy, and touch questions of world order."[20]

The British Broadcasting Corporation notes that not only can plants and their uses be patented but the very genetics of the plants can be nailed down. An article about the patenting of the neem tree published in 2000 on the BBC Web site says, "Genes from nutmeg and camphor have also been patented with the aim of producing their oils artificially—a move which would hit producers in developing countries."[21]

And it's in developing countries where the race to patent indigenous life forms is most rapid, particularly by American-based companies, because U.S. patent law doesn't recognize indigenous use of a product as "prior art," meaning once a use for a plant is "discovered" by an American company—even if that plant has been used in that way for ten thousand years by local tribes, it's considered new and thus patentable. The Web site www.globalissues.org notes, "In Brazil, which probably has the richest biodiversity in the world, large multinational corporations have already patented more than half the known plant species."[22]

The consequences of this behavior are profitable for corporations but can be devastating to the humans who find that their food or medicinal plants are now the property of a multinational corporation. Corporations say that this is necessary to ensure profits, but the thriving herbal products industry— made up mostly of domestic plants that cannot be patented—testifies to the untruthfulness of this assertion. Selling plants may not be as profitable as selling tightly controlled and patented plants, but it can be profitable nonetheless.

This is not to say that plants should or should not be patentable. In a democracy the benefits or liabilities of corporations' patenting life forms would be discussed and decided by popular vote. Because of the *Santa Clara* "decision" and its consequences, however, corporations have exercised their "right" to get patent laws changed and exemptions established that would be difficult to impossible for an ordinary human to accomplish.

Changing Your Citizenship in a Day

For a human to change his or her citizenship from one country to another is a process that can take years, sometimes even decades, and, for most of the world's humans, it is practically impossible. Corporations, however, can change their citizenship in a day. And many do.

The New Hampshire firm Tyco International moved its legal citizenship from the United States to Bermuda and, according to a 2002 report in the *New York Times*, saved "more than $40 million last year alone" because Bermuda does not charge income tax to corporations while the United States does. Stanley Works, which manufactures in Connecticut, will avoid paying U.S. taxes of $30 million. Ingersoll-Rand "saves" $40 million a year.[23]

Offshore tax havens figured big in the Enron debacle, as that corporation spun off almost nine hundred separate companies based in tax-free countries to shelter income and hide transactions. Through this device the company paid no income taxes whatsoever in four of its last five years and received $382 million in tax rebates from Uncle Sam.[24]

Generally, when a human person changes citizenship, he is also required to change his residence—he has to move to and participate in the country where he is a citizen. But Bermuda and most other tax havens have no such requirement. All you need do is be a corporate person instead of a human person, pay some fees (it cost Ingersoll-Rand $27,653), and, as Ingersoll-Rand's chief financial officer told the *New York Times,* "We just pay a service organization" to be a mail drop for the company.[25]

Ironically, the Bush administration justified rounding up human people and holding them incommunicado in jails without normal due process after September 11 because as "nonpersons" they lacked the full protections of citizens under the U.S. Constitution. (Over the weekend of Christmas 2009, the Obama administration successfully argued the same logic, allowing it to constitutionally render persons as "nonpersons" simply by having the president declare them "enemy combatants.")

Similarly, if you or I were to open a post office box in Bermuda and then claim that we no longer had to pay U.S. income taxes, we could go to jail. Corporate persons, however, keep their rights intact when they decide to change citizenship—and save a pile in taxes. And, notes the *New York Times,* "There is no official estimate of how much the Bermuda moves are costing the government in tax revenues, and the Bush administration is not trying to come up with one."

Corporations are taxed because they use public services and are therefore expected to help pay for them.

Corporations make use of a workforce educated in public schools paid for with tax dollars. They use roads and highways paid for with tax dollars. They use water, sewer, power, and communications rights-of-way paid for and maintained with taxes. They demand the same protection from fire and police departments as everybody else, and they enjoy the benefits of national sovereignty and the stability provided by the military and institutions like NATO and the United Nations, the same as all residents of democratic nations.

In fact, corporations are *heavier* users of taxpayer-provided services and institutions than are average citizens. Taxes pay for our court systems—the biggest users of which are corporations, to enforce contracts. Taxes pay for our Treasury Department and other government institutions that maintain a stable currency essential to corporate activity. Taxes pay for our regulation of corporate activity, from ensuring safety in the workplace, to a pure food and drug supply, to limiting toxic emissions.

Taxes also pay (hugely) for our military, which is far more involved in keeping shipping lanes open and trade routes safe for our corporations than protecting you and me from an invasion by Canada or Mexico (our closest neighbors, with whom we've fought wars in the past). It's very difficult to calculate because government doesn't keep track of it, but it's not hard to see that corporate use of our commons—what is funded with our taxes—is well over half of worker use.

Yet, as professor of political economics Gar Alperovitz points out, "In the Eisenhower era, corporations paid an average 25 percent of the federal tax bill; they paid only 10 percent in 2000 and [following the first Bush tax cuts only] 7 percent in 2001."[26]

In a Democracy...

One of the foundational principles of democracy is that all people are treated equally in regard to issues of the law, citizenship, and their access to the commons. As Lawrence Mitchell, a John Theodore Fey research professor of law at the George Washington Law School and author of *Corporate Irresponsibility*, said, "The function of corporations in light of their constitutional personhood is effectively to foreclose access to the commons for most citizens. The entire proposition that a corporation is a person is ridiculous."[27]

CHAPTER 19

Unequal Wealth

I care not how affluent some may be, provided that none be miserable in consequence of it.

—Thomas Paine, 1796

IN THE ABSENCE OF THE CONTROLS RECOMMENDED BY THE FOUNDERS AND early state regulation, corporations have continued to grow in size and power without limit. But they haven't done it just by creating new wealth in the economy. Much of it, instead, has been accomplished by increasingly consolidating existing wealth, moving it out of the hands of the middle class and into the hands of the top few percent of Americans economically. Of course, some new wealth has been generated, but nowhere near enough to explain the observable facts.* The past thirty years has, in fact, seen the largest transfer of wealth from working people to the rich and very rich in the history of both this nation and any nation on earth.

Consolidation: Mergers, Acquisitions, and Interlocking Boards

If you were to define and rank nations according to their gross domestic product, fifty-two of the world's one hundred largest "nations" are actually corporations. Tracking the growth of the largest companies can be problematic because they're constantly merging with or buying other companies. This trend has accelerated in the decreased regulatory environment of the 1980–2010

---

*Many of the statistics in this chapter (unless cited as otherwise) are from Jeff Gates in various sources. Jeff is president of the Shared Capitalism Institute and author of numerous books and articles, all of which I strongly recommend. His Web site is www.shared capitalism.org.

period—just a few generations after Americans busted the trusts during the Populist Movement of Teddy Roosevelt and William Jennings Bryan.

One-third of 1980's Fortune 500 companies no longer existed in 1990—not because they failed but because they had been merged or acquired. This accelerated in the 1990s: two-fifths of the Fortune 500 vanished in the five years from 1990 to 1995. They're still there and still powerful; it's just that now they're even more powerful and wealthy, and they have less competition.[1] Statistics since 1995 are nearly impossible to find because the Clinton administration stopped the tracking of this sort of information and corporations don't publish it. (And conservative think tanks have, over the past decade, systematically employed a small army of Libertarian true-believers to scrub the Internet and rewrite thousands of Wikipedia and other pages.)

The combined GDP of the world's two hundred largest corporations is greater than all but nine nations, and just as the European royal families are interrelated, so too are the boards of directors of most of the world's largest corporations.

Corporate observer Robert A. G. Monks reports that today 86 percent of billion-dollar company boards contain at least one CEO of another company, while 65 percent of outside directors serve on two or more boards. He documents how 89 percent of inside directors are outside directors on other companies' boards, and 20 percent of all directors serve on four or more company boards.[2] Ralph Nader has testified about this extensively before Congress, suggesting that these interlocking boards violate antitrust statutes, and there are entire Web sites devoted to it, such as www.theyrule.net.

For example, the following is a 2002 snapshot showing how interconnected these companies are in that each has at least one board member who's also a board member on another, creating a continuous daisy-chain:[3]

- IBM shares a board member with Coca-Cola

- Which shares a board member with AT&T

- Which shares a board member with Citigroup

- Which shares a board member with Lucent Technologies

- Which shares a board member with Chevron

- Which shares a board member with Hewlett-Packard

- Which shares a board member with Boeing

- Which shares a board member with Sara Lee

- Which shares a board member with Bank One Corporation

- Which shares a board member with Cardinal Health

- Which shares a board member with Freddie Mac

- Which shares a board member with Lehman Brothers Holdings

- Which shares a board member with PepsiCo

- Which shares a board member with Bank of America

- Which shares a board member with Motorola

- Which shares a board member with J. P. Morgan Chase

- Which shares a board member with ExxonMobil

- Which shares a board member with SBC Communications (owns Ameritech, PacBell, and Southwestern Bell, among others)

- Which shares a board member with PG&E Corporation

- Which shares a board member with Home Depot

- Which shares a board member with General Electric

- Which shares a board member with Delphi Automotive Systems

- Which shares a board member with Goldman Sachs Group

- Which shares a board member with Ford Motor Company

- Which shares a board member with Sprint

- Which shares a board member with Allstate

- Which shares a board member with AMR (owns American Airlines)

- Which shares a board member with Aetna

- Which shares a board member with Dell Computer

- Which shares a board member with Prudential Insurance

- Which shares a board member with Dow Chemical

- Which shares a board member with Met Life

- Which shares a board member with Verizon

- Which shares a board member with USX (formerly U.S. Steel)

- Which shares a board member with Lockheed Martin
- Which shares a board member with Enron
- Which at this writing shares board member Ken Lay with Compaq
- Which shares a board member with Dynergy
- Which shares a board member with CVS/Pharmacy
- Which shares a board member with Fannie Mae
- Which shares a board member with Conoco
- Which shares a board member with E. I. du Pont de Nemours
- Which shares a board member with IBM
- Which shares a board member with Coca-Cola (which is where we started)

There is strong evidence that this much concentration of wealth and power is not healthy, and prior to the last century it was considered criminal behavior in many states, as interlocking boards were banned and most states had specific caps on how big a corporation could be.

But that was then and this is now. Today the world's largest two hundred corporations, which employ fewer than 0.8 percent of the world's workforce, account for more than 27 percent of the world's total economic activity, more than all nations in the world combined except the top ten.[4]

The corporations of Samuel Adams's day, like the East India Company, were the bald economic instruments of monarchy and imperial power, but during and after the American Revolution they were put firmly under the control of state legislatures and local municipalities. Today, empowered with human rights, they roam free, with few checks on their power or growth; and they have, in fact, reversed the old East India Company model by becoming the agents that more directly control democracies than do their individual citizens.

- The United Nations reports that "about two-thirds of all world trade" is in the hands of transnational corporations, which "increasingly shape trade patterns" of the planet.[5]

- Corporations reaching out from their home countries and into other countries have become "the main force in international economic integration," according to the U.N.'s Trade and Development Conference.[6]

- Sales of the two hundred largest corporations in the world equal 27.5 percent of the world's economic activity.[7]

- If you added together the sales of every nation in the world except the top ten, the total would be less than the combined sales of the world's two hundred largest corporations.[8]

- The 1999 sales of General Motors were greater than the GDP of 182 nations. The same is true of Wal-Mart, ExxonMobil, Ford Motor, and DaimlerChrysler.[9]

- The eighty-two largest American corporations contributed $33,045,832 to political action committees in the year-2000 election cycle (and that doesn't include "soft money," for which statistics are unavailable), outspending labor unions by 15 to 1. This was apparently useful to candidates: in 94 percent of U.S. House of Representatives races, the candidate who spent the most money won.[10] By the 2008 election it had become much more difficult to track corporate money or that coming from wealthy individuals, particularly when that money was used to fund nonprofit (we pay their share of taxes) astroturf groups that spring up and seem to be grassroots advocacy efforts. A good guess, though, is that the numbers have increased about tenfold.

As this shift in income has happened, along with it came a shift in who owns pretty much everything.

- In 1976 the richest 10 percent of America's population owned 50 percent of American wealth. By 1997 they owned 73 percent. (In other words, 23 percent of America's total wealth shifted from the poor and middle class to the very wealthy in twenty-one years.)[11]

- This was not just because the economic pie got bigger: 44 percent more people work multiple jobs than did in 1970, and American workers are putting in, on average, a full month more at work than they did twenty years ago. And hourly earnings of America's nonsupervisory workers, in 1998 dollars, have fallen by 9 percent since 1973, from $14.09 to $12.77.[12]

- Looking at the same numbers from "the other end of the telescope," in 1976 the lower 90 percent of the population owned half the wealth. By 1997 their share was down to 27 percent.[13]

- In 2000 the top 1 percent of American households had financial wealth greater than that of the bottom 95 percent combined.[14]

- In 1998 the net worth of just one American, Bill Gates, at $46 billion, was greater than the bottom 45 percent of all American households combined.[15]

- It's not just an American phenomenon anymore. Worldwide, according to the United Nations Development Program, the difference between the richest and poorest nations in the world was 1 to 3 in 1820, 1 to 35 in 1950, and 1 to 72 in 1992. The gap has continued to grow since then.[16]

How can this be? What's happening?

Spengler's *The Decline of the West*

In his book *The Decline of the West,* first published in German in 1918 and then in English in 1926, Oswald Spengler suggested that what we call Western civilization was then beginning to enter a "hardening" or "classical" phase in which all the nurturing and supportive structures of culture would become, instead, instruments of the exploitation of a growing peasant class to feed the wealth of a new and growing aristocracy.

Culture would become a parody of itself, people's expectations would decline while their wants would grow, and a new peasantry would emerge, which would cause the culture to stabilize in a "classic form" that, while Spengler doesn't use the term, seems very much like feudalism—the medieval system in which the lord owned the land and everyone else was a vassal (a tenant who owed loyalty to the landlord).

Spengler, considering himself an aristocrat, didn't see this as a bad thing. In 1926 he prophesied that once the boom of the Roaring Twenties was over, a great bust would wash over the Western world. While this bust had the potential to create chaos, its most likely outcome would be a return to the classic, stable form of social organization, what Spengler calls "high culture" and I call neofeudalism.

He wrote:

> In all high Cultures, therefore, there is a *peasantry,* which is breed stock, in the broad sense (and thus to a certain extent nature herself), and a *society* which is assertively and emphatically "in form." It is a set of classes or Estates, and no doubt artificial and transitory. But the history of these classes and estates is

world history at highest potential. It is only in relation to it that the peasant is seen as historyless. [All italics are Spengler's from the original text.][17]

More-recent cultural observers, ranging from billionaire George Soros in his book *The Crisis of Global Capitalism,*[18] to professor Noreena Hertz in *The Silent Takeover: Global Capitalism and the Death of Democracy,*[19] have pointed to deep cracks in the foundational structure of Western civilization, traceable to the current legal status of corporations versus humans. The extent of the problems within our structures is laid bare with startling and sometimes frightening clarity by a wide variety of books.*

The origin of many of modern global society's problems are clearly laid out in *The Trap* by now-deceased billionaire speculator Sir James Goldsmith,[20] and it appears that perhaps that "crazy old coot" (as the media would have us believe) Ross Perot—with his charts and graphs and warnings about corporate money in the political process, GATT, and NAFTA—was right in many regards, at least from a nationalistic American point of view.

The summary version of these and dozens of other books documenting Spengler's decline of the West is this: We're entering a new and unknown but hauntingly familiar era. It's new because it represents a virtual abandonment of the egalitarian archetypes the Founders of the United States put into place in our Constitution and Bill of Rights. And it's hauntingly familiar because it resembles in many ways one of the most stable and long-term of all social structures to have ever established itself in the modern history of Europe—feudalism.

Boston Tea Party participant George R. T. Hewes mentioned the idea that the situation then was beginning to resemble feudalism, and there are those today who have made the same comparison.

The New Feudalism

Feudalism doesn't refer to a point in time or history when streets were filled with mud and people lived as peasants (although that was sometimes the case).

---

*See Sharon Beder, *Global Spin: The Corporate Assault on Environmentalism* (White River Junction, VT: Chelsea Green, 2002); David Helvarg, *The War against the Greens: The "Wise-use" Movement, the New Right, and Anti-environmental Violence* (San Francisco: Sierra Club Books, 1997); Marshall Barron Clinard, *Corporate Corruption: The Abuse of Power* (Westport, CT: Praeger, 1990); and Robert W. McChesney, *Rich Media, Poor Democracy: Communication Politics in Dubious Times* (Champaign: University of Illinois Press, 1999).

Instead it refers to an economic and political system, just like democracy or communism or socialism or theocracy. The biggest difference is that instead of power being held by the people, the government, or the church, power is held by those who own property and the other necessities of life. At its essential core, feudalism could be defined as "of, by, and for the rich."

Marc Bloch is one of the great twentieth-century scholars of the feudal history of Europe. In his book *Feudal Society,* he points out that feudalism is a fracturing of one authoritarian hierarchical structure into another: the state disintegrates as local power brokers take over.

In almost every case, both with European feudalism and feudalism in China, South America, and Japan, "feudalism coincided with a profound weakening of the State, particularly in its protective capacity."[21] Given most accepted definitions of feudalism, feudal societies don't emerge in civilizations with a strong social safety net and a proactive government.

There is a slight debate, in that some scholars like Benjamin Guérard say that feudalism must be land-based, whereas Jacques Flach and others suggest that the structure of power and obligation is the key. But the consensus is that when the wealthiest in a society take over government and then weaken it so that it can no longer represent the interests of the people, the transition has begun into a new era of feudalism. "European feudalism should therefore be seen as the outcome of the violent dissolution of older societies," Bloch says.

Whether the power and wealth agent that takes the place of government is a local baron, lord, king, or corporation, if it has greater power in the lives of individuals than does a representative government, the culture has dissolved into feudalism. Bluntly, Bloch states, "The feudal system meant the rigorous economic subjection of a host of humble folk to a few powerful men."

This doesn't mean the end of government but instead the subordination of government to the interests of the feudal lords. Interestingly, even in feudal Europe, Bloch points out, "The concept of the State never absolutely disappeared, and where it retained the most vitality men continued to call themselves 'free'..."

The transition from a governmental society to a feudal one is marked by the rapid accumulation of power and wealth in a few hands, with a corresponding reduction in the power and the responsibilities of government. Once the rich and powerful gain control of the government, they turn it upon itself, usually first eliminating its taxation process as it applies to themselves. Says Bloch, "Nobles need not pay *taille* [taxes]."

Bringing this to today, consider that in 1982, just before the Reagan-Bush "supply side" tax cut, the average wealth of the Forbes 400 was $200 million. Just four years later, their average wealth was $500 million each, aided by massive tax cuts. Today those four hundred people own wealth equivalent to one-eighth of the entire GDP of the United States.[22]

Extreme Concentrations Are Destabilizing

Too much concentration of anything makes it vulnerable to toppling. Most historians and economists recognize that a root cause of the Great Depression was a severe economic imbalance. The sharp increase in concentration of wealth described in this chapter also has much in common with the statistics of the 1920s.

This is also the history of civilizations. As wealth and power accumulate into fewer and fewer hands, the rest of the populace loses its sense that there's any point in trying to keep up. Whether on a national or a worldwide stage, revolutions and terrorism result when enough people perceive too great a gap between the most rich and the average poor.

In the 1980s the Reagan and Bush administrations effectively ceased enforcement of the Sherman Antitrust Act, just as the Coolidge administration had done in the 1920s. This led to a mania for mergers, acquisitions, and neotrusts, just as happened in the Roaring Twenties, and with a similar reconsolidation of power and wealth and rise in the stock market. In the 2002 edition of this book, the sentence that followed the previous one said: "Hopefully, the same cycle will not play itself out: If we act promptly, we can set in motion forces that will change the direction of the current trend." Unfortunately, we did not act, as the Great Crash of 2008 showed.

The End of the American Dream?

Martin Luther King Jr., in his "I have a dream" speech, referred to how the people who wrote the Declaration of Independence and the U.S. Constitution "were signing a promissory note to which every American was to fall heir." The contents of that note King referred to were identified by Jefferson when he wrote, "We hold these truths to be self-evident, that all men are created equal, that they are endowed by their Creator with certain unalienable Rights, that among these are Life, Liberty and the pursuit of Happiness."

The American Dream is something every schoolchild understands. It's the heart and soul of democracy. It means opportunity and freedom, the ability to raise a family or pursue one's own dreams. It means the strong participate in the protection of the weak, lest they lose their own rights if they become oppressors.

In the Federalist Papers (No. 51), Alexander Hamilton wrote, "In a society under the forms of which the stronger faction can readily unite and oppress the weaker, anarchy may as truly be said to reign"; and under such circumstances, eventually, even "the more powerful factions or parties will be gradually induced, by a like motive, to wish for a government which will protect all parties, the weaker as well as the more powerful."[23]

Are we approaching that time Hamilton mentioned?

- At the same time that the concentration of wealth has taken place over the past three decades, the entry-level wage of an American male high school graduate has declined 28 percent (in real dollars).[24]

- Twenty percent of American workers now earn income below the official poverty rate defined by the U.S. government—and that doesn't include the unemployed.[25]

- The top 20 percent of American families have seen their income go up by 97 percent in the past two decades. Meanwhile, the bottom 20 percent fell 44 percent in their real income, although most were working harder and working longer hours and many carried multiple jobs.[26]

Oswald Spengler noted that cycles of growth and collapse are built into the culture, and at a certain point it "hardens" and then becomes feudal or "classical." The warning signs, he says, are easily seen: replacement of human and spiritual values with slogans and self-indulgence, concentration of wealth into the hands of a few as poverty increases exponentially, citizens who are politically disengaged and ignorant, and a culture that becomes a parody of itself as it obsesses on its slogans and symbols but ceases to live out its ideals.

The fall of the Roman Empire is a classic example, and we may be another.

- In a 1998 survey of American teens, 2.2 percent could name the then–chief justice of the Supreme Court (William Rehnquist), but 59.2 percent could name Curly, Larry, and Moe as the fictional Three Stooges.

- An impressive 74.3 percent of teens knew that Bart Simpson lives in Springfield, Massachusetts, but only 12.2 percent recognized that Abraham Lincoln lived most of his life in Springfield, Illinois.

- Only 21.1 percent knew that there are one hundred U.S. senators, 1.8 percent could identify James Madison as a father of the Constitution, and a thin 25 percent knew what human right the Fifth Amendment protects. But 98.7 percent knew that Leonardo DiCaprio starred in the hit movie *Titanic,* and 75.2 percent knew the ZIP code associated with the popular television show *Beverly Hills 90210.*[27]

Ironically, and probably unknown to the National Constitution Center at the time they designed their poll, the Three Stooges, Bart Simpson, the movie *Titanic,* and the television show *Beverly Hills 90210* were all owned by the same multinational corporation. Such single-corporation influence over popular culture would not have been the case two hundred years ago or even fifty years ago.

To blame all or even most of this on the *Santa Clara* "decision" would be overreaching: Wealth was concentrating and moving around the world well before the modern corporation came along. Rome had concentrations of wealth, as did Sumer and Greece. Medieval Europe and Japan were cultures of extreme wealth and poverty, as was India with its multimillennia caste system. Even Victorian England, not so very long ago, was a hellhole for all but the well born and the industrialists, as Charles Dickens reminds us in graphic, tragic prose. "This is nothing new," some would say.

But there is. The difference between then and now is twofold:

- The wealth in those days had a face and a name. Without corporations to blur who does what, the warlords and nobles and the high caste were identifiable. We know who the kings and queens of old were, from Gilgamesh six thousand years ago in Sumer to the King of France before the revolutionaries executed him and his family. Because that wealth had a face, saying things like "Let them eat cake" could be dangerous for one's survival.

- More important, those governments never claimed to be democratic. In the past six thousand years of modern worldwide agriculture-driven civilization, there were only two governments—Athens for about two centuries, and the United States for a century or so—that rose out of a dominator culture and claimed that they were truly democratic, truly government by the people, even the poorest of the people. Since the American experiment, almost a hundred countries have joined the club in various forms, but it's still very much a new experiment worldwide, one that was tried only once before in all these millennia—Athens, 300 BCE—and they were conquered and thrown back into oppression by the concentrated wealth and power of the warlord who called himself Alexander the Great.

In a Democracy...

The "great experiment" of a democratic republic is at a critical crossroads. Can it recover the "government of, by, and for the people" ideal that it held so recently and implement it again in the halls of governments in America and across the world?

Or has de Tocqueville's worried vision come to pass? Have we become anesthetized and helpless as humans in the presence of a mighty machine that puts on a good face but, when push comes to shove, takes no prisoners and destroys its competitors without a second's thought?

The answer will depend, in some part, on whether the doctrine of corporate personhood is allowed to stand. Will the people take back their government and assert democratic controls over the misdeeds of the fabulously powerful corporations among them?

To some extent, that will depend on whether We the People demand that our elected officials return to the time-tested principles of national trade policy and fair trade instead of the "free for multinationals trade" that has been so aggressively peddled to the world in the past two decades.

CHAPTER 20

Unequal Trade

In the great days of the USA, Henry Ford stated that he wanted to pay high wages to his employees so that they could become his customers and buy his cars. Today we are proud of the fact that we pay low wages. We have forgotten that the economy is a tool to serve the needs of society, and not the reverse. The ultimate purpose of the economy is to create prosperity with stability.

—Billionaire speculator Sir James Goldsmith, 1993[1]

EQUAL TRADE, FAIR TRADE, HONEST, DECENT TRADE REQUIRES REASONABLE balance between trading partners and strong domestic economies. When that happens, Adam Smith's model works pretty well: prices for labor, materials, and finished goods all settle near the area where they "naturally" should be.

But as we've seen from the immensely imbalanced statistics on distribution of wealth in chapter 19, something is not working the way Smith envisioned. Wages appear to be dwindling, and the number of strong, healthy competitors appears to be shrinking.

Teddy Roosevelt Weighs In

President Theodore Roosevelt brilliantly defined the American Dream in the context of the dynamic difference between a business that is a builder of community and one that hollows out community. "We are a business people," Roosevelt said at the Ohio Constitutional Convention in Columbus in 1912.

> The tillers of the soil, the wage workers, the business men—these are the three big and vitally important divisions of our population. The welfare of each division is vitally necessary to the welfare of the people as a whole.

249

The great mass of business is of course done by men whose business is either small or of moderate size.

The middle-sized business men form an element of strength which is of literally incalculable value to the nation. Taken as a class, they are among our best citizens. They have not been seekers after enormous fortunes; they have been moderately and justly prosperous, by reason of dealing fairly with their customers, competitors, and employees. They are satisfied with a legitimate profit that will pay their expenses of living and lay by something for those who come after, and the additional amount necessary for the betterment and improvement of their plant.

The average business man of this type is, as a rule, a leading citizen of his community, foremost in everything that tells for its betterment, a man whom his neighbors look up to and respect; he is in no sense dangerous to his community, just because he is an integral part of his community, bone of its bone and flesh of its flesh. His life fibers are intertwined with the life fibers of his fellow citizens...

So much for the small business man and the middle-sized business man. Now for big business.

It is imperative to exercise over big business a control and supervision which is unnecessary as regards small business. All business must be conducted under the law, and all business men, big or little, must act justly...."Big business" in the past has been responsible for much of the special privilege which must be unsparingly cut out of our national life.

I do not believe in making mere size of and by itself criminal.

The mere fact of size, however, does unquestionably carry the potentiality of such grave wrongdoing that there should be by law provision made for the strict supervision and regulation of these great industrial concerns doing an interstate business, much as we now regulate the transportation agencies which are engaged in interstate business. The antitrust law does good in so far as it can be invoked against combinations which really are monopolies or which restrict production or which artificially raise prices....

The important thing is this: that, under such government recognition as we may give to that which is beneficent and wholesome in large business organizations, we shall be most vigilant never to allow them to crystallize into a condition which shall make private initiative difficult.

It is of the utmost importance that in the future we shall keep the broad path of opportunity just as open and easy for our children as it was for our fathers during the period which has been the glory of America's industrial history—that it shall be not only possible but easy for an ambitious man, whose character has so impressed itself upon his neighbors that they are willing to give him capital and credit, to start in business for himself, and, if his superior efficiency deserves it, to triumph over the biggest organization that may happen to exist in his particular field.

Whatever practices upon the part of large combinations may threaten to discourage such a man, or deny to him that which in the judgment of the community is a square deal, should be specifically defined by the statutes as crimes. And in every case the individual corporation officer responsible for such unfair dealing should be punished.

We grudge no man a fortune which represents his own power and sagacity exercised with entire regard to the welfare of his fellows. We have only praise for the business man whose business success comes as an incident to doing good work for his fellows. But we should so shape conditions that a fortune shall be obtained only in honorable fashion, in such fashion that its gaining represents benefit to the community....

We stand for the rights of property, but we stand even more for the rights of man.

We will protect the rights of the wealthy man, but we maintain that he holds his wealth subject to the general right of the community to regulate its business use as the public welfare requires.[2]

In this speech Roosevelt identified the key distinction and pointed directly to the situation the world finds itself in now.

Corporations have become so large and powerful that We the People—citizens and their governments around the world—no longer have the ability to control or restrain corporate misbehavior when it endangers the common good. And so we have epidemics of cancer, acid rain, ozone holes, and massive species die-offs as multinational corporations roam the world, strip-mining it for human labor, minerals, fossil fuels, and the fragile remaining bounty of its forests and oceans.

The ultimate in unequal trade has ensued from increasing corporate influence. Very large corporations—Roosevelt's "big businesses"—have now become able to sue an entire nation, in a court that they, the companies, lobbied to create, and can overturn the laws of independent nations with virtually no appeal. And unlike any court in the civilized world, this court is as secret, private, and difficult to appeal to as any military tribunal.

Free Trade Ravages National Economies

Free trade is a phrase behind which multinational corporations have essentially strip-mined both the developed and the developing world. That's strong language, but the metaphor holds up under examination. In strip-mining, a company comes in, strips off anything necessary to get at what it wants, and leaves. Similarly, the developing world is being mined for its resources, including human labor. At the same time, the already-developed world is being mined for its wealth, as its middle class and working poor sink farther into debt while multinational corporations become richer than any historic kingdom the planet has ever seen.

To understand what we can do about this, we first need to understand the mechanism. And there most definitely is a mechanism. When properly executed, it works quite reliably.[3]

Every product from shoes to nails to computers requires some human labor to manufacture. This can be done under working conditions that are safe and comfortable (or unsafe and uncomfortable) and using chemicals, techniques, and energy from toxic or safe/renewable sources.

For the cost of one American or European or Australian laborer, a company can hire between fifteen and fifty laborers in a developing country; and as an added bonus, the company can go back to using toxic chemicals banned in the United States over the past fifty years and buying cheap electricity from coal-fired power plants that would be illegal in this country. And when workers are injured or die, there's virtually no cost to the company.

Thus as transnational corporate lobbying succeeded in bringing about a "flat" world opened for free trade, about 4 billion people suddenly came into the same labor market that was once a protected space occupied by about a half-billion, and the other costs of manufacturing fell through the floor.

The first result of this was that companies that moved manufacturing from the developed world to the developing world were able to decrease labor and externality costs and increase earnings (profits). As companies used this principle to their advantage and built empires in industries from shoes to retailing by selling products made in low-labor-cost nations into the retail channels of the high-labor-cost nations, it *seemed* like it was a good thing (it was certainly promoted as a good thing!). Cheaper products were available in the wealthy nations, jobs were created in the poorer nations, and the people who made it all happen got rich.

But there were complications.

- If an American company wanted to compete with the one that had gone offshore for labor or to avoid environmental regulations, it faced only two choices: shut its domestic factories and move manufacturing offshore, or go out of business. The result—on a vast scale—has been that the larger companies have moved offshore and the smaller companies that lacked the resources to do that have gone out of business. The number of competitors has dwindled, and markets have become concentrated in fewer and fewer hands.

- As a consequence well-paying manufacturing jobs in the developed world have evaporated at a startling pace. This echoes all the way up from the local level, through state and national economies, finally showing up as a general lowering of the standard of living in the developed world. Wages drop, benefits vanish, jobs become scarce, and people become insecure.

- Along with the economic changes come social changes. The worst of it shows up at the bottom first—the number of people in prison explodes, as do other negative social indicators. Antidepressant drug use goes up, suicide goes up (particularly among teenagers, who are developmentally most fragile and are watching their future earnings prospects evaporate), and spouses and even children go to work to help support the household. Debt goes up as the society becomes progressively poorer.

- Wealthy nations respond to the offshore challenge by trying to be competitive, which means further lowering wages and benefits. Companies may even cut promised benefits to their longtime employees who have already retired. But even if the local company cuts wages in half (doing enormous damage to the local economy), a transnational corporation is still able to hire a dozen or more workers for the same job in a poor nation. Consequently, the race to the bottom gathers momentum—the bottom is where more than 6 billion people compete for the same work that was, until recently, performed in a tariff-protected economy of 1 billion people (the developed world). Resources won't stretch that far. The bottom is worldwide poverty supervised by a wealthy few, also known as feudalism.

- In the developing nations where these "new jobs are created," people who have been doing traditional farming leave the land for the sweat-shops, and the land is turned over to intensive corporate agriculture. People who in previous generations were independent, self-sufficient farmers become urban slum-dwellers, the working poor, dependent on agribusiness and supermarkets for their food.

- When the new sweatshop nation's urban working poor begin demand-ing higher wages and benefits, clean air and water, and a safe workplace, the corporations move to another country where labor is cheaper and regulations are looser. It happened in the 1990s when a mass exodus of multinational corporations left Korea, Taiwan, and Thailand for the ultracheap labor of Vietnam, Myanmar (Burma), and China, shatter-ing the economies of those former "Asian tigers."* Poverty explodes as slums overflow with crime, drugs, and prostitution—the symptoms of desperate people seeking some sort of income when the real jobs are gone. It is just like strip-mining, and it's a sign of the worst sort of cor-porate citizen—one without the slightest concern for the impact it has.

- In the process the multinational corporations become richer, moving their "mining" activities from one nation to another as profits dictate. As multinational corporate wealth increases, stock prices go up and the top few percent of the socioeconomic pyramid become wealthier. Nations learn to watch the stock market, thinking—in complete error—that it is an accurate indicator of the nation's wealth and economic health. In fact, from the Dutch tulip market collapse in 1637 to the U.S. stock market rises and crashes of 1929 and 2008, rapidly increasing markets have historically been indicators of an economy on the edge of implosion or undergoing radical social transformation.

As Sir James Goldsmith suggested in the epigraph of this chapter, we have forgotten that the purpose of economies—the whole reason why humans began trading with each other from the earliest days—was to provide for social stability. Your country makes good cheese, we make good clothing, another country makes good wine: let's all trade these products with one another so all three of us can enjoy good cheese, clothing, and wine.

---

*The collapse of "the Asian tigers" also had much to do with IMF structural adjustment programs, according to many commentators.

But in a "flat" free-trade world dominated by corporate values instead of human values, social stability is not a consideration unless or until it affects profits. This is the lesson of unequal values. And when a country becomes socially unstable, rather than working to restore the stability of the nation, multinationals simply leave town and go somewhere else, as Asian nations learned in the 1990s and Argentina learned in 2002.

This is not a new model, by the way. It's how the East India Company treated India, the early American colonies, and numerous smaller countries that it considered its property. It reflects the mentality not of communities but of pirates, a mentality that gives birth to phrases like *robber baron, corporate raider,* and *private equity.*

Herman Daly and Robert Goodland used to work at the World Bank. They didn't like what they saw. Consider this prophetic 1992 comment, two years before GATT was approved:

> If by wise policy or blind luck, a country has managed to control its population growth, provide social insurance, high wages, reasonable working hours and other benefits to its working class (i.e., most of its citizens), should it allow these benefits to be competed down to the world average by unregulated trade?...
>
> This leveling of wages will be overwhelmingly downward due to the vast number and rapid growth rate of under-employed populations in the third world. Northern laborers will get poorer, while Southern laborers will stay much the same.[4]

And this is exactly what we have seen happening.

The Corrective, Balancing Power of Tariffs

Historically, nations used tariffs—taxes on imported goods—to equalize differences between nations. Expensive-labor nations would charge tariffs on imported goods that were labor-intensive in their manufacture, to protect their domestic industries. Nations that wanted to protect unique natural resources or strategic products would use import/export policy to ensure their long-term survival and wise use. Trade was possible—it's always happened among nations—but it was fair trade, fair to the humans in the trading nations and in the interest of the nations themselves.

Now multinational corporations have finally succeeded in freeing themselves from the constraints of social commitment to any nation whatsoever.

In the absence of tariffs and self-interested national trade policies, they are free to roam anywhere on a moment's notice, looking for minerals, rain forests, and cheap labor. And because increasingly all money flows through them, they have essentially infinite power in all negotiations.

Finally, in a replay of events on American shores, they have in some cases taken roles in governments around the world. More than 150 countries have joined the WTO, and the giant transnational corporations are now dangling the carrot of cash to the leaders of the poorer nations. We've seen this movie before; it's easy to tell what happens next. These governments readily comply, join the WTO, and subscribe to free trade. But what they get may not be quite what they bargained for. That's what happened to no less a power than America.

How U.S. Legislators React

The world's largest transnational corporations are among the biggest contributors to politicians in America, and most members of Congress have supported the WTO even if they get a bit testy when the Dispute Resolution Panels rule against their favorite legislation. One good example comes from a speech to Congress by Representative John D. Dingell of Michigan on June 21, 2000:

> Our major trading partners, including Japan, Korea, and the EU [European Union nations], have turned the WTO dispute settlement process into a *de facto* appeals court that reviews U.S. trade agency determinations and strikes down our trade laws. Japan and Korea have gone so far as to say they will launch WTO appeals of every U.S. trade determination that is adverse to their interests. Already, WTO decisions are gutting the effectiveness of U.S. trade remedies in ways that the Administration and Congress expressly rejected during the negotiations on the agreement establishing the WTO.

Increasingly, both governments and citizens of nations all over the world are expressing concern about the WTO's process of leveling the corporate playing field across 153 member nations. Corporations manufacturing and exporting from countries that have lax or minimal environmental and labor laws are aggressively challenging and striking down the stronger laws passed in more-developed nations.

Countries with laws that banned the import or marketing of products they consider dangerous to their citizens are finding those laws struck down because other countries with weaker laws can now, to some extent, define the standard to which every WTO-member nation must be held accountable. They do this through WTO's primary trade-law model, which says that a country cannot ban the import of a product because of how or with what type of labor it was produced.

Overturning Our Laws

Thus it's now largely illegal to ban the import of products made by slaves or under inhumane conditions or made with chemicals that poisoned the local environment. This has sparked an explosion of industrial activity in labor-cheap and environmentally lax nations. At the same time, the industrial core of more-developed nations with higher labor and environmental standards has been hollowed out in just the past few decades, leaving vast landscapes of abandoned factories and a populace increasingly on edge about employment security.

In a developing nation where there is little or no cost or penalty to dumping toxins into the air or water, manufacturing is vastly more profitable than in a developed nation where toxins must be captured, stored, tracked, and cleanly disposed of in environmentally responsible ways. In the developed world, we have minimum-wage laws, laws regarding the maximum hours that may be worked per week, and safety and environmental laws. In the past, if an offshore product wasn't made in ways we approved, we either banned its import or added taxes or tariffs to give our cleaner domestic companies a competitively level playing field.

For example, say there's an hour's work in the manufacture of a pair of American-made shoes. In the United States, that hour costs $12.77, including benefits and overhead.[5] That same labor may be 10 cents an hour in Malaysia. So for the past century or so, the United States would have added a tariff, or tax, of $12.67 on any shoe imported from Malaysia that had an hour's labor in it. That way U.S. shoe manufacturers could stay in business. It would level the playing field between the two cultures and nations, thus providing for fair trade.

Nations have often used tariffs to discourage manufacturing operations from moving their factories and jobs to less regulated nations.

But according to WTO, those tariffs are considered "restraint of free trade." It's illegal under WTO rules to consider how or who makes a product or at what level of pay it is manufactured. The loss of jobs to offshore began decades ago, but the elimination of tariffs during the Reagan and Clinton

administrations accelerated it markedly. In the past few decades, more than
20 million Americans in labor-intensive industries have lost their jobs.

The other upshot of this is a dramatic increase in people around the
world who are working either as overt slaves or at a wage rate that makes them
virtual slaves in dangerous and toxic workplaces and living in an environment
of company stores and company housing. The developed world, and particularly the United States, at first appeared to have benefited from this. It allows
our consumer-based economy to continue to hum, with low inflation and rising profits, just as the American South benefited so much from cheap slave
labor before the Civil War. But at best this was a short-term benefit.

The "New World Order"

In most nations of the world today, there are basically two types of political
parties. Those two parties stand on either side of a nearly invisible line—one
party huge and imposing and the other thin and sickly, a political sumo wres-
tler pitted against an aging and infirm Woody Allen. The parties, regardless of
local labels, are "We Who Represent the Interests of Multinational Corporations" and "We Who Represent the Interests of Human Beings." The first group
has gotten laws passed that allow the easy movement of capital from nation
to nation under rules far different and more relaxed than those for humans.

In the United States and most other developed nations, most of the distinctions between politicians are becoming increasingly blurred, and in many
nations all the local politicians have joined the parties of the corporations.
Those parties and politicians that exist to represent the interests of human
beings have been marginalized or overwhelmed by the parties and politicians
that exist to represent the interests of the corporations. The reason for this is
simple: most of the world has followed our lead regarding "free speech" campaign contributions.

After the end of apartheid in South Africa, American corporations
donated the services of corporate lawyers to help draft the new South African
constitution. Pointing to the 1886 *Santa Clara* case, they essentially said that in
America corporations have the same constitutional status as humans, so you
should write this into your constitution, too.

South Africa did that, as have many other countries that have emerged
or developed or separated from the former Soviet Union. It's a challenge to
find the details and the statistics, and I'm hopeful that this book may spur
somebody to do that hard, nation-by-nation, language-by-language research,

but it appears that many of the countries of the world have written corpora-tions-as-persons into their constitutions or laws, thinking that they were following the original intent of the Framers of the U.S. Constitution, which, of course, is not the case.

The result is that corporations have functionally taken control of governments the world over, particularly through their participation in the funding of the electoral process. Thus, corporations have become the honey pot from which many politicians and political parties draw their nourishment.

In a Democracy...

In the 1996 election cycle in the United States, 96 percent of Americans didn't make any direct contribution whatsoever to a politician or political party, and fewer than one-quarter of 1 percent of Americans gave more than $200. By contrast, each of America's top five hundred corporations gave more than $0.5 million to the Democrats and the Republicans during the decade preceding the 1996 elections.

In the 1998 election cycle, which was not even a presidential election year, those corporations contributed $660 million to candidates, while the last remaining organized groups that represent workers—unions, which are not considered persons in the United States and most other countries but are instead regulated as artificial persons—were able to pony up only $60 million in campaign contributions raised from their members.

Unions have to operate under the same types of rules and laws that corporations did before 1886, and, in fact, additional restrictions have been placed on them since then. So-called "paycheck protection" legislation is being promoted by corporate lobbyists that would essentially criminalize union contributions to candidates. And, increasingly, in corporate-controlled nations around the world, unions are being deemed illegal, political, or even labeled as terrorist organizations and ferociously stamped out.

Can it change? I believe so. But only if the word gets out.

CHAPTER 21

Unequal Media

Our liberty depends on the freedom of the press, and that cannot be limited without being lost.

—Thomas Jefferson, letter to James Currie, January 28, 1786

IN RESEARCHING THIS BOOK, I RAN ACROSS AN ASTONISHING PIECE OF WRIT-ing from our nation's early years. It's a fitting prologue for this chapter. In May 1831, a young French aristocrat named Alexis de Tocqueville arrived in the young nation of the United States of America. He was here at a pivotal time in American history. In the "Revolution of 1800," Thomas Jefferson had ousted John Adams's minority Federalist Party (largely made up of what Jefferson called "the rich and the well born") and shifted control of the government to the Jeffersonian Democrats. To de Tocqueville (and most Europeans), American democracy was still very much an unproven experiment. De Tocqueville himself was skeptical that the American Experiment would last, as he thought that the "natural" state of man was to live in an aristocracy, but he was fascinated by the idea of an aristocracy made up of the workers. He was both skeptical and hopeful.

In 1835, just fifty-two years after the end of the American Revolution and forty-six years after the French Revolution, de Tocqueville closed his book *Democracy in America** with a chapter titled "What Sort of Despotism Democratic Nations Have to Fear." Fascinated by that chapter title, which I had first seen on the Internet, I bought an 1862 edition of the book, translated into English. One of the three best-selling books of the entire nineteenth century, it was probably read twenty years earlier by Abraham Lincoln, as it was by almost

---

*Democracy in America is the name by which this work is most commonly known, and that is the title of later printings. The original work, published in 1835, was titled *The Republic of the United States of America, and Its Political Institutions, Reviewed and Examined.*

all American politicians and most citizens. Turning the timeworn pages and reading the young de Tocqueville's thoughts, I was astounded. It was as if he had seen America in the late-twentieth and early-twenty-first centuries.

De Tocqueville had a clear and prescient inkling of danger. He saw a nation where people had become isolated in their own homes, uninformed about the rest of humanity, and addicted to some entertainment that was so powerful it separated them from their fellow humans. He imagined that despotism, in the Spenglerian remnants of a democracy, would take a different form than despotism under authoritarian rule; it would take the form of creating an illusion of choice, and he struggled to find words to express what it would be.

"It would seem that, if despotism were to be established amongst the democratic nations of our days, it might assume a different character; it would be more extensive and more mild; it would degrade men without tormenting them," he wrote.

> I am trying myself to choose an expression which will accurately convey the whole of the idea I have formed of it, but in vain; the old words despotism and tyranny are inappropriate: the thing itself is new; and since I cannot name it, I must attempt to define it.
>
> The first thing that strikes the observation is an innumerable multitude of men, all equal and alike, incessantly endeavoring to procure the petty and paltry pleasures with which they glut their lives. Each of them, living apart, is as a stranger to the fate of all the rest—his children and his private friends constitute to him the whole of mankind; as for the rest of his fellow-citizens, he is close to them, but he sees them not; he touches them, but he feels them not; he exists, but in himself and for himself alone; and if his kindred still remain to him, he may be said at any rate to have lost his country.[1]

His description, written in 1831, sounds astonishingly like our world today, which is so often observed as being centered around gratification—and isolation. And the mechanism for this despotism, he said, is the sort of perpetual gratification that keeps people happy.

He continued, writing about what would or could happen if, for example, large corporations were able to pipe 24/7 entertainment and dumbed-down predigested "news/infotainment" into every home in America:

> Above this race of men stands an immense and tutelary [care-taking] power, which takes upon itself alone to secure their gratifications, and to watch over their fate. That power is absolute, minute, regular, provident, and mild.

It would be like the authority of a parent, if, like that authority, its object was to prepare men for manhood; but it seeks, on the contrary, to keep them in perpetual childhood: it is well content that the people should rejoice, provided they think of nothing but rejoicing....

Thus, it every day renders the exercise of the free agency of man less useful and less frequent; it circumscribes them well within a narrower range, and gradually robs a man of all the uses of himself. The principle of equality has prepared men for these things: it has predisposed men to endure them, and oftentimes to look on them as benefits.

After having thus successively taken each member of the community in its powerful grasp, and fashioned him at will, the supreme power then extends its arm over the whole community.

In an observation that seems to describe the current state of political discourse, where only a very few ever actually get out on the streets and protest, de Tocqueville added, "The will of man is not shattered, but softened, bent, and guided: men are seldom forced by it to act, but they are constantly restrained from acting: such a power does not destroy, but it prevents existence; it does not tyrannize, but it compresses, enervates, extinguishes, and stupefies a people, till each nation is reduced to be nothing better than a flock of timid and industrious animals..."[2]

De Tocqueville also said that the press is the most important of all our democratic institutions; only a free press could preserve American democracy, and the loss of it to government or corporate powers would be the end of the democratic experiment, taking us back to the world of serfs and aristocrats that he considered the natural state of things. "I think that men living in aristocracies may, strictly speaking, do without the liberty of the press: but such is not the case with those who live in democratic countries....servitude cannot be complete if the press is free: the press is the chief democratic instrument of freedom."

The Purpose of a Free Press Is Free Expression

The gadfly of American journalism in the first half of the twentieth century, A. J. "Joe" Liebling, commented, "Freedom of the press belongs to the man who owns one."* It's become even more true today, although you can replace

---

*Many sources say the correct quote is, "Freedom of the press is guaranteed only to those who own one," but the point is the same either way.

the word *man* with the word *corporation*. And today there are fewer of those truly free resources than ever before. This is materially limiting the amount of information available to the public, creating the sort of environment de Tocqueville warned about in the quote above. We'll cover the following issues:

- The effects of consolidation of who owns the presses since fewer presses means fewer different voices reporting the news, and fewer owners means less diversity and dissent

- The effect of heavily financed lawsuits that squelch expression in the media, such as the well-known suit against Oprah Winfrey for her comments about hamburger

- The effects of the press being owned by a business that has pressure to deliver profits

Each of these issues is, in a different way, a consequence of the changes in America that have flowed from the *Santa Clara* "decision."

Is this subject really important to our democracy? Aside from the advice of the far-sighted de Tocqueville, consider these diverse opinions:

- John Adams, our nation's second president (who hated the way he was treated by the press), said, "The liberty of the press is essential to the security of the state."

- Napoleon Bonaparte, who made a serious attempt to conquer his part of the civilized world, was of the opinion that "three hostile newspapers are more to be feared than a thousand bayonets."

- George Orwell, author of *Animal Farm* and *1984*, said, "Freedom of the Press, if it means anything at all, means the freedom to criticize and oppose."

- Richard Nixon said, "The media are far more powerful than the president in creating public awareness and shaping public opinion, for the simple reason that the media always have the last word."

- In a move to block media access, George W. Bush moved his records and papers as governor of Texas into his father's presidential library; and on February 11, 2002, the elder Bush said in a paid speech to roofing contractors that the press was a group "which I now confess I hate."[3]

When people from Adams to Bush, Napoleon to Orwell all have such different ways of saying that the press is immensely powerful, it's a sign that we ought to pay attention to what happens to it. Let's look first at the shrinking diversity of outlets for news and information.

Can I Get a Wide Range of Views in the Media?

Less so than you might think—and far less so than when you were growing up. In 1984, according to media observer Ben Bagdikian, fifty corporations dominated the nation's "daily newspapers, magazines, radio, television, books, and movies." Following the deregulation and merger craze in the 1980s, that number dropped to twenty by 1993. As of 2003 it was just five.

On a longer time scale, the shift is even more startling. Bagdikian observes that in 1946, 80 percent of all American newspapers were owned by individuals and independent local companies. Today it's the opposite: "80 percent [are] owned by corporate chains," and only three corporations control "most of the business of the country's 11,000 magazines."[4]

When NAFTA was before Congress for a vote in 1993, Vermont congressman Bernie Sanders points out that about half of all Americans opposed ratification of the treaty. Of the hundreds of corporate chain–owned city newspapers across the country, only two ran editorials questioning NAFTA, while all the rest, echoing the position of America's largest corporations, came out in support of it.

Looking at all media in the United States, in 2000 Bagdikian noted, "Today, despite more than 25,000 outlets in the United States, twenty-three corporations control most of the business in daily newspapers, magazines, television, books, and motion pictures."[5] Current numbers are hard to come by because the media no longer publish their own numbers (and they've been scrubbed from Wikipedia by the Libertarian think tanks and individuals who have come to dominate Web media) but the number at the end of the first decade of the twenty-first century is certainly smaller than twenty-three corporations.

If you've noticed that no matter where you are in the United States you can hear the same radio shows, there's a reason: the FCC has recently allowed four giant media corporations to buy up radio stations nationwide to the point where those four companies now control 90 percent of total radio advertising revenues.[6]

Only 10 percent of Americans even have a meaningful choice as to their local telephone company. In Vermont a small, local company named Sovernet began offering high-quality local phone service along with DSL Internet access. So, in 2002 lobbyists for the big telecommunications companies got introduced into the Vermont legislature a "freedom in telecommunications" bill that would block Sovernet's access to Verizon's lines, effectively putting Sovernet out of the phone business. The bill was defeated, and Sovernet is still in business, but most Americans have no access to a truly local telephone company.[7]

Many of us are accustomed to viewing the Web as a wellspring of a vast number of information sources, free of restraining influence. Indeed, if properly used by knowledgeable people, it can be. But, in practice, perhaps not as much as we would think. In August 2001 the authoritative Jupiter Media Metrix research company reported on its Web site that just four corporations own the Web sites that more than 50 percent of Americans spend their time viewing.

Meanwhile right-wingers have formed companies to hire people to work from home, spamming Internet message boards and the comment fields on everything from YouTube to Facebook to all the newspapers with online "comment" functions attached to their news stories. One company, called Advantage Consultants, run by a former right-wing radio talk-show host and consultant, as of 2007 ran a Web advertisement that said:

> Are you ready for a blog attack?
>
> Get ahead of your opponent with Professional Blog Warriors.
>
> Be prepared to "flood the zone" with comments from professionals who are ready to put your talking points on the blogosphere 24/7.
>
> Whether it's defense or offense, Advantage Consultants has a dedicated team of experienced blog warriors ready to advance your candidate or campaign.
>
> Why wait for the attack? Launch your attack with a battery of blog and forum comments aimed at all media and blog sites in your district.
>
> Contact us today and let us show you the Advantage in professional blog warfare.[8]

During the 2004 presidential election cycle, my message board at www .thomhartmann.com was really hopping, mostly with listeners to my nationally syndicated radio show. And there were a few people who—often within minutes, always within hours—would respond to *every* liberal/pro-Kerry post with Republican talking points and pro-Bush commentary. They were reasonable, articulate, and not belligerent, so we couldn't get rid of them. A few were actually quite friendly and talked a lot about other issues (movies, sports, relationships, their private lives) in ways that endeared them to our members.

After the election was over, they all vanished. Literally, the day after the election.

A few months later, one of them dropped me a private e-mail, thanking me for keeping him on the message board and telling me that he had been paid 10 to 25 cents per post, depending on the topic and how many people read it, and offering to do the same for me should I ever need his services to spam other people's message boards with pro-Hartmann-radio-show messages.

He said that during that election season and over the course of a few hundred message boards where he was posting, he'd made enough money to cover much of the cost of his next year in college, and he hoped to continue. He'd been paid, he said, by "some political guys" connected with "a big company in D.C."—I'm assuming a political party or lobbying company—but he was unwilling to give me any details.

During the 2008 election cycle, another, similar group of posters appeared on our message boards. And even after the election, they continue to heavily populate all the major news sites that attach "readers' comments" to their news stories.

Although many Internet users think of the World Wide Web as a commons of ideas, it's a commons whose access is now almost entirely controlled by a small number of very large corporations—and their political operatives, ideological partners, and shills, often working from home for a few extra bucks posting comments on message boards, commenting on news articles, and editing open-source information sites like www.wikipedia.org.

Even Internet Search Engines

The once-independent search engines are now selling to the highest bidder the right to be displayed at the top of the list. As a recent ad for search engine placement noted, "Eighty-five percent of all traffic is generated via search queries and over 90 percent of that traffic is driven to the top 30 results. If you're not in the top 30, you're not in a position to compete!"[9] At virtually all the current search engines, top placement, sponsor placement, or top-of-fold ad placement are for sale on keyword searches.

Similarly, much has been written about the homogenizing effects of media mergers, further reducing diversity and trying to find the lowest common denominator to produce the best earnings—at the cost of sacrificing the good reporting that Americans used to take for granted.

The pressure to homogenize is economic, driven by the business incentive to generate economies of scale by being big and by being able to offer advertisers the largest audience size or attractive demographics at a low rate. Another major factor is the increasing amount of capital that's required today to be a broadcaster because of an important change that happened in the 1980s—a change implemented by the government at the request of the corporations. At that time a major piece of the commons was auctioned off to the highest bidder. Not surprisingly, the winners were big corporations.

Who Owns the Airwaves?

The theory used to be that the airwaves over which television and radio signals pass were part of the national infrastructure, just like the highway system or the air-traffic control system. Nobody could own them because they were the ether that floated above the nation, the property of the people, yet some regulation of them was necessary to prevent chaos. Cable systems run under or over public streets, just like the public utilities and the airwaves, and so similarly are part of the public's infrastructure, the commons.

It was also felt that the airwaves were part of the free press that the Founders and the Constitution asserted was so essential and crucial to a vibrant and living democracy and an informed citizenry. Therefore the Federal Communications Commission was formed to regulate the usage and the content of what freely passes over the airwaves of America to Americans.

During the 1980s, however, the media corporations successfully lobbied that the national airwaves should no longer be the shared property of the citizens. Instead, they said, the airwaves and the channels should be carved up by region and frequency and sold off to the highest bidders at frequency auctions. When we auctioned off this part of the commons, it went into the hands of parties that already enjoyed many unequal advantages over humans.

This was followed in 1996 by the Telecommunications Act, the product of prodigious lobbying on Capitol Hill, which, according to media watchdog Ben Bagdikian, "swept away even the minimal consumer and diversity protections of the 1934 act that preceded it."[10]

Auctioning off the airwaves had a secondary effect that was perhaps more important than who owned them. When we auctioned off the airwaves, the corporations that bought them claimed that we gave up the right to have a say in their use. The free press became corporate-owned, and today groups like Fairness and Accuracy in Reporting (FAIR) regularly chronicle examples of news programs and journalists concealing corporate misdeeds and crimes or offering up publicity stories about the products of network owners or major advertisers.[11] It's not just a matter of running flattering stories; it affects the process of filtering which investigative stories get on the air. And this is not just the opinion of a watchdog group; it's reported by those on the inside.

A Pew Center for the People and the Press poll in 2000 found that 61 percent of investigative reporters thought corporate owners influenced news decisions, and 41 percent of reporters could list specific examples of recent times that they themselves had chosen or been forced to change or avoid news stories to further or benefit the interests of their media corporation.[12]

Cost of Access Is Un-democratizing Elections

Along with the airwaves at the auctions went the notion of public service announcements. During the same administration, the FCC requirement that television and radio stations give free time for political debates was repealed. This gave corporations that owned radio and television stations a double wind-fall: they get to own what they had rented and now politicians have to pay for advertising if they want to get their message to the public. Again, the effect is that ordinary humans find it harder than ever to be heard because the previous equal-time provision no longer applies: you have to pay.

And campaign airtime doesn't come cheap. The average U.S. Senate cam-paign now costs more than $6 million, whether the candidate wins or loses. That's $6 million to raise in six years—$1 million a year, $20,000 a week. Can you imagine starting every day in your office knowing, as corporate lobby-ists begin to file in to visit you and promote their causes, that by the end of the day you have to raise another $4,000 or you won't have your job after the next election?

And the price is rising. During the 1998 House and Senate elections, more than $1 billion was paid to media corporations for ads by parties, politi-cians, and interest groups seeking to get their word out to the public. That's double what was spent in 1992 and seven times the amount paid to media corporations by candidates and political parties in the 1978 elections—before the frequency auction and the end of the equal-time rule. In just the first four months of his 2000 campaign, George W. Bush raised and spent more money than Bill Clinton and Bob Dole combined had raised and spent in the entire election cycle four years earlier.[13]

The Obama/McCain election was our nation's first billion-dollar campaign—money far beyond the reach of average citizens. Obama received huge support from people within the financial services industry, and within the first year of his presidency they were repaid with trillions of taxpayer dollars in loans and bailouts, allowing them to pay themselves billions of dollars in bonuses (which could then be recycled, in part, back into more campaign contributions).

There are serious questions about whether the way our government works today is giving everyone in this democracy a fair chance of having their voice heard. Increasingly, the only voices we can hear are those backed by corporations with plenty of money.

The Impact on Local and National Politics

For the most part, average Americans have stopped voting. During the 2000 election, about 55 percent of eligible American voters—more than 100 million people—didn't bother to vote. Ask them why, and you'll most often hear, "What difference does it make?"

According to the Federal Election Commission, in that election about 50 million who were registered didn't show up to vote. In a "To Whom It May Concern" Web letter during the 2000 election, author and political filmmaker Michael Moore wrote about the impact of corporate ownership of the media and corporate influence of the electoral process—and how working Americans are reacting. He addressed his letter to the new American majority—those who have given up on voting.

"The reason you, the majority, no longer vote in America," he wrote, "is because you, the majority, realize there is no real choice on the ballot." He pointed out that more than 80 percent of American voters didn't bother to show up for the primaries—that's more than 160 million nonvoters. He suggests that in a world where "six multinational corporations" deliver the majority of all information Americans get from radio, television, newspapers, and the Internet, American voters apparently feel that their political process no longer offers them any choices worth voting for.[14]

And this is the way some politicians and political parties want it. As the late Paul Weyrich, a Republican consultant who claimed much credit for the wins of Ronald Reagan and both Bushes, told a group of Christian Republican operatives, their job was to discourage all but the most fervent (anti-abortion, anti-gay, pro-gun) base to not vote.

"I don't want everybody to vote," Weyrich said. "Elections are not won by a majority of the people. They never have been from the beginning of our country and they are not now. As a matter of fact, our leverage in the elections quite candidly goes up as the voting populace goes down."[15]

That, of course, is the reason for negative campaigning. Negative campaigns—attack campaigns—rarely cause more people to show up for the person running the attack ad, but they depress the vote overall, causing people to get cynical and say, "They're all crooks; why bother?" and thus allowing fringe-issues-based voters to carry a disproportionate amount of voting power in an election.

We're not as bad as the former Soviet Union, of course, but Moore continues, echoing the widespread American concern that "a handful of companies now call all the shots. They own Congress. They own us....To keep our jobs we have had to give up decent health care, the 8-hour day and time with our kids, the security that we'll even have a job next year, and any unwillingness we may have to compete with a 14-year-old Indonesian girl who gets a dollar a day."[16]

The Effect of the Newsroom's Being a For-profit Enterprise

Earlier we noted that smaller businesses tend, in general, to be focused on the nature of their trade. When they're absorbed into bigger businesses, especially the biggest ones, pressure tends to increase to deliver value for the shareholders—that is, to make money. In news operations almost all the money comes from advertising—and ad prices depend on how many people are watching. So business managers are necessarily required to do what they can to improve income.

Once again the point in pursuing this issue is not to decry profit. The point is that when corporations are allowed to operate with that goal to the detriment of other values, it can harm how well the system performs the functions we depend on, particularly those necessary to a vital democracy.

A month after the September 11 attacks, in a C-SPAN interview with Marvin Kalb on October 13, CBS News anchor and managing editor Dan

Rather made a sobering admission. "We were asleep," he said, speaking of a time that he identified as starting in the 1980s and picking up steam throughout the 1990s and into mid-2001. "We went for titillation," he said, in apparent reference to the Monica Lewinsky and Gary Condit stories the press relentlessly pursued. They had ignored the "clear warnings" of earlier attacks such as the 1993 truck bombing of the World Trade Center, which should have told both America's news and intelligence agencies that there were people intent on harming us.

Rather pointed out that international news bureaus were being closed during the 1990s, and the press had failed to focus on news, going instead for what he called "the sensational" and "the personal."

Legendary newsman Walter Cronkite, who in his time was rated "the most credible man in America," told www.mediachannel.org in the years before he died, "Like you, I'm deeply concerned about the merger mania that has swept our industry, diluting standards, dumbing down the news, and making the bottom line sometimes seem like the only line. It isn't, and it shouldn't be."[17]

But it is, in large part because Ronald Reagan stopped enforcing the Sherman Act or the Fairness Doctrine, which required radio and TV stations to run "real news"—versus infotainment—as a condition of keeping their licenses. The entire process was exacerbated by Bill Clinton's signing the Telecommunications Act of 1996, following which all of the nation's network news departments were merged into the entertainment and profit-making parts of the networks.

Using Lawsuits to Suppress Information

There's a completely different way in which some companies influence what shows up in the media: some will sue to keep people from saying anything bad about them or their products, even if there's plenty of evidence. Because of their unequal resources, they can threaten (and follow through on) lawsuits, which can be effective at squelching criticism. People who fight back may be financially ruined, and many people simply quit before matters reach that point.

The same concern applies to news outlets that might be sued. After all, if a company will weigh the dollar value of a safer gas tank versus the cost of victims' lawsuits, aren't they likely to perform a similar risk assessment here? And if the only parameter that's measured is cash, cash will become the basis of the decision. An engineering decision, or a journalist's editorial decision, becomes a profit decision.

A key turning point on this issue may have been 1989. When CBS's *60 Minutes* reported that a pesticide used on apples may pose health risks to humans, the apple-growing industry lost millions of dollars in sales. In response thirteen states passed "veggie libel laws," making it a crime to disparage the food supply. The most famous case of laws being used in this way was the suit filed by Texas beef producers against Oprah Winfrey for casually remarking (some would say joking) on her show that she was personally going to stop eating hamburgers after interviewing a guest about mad cow disease.

Seattle attorney Bruce Johnson, who defended CBS in the initial suit by the apple industry, said these laws "are designed specifically to stop the Rachel Carsons of the world from alerting the public to food-safety risks. If these were in effect in 1962 [when Carson published *Silent Spring*, her groundbreaking book about the dangers of DDT], they would have sued her and forced her into bankruptcy."[18]

Similarly, in early 1998 when investigative reporters Jane Akre and Steve Wilson produced a three-part series on how a synthetic hormone routinely given to American cattle could be causing cancer in America (and not in Europe, where it's banned), their television station fired them after they refused to "tone down" the story.

Why?

The station is owned by a well-known media conglomerate, and the manufacturer of the chemical—a massive and powerful multinational corporation—apparently threatened to sue if the story ran, which would have decreased the media chain's profits from its news operations.

The Fox News TV outlet was sued by Akre and Wilson for terminating them without just cause, and a jury of their peers unanimously awarded them $250,000. Fox appealed the case, and the Appeals Court determined that the corporation's right to free speech included its right to lie—and to require its employees to lie and to fire them if they didn't. So far that decision stands.[19]

Our representatives have passed whistle-blower laws to protect people who make such discoveries. But if you're in court and you simply don't have the resources to stick with it—the playing field is simply not level with that of a billion-dollar corporation—the law can be defeated by the wealthier party's lawsuits. As it happened, the fired reporters sued under Florida's whistle-blower law and a jury ruled in their favor. But the suits and appeals and countersuits have exhausted these two reporters' funds.

This is a perfect, living example of how the playing field is anything but level when an immortal, nonbreathing corporation is given the same protections as humans.

The Suppression of "Advocacy" Ads

When www.adbusters.org tried to purchase airtime on ABC, CBS, and NBC television networks for their "Buy Nothing Day" commercials, the networks refused them, year after year. The ads have an "in your face" edge to them, but they aren't at all violent or pornographic: they encourage people to "give it a rest"—to take a single-day break from consumerism.

When asked why the networks wouldn't allow the American people to see the ads—for any price—a spokesman at one of the networks said it quite directly: "We don't want to accept any advertising that's inimical to our legitimate business interests."[20] So much for their stewardship of the commons in the public interest.

The vice president of program practices at another of the Big Three networks brought up a more commonly used dodge: "We can't run your ad," he told Adbusters. "It's an advocacy ad."

"I came from Estonia, where you were not allowed to speak up against the government," says former advertising executive Kalle Lasn, head of Adbusters. "Here I was in North America, and suddenly I realized you can't speak up against the sponsor. There's something fundamentally undemocratic about our public airways."[21]

During the run-up to the invasion of Iraq, Americans noticed a sudden explosion of television ads—particularly on the cable news networks—for the companies that make fighter jets and military hardware. There was a similar increase in ads for oil-drilling operations. Because most consumers aren't in a position to go out and buy a billion-dollar jet or a billion-dollar oil rig, some were openly baffled about why these companies would be so heavily advertising on the news networks.

While it's impossible to prove motivations—although most of the ads stopped once Bush began the invasion—those of us who have worked in the media in the years since Reagan and Clinton knocked down the wall that used to separate news from sales/profits understood that what these companies may well have been implicitly saying to the networks was something like, "We'll give you millions in advertising dollars if you don't challenge the coming war, which will be incredibly profitable to us."

Similarly, a cadre of ex-military brass were paraded in front of the TV cameras as "analysts" on the upcoming war, and it was never revealed during the interviews that the men, in aggregate, had been paid tens of millions for their "consulting" work on behalf of military contractors.

Corporate influence of broadcast content happens in radio too. Folksy "man of the people" Jim Hightower's radio show was syndicated by one of the Big Three American networks in 150 markets with more than 2 million listeners until that network was bought out by an even larger entertainment conglomerate. Hightower mentioned on the air that his new parent corporation had replaced some of its full-time workers with contract laborers recruited from a local homeless shelter. On another show, he accused his network of "bending down and kissing the toes" of a tobacco company advertiser. Soon his show was canceled.

The reason given to the press was that his show wasn't making enough money from advertising, but Hightower pointed out that he would have been very profitable if the network had allowed him to run $250,000 worth of ads that the unions had tried to buy. Those ads, however, were "advocacy advertising," the network said, so they never made it to the air.[22] Remember, unions are not persons under the Fourteenth Amendment.

The Effect on Crime Reporting

Corporate influence on news content continues to have serious ramifications on what we know—and thus how well prepared we are to make fundamental decisions for our communities and ourselves.

Consider crime reporting. Everybody who watches American television knows about the repeated troubles of Rodney King since his famous (and much-televised) beating by the Los Angeles police or Mike Tyson's difficulties with rage. But how many Americans know that in a 1982 study of America's five hundred largest corporations, it was found that in the past ten years 23 percent of them had been convicted of a major crime or had paid more than $50,000 in penalties for serious misbehavior or both?[23]

Stories about welfare moms make the news with no problem, but stories of the billions in taxpayer money given to oil companies appear mainly in the business press—where they're recognized as triumphs for the companies involved, events that will favorably raise their stock value.

As I watched Kalb's interview of Dan Rather, it seemed that Rather often came close to raising these topics, but that neither man wanted to step into the role of the fictional Howard Beal in the startlingly predictive movie *Network,* when he yelled about corporate/political influence on news, "I'm mad as hell and not going to take it anymore!"

Doesn't the FCC Protect the First Amendment?

In early 2001 George W. Bush appointed as the chairman of the Federal Communications Commission a young man named Michael Powell, the son of Secretary of State Colin Powell, himself a former member of the board of directors of media giant AOL. Michael Powell was apparently rather new to the ideas of de Tocqueville and Jefferson when he took his job. As the *Columbia Journalism Review* reported in 2001, "Asked at his maiden news conference for his definition of 'the public interest,' Powell joked, 'I have no idea.' The term can mean whatever people want it to mean, he said. 'It's an empty vessel in which people pour in whatever their preconceived views or biases are.'"[24]

Those biases at the FCC since became clear, as Powell's team showed. Other FCC commissioners included two former industry lobbyists.[25] Powell's chief of staff was a former Disney lobbyist, and his legal adviser was a former lobbyist for another media giant.[26]

The week of Powell's appointment, media analyst Tom Wolzien said, "I think you'll see a little bit more of a free-market approach, perhaps less attention to consumer groups and more of letting companies do more of what they want."[27]

According to Fairness and Accuracy in Media (FAIR), "One of Powell's first acts as chairman was to approve 62 pending radio station acquisitions, handing still more outlets to two of the country's largest and grabbiest conglomerates..."[28]

On April 24, 2001, Powell told the Associated Press, "There is something offensive to First Amendment values about that limitation [on concentration of television station ownership]" because, FAIR notes, "it restricts the number of people one company can talk to."

In a December 2000 speech before a corporate-sponsored group in Washington, Powell said, as quoted by the *Chicago Tribune,* "Our bureaucratic process is too slow to respond to the challenges of Internet time. One way to do so is to clear away the regulatory underbrush to bring greater certainty and regulatory simplicity to the market."[29]

When the proponents of corporations having personhood suggest that corporations should have the ability to aggregate media so that the largest multinational corporations among us will have free speech, they often trot out the argument that deregulating the media (or any other industry) encourages competition. The actual effect, as Ben Bagdikian so eloquently documents, is the reverse: there are fewer and fewer competitors, less variety and fewer viewpoints for consumers to choose among, and a massive grab of media by a small number of huge multinational corporations.

One of the most visible results of this is that business coverage has become an important part of every corporate-owned newspaper and broadcast network (even though 42 percent of stock market gains between 1989 and 1997 went to America's top 1 percent of individuals, and 86 percent of stock market gains went to the top 10 percent, and numbers in the twenty-first century are even a bit more heavily weighted toward rich individuals), reflecting the prime moral value of corporate culture: profit.[30] At the same time, the 100 percent of American citizens who are consumers and who confront a one-in-three chance of contracting cancer in their lifetimes find virtually no mention in the mainstream corporate-owned media of issues relating to shoddy products, criminal business practices, or environmental toxins.

Indeed, as Bagdikian notes, "From 1987 to 1994, the purchasing power of the minimum wage dropped 35 percent," an issue that hits 12 million more Americans in a much more real and powerful way than the Dow Jones Industrial Average (even considering stocks in pension plans held by the middle class). "If the Dow Jones Industrial Average had dropped 35 percent in seven years it would have been an ongoing and urgent issue in newscasts and on page one in newspapers, with insistence that official action be taken," Bagdikian says.[31] But these are not issues that hurt profits—they enhance profits. So instead we hear that when more people become unemployed, the Dow goes up because it means corporations can then negotiate lower labor costs. The human toll is apparently not an issue.

And that media competition extolled by FCC Chairman Powell? FAIR remarks, "Powell opposed the opening of the bandwidth to new microradio [small, local community stations with limited transmission range] voices on grounds that it might dilute audience share (and ad revenue) for commercial stations." (Although, in fairness, it should be noted that one of the groups that has historically most strongly argued against the expansion of micro-stations is the Corporation for Public Broadcasting, which sees them as competition for its PBS and NPR brands.)[32]

In a Democracy...

As the twentieth century came to a close, corporate-controlled media was reaching the most distant corners of the world, and its effects were seen in strange ways. In 1995 parts of the island of Fiji, which had never before seen television, got the tube. Three years later researchers talked with several groups of Fijian girls whose average age was seventeen. They found that before television, only 3 percent had ever thrown up to try to control their weight. After three years of television, however, 15 percent of those teenage girls were clinically bulimic.[33]

The first step in a values-driven advertising campaign is to disempower humans—convince people that there's something wrong or deficient about them. The teenage girls of Fiji sure got the message and got it quickly. In the United States, with its own startlingly high prevalence rate of bulimia among young girls, we say, "It's a serotonin deficiency" that can be cured with antidepressant drugs, but the Fiji example tells us it may be easier to cure it by removing the television set.

After you read this page, set down this book and walk around for the next five minutes—indoors or out—and notice how many advertising messages and logos you see or hear. Have any of them suggested that you should slow down your life, spend more time with your family, or seek deeper meaning and richer states of consciousness? Or are they all "Buy from us—we'll make you happy" messages?

Daily exposure to such messages has produced—no doubt as an unintended consequence but real nonetheless—a deep angst and existential emotional and spiritual crisis around the world. We will successfully confront this existential angst when corporations no longer have the same rights as humans.

Then our politicians can go back to being statesmen and stateswomen, and our doctors won't have to deal with an insurance industry that controls life-and-death decisions based solely on cost. Then our commons can be clean because we—the people—decided that's how it should be.

Then making money will be back in perspective: a fine thing to do—but please don't overwhelm our media, wreck our world, and harm our children's future in the process.

CHAPTER 22

Unequal Influence

The resources in the treasury of a business corporation...are not an indication of popular support for the corporation's political ideas. They reflect instead the economically motivated decisions of investors and customers. The availability of these resources may make a corporation a formidable political presence, even though the power of the corporation may be no reflection of the power of its ideas.

—U.S. Supreme Court Justice William J. Brennan Jr.[1]

THE PEOPLE HAVE GOT TO KNOW IF THEIR PRESIDENT IS A CROOK," U.S. PRESI-dent Richard Nixon told a national television audience on November 11, 1973, when asked at a press conference if donations from the dairy industry had caused him to reverse his position on dairy price supports. He added, "Well, I am not a crook."

A bit over two years earlier, however, Nixon had a meeting at the White House with representatives of the dairy industry, who had apparently just given him a $2 million campaign pledge. With the tape running on March 23, 1971, Nixon said, "Uh, I know...that, uh, you are a group that are politically very conscious...And you're willing to do something about it. And, I must say a lot of businessmen and others...don't do anything about it. And you do, and I appreciate that. And I don't have to spell it out."

When the men from the trade association left, John Connally, one of Nixon's advisers who didn't realize that Nixon had bugged his own office, said to Nixon, "They are tough political operatives. This is a cold political deal."

Two days later, as Dairy Education Board Executive Director Robert Cohen documents, Nixon announced to his cabinet a stunning change in administration position that would bring the dairy industry more than

$300 million in additional revenue for the following year.[2] It's an old political equation: invest a million dollars in a politician and see a three-hundred-fold or more return on your investment. Good business.

Similarly, as somebody involved in education issues (I'm on the board of directors of a private school in New Hampshire and have written seven education-related books), I had wondered why the Bush administration would propose doubling the testing burden on public schoolchildren when both good science and common sense say that decreasing classroom size, increasing teacher training and resources, and other less expensive and more local methods are far more effective at helping children learn.[3]

Then the office of Senator Jim Jeffords gave me a study from the Congressional Research Service from July 9, 2001, titled "Educational Testing: Bush Administration Proposals and Congressional Response." The report, produced for members of Congress and not generally available to the public, noted, "Estimated aggregate state-level expenditures for assessment programs in FY2001 are $422.8 million."[4]

Suddenly, it all made sense: most standardized tests are sold to schools by a small number of very large corporations, and those corporations would make hundreds of millions more dollars under the Bush proposals.

In fact, the report notes that the Senate version of the Bush plan would "authorize a total of $400 million for state assessment development grants for FY2002"; "authorize $110 million for expansion of NAEP [National Assessment of Educational Progress] state assessments"; and "authorize $50 million for state performance awards"—all in addition to the current $422 million that the states were already spending on testing. The testing industry would more than double in size in a single year, helping a handful of large corporations get very much richer from this redistribution of tax dollars, whether it helps kids learn or not.

George W. Bush's brother, Neil, in fact, was then getting into the education business. And educational testing, now in 2010, as a result of No Child Left Behind, is a more than $2 billion a year industry.

The daily payoffs in Washington—the hundreds of millions that are funneled from corporate bank accounts to politicians' campaigns, often producing results that are of questionable benefit to anybody but the donor corporations—evoke a response of cynicism among most Americans.

A Political Backlash

Political optimists see a different possibility than today's rampant cynicism. And although most registered voters no longer bother to vote, some do believe that politicians who are truly dedicated to the public good can return power to the people. Those who believe that it is the role of government and not corporations to ensure our rights to "life, liberty, and the pursuit of happiness" view the increasingly populist talk of some national politicians as good news.

For example, Vermont Congressman Bernie Sanders published an article on his Web site on August 17, 2001, titled "The U.S. Needs a Political Revolution." He wrote,

> At a time when more and more Americans are giving up on the political process, and when the wealthy and multi-national corporations have unprecedented wealth and power, it is imperative that we launch a grass-roots revolution to enable ordinary Americans to regain control of their country....
>
> It is no accident that while pharmaceutical and insurance companies donate huge sums of money into the political process, American citizens must pay, by far, the highest prices in the world for prescription drugs. Those same companies and their political donations ensure that the United Stares remains the only industrialized nation that does not have a national health care program providing health care to all.
>
> The rich hold $25,000-a-plate fundraisers for their candidates. Why would they pay so much for a chicken dinner? The answer is, they want access and special favors. It is no accident that after raising more money from the wealthy for his campaign than any candidate in history, President Bush and the Republican leadership passed a $1.3 trillion dollar tax bill which provides $500 billion in tax breaks for the wealthiest 1 percent of Americans.
>
> It is no accident that, rather than raising the minimum wage, the President and congressional leadership are providing billions in tax breaks and subsidies to the major oil, gas, and coal companies. It is also, sadly, no accident that almost 20 percent of our children live in poverty, schools throughout the country are physically deteriorating, college graduates begin their careers deeply in debt, and millions of working class people are unable to find affordable housing.

My read of it is that Sanders is suggesting that we again try real "republican democracy"—a government truly of, by, and for humans—that we begin to put people first and the rights and the powers of corporations (and governments, churches, and any other human-made institutions) second.

This brings us back to those two meta-political parties: the politicians who work on behalf of corporations and the politicians who work on behalf of humans. Increasingly, citizens of democratic nations are setting aside labels like *Republican, Democrat, Tory,* and *Labour* when considering their politicians. Instead the labels in people's minds are: *working in the interests of corporations* and *working in the interests of individual citizens.*

How Public Opinion Is Influenced by Concentrated Money

Poll after poll has shown that Americans overwhelmingly support reform of our health-care system. People are concerned about costs and quality of care. Yet in 1993, when President Bill Clinton proposed that the government offer some form of health-care protection to the nation's 40-plus-million uninsured, the insurance industry spent an estimated $100 million on lobbying and $60 million on advertising and provided members of Congress with about 350 free trips.

What actually happened as a result of all this spending is extraordinarily ironic. Industry polls showed that people cared more about being able to choose their own doctor than most other medical issues. Taking advantage of this, an infamous series of ads featuring "Harry and Louise" warned Americans that under a government-run health insurance program they would lose their ability to select the doctor of their choice.

The advertising worked. People panicked, and American public opinion swung from strong support for Clinton's proposals to overwhelming fear of them. The Internet became flooded with insulting e-mails about the evils of "Hillary's" insurance proposal.

Even more ironically, those fears have been realized today—without the Clinton proposal. Back in 1993 you could pretty much go to any doctor you wanted (assuming you were insured), and your insurance would almost always pay for it. Overtly restricting that ability was never part of the Clinton proposal, but because of the power of the Harry and Louise ads people came to believe that it was.

And within a few years, insurance companies and HMOs (health maintenance organizations) began to crack down on consumers who wanted to select their own doctors. Today fewer Americans have that privilege than in 1993, even though it's fully available to citizens of virtually every country that has a national health-care program...which is every developed country in the world except the United States.

It turns out there is a strong reason why the insurance industry was eager to invest so much cash in advertising and lobbying to keep the government from competing with it in the realm of health care: profits. For every $100 that passes through the hands of the government-administered Medicare programs, between $2 and $3 is spent by Medicare on administration, leaving $97 to $98 to pay for medical services and drugs. But of every $100 that flows through corporate insurance programs and HMOs, $10 to $45 sticks to corporate fingers along the way. As Yale University Professor of Public Policy Theodore R. Marmor, author of *The Politics of Medicare*, said, "The costs of administering private insurance are somewhere between 5 and 10 times the costs of administering Medicare."[5]

After all, Medicare doesn't have lavish corporate headquarters and corporate jets, nor does it pay expensive lobbying firms in Washington to work on its behalf. It doesn't pay out profits in the form of dividends to its shareholders. And it doesn't compensate its top executives with more than $1 million a year, as does each of the largest of the American insurance companies. The result, as Professor Marmor points out, is that Canadians—who receive health care at one-half the cost of comparable services in the United States because no insurance companies are in the middle—"are somewhat healthier than citizens of the United States, use more hospital days per thousand, and visit their physicians more often" because services are freely available.[6]

Yet most citizens of the United States have no idea what it's like to live in a country with national health care. When our family lived in Germany for a year in the late 1980s, we were amazed at how smoothly its health-care system worked: we could make any appointment with any physician, and they were excellent at what they did. But even describing the reality of that experience draws uncomprehending stares from Americans, who have been fed a steady corporate diet of very one-sided information.

This is why when President Obama decided he wanted one of the main legacies of his presidency to be a solution to America's health-care mess, he first met privately and secretly with the pharmaceutical, hospital, and health insurance industries. He cut a deal with them, if news reports are to be believed (and they were not denied by the Obama administration), that he would protect their interests and give them tens of millions of new customers if they would hold back and not spend hundreds of millions of dollars to destroy his attempts the way they had with Clinton.

Something really rotten has taken hold of the American political system when the president of the United States must go to big corporations on bended knee and get their approval before suggesting legislation.

Polluters Pass "Go"

In 1995 the new governor of Texas responded to the needs of the "polluting industries" that had contributed more than $4 million (about 20 percent of his total) to his election campaign the year before. Thus, as soon as he was in office, George W. Bush signed into law the Texas Environmental Health and Safety Audit Privilege Act, also known as the "polluter immunity law." This new law, which has since been emulated in twenty-five other states and was tried at the federal level during the Bush presidency, allows polluting industries to avoid prosecution for pollution violations if they themselves report their own crimes to themselves in an internal audit. It also gives them the ability to prevent the public from knowing about their violations.

As Arizona's assistant attorney general, David Ronald, said, "Only the business with something to hide would benefit from a law that turns data gathered from environmental audits into secret information."[7] Some of these laws even provide for a year in jail and a $10,000 fine for any *human* who reveals to the public or to government agencies any corporate pollution discovered in an audit, thus discouraging investigative reporting or whistle-blowing employees.

Like with health-care policy, these laws that increase the power and the profitability of the nation's largest corporations at the expense of smaller companies who play by the rules—and to the detriment of average citizens—from the beginning are influenced by enormous amounts of "corporate free speech" in the form of cash for politicians and political parties.

In a Democracy...

The point for a democracy is, "What is the will of the people?" That will may change over time, but it is undemocratic when it is shaped by the single voice that shouts the loudest because there are profits to be made. Democracy is more important than any single debate, and this is a classic example of how democratic republican processes have been twisted because of the concept of corporate personhood.

PART IV

Restoring Personhood to People

The Fourteenth Amendment followed the freedom of a race from slavery....The amendment was intended to protect the life, liberty, and property of human beings. The language of the amendment itself does not support the theory that it was passed for the benefit of corporations.

—U.S. Supreme Court Justice Hugo Black, 303 U.S. 77 (1938)

CHAPTER 23

Capitalists and Americans Speak Out for Community

In America, no other distinction between man and man had ever been known but that of persons in office exercising powers by authority of the laws, and private individuals. Among these last, the poorest laborer stood on equal ground with the wealthiest millionaire, and generally on a more favored one whenever their rights seem to jar.

—Thomas Jefferson: Answers to de Meusnier Questions, 1786

ALTHOUGH WE HAVE MUCH THAT WE MIGHT CHANGE ABOUT OUR GOVERN-ment and business, it's clear that we also have a great and noble heritage on which to build and many great leaders in whose footsteps we can follow. Unlike America's Founders, however, we don't have to start from a blank piece of paper.

The Founders set the principles for us, and they inspired the world over—from the French Revolution to Tiananmen Square. Our job is to pick up the torch of liberty.

In this chapter we ask, "Is this a biased view, or do others see a problem, too?" This time we look to three powerful proponents of capitalism and free enterprise: a billionaire, a Nobel laureate who was chief economist of the World Bank, and *Business Week* magazine.

The Charitable Billionaire

George Soros is one of the most successful capitalists in history. He has made billions and has given away enormous amounts to charity. He clearly understands how the system works—his financial success is proof of that—and he is worried about it, on a global scale.

Soros wrote the cover story for the February 1997 issue of *Atlantic Monthly*. The subtitle asked: "What kind of society do we want? 'Let the free market decide!' is the often-heard response. That response, a prominent capitalist argues, undermines the very values on which open and democratic societies depend."

Soros's article, titled "The Capitalist Threat," directly addressed the issue of whether government should intervene in economic affairs, or if corporations should be unconstrained by elected officials (often referred to as laissez-faire capitalism). He wrote, "Although I have made a fortune in the financial markets, I now fear that the untrammeled intensification of laissez-faire capitalism and the spread of market values into all areas of life is endangering our open and democratic society. The main enemy of the open society, I believe, is no longer the communist but the capitalist threat."[1]

Four years later he wrote in *Newsweek,* "We need new ideas for fighting global poverty, ideas as sweeping as those that set the stage for global recovery after World War II....The globalization of financial markets makes it more difficult for individual states to provide public goods. National governments find it harder to impose taxes and regulations because capital can go elsewhere."

He went on to propose the creation of a fund managed by the International Monetary Fund, which would serve three types of programs: "global campaigns to provide such public benefits as eliminating HIV/AIDS," "government-sponsored programs to alleviate poverty," and "nongovernmental development programs [which] would be particularly valuable in countries with repressive or corrupt regimes."[2]

Clearly, the principles of the common good proposed by Jefferson and the other Founders, and espoused by so many of our presidents, are not at all incompatible with modern capitalist thinking. The problem, according to this billionaire, is in restriction of choices and excessive concentration of corporate power.

The Nobel Laureate from the World Bank

Stanford University Professor Emeritus Joseph E. Stiglitz won the Nobel Prize for Economics in 2001 just after quitting his job at the World Bank. His remarks were timely:

> As the chief economist at the World Bank from 1997 to 2000, I have seen first-hand the dark side of globalization—how the liberalization of capital markets,

by allowing speculative money to pour in and out of a country at a moment's whim, devastated East Asia; how so-called structural-adjustment loans to some of the poorest countries in the world "restructured" those countries' economies so as to eliminate jobs, but did not provide the means of creating new ones, leading to widespread unemployment and cuts in basic services.... The voices of those most affected by globalization are barely audible in discussions about how the table should be reshaped and who should have a seat at it.[3]

Once again, true democracy is being thwarted by the influence of decisions being made on the basis of corporate income regardless of human cost. Those are exactly the sorts of decisions the Founders fought against at great peril to themselves. They literally put their lives and personal fortunes on the line, risked everything, to fight the corporate and political tyranny of the day and gain democracy. Stiglitz gave up his position as chief economist of the World Bank. Clearly, compassion and concern for one's community are not incompatible with capitalist thinking—even for a world-leading economist.

Business Week Poll of the American Public

Finally, we turn to the American public, to gauge its mood. Has big business overstepped its bounds? Should it behave responsibly toward its community? What do Americans think?

In September 2000 a *Business Week*/Harris poll asked whether "business has gained too much power over too many aspects of American life." Between 72 and 82 percent of Americans said yes, and 95 percent of Americans agreed that American corporations "owe something to their workers and the communities in which they operate, and should sometimes sacrifice profit for the sake of making things better."[4]

By any measure, 72 to 82 percent of public opinion is an overwhelming majority, and the remarks of Soros and Stiglitz show that reasonable restrictions on businesses are not at all incompatible with success in business. Yet we see around us the sort of imbalance and injustice that our early presidents warned us about, in which so many large corporations misuse the protections that were created to protect humans from the biggest and most powerful. As Justice Black said, it was never meant to be this way.

In a Democracy...

We must level the playing field and return to the balance envisioned by our Founders, in which the highest priority actually accrues to humans and their communities—not to any massive authority, be it government or business.

The first step in getting back to those values will be to end corporate personhood.

CHAPTER 24

End Corporate Personhood

We are made wise not by the recollection of our past, but by the responsibility for our future.

—George Bernard Shaw

ARIZONA CHANGED ITS LAW AFTER 1886 SO THAT THE WORD *PERSON* WOULD include nonliving as well as living legal entities: "'Person' includes a corporation, company, partnership, firm, association or society, as well as a natural person."[1]

Many states have varying definitions of *person* depending on the part of law at issue. For example, there was a 1998 U.S. Supreme Court case in which a large part of the argument had to do with whether the Federal Trade Commission had the authority, under California law, to act as a person in enforcing a judgment against a telemarketer.[2]

Limit-setting Legislation Isn't Enough

As we've seen through the history of the Sherman Antitrust Act and other legislative attempts to control corporate behavior, the problem faced by citizens as well as directors and stockholders of corporations is systemic and rooted in how corporations are defined under the law.

Virtually every legislative session since the 1800s has seen new attempts to regulate or control corporate behavior, starting with Thomas Jefferson's unsuccessful insistence that the Bill of Rights protect humans from "commercial monopolies." Ultimately, most have either failed or been co-opted because they didn't address the underlying structural issue of corporate personhood.

To solve this problem, then, new laws controlling corporations aren't the ultimate answer. Instead what is needed is a foundational change in the definition of the relationship between living human beings and the nonliving legal fictions we call corporations. Only when corporations are again legally subordinate to those who authorized them—humans and the governments representing them—will true change be possible.

To bring this about will require a grassroots movement in communities all across America and the world to undo corporate personhood, leading to changes in the definitions of the word *person*.

Persistence

I'm not so naive as to think that this is something that will happen quickly or easily or will start at a national level. It will begin with you and me, at a local level, and percolate up from there, just as every substantial reformation movement has, from the American Revolution to the trust-busting Populist Movement of Teddy Roosevelt's era to the Civil Rights Movement. Change happens when citizens stand up and say "I won't have it anymore."

If history is any indicator, it won't be a short or direct path. It may be in my children's or their children's lifetime that humans finally take back their governments and their planet from corporations, and it may even be generations beyond that, although the growing global climate crisis may galvanize people the world over to far more rapid action.

Along those lines sometimes the Constitution is amended quickly in response to an overall public uprising, as happened with the amendment to end Prohibition and the amendment to lower the voting age to eighteen, which was passed in response to the rage of teenagers being forced to serve in the Vietnam War over which they had no voting power.

Townships Fight Back

In 2001 several townships in Pennsylvania passed ordinances forbidding corporations from owning or controlling farms in their communities. "They chose to go that route instead of the regulatory route," said attorney Thomas Linzey of the Community Environmental Legal Defense Fund (CELDF). "If we just got a regulation passed about, for example, odor from factory farms, then the entire debate from then on would be about odor. But what we want to challenge is the right for these huge corporate farming operations to exist in our communities in the first place."[3]

In December 2001, Gene Mellott, the secretary for Thompson Township, Pennsylvania, told me that his township had adopted several such ordinances, including "an ordinance forbidding confined animal-feeding operations from being owned and operated by a corporation" and "one that deals with corporations who have a previous history of violations, denying them access to starting up an animal-feeding operation."

Mellott noted at the time of our interview that one farmer was actually going through the processes specified by the ordinance, cooperating with the township, prior to opening a new animal-feeding operation.

Other townships weren't so lucky, though, Mellott said. "In one township the agribiz corporations threatened to sue the directors of the township, both as directors and personally. They didn't have the personal funds to fight that, so they decided not to pass the ordinance."[4]

I asked Linzey how a corporation could sue a township official for proposing legislation, and he said, "They allege that the township officials are planning to infringe on their civil rights."

"Civil rights?"

"Yes, civil rights. Because they claim they're persons, just like the township officials, so they can sue them, person to person, so to speak. That also immediately throws it into federal court, where the local officials will have to pay more for defense and won't have the easy support of their local community."[5]

If corporations weren't persons, they couldn't use such forms of harassment to prevent local officials from trying to protect their citizens from what may be unpleasant corporate neighbors.

And that's really the bottom line for township officials like Mellott, who said, "These ordinances were passed *to protect our citizens* [italics added] from pollution or side-effects of factory farms, water usage problems where they may draw down our reserves and making wells go dry—that sort of thing. We felt that a business that large should be regulated. I've heard the Farm Bureau is opposed to this, but the majority of the citizens of the township are in favor of them if they're passed, and they're the ones who elected us to represent their interests."[6]

In the decade since I wrote the first edition of this book, Linzey has been busy. CELDF has become one of the foremost organizations in the country advocating for the rights of humans over corporations. It has helped start a "Democracy School" that trains citizen-activists (and goes way deeper than this book into the history of corporate power in America) and has helped or inspired hundreds of communities to directly take on corporate personhood.

Here are a few headlines from www.celdf.org circa January 2010:

- Maine Town Passes Ordinance Asserting Local Self-governance and Stripping Corporate Personhood

- Spokane Considers Community Bill of Rights

- PA Citizens Denied Ballot Question to Add Local Bill of Rights: They Sue County Board of Elections, August 28, 2009

- Pennsylvania Town Fights Big Coal on Mining Rights

- Pittsylvania County, VA Citizens to County Government: Ban Uranium Mining, or Step Aside and We'll Govern Under a New County Constitution!

- Beccaria Township Citizens Appalled: Elected Official Calls Constituents "Traitors" and "A Mob" for Claiming Citizens Have Rights and Corporations Do Not

- Newfield, Maine Citizens Adopt Local Law to Stop Corporate Takeover of Ground Water

- Ecuador's Constitutional Assembly Calls on CELDF to Assist in Drafting Rights of Nature Language

- The Right to Local Self-government: PA Attorney General Corbett Denies It Exists

As you can see, the battle continues. But more and more people are waking up to the issues, which in itself is progress!

Changing Local Laws First

So how do we make these changes? As with the family farmers in Pennsylvania with their and CELDF's battle against corporate factory-farming operations that risk fouling their air, polluting their wells and river waters, and degrading their land, it will start at the local level.

I've helped fund an effort by attorneys Daniel Brannen and Thomas Linzey to check the laws of every single state in the union and Washington, D.C., to figure out how to best phrase local ordinances denying corporate personhood. You'll find the proposed Model Ordinances to Rescind Corporate

Personhood at www.thomhartmann.com; and there is a virtual encyclopedia of information on corporate personhood and what can be done about it at Linzey's Web site, www.celdf.org.

In many communities you'll have to get a city councilperson or other elected official to propose the law; in others, individuals themselves can place initiatives on ballots or before town meetings. Call your town hall to find out; ask, "How do I go about submitting a new law? What's the process?" In so doing you will be joining all those down through the centuries who have initiated change in democracies around the world.

And just as those who worked for civil rights for specific groups of humans came up against resistance, there may be opposition to your proposal.

When Linzey helped local farmers and elected officials pass ordinances keeping corporate factory farms out of their communities, he said, "A ranking Republican state senator demanded that CELDF be banned from [speaking out in public] panels. The Farm Bureau actively interfered in one local government's effort to pass the ordinance. And factory farm operatives began attending local government meetings."

But that was just the beginning, Linzey notes. Next, "The Pennsylvania Chamber of Commerce became more active, doing what the Chamber is designed to do—painting people like me and public officials who believe in democracy as rabble-driven advocates of no growth and no jobs. The Chamber also labeled as 'anti-agriculture' residents who supported our ordinance."

And then the corporate public relations (PR) machine turned itself on. Linzey says, "Our work made the cover of the Chamber's monthly *Advocate for Pennsylvania Business,* with an article titled 'There's No Business Like No-Bizness in Wayne Township' and a graphic of the township surrounded by barbed wire."[7]

Nonetheless, remembering former Speaker of the House of Representatives Tip O'Neill's comment, "All politics is local," there's little doubt that the best strategy is to start where we humans live, town by town, city by city, county by county. Corporations may have corrupted many of our political processes, but you and I still retain the right to vote. The ballot box has the potential to be the great leveler, the remedy of past errors and current inequalities.

Changing State Laws

When enough local communities have passed laws denying corporate personhood, eventually a corporation will challenge one of these laws and it'll end up before the Supreme Court. This could be a golden opportunity for the court to rectify the error made by reporter J. C. Bancroft Davis in his headnote for the 1886 *Santa Clara* case. If the Court were to rule that the Founders didn't intend to give corporations human protections under the Bill of Rights and the Fourteenth Amendment, step one would be finished.

But if the Court rules that the new anti–corporate personhood laws are unconstitutional, it will be necessary to move up the ladder and amend the state and federal constitutions. To support that effort, you'll also find ready-to-use draft amendments at www.thomhartmann.com.

I've spoken with a number of attorneys, constitutional scholars, and a few politicians about all this, and most agree that starting on a local level is probably best. But most also suggest that people should concurrently begin the process of amending state constitutions because corporate charters are issued and controlled by—in virtually all cases—the states themselves.

Making Change Happen

Taking on the conventional wisdom and a hierarchical power structure is no small or easy task. The Civil Rights and Women's Rights movements tell us how true social change happens: from the bottom up. The Supreme Court, for example, doesn't just go out and right social or legal wrongs. Instead legislatures pass laws, and people challenge those laws. When the challenges have worked their way up through the courts, they end up before the Supreme Court, which then has an opportunity to rule on the laws in the context of their relationship to the Constitution.

For humans to take back control of our governments by undoing corporate personhood, we'll have to begin with the governments that are the closest and most accessible to us. It's almost impossible for you or me to go to Washington, D.C., and have a meeting with our senator or representative—most of us usually can't even get them on the phone unless we're a big contributor. But most of us can meet with our city council members or show up at their meetings. Lobbying within the local community is both easy and effective. Local politicians are the closest to—and generally the most responsive—to the people they represent.

When enough local communities have passed ordinances that directly challenge corporate personhood, state legislatures will begin to notice. As with the issues of slavery, women's suffrage, and Prohibition (among others), when local communities take actions that are followed by states, eventually the federal government will get on board.

An Opportunity for the Supreme Court to Now Right a Wrong

These new laws will surely meet with lawsuits, which will bring the question back to the courts. Just as the railroads themselves sought change in the courts, ordinary citizens across the land are standing up and saying, "This is not what we want." It may take decades, as it did to create the wrong in the first place, but eventually the movement will lead to explicit legislation, or an amendment to the U.S. Constitution, or to the Supreme Court's reversing the *Santa Clara* precedent as it has reversed so many other error-filled cases over the years.

The ultimate change would be to clarify that the Fourteenth Amendment's reference to "persons" meant "natural persons" with what Locke and Jefferson called our natural rights as human persons.

The result could be a new flowering of freedom, democracy, and economic opportunity in America and around the world.

CHAPTER 25

A New Entrepreneurial Boom

To widen the market and to narrow the competition is always the interest of the dealers....The proposal of any new law or regulation of commerce which comes from this order, ought always to be listened to with great precaution, and ought never to be adopted, till after having been long and carefully examined, not only with the most scrupulous, but with the most suspicious attention.

It comes from an order of men, whose interest is never exactly the same with that of the public, who have generally an interest to deceive and even to oppress the public, and who accordingly have, upon many occasions, both deceived and oppressed it.

—Adam Smith, *The Wealth of Nations,* Book I, Chapter XI

FOR SOME PEOPLE, PARTICULARLY THE YOUNG AND THE OLD, THE LOCAL MALL or big-box retailer or superstore is an important part of their social lives. They get exercise by walking up and down the aisles, greet friends they see only there, and have a special and often inexpensive meal. They notice what's on sale and what's new in stock, making both intentional purchases and the occasional impulse buy.

Are Superstores and Malls "the New Downtown"?

In a way, a mall or superstore is like a small town's downtown. Instead of a library, there's the bookstore where you can browse books, thumb through magazines, and read today's newspapers. Instead of the old corner coffee shop, there's the food court. Most of the retail categories in a traditional downtown area are represented, from the clothing stores to the drugstore to the optometrist. The mall has its own police force and its own street-sweepers and maintenance crew. There are even sitting areas—the equivalent of the old parks—although they're usually lacking in squirrels and pigeons.

Shopping malls and big-box retailers are so much like downtowns that in most of the world's suburban communities where they exist, they've replaced the downtown areas of previous centuries. From the outside it looks like a change of location and style, but not one of great significance. So people now shop at the mall instead of downtown. So what? Isn't it just one business replacing another? Isn't that the way of commerce? Well...no. It's not the same thing.

The Local Money Recycling System We Lost

There is one huge difference between a mall full of chain stores or a big-box retailer and a downtown area full of small businesses, and it's a difference that is destroying local communities on the one hand and creating mind-boggling wealth for a very few very large corporations on the other. Here's how it works.

When I shop in downtown Montpelier, Vermont, and buy a pair of pants, for example, at the Stevens Clothing Store on Main Street, at the end of the day the store's owner, Jack Callahan, takes his proceeds down to the Northfield Savings Bank and deposits them. From Stevens, I walk next door to Bear Pond Books and buy today's newspaper, a magazine, and a copy of Thomas Paine's *Rights of Man,* a book that is as fascinating today as when it was first written in 1791. At the end of the day, Bear Pond's manager, Linda Leehman, will take my money down to the Chittenden Bank and deposit it. From Bear Pond I go to one of the dozen or so local restaurants and exchange some of my cash for a good meal. At day's end that cash, too, will end up in one of Montpelier's local banks.

The next day Montpelier's banks are richer by my purchases, as are Stevens, Bear Pond, and the restaurant. If my daughter the Web designer wanted to start her own design firm in an office on Main Street (or from her home), she could visit one of those banks, and, if her credit was good, they could loan her some of the money that was deposited with them the night before from the townspeople's purchases.

If her work is good, Stevens or Bear Pond or the restaurant may decide they want to hire her to design their Web site, using the profits they made from my and others' purchases to pay for her work. She'll put her money into the local bank, increasing its deposits available for local lending. Thus, by keeping money within the community, the community grows. This is how communities in America and most of the rest of the world have historically grown.

In the process of patronizing local businesses, people get their social and exercise needs met by walking into and around in downtown areas, and they contribute wealth to the local community, which eventually recycles back to them in the form of an improved quality of life, local taxes for local services like schools and police and parks, and a thriving entrepreneurial environment. That's a healthy local economy.

The Out-of-town Money Vacuum

Consider, though, if my shopping trip had been to a mall full of chain stores or to a national superstore. Strict management of cash flow is the name of the game for such businesses, and some of them make deposits several times a day. But the money stays in town for only a day at best.

At the end of every day, somebody somewhere pushes a button and all the money from each of the national or international chain's outlets all over the world goes *whoosh* to a distant location (usually near the headquarters of the chain). Of course, some of the money comes back into the local community in the form of wages, rent, taxes, and purchased services, but it's a fraction of what it would be had it all stayed in the community from beginning to end. And none of the profit ever finds its way back into the local community unless, coincidentally, there are local stockholders (and except in the most extraordinary of cases, the amount would be minuscule).

At the moment one of the main things that prevent local communities from defining and protecting their own local economies from these cash vacuums is based on the concept of corporate personhood.

How Corporate Personhood Set the Stage

When Thomas Jefferson pushed so hard for two years for the Bill of Rights to include "freedom from monopolies," he may well have anticipated the very problem I just identified: the dominance of distant mega-merchants (such as the East India Company) over local merchants. On the other hand, his Federalist opponents thought a strong central government could prevent the rise of monopolies while controlling the entrepreneurial engine that could drive great prosperity for a new nation in a vast, relatively untouched commons.

As America industrialized through the 1800s, it went from a minor agricultural nation to an industrial powerhouse central to the world's economy. This brought vast and rapid leaps in what we would call progress, but it also left huge areas soiled by industrial waste and strip-mining and resulted in one of the most rapid and dramatic losses of topsoil in the history of the world. Overall, though, most Americans today would consider it a good foundation laid for contemporary comforts.

While our history books tend to focus on the rich and powerful of the past—the John Rockefellers, Andrew Carnegies, and Prescott Bushes—the reality is that hundreds of thousands of small businesspeople built much of America and the rest of the modern industrial world.

These small businessmen and women didn't just create personal wealth for their families; they also kept wealth circulating in the communities where they lived. They provided employment, improvements, and economic vigor to their towns or neighborhoods, and they responded to the needs of those communities—because they lived in them.

State and local governments recognized the value and the importance of having local entrepreneurs responsible for the local business, rather than out-of-state monopolies, chains, or multinational corporations. During the 1920s and 1930s, in a wave of anti-chain-store populist sentiment, more than twenty-five states passed laws that taxed out-of-state or multinational businesses at a higher rate than local entrepreneurs, to discourage the distant and encourage the local.

But this was overthrown in 1935 when the Lane Drug Store chain sued the state of Florida, claiming that because its corporation was actually a person under the Constitution it was illegal discrimination under the Fourteenth Amendment for a state to give preferential treatment to a person in that state while not offering the same treatment to a person from out of state. The Supreme Court, looking back to 1886, sided with the Lane corporation, and now states and local communities all over the nation find themselves without the legal tools to encourage and nurture local businesses.[1]

Like the *Santa Clara* case, this one too went all the way to the Supreme Court because a very large corporation could litigate over an astonishingly small amount of money: $25. At that time local businesses were assessed a $5 annual fee and out-of-state businesses were charged up to $30 in Florida.

Chains and Category-killers: No More Building for Posterity

The fallout from that 1935 decision has been far-reaching. Just as individual humans are woefully outmatched by a corporation that wants to fight them, so are local communities outmatched.

A related effect is that individuals today are far less able to build an enterprise that will last in their community. And due to the attraction of enormous amounts of money from distant areas, they're often not even interested in doing so.

I first noticed the change in the mid-1980s, although it was probably under way for a decade or more. A young friend was pursuing the American Dream—starting his own business—and as a fellow entrepreneur he had adopted me as a mentor.

"People who start businesses aren't always the best to run them as they get larger," I advised him. "Leadership and management are two different skill sets, and only in very rare individuals do you find both together. When your company gets large enough that it needs real, day-to-day management of the details, I recommend you plan in advance now to hire somebody to replace yourself so that you can move into sales, idea-hatching, or some other function that you still find fun but that doesn't get in the way of the bean counters you'll need to bring in."

"Not gonna be a problem for me," he said. "I have no intention of keeping this business beyond its initial growth phase."

"Why not?" I said, reflecting that small businesses were what had built and sustained virtually every American community over the past three hundred years. Why go to the trouble of starting one if you weren't going to let it sustain you for your lifetime?

"Because that's not how things work anymore," he said, reversing our advice-giving roles:

> People don't start businesses anymore thinking they'll have security for their old age or something to pass along to their children. Whether it's a restaurant or a retail store or a software company, the plan now is to grow big enough and fast enough to be noticed by one of the big guys, and then cash out before they squash you like a bug. Make it easier and cheaper for them to buy you out than for them to spend the time and effort running you out of business or simply stealing your idea. And to succeed, you've gotta do it quickly.

After that meeting, while driving home in suburban Atlanta, I noticed with new eyes the stores that lined the main roads. Nearly all were large corporate chains, from the video stores to the bookstores to the fast-food outlets. The crafts store was a chain, as was the bicycle store. Nearly all the entrepreneurial ventures that had populated the area up until the late 1970s and mid-1980s had died, replaced by such a numbing sameness of product and presentation that

I could just as easily have been driving down a suburban street in Dallas, San Diego, Seattle, Memphis, Detroit, or Boston. Or, increasingly, Paris, London, Frankfurt, Rio, or Taipei.

Retail has been taken over. There's a good reason why national super-store chains are known in the business press as "category-killers." When such a chain enters an industry, whether it's hardware or stationery or anything else, it typically puts dozens to hundreds of local, family-owned businesses into bankruptcy. Other local merchants, having seen the fate that awaits them, "get while the getting's good," closing down before they lose everything they've earned in decades of business. In either case, the category-killer relocates locally generated profits to its distant corporate headquarters, and the local, community-oriented, full-service merchants are gone.

Manufacturing too has been moved far away from the local economy to labor-cheap countries. Taking Amtrak from Boston to New York, you see miles of empty, decaying, vandalized factory buildings once serviced by the railroads, their products now manufactured in China or Indonesia, their former workers now flipping burgers or unemployed. And even when the foreign companies do their manufacturing in the United States (like Toyota and Kia have done—and extol in their advertising), the *profits* from all that manufacturing effort go back to Japan or South Korea or whatever the corporation's country of origin may be. The principle is pretty much the same.

Big, nonlocal corporations have largely inhaled even service industries, traditionally the last bastion of lower-paying local labor: fast-food chains, day-care and learning-center chains, home-service franchises, and hospital and medical chains.

Relocalizing Our Economies

In summary, consider these benefits of local communities being allowed to give special breaks to local companies, or to regulate out-of-town companies, to support their local economy:

- They keep cash local.

- Local companies are more sensitive and responsive to regional issues—they are far less likely to be "bad citizens" because their families have to live with the consequences.

- They are more heterogeneous and responsive in the services and the products supplied.

- They preserve regional culture, personality, and perspective.

- They provide greater stability, given that the economies become more self-contained. The demise of a business or two won't prove nearly as devastating as when a large employer decides to shut down a plant and move production to Mexico.

This is not to say we shouldn't have large businesses. Instead, as Teddy Roosevelt pointed out, they must be kept in an appropriate context and submit to regulation by the local communities in which they operate.

Recovering an Entrepreneurial Boom

According to the U.S. Small Business Administration (SBA), "Industries dominated by small firms created jobs at a rate almost 60 percent faster than those dominated by large businesses." The report adds, "Approximately 86 percent of small businesses are legally organized as proprietorships or partnerships."[2]

The same trends are found worldwide and attested to by the enormous success of microlending projects such as run by the Grameen Bank in Bangladesh, which was started in 1976 when Bangladeshi economics professor Muhammad Yunus loaned $26 to forty-two Bangladeshi villagers, thus starting the Grameen Bank. As of January 2010, Yunus's bank has more than 8 million borrowers, 97 percent of whom are women. Since its inception it has loaned $8.74 billion, with an average loan size of $160 and a repayment rate (including interest) of 97 percent. Through the small businesses that have been started with these microloans, more than one-third of Grameen's clients have now been raised out of poverty, and microlending is a growing tool of non-profits and charities around the world.[3]

The challenge to a new entrepreneurial boom is found in the type of neoliberal corporate person–based economics practiced by the World Bank, WTO, and big-business advocates of what is called free trade. It's a system that does exactly what corporations are chartered to do: move and aggregate wealth into the corporation. But with corporate personhood openly allowing corporations to corrupt political processes and roam the world unrestrained, the consequences have been unhealthy for humans. The result of today's situation is well summarized by Jeff Gates, author of *Democracy at Risk*, in an article published in *Reflections*, MIT's journal of the Society for Organizational Learning.[4] Gates notes the following nine clear and troubling trends, which all track back to the current corporate laws and structures for the very largest of the corporations we allow to do business here:*

1.   **From the bottom to the top.** The wealth of the Forbes 400 richest Americans grew an average $1.44 billion each from 1997 to 2000, for a daily increase in wealth of $1,920,000 per person.[5] The financial wealth of the top 1 percent now exceeds the combined household financial wealth of the bottom 95 percent. The share of the nation's after-tax income received by the top 1 percent nearly doubled from 1979 to 1997.[6] By 1998, the top-earning 1 percent had as much combined income as the 100 million Americans with the lowest earnings. The top fifth of U.S. households now claim 49.2 percent of the national income while the bottom fifth gets by on 3.6 percent.[7] Between 1979 and 1997, the average income of the richest fifth jumped from 9 times the income of the poorest fifth to 15 times.[8] The pay gap between top executives and their average employees in the 365 largest U.S. companies widened from 42 to 1 in 1980 to 531 to 1 in 2000.[9]

2.   **From democracies to plutocracies.** Today's capital markets–led "emerging markets" development model is poised to replicate U.S. wealth patterns worldwide. For instance, World Bank research found that 61.7 percent of Indonesia's stock market value is held by that nation's 15 richest families. The comparable figures are 55.1 percent for the Philippines and 53.3 percent for Thailand. Worldwide, there is now roughly $60 trillion in securitized assets (stocks, bonds, and so on), with an estimated $90 trillion in additional assets that will become securitizable as this model spreads.[10]

3.   **From the future to the present.** Unsustainable production methods are now standard practice worldwide, owing largely to globalization's embrace of a financial model that insists on maximizing net present value (chiefly, what stock values represent). That stance routinely and richly rewards those who internalize gains and externalize costs such as paying a living wage or cleaning up environmental toxins.

---

*Quoted verbatim from Jeff's article with permission.

4. **From poor nations to rich.** This version of globalization assumes that unrestricted economic flows will benefit the 80 percent of humanity living in developing countries as well as those 20 percent living in developed countries. Yet the U.N. Development Program reports that the richest fifth of the global population now accounts for 86 percent of all goods and services consumed, while the poorest fifth consumes just over 1 percent.[11]

5. **From developing nations to developed nations.** In all three ecosystems suffering the worst declines (forests, freshwater, and marine), the most severe damage has occurred in the southern temperate or tropical regions. Industrial nations (located mainly in northern temperate zones) are primarily responsible for the ongoing loss of natural capital elsewhere in the world. In its July 2001 report, the International Panel on Climate Change confirms that relentlessly rising global temperatures—due primarily to hydrocarbon use in the 30 most developed economies—are poised to create catastrophic conditions worldwide. Agriculture, health, human settlements, water, animals—all will feel the impact on a planet that is warming faster than at any time in the past millennium. Throughout the panel's 2,600 pages of analysis, one theme remains constant: The poor of the world will be hardest hit. According to GEO 2000, a U.N. environmental report, "The continued poverty of the majority of the planet's inhabitants and excessive consumption by the minority are the two major causes of environmental degradation."[12]

6. **From families to financial markets.** The work year for the typical American has lengthened by 184 hours since 1970. That's an additional 4½ weeks on the job for about the same pay. Parents in the United States also spend 40 percent less time with their children than in 1970.

7. **From free-traders to protectionists.** OECD nations channel $362 billion a year in subsidies to their own farmers while restricting agricultural imports from developing countries and insisting that debtor nations repay their foreign loans in foreign currency, which they can earn only by exporting.[13]

8. **From debtors to creditors.** In 1999, leaders of the G7 nations agreed to a debt initiative for Heavily Indebted Poor Countries, aiming to cap

debt service for the world's 41 poorest countries at [a steep] 15 to 20 percent of [their] export earnings. By comparison, after World War I, the victors set German reparations at 13 to 15 percent of exports.[14]

9. **From law abiders to law evaders.** Roughly $8 trillion is held in tax havens worldwide, ensuring that globalization's most well-to-do can harvest the benefits of globalization without incurring any of the costs.[15]

Denying corporate personhood isn't a panacea, but it's a huge first step. Corporations will still have extraordinary constitutional protections (the contracts clause and the commerce clause, for example), as they have had from the founding of the United States. Personhood status won't by any means leave them unprotected in court any more than they were before 1886.

But when states, counties, townships, and communities can once again define corporate behavior, they can again encourage entrepreneurial activity. Then people can start and run small businesses without worrying that a giant corporation will come along and crush them without the slightest thought.

Communities will see the money spent in their neighborhoods circulate and be reinvested in their own area, building strong and vital towns, counties, and states. And corporations won't be able to intimidate local politicians by suing them personally for violations of the very civil rights laws that were first enacted to protect human beings.

An entrepreneurial boom awaits America and the rest of the world.

- The U.S. State Department notes that only 1 percent of the corporations in America (and most other developed nations) are "large" (more than five hundred employees); 99 percent of all American companies are small businesses.

- That 99 percent accounts for 52 percent of all nonfarm jobs (keep in mind that about one-third of all other workers are employed by governments and nonprofits) and 47 percent of all sales.

- America's five hundred largest manufacturing firms cut almost 2 million workers from their payrolls in the United States between 1986 and 1994 (after that the statistics gathering system changed, and it's not broken out anymore) as the focus of large companies moved from making things in America to selling them in America.

- But during the years 1990 to 1995 (the last years for which there are current statistics broken out in this fashion), more than three-quarters of all new jobs were created by small businesses.[16]

- The U.S. Small Business Administration says, "Overall, employment in establishments owned by small firms grew 10.5 percent over the period (noted above), compared with 3.7 percent employment growth in establishments owned by firms with more than 500 employees."[17]

- Small businesses obtain more patents per sales dollar than large firms and produce 55 percent of all significant innovations.[18]

- The Bureau of Labor Statistics projects that 88 percent of all new job creation in the years up to 2005 will come from small businesses.[19]

- As the SBA notes in its "Annual Report on Small Business and Competition," small firms make two indispensable contributions to the American economy:

  First, they are an integral part of the renewal process that pervades and defines market economies. New and small firms play a crucial role in experimentation and innovation that leads to technological change and productivity growth....

  Second, small firms are the essential mechanism by which millions enter the economic and social mainstream of American society. Small businesses enable millions, including women, minorities, and immigrants, to access the American Dream....In this evolutionary process, community plays the crucial and indispensable role of providing the "social glue" and networking opportunities that bind small firms together in both high tech and "Main Street" activities.[20]

And few to none of these small businesses would be affected in an adverse way by the elimination of corporate personhood.

- Small businesses don't have the time or money to field full-time lobbyists in Washington or to funnel millions of dollars to presidential or congressional campaigns and thus don't assert First Amendment personhood rights. (Or, if they do, it's usually the business owner who contacts an elected official as a private citizen with a concern.)

- They don't claim the First Amendment right to free speech in spending hundreds of millions on national advertising designed to affect the political processes.

- They don't sue the government, declaring a person's Fourth Amendment right to privacy as a means to prevent OSHA or EPA inspectors from looking into toxic wastes or labor practices in chemical factories or steel mills.

- They don't demand Fourteenth Amendment rights of equal protection to knock down local community laws designed to keep out large corporations that have been convicted of corporate crimes or have the ability to unfairly compete.

- They don't sit on the councils of NAFTA and the WTO and make decisions that wipe out domestic high-paying jobs and create offshore kingdoms in tax havens or low-wage nations.

- Most small businesses don't even make use of the limited-liability provisions of corporate law: banks and venture capitalists almost always demand that a small-business owner—an individual—personally sign for and secure loans and other transactions.

In fact, small and medium-sized businesses make little to no use whatsoever of corporate personhood. Eliminating corporate personhood would help them inasmuch as it could help restore democratic processes, empower local communities in which small businesses are rooted, and enable politicians to begin anew to enforce anti-monopoly legislation.

Denying the personhood of the handful of very large corporations that exploit it will allow the passage of laws getting them out of undue influence in politics, which in turn will hinder efforts to influence government to maintain trust and monopoly status. Federal, state, and local governments will be able to enforce laws, if the citizens want, that require corporations to operate to the benefit of the states and the communities in which they are incorporated and do business.

This will open millions of doors of opportunity for the entrepreneurial energies and imagination of people all over the world and could easily create a boom every bit as dramatic as the Agricultural Revolution, the Industrial Revolution, or the Technological Revolution.

CHAPTER 26

A Democratic Marketplace

*The prevalence of the corporation in America has led men of this
generation to act, at times, as if the privilege of doing business in
corporate form were inherent in the citizen; and has led them to accept
the evils attendant upon the free and unrestricted use of the corporate
mechanism as if these evils were the inescapable price of civilized life,
and, hence, to be borne with resignation.*

Throughout the greater part of our history a different view prevailed.

*Although the value of this instrumentality in commerce and industry
was fully recognized, incorporation for business was commonly denied
long after it had been freely granted for religious, educational, and
charitable purposes.*

*It was denied because of fear. Fear of encroachment upon the liberties
and opportunities of the individual. Fear of the subjection of labor
to capital. Fear of monopoly. Fear that the absorption of capital by
corporations, and their perpetual life, might bring evils similar to those
which attended mortmain [immortality]. There was a sense of some
insidious menace inherent in large aggregations of capital, particularly
when held by corporations.*

—U.S. Supreme Court Justice Louis Brandeis, 1933[1]

ALTHOUGH THE INCREASINGLY UNRESTRAINED MARKETPLACE THAT TEDDY
Roosevelt and Louis Brandeis warn of makes it hard for many companies to
emphasize community values, some still do. Others are recognizing the need
to respond to human demands for a cleaner, safer, less toxic world.

Additionally, many people are fortunate enough to work in an industry
they love, and the love of railroads or automobiles or flying or medicine has

motivated the start-up and the ongoing operation of many of what are now the world's best companies.

In my experience in business, it's the people who care about their industry or area of expertise who are the most likely to be successful. And companies with mission statements and standards of behavior that let people ethically live out their passions can be wonderful places to work.

As people take back control of their governments and begin to again regulate how far businesses can go, the vast majority of ethical and appropriately run corporations can begin to operate in ways that are more long-term and more community oriented.

Revoking Corporate Charters Is Not at All New

The process of revoking corporate charters goes back to the very first years of the United States. Beginning in 1784 (four years before the U.S. Constitution was ratified), Pennsylvania demanded that corporations include a revocation clause in corporate charters.[2]

As the United States grew, laws were passed requiring revocation clauses in the corporate charters (permissions) of insurance companies in 1809 and banks in 1814. From the founding of America to the late 1800s, governments routinely revoked corporate charters, forcing the liquidation and the sale of assets. Banks were shut down for behaving in a "financially unsound" way in Ohio, Mississippi, and Pennsylvania. And when corporations that ran the turnpikes in New York and Massachusetts didn't keep their roads in repair, those states gave the corporations the death sentence.

In 1825 Pennsylvania passed laws making it even easier for that state to "revoke, alter, or annul" corporate charters "whenever in their opinion [the operation of the corporation] may be injurious to citizens of the community," and by the 1870s nineteen states had gone through the long and tedious process of amending their state constitutions expressly to give legislators the power to terminate the existence of corporations that originated in those states.

Presidents have even run for public office and won on platforms that included the revocation of corporate charters. One of the largest issues of the election of 1832 was Andrew Jackson's demand that the corporate charter of the Second Bank of the United States not be renewed.

Following his lead states across the nation began examining their banks and other corporations; and in just the year 1832 Pennsylvania pulled the charters of ten corporations, sentencing them to corporate death "for operating contrary to the public interest."

Oil corporations, match manufacturers, whiskey trusts, and sugar corporations all received the corporate death penalty in the late 1800s in Michigan, Ohio, Nebraska, and New York. And when, in 1894, the Central Labor Union of New York City campaigned for the New York State Supreme Court to revoke the charter of Standard Oil Trust of New York for "a pattern of abuses," the court agreed and dissolved the company.

It was the beginning of a bandwagon that ended only, for all practical purposes, with the election of President Warren G. Harding in 1921, with his promise to have "less government in business and more business in government."

Legislative Remedies

Whether the threat is one of economic penalty, regulation, or even dissolution, the fact is that laws do change corporate behavior. For example, literally millions of corporate decisions are made daily around the world in response to tax laws. In Germany, where a government-imposed energy tax causes oil and gasoline to cost more than twice what it does in the United States, industry is roughly twice as energy-efficient as American companies and with significantly lower toxic and atmosphere-destabilizing discharges as a result. When the three-martini lunch became no longer deductible under U.S. tax law, most American companies changed their guidelines for employee behaviors and reimbursements.

Thus, if humans were to again decide that they wanted corporations to behave in a way that protected the living environment that sustains all life forms (including humans), we could indeed pass laws making it unprofitable or dangerous for corporations to do otherwise. Taking it a step further, we could even pass laws that give corporations incentives to actively help the environment.

With the end of corporate personhood, it will be possible for the humans of the United States and every nation in the world to define the terms of a new economy. With natural persons once again in charge of government, we can redefine the rules of business so that corporations are profitable when their actions lead to sustainability and a clean environment, respond to values defined by local communities, and promote and develop renewable forms of energy. We can strip out the strings and the harnesses put into regulatory law by corporate lobbyists so that the government agencies charged with protecting us from malefactors and criminals can once again work.

Eliminating Corporate Personhood

Once corporate personhood is eliminated and corporations are again seen as they really are—the fictitious legal creatures of the states that authorized and created them—all this can change. The rightful representatives of humans— our governments—can then pass laws like the ones that were once part of this nation and its states, forbidding corporations from attempting to influence the laws and the regulatory agencies that oversee their activities.

As stated in the Wisconsin law that stood until it was finally noticed and struck down in 1953,

> No corporation doing business in this state shall pay or contribute, or offer, consent or agree to pay or contribute, directly or indirectly, any money, property, free service of its officers or employees or thing of value to any political party, organization, committee or individual for any political purpose whatsoever, or for the purpose of influencing legislation of any kind, or to promote or defeat the candidacy of any person for nomination, appointment or election to any political office.[3]

Returning Political Power to the People

When decisions are made locally, their full range of impacts, including all present and future costs, are more likely to be considered. If a community knows that extracting a mineral from its soil will produce environmental damage, it can require the mining corporation to pay for that damage in advance or as product is extracted—without worrying that, because some other community has chosen not to so tax the corporation, the community is trampling the "rights" of the corporation under the Fourteenth Amendment's equal protection clause.

German historian and author Wolfgang Sachs noted in an interview with former California governor Jerry Brown, "Nature has only been minimally present in the market. The market thrives on the fact that nature doesn't cost anything."[4] Except it does cost something to the local communities, who must suffer with the effects of strip mining, toxic waste, loss of topsoil, and the destruction of their ecosystems.

When corporations are changed from natural-person to artificial-person status, the natural persons who live in these regions can begin to legislatively regulate the actions of any corporation that seeks to exploit their nature.

Once again in America, as Thomas Jefferson hoped would always be the case, "the people, being the only safe depository of power, should exercise in person every function which their qualifications enable them to exercise, consistently with the order and security of society."[5]

Democracy in the Global Marketplace

On January 20, 1949, President Harry S. Truman in his inaugural address committed the United States to helping lift much of the world out of poverty.[6] It was the first time a national leader had used the word "development" to describe a national goal outside the United States, or "undeveloped" to describe what we now call the third world or the developing world. Truman was quite clear and specific about his vision:

> We must embark on a bold new program for making the benefits of our scientific advances and industrial progress available for the improvement and growth of underdeveloped areas. More than half the people of the world are living in conditions approaching misery. Their food is inadequate. They are victims of disease. Their economic life is primitive and stagnant. Their poverty is a handicap and a threat both to them and to more prosperous areas.

Pointing out that the United States had the resources and the knowledge to help lift people around the world out of poverty and misery, Truman demanded that corporations that had an eye to exploiting the developing world be restrained. He said, "The old imperialism—exploitation for foreign profit—has no place in our plans."

Instead, he added, the poorer people of the world must have the ability to determine their own fates and control for themselves the extent of our companies' participation in their nations as well as the extent of their own development. "Democracy alone can supply the vitalizing force to stir the peoples of the world into triumphant action," Truman said, "not only against their human oppressors, but also against their ancient enemies—hunger, misery, and despair."

The role of government is to protect, defend, and represent the interests of its own people, he said. "Democracy maintains that government is established for the benefit of the individual, and is charged with the responsibility of protecting the rights of the individual and his freedom in the exercise of his abilities." Citing Locke's concept of natural rights, he added, "Democracy is based on the conviction that man has the moral and intellectual capacity, as well as the inalienable right, to govern himself with reason and justice."

Truman's vision was a challenge to corporate personhood, but NAFTA, GATT, WTO, and fast-track authority have sidetracked it. Ending corporate personhood would allow communities to correct this situation and empower them to enforce ethical and socially responsible corporate behavior.

CHAPTER 27

Restoring Government of, by, and for the People

All constitutions, those of the States no less than that of the nation, are designed, and must be interpreted and administered so as to fit human rights.

—Theodore Roosevelt, in a speech given on February 12, 1912

CAN WE RECLAIM THE DREAM OF FREEDOM AND INDIVIDUAL LIBERTY IN THE land of its birth? I believe we can.

Every culture and every religion of what we call the civilized world carries, in one form or another, a mythos or story about a time in the past or future when humans lived or will live in peace and harmony. Whether it's referred to as Valhalla or Eden, Shambhala or One Thousand Years of Peace, the Satya Yuga or Jannat, stories of past or coming times of paradise go hand-in-hand with hierarchical cultures.

Such prophecies were clearly in the minds of America's Founders when they first discussed integrating Greek ideas of democracy, Roman notions of a republic, Masonic utopian ideals, and the Iroquois Federation's constitutionally organized egalitarian society, which was known to Jefferson, Washington, Adams, and Franklin. The creation of the United States of America brought into the world a dramatic new experiment in how people could live together in a modern state.

While most of the rest of the world watched this new experimental democracy with skepticism, the citizens of France took our revolution to heart and initiated the French Revolution just six years after ours ended.

America grew swiftly and steadily for nearly a century, and many other countries of the world began to experiment with their own versions of democracy. As America was convulsed by the Civil War, the world held its breath, but America remained intact and the period of industrialization following the war led to one of the most rapid periods of worldwide growth in history. This growth cemented for the world the concept of the American ideal, as millions escaped their homelands to settle in the new "land of opportunity and freedom."

Thus America has come to represent the world's archetypal concept of freedom and egalitarianism. On May 29, 1989, twenty thousand people gathered around a 37-foot-tall statue in Beijing's Tiananmen Square. They placed their lives in danger, but that statue was such a powerful representation that many were willing to die for it...and some did. They called their statue the Goddess of Democracy: it was a scale replica of the Statue of Liberty that stands in New York harbor on Liberty Island.

From the French Revolution in 1789 to the people's uprising in Beijing in 1989 to the various "color" revolutions in former Soviet republics and Iran, people around the world have used language and icons borrowed from the pen of Thomas Jefferson and his peers. Even if we didn't implement it fully in our early efforts, and even if it's been strained since its inception, the Greek-Roman-Masonic-Iroquois-American idea of a government "deriving its just Powers from the Consent of the Governed" is probably one of the most powerful and timeless ideas in the world today. It is the Global Dream.

While there are pockets of those in the world who hate us and even foist terrorist acts upon us, there are billions more who desperately wish to embrace the principles upon which our nation was founded. We in the United States of America hold a sacred archetype for the world: the dream of freedom and individual liberty.

Change Is in the Air

Thanks to the hegemony of corporate personhood, that dream is in jeopardy. History, however, has shown that change *is* possible when citizens speak out and work to change the Constitution. In the previous century, a citizen-led effort resulted in the passage and the ratification of the Nineteenth Amendment, guaranteeing women the right to vote—despite long tradition and past court decisions. Similar efforts led to constitutional amendments banning, and then rescinding the ban on, alcohol. Most recently, the Twenty-sixth Amendment lowering the voting age from twenty-one to eighteen was ratified, in part in response to demands from servicemen and women in Vietnam and veterans of that war. And a popular protest song, "The Eve of Destruction," was a prominent voice for this popular sentiment, proclaiming, "You're old enough to kill, but not for votin'."

More recently, a growing movement has begun in the United States to bring back the Global Dream, restoring human personhood to its rightful place at the top of the priority list. For example, on April 25, 2000, the city of Point Arena, California, passed a City Council Resolution on Corporate Personhood, "rejecting the notion of corporate personhood," in which they "urge other cities to foster similar public discussion" on the issue.[1]

As mentioned earlier, the Community Environmental Legal Defense Fund (www.celdf.org) has been working with hundreds of communities across the nation to fight corporate personhood. Other groups—such as Jeff Milchen's ReclaimDemocracy.org and former Green Party presidential candidate and pro-democracy activist (and lawyer) David Cobb's Democracy Unlimited of Humboldt County (www.duhc.org) and Campaign to Legalize Democracy (www.movetoamend.org)—are undertaking serious efforts to raise awareness about the issue. Even one of our recent vice presidents has taken notice and is shouting a call for change. Al Gore, in his book *The Assault on Reason,* writes:

> The 1886 Supreme Court decision *Santa Clara County v. Southern Pacific Railroad* has been cited for decades—especially since the conservative takeover in 1980—to uphold the proposition that corporations are, legally speaking, "persons" and thus protected under the Fourteenth Amendment. It was one of many developments that marked the ascendancy of corporate power in both the economic and political spheres of American Life. By the end of the nineteenth century, the "monopolies in commerce" that Jefferson had wanted to prohibit in the Bill of Rights were full-blown monsters, crushing competition from smaller businesses, bleeding farmers with extortionate shipping costs, and buying politicians at every level of government.[2]

The dream of egalitarian democracy in America as articulated in the Declaration of Independence (against the East India Company) has been taken captive, but it lives on. Today the captivity is so obvious that as the twenty-first century began people protested in Seattle and Genoa, facing police beatings to register their hope that the dream be reawakened. They faced risks similar to those of the Americans who stood up against tyranny at the Boston Tea Party and have continued to do so at every major meeting of world leaders and multinational corporate heads.

Fighting the New Feudalism

As Richard Cohen noted in a January 21, 2002, article in the *Washington Post* about the Enron debacle, "What we have here is an updated form of feudalism."[3] And like the feudal systems that held Europe, Asia, South America, and Japan in their grip for centuries, this new feudalism isn't going to easily submit to transformation or simply morph back into the representative republican democracy from which it emerged and has now largely taken over.

Instead it will fight back, and if Alexis de Tocqueville was right, the main tool it will use will be the media it owns or has easy access to with its advertising and PR dollars, keeping people passively lulled into the twin beliefs that they are powerless and that the world's largest corporations do know, after all, how to run the planet and therefore everything is just fine and there's no need to worry about or do anything.

But no matter how much they try to convince us that "global warming is a good thing"[4] or "toxic sludge is good for you,"[5] humans know. Thomas Paine said it best: individual persons should be more powerful than any other institution.

"It has been thought," he wrote in *The Rights of Man* in 1791,

> that government is a compact between those who govern and those who are governed; but this cannot be true, because it is putting the effect before the cause; for as man must have existed before governments existed, there necessarily was a time when governments did not exist, and consequently there could originally exist no governors to form such a compact with.

> The fact therefore must be, that the individuals themselves, each in his own personal and sovereign right, entered into a compact with each other to produce a government: and this is the only mode in which governments have a right to arise, and the only principle on which they have a right to exist.[6]

We've figured out that Paine's ideals and dreams, and those of Jefferson and Madison, Washington, and Adams—even allowing for their differences—have been stolen.

Change Starts at the Grassroots

To reclaim the dream, we need to be fostering grassroots efforts to fight corporate personhood.

Many of the problems of corporate personhood could be solved—or at least begin to be solved—by the passage of an amendment to the Fourteenth

Amendment to insert the word *natural* before the word *person* or by the passage of a standalone amendment that explicitly states that only humans have human rights and that corporations and other artificial forms of organization don't.

Article V of the U.S. Constitution states that a constitutional amendment may be offered to the states for approval when it's been approved by two-thirds of both the House of Representatives and the Senate or submitted to the Congress by two-thirds of the states. To become law and actually amend the Constitution, three-quarters of the states must then approve, or ratify, the amendment. Those two-thirds and three-quarters thresholds have proven a substantial (and intentional) obstacle to changing the Constitution of the United States.

As of this writing, the most recent successful amendment to the Constitution became law in 1992, an amendment to ensure that when legislators vote themselves a pay raise, they don't enjoy the benefits of it until after the next election cycle. More than eighteen thousand amendments have been proposed in Congress, but since 1789 only thirty-three have emerged with the required two-thirds majority of both the House and the Senate (or submitted by the states) to be passed along to the states for ratification. Of those thirty-three only twenty-seven have been ratified into law by three-quarters of the states.*

As with nearly all social movements, most of these started at a grassroots level and grew from there. People passed or defied laws on a local level that echoed all the way up to the federal legislature or Supreme Court. The effort to again put people first in America and the rest of the free world will no doubt work in the same way. As anthropologist Margaret Mead said, "Never doubt that a small group of thoughtful, committed citizens can change the world. Indeed, it is the only thing that ever has."[7]

Nonetheless a grassroots revolution won't be rapid or easy. Consider the history of another group who set out to establish equality in America: women of the Revolutionary Era and their successors.

The Battle for Human Rights as a Model

The history of the Women's Rights Movement, like that of the Civil Rights Movement, is complex and well beyond the scope of this book, but it claimed its first major victory in 1920 with the passage of the Nineteenth Amendment, which gave women the right to vote.

---

*Amending America by Richard B. Bernstein is a brilliant book on the process.

But that was just the beginning. A hundred and one years after Susan B. Anthony was arrested for casting a vote, the U.S. Supreme Court referenced the Fourteenth Amendment a total of seventeen times regarding people in the 1973 *Roe v. Wade* case, as the Court finally decided that men don't have the power to control the behaviors of women. That decision, combined with broad changes in public sentiment and corporate behavior, effectively overturned the 1873 *Bradwell v. State* Supreme Court decision which had said that "the Law of the Creator" defined the "paramount destiny and mission" of women as limited to "the noble and benign offices of wife and mother."

The process began with a small group of dedicated people, and America and the world are the better for it, even as the Women's Rights Movement continues to work for full equality in the United States and recognition in those nations where women are still in slavery under religious law or male-dominated dictatorships.

Similarly, as Martin Luther King Jr. and Mohandas Gandhi well understood, changing laws is a process that requires enormous and broad grassroots support. Recent events have shocked and awakened many people in the world, and expressions of a desire for change—from riots at WTO meetings to tectonic shifts in the politics of nations—are increasingly obvious.

But many of these efforts to protest globalization or poverty or corporate crimes are less than effective because they attack the symptoms of the problem rather than its cause.

The new feudalism is not the result of bad people or even bad corporations. It's the result of a structure that's broken down. A system of laws put in place in the United States and other nations in the late 1700s and early 1800s that had controlled the size, power, and political influence of the newly emerging business corporations was thrown aside first by the pen of J. C. Bancroft Davis in 1886 and then by hundreds of other advocates of corporate power and great wealth, from the railroad tycoons and robber barons to many of the members of today's Supreme Court and Congress.

At its core it's the result of a dysfunctional cultural story—that corporations are persons—and that is the level at which it must be healed.

Our best hope for changing the current situation of the world is in restoring the story and the vision of Jefferson and Madison—that corporations (and governments and all institutions) are subservient to the will of We the People. Restoring the control mechanism for this—effectively struck down by the *Santa Clara* ruling—means changing our laws and, ultimately, probably will require amending our Constitution.

Reclaiming Democracy

What should our new Constitution look like? Several proposals are on that table, but I particularly recommend the models put forth by Jeff Milchen and David Cobb. Jeff's Web site, www.reclaimdemocracy.org, is one of the leading resources on the issues of corporate personhood; and David's site, www .movetoamend.org, incorporates Jeff's proposed Constitutional amendment below as well as several other options. Milchen's proposed constitutional amendment, more explicitly than simply inserting the word *natural* before the word *person* in the Fourteenth Amendment, could seriously begin the process of turning the United States into a democratic republic responsive and responsible to its citizens instead of its most powerful corporations. The proposed amendment states:

> **Section 1.** The U.S. Constitution protects only the rights of living human beings.
>
> **Section 2.** Corporations and other institutions granted the privilege to exist shall be subordinate to any and all laws enacted by citizens and their elected governments.
>
> **Section 3.** Corporations and other for-profit institutions are prohibited from attempting to influence the outcome of elections, legislation or government policy through the use of aggregate resources or by rewarding or repaying employees or directors to exert such influence.
>
> **Section 4.** Congress shall have power to implement this article by appropriate legislation.

Other variations on this amendment, some simpler and some more complex, can be found at www.movetoamend.org.

Prepare for SCOTUS Resistance

Grassroots groups who mobilize to defeat corporate hegemony should prepare to encounter a hostile U.S. Supreme Court. The Constitution does not give the Supreme Court the power to strike down laws as "unconstitutional" or to interpret the Constitution in their own unique way (which invariably changes from Court to Court). As noted earlier, that power was taken on by the Court in 1803 by Chief Justice John Marshall in the case of *Marbury v. Madison* and caused then-president Thomas Jefferson to cry out in anguish that the single unelected branch of government had taken onto itself such power that the Constitution itself was now in danger.

Eighteen years later former-president Jefferson still saw an unelected Court with the power to overrule Congress and the president as a threat to democracy in America. On November 23, 1821, in a letter to his old friend Nathaniel Macon, one of the most outspoken of the Founders against the power of the Marshall Court, Jefferson wrote: "Our government is now taking so steady a course as to show by what road it will pass to destruction, to wit: by consolidation first, and then corruption, its necessary consequence. The engine of consolidation will be the federal judiciary; the two other branches, the corrupting and corrupted instruments."[8]

And by granting corporate personhood—a doctrine never ever laid out in legislation, state or federal, and never proposed by any president—the unelected Court has led us directly to Jefferson's corrupting consolidation of power in the hands of transnational corporate "persons."

The Court has occasionally used this power, which was not explicitly granted to it in the Constitution, to be ahead of the curve of social change, beating federal legislatures to the punch on things like desegregation of schools in 1954 (*Brown v. Board of Education of Topeka*) and legalizing birth control in 1965 (*Griswold v. Connecticut*) and abortion in 1973 (*Roe v. Wade*).

On the other hand, it has also used the power in very regressive fashions, striking down as unconstitutional laws that protected unionization (*Adair v. United States*, 1908), a minimum wage (*Adkins v. Children's Hospital*, 1923), and full rights of African Americans (*Dred Scott v. Sanford*, 1858, and *Plessy v. Ferguson*, 1896).

Since *Marbury* in 1803, the "solution" to the "problem" (perceived by both the right and the left) of the Court's overreaching power has been either to amend the Constitution (the one thing to which the Court *must* defer) or to elect a president who would appoint Supreme Court justices more in tune with the times.*

Legislative Solutions

British history offers one potentially useful legislative solution that I'd strongly recommend reviving (though perhaps without the snakes): the "Bubble Act"

---

*When, during the New Deal, the Supreme Court struck down some of FDR's progressive legislation, he contemplated expanding the number of members of the Court—something that could legally be done, as the number of justices is not specified in the Constitution—but the political blowback from his attempt to "pack the Court" was so severe that it cost him and the Democratic party dearly.

was the first and arguably last pushback against corporate power in the United Kingdom. It was desperately needed, and it worked for as long as citizens let it stand.[9]

When the British East India Company was incorporated in 1601, it was the first of many. By 1710 corporations were being created left and right in England, and the following year one particularly toxic one—the Enron of its day—was formed: the South Seas Company.

Like Enron or AIG, the company was running a series of major "betting" ("insurance" or "derivitive") scams, and like Enron and AIG its stock value exploded—only to crash in 1720, a crash so bad that it endangered the entire British economy.

Mobs turned out in the streets of London and other British cities. John Blunt, one of the company's more high-profile directors, was shot dead. A member of Parliament publicly called for the rest of the directors of the company to be sewn into bags along with snakes and drowned in the Thames.

Like in 1929 and 2008, average investors were rushing into the growing stock market. "Women sold their jewels" to buy stock in the company, and the well-off like Jonathan Swift were burned terribly when the company crashed in 1720—bringing with it the entire British stock market. Swift even wrote a famous poem about the experience, titled *The Bubble.*

Parliament responded to the entire mess by making illegal *all* corporations except those, like the British East India Company, that had been explicitly chartered and authorized by Parliament itself. The 1720 "Bubble Act" lasted more than a century, until corporations engineered its repeal in 1825.

The question Americans face now is whether our politicians have the power and the will to pass this nation's and this generation's equivalent of the Bubble Act (or a variation thereof) or whether corporate power—particularly given the recent *Citizens United* case—has grown so great that it is now impossible for any politician to step out of line without getting politically squashed like a bug. There is in fact recent precedent for just that, in a time when corporations had even less legal power (but, arguably, more extralegal power) than they do today.

An American Coup Attempt

Similarly, in the mid-1930s in the United States, following the Roaring Twenties stock market bubble that ended in the Great Crash of 1929 and the Republican Great Depression, President Franklin D. Roosevelt directly took on corporate power in the United States for the first time since the presidency of Zachary Taylor.

The corporate response was ferocious, and the memory of that may be why no president since has followed in Roosevelt's footsteps.

The summer of 1934 was a watershed. In July of that year, the cover story of *Fortune* magazine sang the praises of Mussolini's new economic/political invention. The opening paragraph read:

> "Fascism is a religion," says Mussolini. And he also says, "The twentieth century will be known in history as the Century of Fascism." To look at these two statements and then to realize that Fascism has all but conquered half of Europe and part of Asia is to wonder whether Fascism is achieving in a few years or decades such a conquest of the spirit of man as Christianity achieved only in ten centuries.

The article closed with this summary, reflecting an opinion held by many of America's business elite. After qualifying that, "No 100 percent journalist can be more than a few percent Fascist," the magazine's concluding paragraph said: "But the good journalist must recognize in Fascism certain ancient virtues of the race, whether or not they happen to be momentarily fashionable in his own country. Among these are Discipline, Duty, Courage, Glory, Sacrifice."[10]

As General Motors was building trucks for Hitler, and IBM was helping him organize lists of Jews across Germany, a group of American businessmen decided to stop Franklin Roosevelt from trying to limit the power of their corporations.

August 22, 1934, was a beautiful summer day in Philadelphia. The sky was clear, the afternoon air 81 degrees after a comfortable 68-degree overnight. The nation's most famous and highly decorated Marine general, Smedley Butler, walked through the sunny afternoon to the Bellevue Hotel, where, in the elegant lobby, he met a bond trader by the name of Gerald MacGuire.

Retiring to a quiet corner of the hotel's café, the two men talked. MacGuire explained how a group of businessmen wanted to organize as many as a half-million military veterans to come together with Butler as their leader and overthrow Roosevelt as president. "We might go along with Roosevelt and then do with him what Mussolini did with the king of Italy,"[11] MacGuire told Butler, going on to say that the group of businessmen he represented could put $3 million on the table that day and had up to $300 million if necessary (well over $300 billion in today's money).

MacGuire was employed by Grayson Murphy, the director of the American Liberty League, a group incorporated to "generally foster free enterprise,"[12] whose executives were also executives at J. P. Morgan and DuPont, with funding from "the Pitcairn family, Andrew Mellon Associates, Rockefeller Associates, E. F. Hutton Associates, William Knudsen of General Motors, and the V. Pew family."[13]

Butler turned down the offer and went public with the plot, stopping it in its tracks. Congress held hearings into it for a few days, but Roosevelt stopped them, concerned that with all the publicity others may get the same idea and try to end his presidency. As a result, most Americans today don't even know about the very real and serious plot to overthrow constitutional democracy and replace it with fascism in the United States of America.

Today many politicians avoid the threat of a coup—or of being destroyed politically by an industry carpet-bombing the nation with television advertising, as the health insurance industry did in the first years of the Clinton administration—by publicly being populists but legislatively going along with the biggest corporations in America.

Pushing Back against Third Way Politics

In the decade following the "Reagan revolution" in the United States and the "Thatcher revolution" in the United Kingdom, both Tony Blair and Bill Clinton faced a problem. The traditional constituencies of both Labour in the U.K. and the Democratic Party in the U.S. had been organized labor—unions; and when Reagan declared war on organized labor by busting PATCO in 1981, and Maggie Thatcher took on and beat Britain's largest and most powerful union (the coal miners) in 1984, by the early 1990s organized labor was on life support.

Corporate support had gone totally in the direction of the Conservatives in the United Kingdom and the Republicans in the United States, and the amounts of money it was starting to cost in the new TV era to run a national campaign (particularly in the U.S.) were beyond what could be raised just from a union and union-household base.

So Blair and Clinton came up with something new. Blair coined it "Third Way" politics, renaming his faction of his party "New Labour," while Bill Clinton's "Third Way" meant plugging himself into the Democratic Leadership Council (DLC) and calling himself a "New Democrat." What both meant was that while they still spoke up for the little guy, they were mostly for sale to the highest corporate bidder and would ensure that the wheels of industry were well greased.

Blair continued the pressure on the unions, while Clinton famously "ended welfare as we know it" and rolled back other New Deal and Great Society programs that both conservatives and corporations found offensive.

Banks and investment houses in the United States were allowed to merge in 1999 when the Gramm-Leach-Bliley Act blew up Glass-Steagall; and in 2000, with the passage of the Commodities Futures Modernization Act, these now-can-gamble banks were allowed to "invent" a new "commodity" they could sell in virtually unlimited fashion: bets on bets on bets on mortgages called credit default swaps and collateralized debt obligations. The economy boomed, or at least seemed to until the bubble inflated in 1999 burst in 2008.

One of the strongest forces supporting the continuing domination of corporations over our nation is the misplaced faith in toxic Third Way politics, in which Democratic politicians accomplish traditionally Republican goals of increasing corporatism. Sometimes it gets hard to tell who's who on the scorecard.

For example, during the big health-care debate of 2009/2010, forty-two Republican state legislators in Florida united their efforts to amend the Florida Constitution to exempt the state from any health-care reforms that the Obama administration may pass. In this they were following the efforts suggested by the American Legislative Exchange Council, which had already helped get such constitutional amendments or laws on the legislative agendas of fourteen states—before any health-care legislation had even been voted on by both houses of Congress.

In the last week of 2009, David D. Kirkpatrick, writing for the *New York Times,* pointed out some troubling dimensions of these actions. In his article, "Health Care Industry Takes Fight to the States," Kirkpatrick wrote that the forty-two Florida Republican legislators "were almost all recipients of outsize campaign contributions from major health care interests, a total of about $765,000 in 2008..."[14]

And the American Legislative Exchange Council? "Five of the 24 members of its 'free enterprise board' are executives of drug companies and its health care 'task force' is overseen in part by a four-member panel composed of government-relations officials for the BlueCross BlueShield Association of insurers, the medical company Johnson & Johnson and the drugmakers Bayer and Hoffman–La Roche."[15]

Every industrialized country in the world—and some not so industrialized, like Costa Rica (which has lower health-care costs than the United States and better outcomes)—has defined health care as a *right* rather than a *privilege*. Rights are defended by governments; it's one of the main reasons for creating governments, along with defending the commons.

Historically in the United States, conservatives and liberals differed—in terms of public policy—on one major philosophical point. Both agreed that the U.S. government was founded on the principle of protecting rights and the commons, commonly referred to as the "public good"—the "general welfare" that is spelled out twice in the Constitution—but conservatives and liberals historically looked at the dimensions of that public good, and how it should be protected and delivered, in very different ways.

Conservatives felt that government involvement in the public good should be limited to police and the military. Most were even wary of public schools and fire departments, preferring to let corporations handle such functions.

Liberals, on the other hand, felt that the public good included a wider array of public services, including the right to health care, education, freedom from hunger and homelessness, and, of course, police and the military. All of these functions, liberals believe, are among the obligations of government and thus should fall within the functions of government rather than private corporations.

But when Third Way politics began to arise in the 1980s, it brought with it the curious doctrine that *all* government functions—even the military and police—could be better handled by private corporate interests than by government itself, that government was inherently an evil force that never produced any good whatsoever, or at least when it tried it did so inefficiently. Therefore the military should be augmented by, and ultimately replaced by, private mercenaries. The Postal Service should be privatized. Ditto for Social Security and Medicare and public schools.

At their core Third Way politicians assert that the liberal perspective on the responsibility of government is correct—government should make sure that people are free from fear of illness, homelessness, and hunger and have access to a good education. But, unlike traditional liberals, they believe that all of these functions should be *paid for* by the government but actually *provided* by private corporations.

In this the Third Way movement represents a merging of business and governmental interests; it offends conservatives because taxes must be raised to pay for all these things, and it causes liberals to talk of Mussolini's "corporate state" because of the close merger of corporate and political interests.

Bill Clinton pursued Third Way politics by transforming welfare into workfare, pushing the charter school agenda, proposing a government-paid-for but privately run health-care system (which was not passed), pushing through Congress the GATT and NAFTA agreements, and embracing the use of private contractors for military operations. President George W. Bush, while publicly saying that he was a conservative, continued and dramatically expanded the Third Way initiatives of Clinton, although he did so in such a fiscally irresponsible way that he turned an inherited budget surplus into the largest budget deficit in the world and in the history of the United States.

President Barack Obama has continued many of Clinton's and Bush's programs, along with promoting more Third Way programs such as his health-care initiative, which could end up with American workers in the middle class paying more to private insurance companies every year than they pay in taxes.

The Third Way is ultimately toxic to democracy. On the other hand, given how an unelected Supreme Court has so fundamentally changed the historic relationship between We the People and corporations, it's about the only way that Democratic (or Republican) politicians can raise enough money to win elections. Even ethical Democrats find themselves in a terrible bind.

This is why it's so important to roll back these Supreme Court decisions and why the most effective way to do that will be a constitutional amendment unambiguously asserting that corporate persons are not the same as human persons, the latter having "rights" while the former have only those "privileges" that We the People choose to confer on them—and that one of the rights that corporations do *not* have is "free speech."

Then the Big Work Begins

Once corporations are again under the authority of We the People who sanctioned their formation, the real work begins. A whole realm of issues will then become truly open for honest and vigorous debate.

The entire spectrum of human issues that humans should discuss with the governments they have empowered to represent them will once again be open for debate: this is the really vital work that must be done but which cannot be done freely until *Santa Clara* and all her heirs are reversed, whether by Supreme Court decree or by citizens joining together to replace the word "*persons*" in the Fourteenth Amendment with the phrase *natural persons*.

Because *Santa Clara* and its derivatives have been with us for more than a century, correcting it won't instantly change common and case law, but it will provide a basis for us to begin making the changes that could reinvigorate both democracy and free enterprise—and not just in the United States but across the world in the many nations where democracies thrive.

As America goes, to a large extent so goes the world, and it's been that way ever since France followed the American colonists by just six years in revolting against royal institutions that denied human rights to all individuals and reserved them for the rich and powerful.

Alastair McIntosh, a Fellow of the Centre for Human Ecology in Edinburgh, Scotland, points out on his Web site that a multinational corporation recently demanded protection from Scotland's Court of Session (the Scottish supreme court), claiming Article 6 of the European Convention of Human Rights.

"Mammon [material wealth] got up in court and claimed human attributes," McIntosh writes. "It makes instant mockery of our new human rights protection." He points out that the trend of corporations claiming human rights "can be traced across the Atlantic to the case of *Santa Clara County v. Southern Pacific Railroad, 1886.*"[16]

While the exact language of the amendments proposed in this book may not be applicable in all nations that claim democratic principles, similar ones can be passed. It is my hope that this book will inspire people around the world to come up with their own, appropriate language and begin the process of local and national legislative reform in their own nations.

As with the Twenty-sixth Amendment (giving eighteen-year-olds the right to vote), we may get lucky. It could be that so many people are motivated to restore the balance to public discourse that change will happen quickly.

Let Us Begin

The process of reclaiming our lives from corporate domination will most likely take time, and it will surely be fraught with dispute and unintended consequences. Who could have guessed, for example, that a constitutional amendment to free the slaves would end up empowering corporations?

When I was very young, I first discovered the writings of Thomas Jefferson. It was about the same time I was reading Henry David Thoreau and

Ralph Waldo Emerson, and I was entranced with the thoughts of the Transcendentalist Movement in early America. I was touched by Thoreau's vision of the natural world, Emerson's notions about an understanding of the eternal, and Jefferson's romance with the idealisms of his Saxon ancestors; the idealism of all three seemed made of the same cloth.

As Emerson said in 1842, "The light is always identical in its composition, but it falls on a great variety of objects, and by so falling is first revealed to us, not in its own form, for it is formless, but in theirs; in like manner, thought only appears in the objects it classifies."[17]

I'm convinced that the light of idealism and hope is within all of us. In some it shines as the noble desire to build institutions that may both help humanity and enrich the helpers; a desire that, it seems, sometimes extends beyond prudence. In others it shines as the light of a passion to protect loved ones or the natural world of which we are a part.

Addressing the conflict between these two, Emerson added, "Amidst the downward tendency and proneness of things, when every voice is raised for a new road or another statute, or a subscription of stock, for an improvement in dress, or in dentistry, for a new house or a larger business, for a political party, or the division of an estate, will you not tolerate one or two solitary voices in the land, speaking for thoughts and principles not marketable or perishable?"[18]

As Delphin M. Delmas reminds us in his impassioned 1901 defense of the California redwoods, and Gilgamesh's six-thousand-year-old ghost tells us in his tale of weather changes and the destruction of a civilization by commercial practices, this is not a new debate. These are, to again quote Emerson, "but the very oldest of thoughts cast into the mould of these new times."

Rescinding corporate personhood is the first step toward a larger vision of reclaiming and reinvigorating democracy around the world. It is a noble effort, but not the only effort. It is a start, not an end. And if we are to respond usefully to its challenges and to its perhaps unintended consequences, we must do so in the context of the larger vision of egalitarian society and the principles upon which the first democratic republics were founded. (On my Web site at www.thomhartmann.com you'll find a list of grassroots organizations working to end corporate personhood.)

As John F. Kennedy said about the ambitious goals he set for his new administration, "All this will not be finished in the first 100 days. Nor will it be finished in the first 1,000 days, nor in the life of this Administration, nor even perhaps in our lifetime on this planet.

"But let us begin."[19]

Acknowledgments

Today the business once transacted by individuals in every community is in the control of corporations, and many of the men who once conducted an independent business are gathered into the organization, and all personal identity, and all individualities lost. Each man has become a mere cog in one of the wheels of a complicated mechanism. It is the business of the corporations to get money. It exacts but one thing of its employees: Obedience to orders. It cares not about their relations to the community, the church, society, or the family. It wants full hours and faithful service, and when they die, wear out or are discharged, it quickly replaces them with new material.

The corporation is a machine for making money, but it reduces men to the insignificance of mere numerical figures, as certainly as the private ranks of the regular army.

—Fighting Bob La Follette, speech on the Dangers
Threatening Representative Government,
Mineral Point, Wisconsin, July 4, 1897

I AM DEEPLY INDEBTED TO A NUMBER OF PEOPLE FOR THEIR HELP IN THE creation of this book. Those who particularly helped form and organize my thinking on the subject include David Korten, Richard Grossman of POCLAD, and Thomas Linzey of CELDF. Richard B. Bernstein provided me with many excellent leads, and I was challenged to dig deeper and deeper by our correspondences. Dave deBronkart, who has helped edit several of my books, helped the first edition of this one into its final form, and Neil Wertheimer helped give it birth and structure.

Johanna Vondeling was one of the best editors I've ever worked with—she helped birth this Second Edition, which includes a substantial rewrite of the original book and huge chunks of new material—and I'm honored that a person of her experience and stature would work with me on this. Other people at Berrett-Koehler who helped bring this book into print in its new and improved form include Richard Wilson, Dianne Platner, and Jeevan Sivasubramaniam. Many thanks and much gratitude to a couple of real pros—Gary Palmatier and Elizabeth von Radics of Ideas to Images—for the book's design and copyediting.

So many writers I know these days complain that their editors no longer edit, but that was not my experience with the first edition, for which I'm very grateful to Rodale and to their and my editor, Troy Juliar. Stephanie Tade, Tom Mulderick, Kelly Schmidt, Leslie Schneider, Dana Bacher, and Cindy Ratzlaff of Rodale helped move the first edition of this book along as well—thanks!

Paul Hannam, Tim King, Michael Pottinger, and Rob Kall provided particularly valuable input and suggestions. Thanks to Jayne Kennedy for her research work, to Paul Donovan and Marge Zunder for helping me track down arcane documents in the library in the Vermont Supreme Court building, and to Jane Anne Morris for sharing her illuminating documentation of former laws in the state of Wisconsin.

Daniel Brannen of CELDF spent many long hours with law books from every state in the union in putting together the proposed ordinances and constitutional amendments in the first edition, for which I am very grateful. My agent, Bill Gladstone, helped move this project along and provided valuable input. Special thanks to Michael Kinder, who waded through piles of nineteenth-century documents in the Library of Congress to find the personal correspondences of Morrison R. Waite and J. C. Bancroft Davis that were pivotal to a chapter of this book. Thanks also to Paula Bennet, who provided valuable insights into the women's suffrage movement, and to Kathy Roeder of the AFL-CIO, who took the time to track down details for me and return my calls.

I'm very grateful to Jock Gill, Jack Rieley, and Jaye Mueller, who often pointed me in the right directions and kept me focused on track and on issue, and to Judy Kahrl, who brought to my attention the important difference between citizenship and personhood in relation to the Fourteenth Amendment. William Meyers has done us all a great service by writing and publishing in the public domain his paper "Santa Clara Blues," on the Internet at www.iiipublishing.com, and I gratefully thank him for the added permission to reprint. Jeff Gates also gave me the valuable gift of allowing republication of more than just a "fair use" portion of his words, and I both thank him and recommend to you his several books and his Web site at www.sharedcapitalism.org.

Chanin Rotz sent articles from the *Fulton County News,* Roger C. Parker gave valuable editorial suggestions and encouragement, and Scott Berg and

Bob Koski were particularly important sources of information and reference. Thanks to Booth Gunter and Shannon Little of Public Citizen and to B. J. Kinkade for sharing her story with me. And the folks at Bear Pond Books and Montpelier's Kellogg-Hubbard Library were also very helpful in my early research efforts. Thank you all.

Throughout the research and writing of this book, I've tried to be as clear and accurate as possible. No doubt there are errors in a work of this size, and the responsibility for them is mine, and not that of the people I thanked above.

Notes

Introduction: The Battle to Save Democracy

1. W.E.B. Du Bois' *Black Reconstruction in America 1860–1880* (1935; New York: Free Press, 1998) puts this in context brilliantly and includes long and detailed quotes from and commentary on Thaddeus Stevens's floor speeches on this topic.

2. http://www.youtube.com/watch?v=iivL4c_3pck&.

3. Alexander Hamilton, Federalist Papers (No. 84), http://www.foundingfathers.info/federalistpapers/fed84.htm.

4. Ibid.

CHAPTER 1: *The Deciding Moment?*

1. *Santa Clara County v. Southern Pacific Railroad Co.,* 118 U.S. 394 (1886), http://caselaw.lp.findlaw.com/scripts/getcase.pl?court=US&vol=118&invol=394.

2. D. M. Delmas, *Speeches and Addresses* (San Francisco: A. M. Robinson, 1901). A first edition is in the library of the author. Delmas's quotations in this section come from this volume.

3. Blackstone, Book I, 123 (reference from Delmas; see note 2 above). Blackstone's *Commentaries to the Constitution and Laws of the Federal Government of the United States* (Philadelphia: Birch and Small, 1803).

4. *Connecticut General Life Insurance Company v. Johnson,* 303 U.S. 77 (1938).

5. *Wheeling Steel Corp. v. Glander,* 337 U.S. 562 (1949). Justice Douglas dissents. Regarding the ruling that corporations are given rights as persons under the Fourteenth Amendment, he said, "There was no history, logic or reason given to support that view nor was the result so obvious that exposition was unnecessary."

6. Grover Cleveland, State of the Union address, December 3, 1888, http://stateoftheunion address.org/category/grover-cleveland.

7. *First National Bank of Boston v. Bellotti,* 435 U.S. 765 (1978).

8. Associated Press, "Rehnquist Challenged Minority Voters, 3 Say," *Toledo Blade,* July 26, 1986. The article asserts that Rehnquist "directed ballot security programs for Republicans in Phoenix from 1958 through 1964" and, according to three of his then-colleagues, was "a young eager beaver, a highly partisan Republican who was going to try and stop as many Democratic votes as he could." The eyewitnesses testified that "Justice Rehnquist 'approached a black gentleman and said: "Are you qualified to vote?" He (the black man) quietly left the line, and it happened again,' Mr. Pine recounted."

9. Richard L. Grossman and Frank T. Adams, *Taking Care of Business: Citizenship and the Charter of Incorporation* (S. Yarmouth, MA: Charter Ink, 1999), http://www.ratical.org/corporations/TCoB.txt.

10. Charles Beard and Mary Beard, *The Rise of American Civilization* (1927; Whitefish, MT: Kessinger, 2005).

11. Howard Jay Graham, *Everyman's Constitution: Historical Essays on the Fourteenth Amendment, the "Conspiracy Theory," and American Constitutionalism* (Madison: State Historical Society of Wisconsin, 1968).

334

CHAPTER 2: *The Corporate Conquest of America*

1. *First National Bank of Boston v. Bellotti,* 435 U.S. 765 (1978).
2. *Marshall v. Barlow's, Inc.,* 436 U.S. 307 (1978).
3. *Liggett v. Lee,* 288 U.S. 517 (1933).
4. The correspondence between Abigail Adams and John Adams is available at http://www.masshist.org/digitaladams/aea/letter.
5. For more on this subject see http://lcweb2.loc.gov/ammem/awhhtml/awlaw3/property_law.html.
6. Quoted in Sharada Rath, *Women in Public Administration of the American States: A Study of their Administrative Values* (New Delhi: M.D. Publications, 1998), 41.
7. *Plessy v. Ferguson,* 163 U.S. 537 (1896).
8. *Connecticut General Co. v. Johnson,* 303 U.S. 77 (1938).

CHAPTER 3: *Banding Together for the Common Good*

1. Bruce Bower, "'Modern' Humans Get an Ancient, Nonhuman Twist: Two New Reports Suggest That Hominids Other Than *Homo Sapiens* Made Complex Stone Tools and Fancy Necklaces," *Science News,* January 16, 2010, http://www.sciencenews.org/index/generic/activity/view/id/54973/title/Modern_humans_get_an_ancient%2C_nonhuman_twist.
2. For a full searchable text of the Kojiki, see http://sunsite.berkeley.edu/jhti/Kojiki.html; for more on the Nihon Shoki, see http://www.search.com/reference/Nihon_Shoki.
3. See http://en.wikipedia.org/wiki/Pachacuti and http://www.mythicjourneys.org/bigmyth/myths/english/eng_inca_culture.htm.
4. L. L. Blake, *The Young People's Book of the Constitution* (London: Sherwood Press, 1987).

CHAPTER 4: *The Boston Tea Party Revealed*

1. Albert J. Beveridge, *Abraham Lincoln: 1809–1858* (Cambridge, MA: Riverside Press, 1928). From the introduction by his wife, quoting him at an earlier date.
2. R. Buckminster Fuller, *Grunch of Giants* (Summertown, TN: Book Publishing Company, 2004), http://www.bfi.org/?q=node/408.
3. Ibid.
4. The history of the East India Company is well documented in innumerable sources. Much of this information comes from the company's own Web site at http://www.theeastindiacompany.com.
5. From http://www.theeastindiacompany.com. (This quote has since been taken off the company's Web site, but it can likely be found in any of the six books the East India Company has written about itself, published by HarperCollins.)
6. From *Encyclopedia Britannica Online* at http://www.britannica.com/EBchecked/topic/74947/Boston-Tea-Party.
7. From http://www.theeastindiacompany.com (circa 2002).
8. Ibid.
9. Unless otherwise noted, all quotations in this discussion of George R. T. Hewes are from Esther Forbes, *Paul Revere and the World He Lived In* (Boston: Houghton Mifflin, 1942).

10. *A Retrospect of the Boston Tea-Party with a Memoir of George R. T. Hewes, a Survivor of the Little Band of Patriots Who Drowned the Tea in Boston Harbour in 1773* (New York: S. S. Bliss, 1834). All subsequent quotes from Hewes in this chapter are from this volume.

11. *The Alarm* pamphlet signed by Rusticus (May 27, 1773). *Rusticus* is slang term of the time for *peasant,* based on the 1577 *Rusticus in Gallia* drawing of a French peasant from *Habitus,* a book on the dress of the nations of Europe by Hans Weigel. There is an impressive online collection of *The Alarm* and other broadsides and pamphlets at http://memory.loc.gov/ammem/rbpehtml.

12. Ibid.

13. *The Alarm* pamphlet signed by Hampden (October 27, 1773). This one can be viewed at http://hdl.loc.gov/loc.rbc/rbpe.1050090d.

14. From *Encyclopedia Britannica Online* at http://www.britannica.com/EBchecked/topic/74947/Boston-Tea-Party.

CHAPTER 5: *Jefferson versus the Corporate Aristocracy*

1. James Madison, speech in the House of Representatives, April 9, 1789, in James Madison, *The Writings of James Madison,* vol. 5., ed. Gaillard Hunt (New York: G. P. Putnam, 1900): 342–45.

2. James Madison, "Republican Distribution of Citizens," *National Gazette,* March 3, 1792, http://olldownload.libertyfund.org/?option=com_staticxt&staticfile=show.php%3F title=875&chapter=63884&layout=html&Itemid=27.

3. Andrew Jackson, fifth annual message to Congress, December 3, 1833, http://miller center.org/scripps/archive/speeches/detail/3640.

4. James Madison to James K. Paulding, March 10, 1827, http://oll.libertyfund.org/ ?option=com_staticxt&staticfile=show.php%3Ftitle=1940&chapter=119324&layout= html&Itemid=27.

5. A statement by Albert Gallatin, who later became secretary of the Treasury after the Federalists lost power.

6. This early draft of the Declaration of Independence can be viewed at http://www.us history.org/declaration/document/rough.htm.

7. Thomas Jefferson to James Madison, December 20, 1787, http://teachingamerican history.org/library/index.asp?document=306.

8. Thomas Jefferson to Alexander Donald, February 7, 1788, http://press-pubs.uchicago .edu/founders/documents/a7s12.html.

9. Thomas Jefferson to Mr. Dumas, February 12, 1788.

10. Thomas Jefferson to James Madison, July 31, 1788, http://teachingamericanhistory.org/ library/index.asp?document=998.

11. Thomas Jefferson to Francis Hopkinson, March 13, 1789, http://www.let.rug.nl/usa/P/ tj3/writings/brf/jefl75.htm.

12. Thomas Jefferson to John Adams, October 28, 1813, http://www.let.rug.nl/usa/P/tj3/ writings/brf/jefl223.htm.

CHAPTER 6: *The Early Role of Corporations in America*

1. Alfons J. Beitzinger and Edward G. Ryan, *Lion of the Law* (Madison: State Historical Society of Wisconsin, 1960), 115–16. From an 1873 address to the graduating class of the University of Wisconsin Law School.

2. Jane Anne Morris is a brilliant researcher, and I gratefully owe much of the Wisconsin-related content of this chapter to her work and thank her for her generous permission to share it with you. The examples in this list are from her "Fixing Corporations: The Legacy of the Founding Parents" at http://www.populist.com/6.96.Fixing.Corps.html.

3. Wis. G.L. 1864, Ch. 166, Sec. 7; Wis. R.S. 1878, Sec. 1767. See the "reserved power" clause.

4. Wis. AG. Op. (1913), Vol. 2, 169.

5. Act of August 21, 1848, Wis. Laws, p. 148 (Gen. Incorp. for Plank Roads).

6. State ex rel. *Kropf v. Gilbert,* 251 N. W. 478 (1934).

7. Dudley O. McGovney, "A Supreme Court Fiction: Corporations in the Diverse Citizenship Jurisdiction of the Federal Courts," *Harvard Law Review* 16 (1943): 853–98, 1090–1124, 1225–60.

8. Wis. R.S. 1878, Sec. 1776; Wis. Stat. 1931, 180.13.

9. Wis. G.L. 1864, Ch. 166, Sec. 9.

10. Wis. G.L. 1864, Ch. 166, Secs. 4, 33.

11. Wis. R.S. 1878, Sec. 1775.

12. Wis. R.S. 1849, Ch. 54 Sec. 7; Wis. G.L. 1864, Ch. 166, Secs. 6, 15.

13. And it was a felony to do so. Wis. State 1953, Ch. 346.12–346.15.

14. For example, Wis. G.L. 1864, Ch. 166, Sec. 7.

15. *Stone v. State of Wisconsin,* 94 U.S. 181 (1876).

16. Wis. R.S. 1849, Ch. 54, Sec. 22.

17. Lyman J. Nash, ed. *Wisconsin Statutes 1919, Volume II: Embracing All General Statutes in Force at the Close of the General and Special Sessions of 1919, Consolidated and in Part Revised Pursuant to Sections 43.07, 43.03, 35.18 and 35.19 of These Statutes* (Madison: State of Wisconsin, 1919), sec. 4479a, 1771–1775, http://books.google.com/books?id=6ZCxAAAAMAAJ&pg=PA2299&lpg=PA2299&ots=WxkbUWGxMn&dq=wisconsin+1905+section+4479a&output=text.

18. Richard L. Grossman and Frank T. Adams, *Taking Care of Business: Citizenship and the Charter of Incorporation* (S. Yarmouth, MA: Charter Ink, 1999), http://www.ratical.org/corporations/TCoB.txt.

19. Charles Beard and Mary Beard, *The Rise of American Civilization* (1927; Whitefish, MT: Kessinger, 2005).

20. Thomas Jefferson to Judge Spencer Roane, September 6, 1819, http://teachingamerican history.org/library/index.asp?document=2192.

21. Alexander Hamilton, Federalist Papers (No. 23), http://www.foundingfathers.info/federalistpapers/fed23.htm.

22. James Madison, Federalist Papers (No. 39), http://www.foundingfathers.info/federalist papers/fed39.htm.

23. *McCulloch v. Maryland,* 17 U.S. 316 (1819).

24. *Trustees of Dartmouth College v. Woodward,* 17 U.S. 518 (1819).

25. James Willard Hurst, *The Legitimacy of the Business Corporation in the Law of the United States, 1780–1970* (Charlottesville: University Press of Virginia, 1970).

26. Most of the information in this and the following two paragraphs is from Grossman and Adams, *Taking Care of Business;* see note 18 above.

27. James Madison to Edmund Randolph, September 30, 1783.

28. James Madison, speech in the House of Representatives, April 9, 1789, in James Madison, *The Writings of James Madison, vol.* 5., ed. Gaillard Hunt (New York: G.P. Putnam, 1900): 342–45.

29. From Elizabeth Fleet, "Madison's 'Detatched Memoranda,'" *William and Mary Quarterly* 3, no. 4 (1946), 551–62. See http://www.worldpolicy.org/projects/globalrights/religion/madison-detachedmem.html.

30. James Madison to James K. Paulding, March 10, 1827, in *James Madison's "Advice to My Country,"* ed. David B. Mattern (Charlottesville: University of Virginia Press, 1997).

31. Thomas Hobbes, *Leviathan* (1651; New York: Oxford University Press, 1996). Here's the quote in context (chapter 29):

> Another infirmity of a Commonwealth is the immoderate greatness of a town, when it is able to furnish out of its own circuit the number and expense of a great army; as also the great number of corporations, which are as it were many lesser Commonwealths in the bowels of a greater, like worms in the entrails of a natural man. To may be added, liberty of disputing against absolute power by pretenders to political prudence; which though bred for the most part in the lees of the people, yet animated by false doctrines are perpetually meddling with the fundamental laws, to the molestation of the Commonwealth, like the little worms which physicians call ascarides.

32. Thomas Jefferson to George Logan, November 12, 1816, http://oll.libertyfund.org/?option=com_staticxt&staticfile=show.php%3Ftitle=808&chapter=88352&layout=html&Itemid=27.

33. Martin Van Buren, first annual message to Congress, December 5, 1837, http://www.presidency.ucsb.edu/ws/index.php?pid=29479.

34. Abraham Lincoln to Thompson R. Webber, September 12, 1853, in *The Collected Works of Abraham Lincoln,* ed. Roy P. Basler (Piscataway, NJ: Rutgers University Press, 1953), 2:202.

35. Ibid.

36. Abraham Lincoln to Mason Brayman, September 12, 1853, in Basler, *Collected Works,* 2:205.

37. *Illinois Central Railroad v. County of McLean,* 17 Ill. 291 (1856).

38. Charles L. Capen to John G. Drennan, April 6, 1906, MSS. Files Legal Dept. I.C.R.R.Co.

39. Adlai E. Stevenson's statement, April 6, 1906, MSS. Files Legal Dept. I.C.R.R.Co.

40. I.C.R.R.Co. notice published in the New York papers and signed by the railroad's treasurer, J. N. Perkins.

41. *Central Illinois Gazette,* April 14, 1858.

42. Henry Clay Whitney to William H. Herndon, August 27, 1887, in Albert J. Beveridge, *Abraham Lincoln* (Riverside Press, 1928).

43. Ibid.

44. Ibid.

45. John F. Stover, *History of the Illinois Central Railroad* (New York: Macmillan, 1976).

46. Ibid.

47. Ibid.

48. Carl Sandburg, *Abraham Lincoln* (New York: Harcourt, Brace, and World, 1926).

49. Emanuel Hertz, *Abraham Lincoln: A New Portrait* (New York: Horace Liveright, 1931), 2:954. In my 1931 first-edition copy of this book, this note by Lincoln is not addressed and is unsigned. Dale Carnegie tells a famous story, in his book *How to Win Friends and Influence People,* about how Lincoln would often write letters to others or even to himself expressing his greatest concerns and then hide them away, often to be later destroyed. It's my guess that this letter was one of those, later found by Hertz as he collected Lincoln's personal effects in the early decades after Lincoln's death. From its order in Hertz's book, this letter sits between a signed and dated letter to Secretary of War Edward Stanton on November 10, 1864, and a signed note about Colonel Ward Hill Lamon dated November 29, 1854. Hertz certifies it is in Lincoln's hand but gives us no clues as to whom he wrote the note to or how he planned to send or dispose of it before his death.

50. Abraham Lincoln, fourth annual message to Congress, December 6, 1864, http://www .presidency.ucsb.edu/ws/index.php?pid=29505.

51. Howard Zinn, *A People's History of the United States: 1492–Present* (New York: Harper-Perennial, 2001).

52. Chester Arthur, second annual message to Congress, December 4, 1882, http://www .presidency.ucsb.edu/ws/index.php?pid=29523.

53. "Slaughterhouse Cases," 83 U.S. 36, 81 (1873).

54. The cases, all in 1877, are: *Chicago, Burlington, and Quincy Railroad Company v. Iowa,* 94 U.S. 155; *Peik v. Chicago and North-Western Railway Company,* 94 U.S. 164; *Chicago, Milwaukee, and St. Paul Railroad Company v. Ackley,* 94 U.S. 179; and *Winona and St. Peter Railroad Company v. Blake,* 94 U.S. 180.

55. *San Mateo County v. Southern Pacific Railroad,* 83 U.S. 36 (1873).

56. *Connecticut General Life Insurance Company v. Johnson,* 303 U.S. 77 (1938).

CHAPTER 7: *The People's Masters*

1. http://www.monthlyreview.org/598einstein.php.

2. Peter Kellman, *Building Unions: Past, Present, and Future* (New York: Apex Press, 2001).

3. Howard Zinn, *A People's History of the United States: 1492–Present* (New York: Harper-Perennial, 2001).

4. Ibid.

5. Grover Cleveland, fourth annual message to Congress, December 3, 1888, http://www .presidency.ucsb.edu/ws/index.php?pid=29529&st=cleveland&st1=. All of Cleveland's quotations in this section are from this speech.

6. Report of the Committee on General Laws on the Investigation Relative to Trusts, March 6, 1888.

7. House Trust Investigation, 1888, 316, 317.

8. Ibid.

9. Ibid.

10. Senator John Sherman quoted in Frederick M. Rowe, "The Decline of Antitrust and Delusions of Models: The Faustian Pact of Law and Economics," *Georgetown Law Journal* 72 (June 1984): 1511.

11. Theodore Roosevelt, sixth annual message to Congress, December 3, 1906, http:// www.presidency.ucsb.edu/ws/index.php?pid=29547.

12. Theodore Roosevelt, seventh annual message to Congress, December 3, 1907, http://www.presidency.ucsb.edu/ws/index.php?pid=29548.

13. Greg Coleridge, *Citizens over Corporations: A Brief History of Democracy in Ohio and Challenges to Freedom in the Future* (Ohio Committee on Corporations, Law, and Democracy: 1999).

14. Carl Sandburg, *Abraham Lincoln* (New York: Harcourt, Brace, and World, 1926).

15. James Willard Hurst, *The Legitimacy of the Business Corporation in the Law of the United States, 1780–1970* (Charlottesville: University Press of Virginia, 1970).

16. State of Delaware Web site at http://corp.delaware.gov/default.shtml.

17. Ralph Nader, Mark Green, and Joel Seligman, *Corporate Power in America* (Norton, 1976).

CHAPTER 8: *Corporations Go Global*

1. Raymond F. Mikesell, *The Bretton Woods Debates: A Memoir* (Princeton: International Finance Section, Department of Economics, Princeton University, 1994).

2. Ibid.

3. Ibid.

4. John Foster Dulles, before a Louisville, Kentucky, American Bar Association meeting, April 11, 1952.

5. Charles Alexander, Evan Thomas, and Frederick Ungeheuer, "Big Doubts about Big Deals," *Time,* August 3, 1981, http://www.time.com/time/magazine/article/0,9171,949280-3,00.html.

6. George Gilder, *Wealth and Poverty* (Richmond, CA: ICS Press, 1993).

7. Comments of Senator Hank Brown in response to his acceptance of Ralph Nader's "$10,000 to Charity GATT Challenge" of November 28, 1994, in which he challenged any member of Congress to actually read the treaty. Brown was the only U.S. senator to accept Nader's challenge, and this is part of his response to Nader, from a 1994 pamphlet from Nader in the author's library.

8. See note 1 above.

9. Thanks to Mark J. Palmer of Earth Island Institute for this information. See http://www.earthisland.org/dolphinSafeTuna.

10. Noreena Hertz, PhD, *The Silent Takeover: Global Capitalism and the Death of Democracy* (London: Heinemann, 2001).

11. Bernie Sanders, "'Fast Track' Hurts Here and Abroad," *Burlington Free Press,* December 14, 2001.

12. Ibid.

13. Paul Geitner, Associated Press, "WTO Rules Against U.S. Law on Tax Breaks," *Burlington Free Press,* January 15, 2002.

14. http://www.epa.gov.

15. http://www.aidc.org.za.

16. Private correspondence with the author, January 2002.

17. Theodore Roosevelt, "A Charter for Democracy" speech at the Ohio State Constitutional Convention, February 21, 1912, http://teachingamericanhistory.org/library/index.asp?document=1126.

18. http://www.un.org/millennium/sg/report/full.htm.

19. Simon Romero, "Union Killings Peril Trade Pact With Colombia," *New York Times,* April 14, 2008, http://www.nytimes.com/2008/04/14/world/americas/14colombia.html.

20. Russ Baker, "Two Years Before 9/11, Candidate Bush was Already Talking Privately About Attacking Iraq, According to His Former Ghost Writer," *CommonDreams.org,* October 28, 2004, http://www.commondreams.org/headlines04/1028-01.htm.

21. James Madison, from "Political Observations," April 20, 1795, in *Letters and Other Writings of James Madison,* vol. 4 (1965).

22. Dwight D. Eisenhower, Farewell Address to the Nation, January 17, 1961, http://mc adams.posc.mu.edu/ike.htm.

23. Dwight D. Eisenhower, "The Chance for Peace," speech before the American Society of Newspaper Editors, April 16, 1953, http://www.informationclearinghouse.info/article9743.htm.

CHAPTER 9: *The Court Takes the Presidency*

1. None dare call it stolen. See Mark Crispin Miller, "Ohio, the Election, and America's Servile Press," *Harper's,* August 2005, http://www.harpers.org/archive/2005/08/0080696.

2. Evan Thomas and Michael Isikoff, "The Truth Behind the Pillars: The Final Act: They Cultivate an Olympian Air, but the Justices Are Quite Human—and Can Be Quite Political," *Newsweek,* December 25, 2000, http://www.newsweek.com/id/104964.

3. Christopher Marquis, "Contesting the Vote: Challenging a Justice; Job of Thomas's Wife Raises Conflict-of-interest Questions," *New York Times,* December 12, 2000, http://www.nytimes.com/2000/12/12/us/contesting-vote-challenging-justice-job-thomas-s-wife-raises-conflict-interest.html.

4. Patrick Martin, "Family Ties, Political Bias Linked U.S. Supreme Court Justices to Bush Camp," *WSWS.org,* December 22, 2000, http://www.wsws.org/articles/2000/dec2000/sup-d22.shtml.

5. Robert Parry, "Rehnquist—Political Puppeteer, *Consortiumnews.com,* January 29, 2001, quoting a U.S. Senate inquiry at the time of the Rehnquist nomination, http://www.consortiumnews.com/2001/012901a.html.

6. Ibid.

7. From http://en.wikipedia.org/wiki/Anthony_Kennedy.

8. Ford Fessenden and John M. Broder, "Study of Disputed Florida Ballots Finds Justices Did Not Cast the Deciding Vote," *New York Times,* November 12, 2001, http://www.nytimes.com/2001/11/12/politics/12VOTE.html?pagewanted=all.

9. Ford Fessenden, "Ballots Cast by Blacks and Older Voters Were Tossed in Far Greater Numbers," *New York Times,* November 12, 2001; http://www.nytimes.com/2001/11/12/politics/recount/12NUMB.html.

10. See note 8 above.

11. Marc Caputo, "Roberts Had Larger 2000 Recount Role," *Miami Herald,* July 28, 2005, http://bellaciao.org/en/article.php3?id_article=7228.

12. *Bush v. Gore,* 531 U.S. 98 (2000).

CHAPTER 10: *Protecting Corporate Liars*

1. http://www.reclaimdemocracy.org/nike/kucinich_nike_colleague_letters.pdf.

2. http://www.corpwatch.org/article.php?id=3448.

3. Ibid.

4. Josh Richman, "Greenwashing on Trial," *Mother Jones,* February 23, 2001, http://mother jones.com/politics/2001/02/greenwashing-trial.

5. http://supreme.lp.findlaw.com/supreme_court/briefs/02-575/02-575.mer.ami.usa.rtf.

6. http://reclaimdemocracy.org/nike/nike_brief_us_supreme.pdf.

7. http://www.reclaimdemocracy.org/personhood/reclaim_kasky_brief.pdf.

CHAPTER 11: *Corporate Control of Politics*

1. Jeffrey Toobin, "No More Mr. Nice Guy," *New Yorker,* May 25, 2009, http://www.new yorker.com/reporting/2009/05/25/090525fa_fact_toobin.

2. Robert Barnes, "Justices to Review Campaign Finance Law Constraints," *Washington Post,* June 30, 2009, http://www.washingtonpost.com/wp-dyn/content/article/2009/06/29/AR2009062903997.html.

3. *Federal Election Commission v. Wisconsin Right to Life,* 551 U.S. 449 (2007), http://www.law.cornell.edu/supct/pdf/06-969P.ZC1.

4. http://www.law.cornell.edu/supct/pdf/06-969P.ZO.

5. http://www.law.cornell.edu/supct/pdf/06-969P.ZD.

6. *Citizens United v. Federal Election Commission,* 558 U.S. __ (2010), http://www.supreme courtus.gov/opinions/09pdf/08-205.pdf.

7. David D. Kirkpatrick, "In a Message to Democrats, Wall St. Sends Cash to G.O.P.," *New York Times,* February 7, 2010, http://www.nytimes.com/2010/02/08/us/politics/08lobby.html.

8. Greg Palast, "Supreme Court to OK Al Qaeda Donation for Sarah Palin?" December 15, 2009, http://www.opednews.com/articles/Supreme-Court-to-OK-Al-Qae-by-Greg-Palast-091215-29.html.

9. Bill Moyers and Michael Winship, "What Are We Bid for American Justice?" *Huffington Post,* February 19, 2010, http://www.huffingtonpost.com/bill-moyers/what-are-we-bid-for-ameri_b_469335.html.

10. Ibid.

11. From Henry A. Wallace, *Democracy Reborn,* ed. Russell Lord (New York: Reynal & Hitchcock, 1944), http://www.newdeal.feri.org/wallace/haw23.htm.

12. Franklin D. Roosevelt, "A Rendezvous with Destiny," speech before the 1936 Democratic National Convention, Philadelphia, Pennsylvania, June 27, 1936.

13. Ibid.

CHAPTER 12: *Unequal Uses for the Bill of Rights*

1. Jeffrey H. Birnbaum, "The Road to Riches Is Called K Street: Lobbying Firms Hire More, Pay More, Charge More to Influence Government," *Washington Post,* June 22, 2005, http://www.washingtonpost.com/wp-dyn/content/article/2005/06/21/AR2005 062101632.html.

2. Ibid.

3. The foregoing examples cited are from Anne C. Mulkern, "When Advocates Become Regulators: President Bush Has Installed More Than 100 Top Officials Who Were Once Lobbyists, Attorneys, or Spokespeople for the Industries They Oversee," *Denver Post,* May 23, 2004, http://www.commondreams.org/headlines04/0523-02.htm.

4. Committee on Communications, American Academy of Pediatrics, "Children, Adolescents, and Advertising," *Pediatrics* 95, no. 5 (1995): 295–97.

5. *Pacific Gas & Electric Co. v. Public Utility Commission of California,* 475 U.S. 1 (1986).

6. Ralph Nader and Carl J. Mayer, "Corporations Are Not Persons," *New York Times,* April 9, 1988.

7. *Marshall v. Barlow's, Inc.,* 436 U.S. 307 (1978); and *See v. City of Seattle,* 387 U.S. 541 (1967).

8. *Hale v. Henkel,* 201 U.S. 43 (1906).

9. William Meyers, *The Santa Clara Blues: Corporate Personhood versus Democracy* (Gualala, CA: III Publishing, 2000), http://www.reclaimdemocracy.org/pdf/primers/santa_clara_blues.pdf.

10. Cited by Nader in the *New York Times* (see note 6 above).

11. *Dow Chemical v. The United States,* 476 U.S. 227 (1986).

12. See note 9 above.

CHAPTER 13: *Unequal Regulation*

1. Robert A. G. Monks and Nell Minow, *Power and Accountability* (New York: Harper-Collins, 1991), http://www.ragm.com/archives/books/poweracc/cover.html.

2. Kurt Eichenwald, "Redesigning Nature: Hard Lessons Learned; Biotechnology Food: From the Lab to a Debacle," *New York Times,* January 25, 2001, http://www.nytimes.com/2001/01/25/business/redesigning-nature-hard-lessons-learned-biotechnology-food-lab-debacle.html?pagewanted=1.

3. Ibid.

4. Ibid.

5. Ibid.

6. Marian Burros, "Shoppers Unaware of Gene Changes," *New York Times,* July 20, 1998, http://www.nytimes.com/1998/07/20/world/shoppers-unaware-of-gene-changes.html?scp=1&sq=Marian%20Burros,%20%E2%80%9CShoppers%20Unaware%20of%20Gene%20Changes,%E2%80%9D%20New%20York%20Times,%2020%20July%201998&st=cse.

7. http://www.commondreams.org/headlines04/0523-02.htm.

8. Paul Hawken, *The Ecology of Commerce* (New York: HarperCollins, 1994).

9. Anne Platt McGinn, "Detoxifying Terrorism," *Worldwatch.org,* November 16, 2001, http://www.worldwatch.org/node/1711.

10. Ibid.

11. http://secret-of-life.org/too-big-to-fail.

12. Julie Brussell, "Our Family Farms: A Final Requiem or a Route to Recovery?" *Conscious Choice,* May 2001, http://www.lime.com/magazines?uri=consciouschoice.com/lime/2001/cc1405/ourfamilyfarms1405.html.

13. Interview with Thomas Linzey, Esq., and POCLAD published in *Defying Corporations, Defining Democracy,* ed. Dean Ritz (New York: Apex Press, 2001).

CHAPTER 14: *Unequal Protection from Risk*

1. *Terry v. Little,* 101 U.S. 216, 217, 25 L.Ed. 864 (1879).

2. Joel Seligman, "A Brief History of Delaware's General Corporation Law of 1899," 1 Del. J. Corp. L. 249, 255–56 (1976).

3. http://www.abanet.org/buslaw/library/onlinepublications/mbca2002.pdf.

4. *Fields v. Synthetic Ropes, Inc.,* 215 A.2d 427, 433 (Del. 1965).

5. Dan Brannen Jr., personal correspondence with the author (ca. 2001).

6. *United States v. Best Foods et al.,* 524 U.S. 51 (1998), http://ftp.resource.org/courts.gov/c/US/524/524.US.51.97-454.html.

7. *Cape Cod Times,* March 27, 1999.

8. http://www.environmentaldefense.org.

9. From a Bill Moyers documentary on the chemical industry titled *Trade Secrets.* A transcript is available at http://www.pbs.org/tradesecrets.

10. David Appell, "The New Uncertainly Principle: For Complex Environmental Issues, Science Learns to Take a Backseat to Political Precaution," *Scientific American,* January 2001, http://www.scientificamerican.com/article.cfm?id=the-new-uncertainty-princ.

11. Bryan A. Garner, ed., *Black's Law Dictionary,* 7th ed. (St. Paul: West Group, 1999), 1393.

CHAPTER 15: *Unequal Taxes*

1. http://www.newportmansions.org.

2. http://www.nps.gov/archive/vama/house_of.html.

3. Annie S. Daniel, "The Wreck of the American Home: How Wearing Apparel Is Fashioned in Tenements" *Charities* 14, no. 1 (April 1905): 624–29.

4. http://www.aflcio.org (ca. 2001).

5. Ibid.

6. John Irons, "Corporate Tax Declines and U.S. Inequality" *EPI.org,* April 9, 2008, http://www.epi.org/economic_snapshots/entry/webfeatures_snapshots_20080409.

7. http://www.aflcio.org (ca. 2001).

8. David C. Korten, *When Corporations Rule the World* (West Harford, CT: Kumarian Press, 2001).

9. http://www.commoncause.org.

10. The Institute on Taxation and Economic Policy 2001 report at http://www.auschron.com.

11. Richard Cohen, "Enron: No Taxes," *Washington Post,* January 22, 2002.

12. From a 2008 study by the GAO, "Comparison of the Reported Tax Liabilities of Foreign- and U.S.-controlled Corporations, 1998–2005," http://www.gao.gov/new.items/d08957.pdf.

13. Ibid.

14. http://www.aflcio.org (ca. 2001).

15. William Ahern, Tax Foundation, "Comparing the Kennedy, Reagan and Bush Tax Cuts," http://www.taxfoundation.org/news/show/323.html.

16. Ibid.

17. All figures taken from Paul A. Gusmorino III, "Main Causes of the Great Depression," *Gusmorino World,* May 13, 1996, http://www.gusmorino.com/pag3/greatdepression/index.html.

18. "Political Dynamite Fails to Explode: Extreme Proposals of Treasury's O'Neill Mostly Unreported," *FAIR.org,* June 13, 2001, http://www.fair.org/activism/o%27neill.html.

19. Paul Vitello, *Newsday,* May 24, 2001. See also note 18.

20. The phone number for the Public Liaison Office of the secretary of the Treasury is (202) 622-1680.

21. Hawken and I had this conversation when he was working on his article "Natural Capitalism" for *Mother Jones* magazine (published in the March/April 1997 issue). The article was later expanded to a book of the same name; see http://www.natcap.org.

22. David Barboza, "Chicago, Offering Big Incentives, Will Be Boeing's New Home," *New York Times*, May 11, 2001, http://www.nytimes.com/2001/05/11/business/chicago-offering-big-incentives-will-be-boeing-s-new-home.html?pagewanted=1.

23. Stephen Moore and Dean Stansel, "How Corporate Welfare Won," Cato Institute, 1996.

24. David C. Korten, *The Post-corporate World* (San Francisco: Berrett-Koehler, 1999).

25. Borden Chemicals, noted by Noreena Hertz, PhD, in *The Silent Takeover* (London: Heinemann, 2001).

26. *New York Times*, September 21, 1995.

27. Donald L. Barlett and James B. Steele, "Corporate Welfare," *Time*, November 9, 1998, http://www.time.com/time/magazine/article/0,9171,989508,00.html.

28. Ibid.

29. Ibid.

30. Ibid.

31. Charles V. Bagli, "Companies Get Second Helping of Tax Breaks," *New York Times*, October 17, 1997, http://www.nytimes.com/1997/10/17/nyregion/companies-get-second-helping-of-tax-breaks.html?pagewanted=1.

32. Greg LeRoy, "No More Candy Store: States and Cities Making Job Subsidies Accountable" (Washington, DC: Good Jobs First, 1994), http://www.goodjobsfirst.org/pdf/nmcs.pdf.

33. Ibid.

34. Joseph G. Lehman, "MEGA Program Shifts Jobs to Where They Are Needed Least," *Mackinac.org*, April 7, 1999, http://www.mackinac.org/1669.

35. See note 31 above.

36. Micah L. Sifry, "At a Time of Sacrifice, Corporations Are Picking Our Pockets," Knight Ridder News Service, November 5, 2001, http://www.progressive.org/media_1731.

37. "Political Donors Profiteering in the Name of Economic Stimulus: Stimulus Legislation Is Lobbying Opportunity of a Lifetime, Says Common Cause," news release, October 25, 2001.

38. http://www.commoncause.org.

39. Sarah Anderson and John Cavanagh, "Top 200: The Rise of Corporate Global Power," The Institute for Policy Studies, December 4, 2000, http://www.corpwatch.org/article.php?id=377; http://s3.amazonaws.com/corpwatch.org/downloads/top200.pdf.

40. Editorial, "Another Casualty of the Left," *Washington Post*, March 15, 1999.

41. Julian Borger, "For Sale: The Race for the White House," *Guardian*, January 7, 2000.

42. Charles Lewis, *The Buying of the President* (New York: Avon Books, 2000).

CHAPTER 16: *Unequal Responsibility for Crime*

1. Peter Montague, "New Strategy Focuses on Corporations," *Rachel's Hazardous Waste News* #309, October 28, 1992, http://www.ratical.com/corporations/RHWN309.html.

2. *Corporate Crime Reporter,* 1998, published by Russell B. Mokhiber, http://corporate crimereporter.com/top100.html.

3. Ibid.

4. Russell Mokhiber and Robert Weissman, "Ball Park Franks Fiasco: 21 Dead, $200,000 Fine," July 26, 2001, for Common Dreams News Center at http://www.common dreams.org.

5. Ibid.

CHAPTER 17: *Unequal Privacy*

1. Elinor Mills, "Privacy Advocate Seeks FTC Probe of Microsoft: Federal Trade Commission Will Pay 'Serious Attention' to Data-gathering Practices," IDG News Service, March 24, 1999, http://www.pcworld.com/article/10262/privacy_advocate_seeks_ftc_probe_of_microsoft.html.

2. Sarah Anderson and John Cavanagh, "Top 200: The Rise of Corporate Global Power," The Institute for Policy Studies, December 4, 2000, http://www.corpwatch.org/article .php?id=377; http://s3.amazonaws.com/corpwatch.org/downloads/top200.pdf.

CHAPTER 18: *Unequal Citizenship and Access to the Commons*

1. Centers for Disease Control and Prevention. Web-based Injury Statistics Query and Reporting System (WISQARS) (2002). National Center for Injury Prevention and Control, Centers for Disease Control and Prevention (producer), March 27, 2003, http://www.cdc.gov/ncipc/wisqars.

2. J. S. Hacker, *The Great Risk Shift: The New Insecurity and the Decline of the American Dream* (New York: Oxford University Press, 2006).

3. http://www.ilo.org.

4. http://www.who.org (June 2001).

5. Elizabeth Warren, "America without a Middle Class, *HuffingtonPost.com,* December 3, 2009, http://www.huffingtonpost.com/elizabeth-warren/america-without-a -middle_b_377829.html.

6. Lauren E. Glaze and Thomas F. Bonczar, Bureau of Justice Statistics, "Probation and Parole in the United States, 2006" (Washington, DC: U.S. Department of Justice, December 2000), http://bjs.ojp.usdoj.gov/content/pub/ascii/ppus06.txt.

7. Bureau of Justice Statistics, "Prisoners in 1996" (Washington, DC: U.S. Department of Justice, 1997).

8. Bureau of Justice Statistics, "Sourcebook of Criminal Justice Statistics, 1996" (Washington, DC: U.S. Department of Justice, 1997), 20; Executive Office of the President, Budget of the United States Government, Fiscal Year 2002 (Washington, DC: U.S. Government Printing Office, 2001), 134.

9. Stephen Nathan, "The Prison Industry Goes Global," *Yes!,* Fall 2000, http://www.yes magazine.org/issues/is-it-time-to-close-the-prisons/the-prison-industry-goes-global.

10. http://www.doc.state.or.us and http://www.cdc.gov.

11. Wackenhut Corporation, news release, February 8, 2002.

12. Michael Grunwald, "How Enron Sought to Tap the Everglades," *Washington Post,* February 8, 2002.

13. James Flanigan, "Enron Is Blazing New Business Trail," *Houston Chronicle,* January 26, 2001.

14. See http://www.ratical.com/ratville/CAH/BechtelBlood.pdf and http://en.wikipedia
.org/wiki/2000_Cochabamba_protests.

15. David C. Korten, "Money versus Wealth," *Yes!,* Spring 1997.

16. Ibid.

17. Maggie McDonald, "International Piracy Rights," review of *Protect or Plunder? Understanding Intellectual Property Rights* by Vandana Shiva, *New Scientist,* January 12, 2002, 23, http://www.newscientist.com/article/mg17323254.500-out-in-paperback.html.

18. Ibid.

19. "Patently Rewarding Work," *New Scientist,* January 12, 2002, 50.

20. Ibid, 51.

21. Karen Hoggan, "Neem Tree Patent Revoked," *BBC News,* May 11, 2000, http://news
.bbc.co.uk/2/hi/science/nature/745028.stm.

22. Anup Shah, "Food Patents—Stealing Indigenous Knowledge?" (September 26, 2002), http://www.globalissues.org/article/191/food-patents-stealing-indigenous-knowledge.

23. David Cay Johnston, "U.S. Companies File in Bermuda to Slash Tax Bills," *New York Times,* February 18, 2002, http://www.nytimes.com/2002/02/18/business/18TAX.html
?pagewanted=all.

24. David Cay Johnston, "Enron's Collapse: The Havens; Enron Avoided Income Taxes in 4 of 5 Years," *New York Times,* January 17, 2002, http://www.nytimes.com/2002/01/17/
business/enron-s-collapse-the-havens-enron-avoided-income-taxes-in-4-of-5-years
.html?pagewanted=1.

25. See note 23.

26. Gar Alperovitz, "Tax the Plutocrats!" *The Nation* 276, no. 3 (January 27, 2003), http://
www.bsos.umd.edu/gvpt/alperovitz/taxplutocrats.html.

27. Lawrence Mitchell, in a discussion with the author, February 2002.

CHAPTER 19: *Unequal Wealth*

1. Harold James, *The End of Globalization: Lessons from the Great Depression* (Cambridge, MA: Harvard University Press, 2001).

2. Robert A. G. Monks and Nell Minow, *Corporate Governance* (Malden, MA: Blackwell Publishers, 1999), 267.

3. From the map titled "Big Loop" at http://www.theyrule.net (circa 2002).

4. Sarah Anderson and John Cavanagh, "Top 200: The Rise of Corporate Global Power," The Institute for Policy Studies, December 4, 2000, http://www.corpwatch.org/article
.php?id=377; http://s3.amazonaws.com/corpwatch.org/downloads/top200.pdf.

5. United Nations Conference on Trade and Development report, "Foreign Direct Investment Soars," September 18, 2001.

6. Ibid.

7. See note 4 above.

8. Ibid.

9. Ibid.

10. Ibid.

11. "Working America: The Current Economic Situation," http://www.aflcio.org.

12. Ibid.

13. Jeff Gates, *Democracy at Risk: Rescuing Main Street from Wall Street* (Cambridge, MA: Perseus, 2000).

14. Ibid.

15. Morris Berman, *The Twilight of American Culture* (New York: W. W. Norton, 2001), http://www.nytimes.com/books/first/b/berman-culture.html.

16. "Human Development Report 2000," United Nations Development Program, http://www.undp.org.

17. Oswald Spengler, *The Decline of the West* (New York: Oxford University Press, 1918, 1991).

18. George Soros, *The Crisis of Global Capitalism: Open Society Endangered* (New York: PublicAffairs, 1998).

19. Noreena Hertz, PhD, *The Silent Takeover: Global Capitalism and the Death of Democracy* (London: Heinemann, 2001).

20. Sir James Goldsmith, *The Trap* (New York: Carroll & Graf, 1994).

21. Marc Bloch, *Feudal Society,* trans. L. A. Manyon (Chicago: University of Chicago Press, 1961). All subsequent quotes from Bloch in this chapter are from this book.

22. Statistics from http://www.aflcio.org.

23. Alexander Hamilton, Federalist Papers (No. 51), http://www.foundingfathers.info/federalistpapers/fed51.htm.

24. See note 22 above.

25. "Estimates of Federal Tax Liabilities for Individuals and Families," Congressional Budget Office Memorandum, May 1998, cited by Gates, *Democracy at Risk.*

26. See note 22 above.

27. All statistics for the 1998 survey of American teens are from the National Constitution Center, http://www.constitutioncenter.org.

CHAPTER 20: *Unequal Trade*

1. Sir James Goldsmith in an interview with Yves Messarovitch, published as *The Trap* (New York: Carroll & Graf, 1994).

2. Theodore Roosevelt, "A Charter for Democracy" speech at the Ohio State Constitutional Convention, February 21, 1912, http://teachingamericanhistory.org/library/index.asp?document=1126.

3. A more detailed explanation of the concepts in these points is found in Goldsmith's *The Trap* (see note 1 above).

4. Herman Daly and Robert Goodland, "An Ecological-economic Assessment of Deregulation of International Commerce under GATT" (Washington, DC: World Bank, 1992), quoted in *The Trap* (see note 1 above).

5. Example from http://www.aflcio.org.

CHAPTER 21: *Unequal Media*

1. Alexis de Tocqueville, *The Republic of the United States of America, and Its Political Institutions, Reviewed and Examined* (New York: A. S. Barnes, 1862).

2. Ibid.

3. Maureen Dowd, "The Axis of No Access," *New York Times,* February 13, 2002, http://www.nytimes.com/2002/02/13/opinion/13DOWD.html.

4. Ben H. Bagdikian, *The Media Monopoly* (Boston: Beacon Press, 2000).

5. Ibid.

6. Brendan I. Koerner, "Losing Signal," *Mother Jones,* September/October 2001, http://motherjones.com/politics/2001/09/losing-signal.

7. Ibid.

8. The 2007 ad is archived at http://www.politicsandtechnology.com/2007/07/make-no-mistake.html. The company's Web site is http://www.advantageconsultants.org.

9. From an e-mail received by the author.

10. Ben H. Bagdikian, *The New Media Monopoly* (Boston: Beacon Press, 2005).

11. http://www.fair.org.

12. Pew Research Center for People & the Press, "Self Censorship: How Often and Why—Journalists Avoiding the News," April 30, 2000, a survey in association with the *Columbia Journalism Review,* http://people-press.org/report/39/.

13. http://fecweb1.fec.gov.

14. Michael Moore, "A Letter from Michael Moore to the Non-voters of America," July 19, 2000, http://www.michaelmoore.com/words/mikes-letter/bush-and-gore-make-me-wanna-ralph.

15. http://www.youtube.com/watch?v=8GBAsFwPglw.

16. See note 14 above.

17. http://movingimages.wordpress.com/2009/07/18/walter-cronkite-1916-2009-and-thats-the-way-it-is.

18. Martha Groves, "Push Grows for Law on 'Veggie Libel,'" *Los Angeles Times,* August 20, 1997, http://articles.latimes.com/1997/aug/20/news/mn-24164.

19. The history of the event is on the Web at http://www.foxBGHsuit.com.

20. Adbusters, November 14, 1996. You can listen to various network rejections of the ads at https://www.adbusters.org/campaigns/bnd.

21. http://www.adbusters.org.

22. Eric Alterman, "Radio squelch (radio talk show host Jim Hightower)," *The Nation,* October 16, 1995.

23. Russell Mokhiber, *Corporate Crime and Violence: Big Business and the Abuse of the Public Trust* (San Francisco: Sierra Club Books, 1988), 18, 19; cited in Robert A. G. Monks and Nell Minow, *Power and Accountability* (New York: HarperCollins, 1991), http://www.ragm.com/archives/books/poweracc/cover.html.

24. Neil Hickey, "Unshackling Big Media," *Columbia Journalism Review,* May/June 2001.

25. Kathleen Abernathy, "a longtime Telco lobbyist" according to *Broadcast and Cable* magazine, May 21, 2001; and Michael Copps, a former lobbyist for a trade group and a Fortune 500 plastics company.

26. Marsha Macbride is a former Disney lobbyist, and Susan Eid is a former lobbyist for MediaOne Group.

27. Tom Wolzien of Sanford C. Bernstein and Co., quoted in Tim Jones, "More Media Freedoms Seen Under New FCC Chairman," *Chicago Tribune,* January 24, 2001.

28. Janine Jackson, "Their Man in Washington," *FAIR Extra!,* September/October 2001, http://www.fair.org/extra/0109/powell.html.

29. Ibid.

30. David Wessel, "U.S. Stock Holdings Rose 20 Percent in 1998," *Wall Street Journal,* March 15, 1999.

31. Ben H. Bagdikian, *The Media Monopoly* (Boston: Beacon Press, 2000).

32. See note 28 above.

33. Anne E. Becker, MD, PhD; Rebecca A. Burwell, MPhil; Stephen Gilman, BA; David B. Herzog, MD; and Paul Hamburg, MD, "The Impact of Television on Disordered Eating in Fiji," a paper presented at the 2000 meeting of the International Conference on Eating Disorders, New York.

CHAPTER 22: *Unequal Influence*

1. *Federal Election Commission v. Massachusetts Citizens for Life, Inc.,* 479 U.S. 238 (1986).

2. Michael T. McMenamin and Walter McNamara, *Milking the Public* (Chicago: Nelson-Hall, 1980).

3. Thom Hartmann, *Thom Hartmann's Complete Guide to ADHD* (Nevada City, CA: Underwood Books, 2001).

4. Wayne Clifton Riddle, Specialist in Education Finance, Domestic Social Policy Division, "CRS Report for Congress," Order Code RL30942.

5. From an interview with the author, February 18, 2002.

6. Ibid.

7. See Christopher Bedford, "Dirty Secrets: The Corporations' Campaign for an Environmental Audit Privilege," Environmental Action Foundation, the Good Neighbor Project for Sustainable Industries and Communities Concerned about Corporations, February 1996, http://www.mapcruzin.com/scruztri/docs/r2.htm.

CHAPTER 23: *Capitalists and Americans Speak Out for Community*

1. George Soros, "The Capitalist Threat," *Atlantic Monthly,* February 1997, http://www.theatlantic.com/issues/97feb/capital/capital.htm.

2. George Soros, "The Free Market for Hope," *Newsweek,* October 2001.

3. Joseph Stiglitz, "Thanks For Nothing," *Atlantic Monthly,* October 2001, http://www.theatlantic.com/doc/200110/stiglitz.

4. "Business Week/Harris Poll: How Business Rates: By the Numbers," *Business Week,* September 11, 2000, http://www.businessweek.com/2000/00_37/b3698004.htm.

CHAPTER 24: *End Corporate Personhood*

1. Arizona Statute, I-29 (definitions).

2. *Frontier Pacific Insurance Co. v. Federal Trade Commission,* 98-713 (1998).

3. Comments by Thomas Linzey, published as "Turning the Tables on Pennsylvania Agricorporations" in *Defying Corporations, Defining Democracy,* ed. Dean Ritz (South Yarmouth, MA: POCLAD/Apex Press: 2001).

4. Gene Mellott, from an interview with the author, December 2001.

5. Thomas Linzey, personal communication with the author.

6. See note 4 above.

7. See note 3 above.

CHAPTER 25: *A New Entrepreneurial Boom*

1. *Lane Drug Stores v. Lee*, 11 F. Supp. 672 (N. D. Fla. *1935*).

2. Statistics for 1998, the most recent year available in early 2002. From "The State of Small Business: A Report by the President," U.S. Government Printing Office, 1999.

3. http://www.grameen-info.org.

4. Jeff Gates, "Globalization's Challenge: Attuning the Global to the Local," *Reflections/ The SoL* [Society for Organizational Learning] *Journal* 3, no. 4 (2002): 35–37.

5. E. N. Wolff, "Recent Trends in Wealth Ownership," a paper for the conference Benefits and Mechanisms for Spreading Asset Ownership in the United States, December 10–12, 1998, New York.

6. "Estimates of Federal Tax Liabilities for Individuals and Families by Income Category and Family Type for 1995 and 1999" (Washington, DC: Congressional Budget Office Memorandum, May 1998).

7. http://www.census.gov ("income" at Table H-2).

8. Reported in the *Economist*, June 16–22, 2001.

9. "Executive Pay Special Report," *Business Week*, April 9, 2001, cited by Jeff Gates in the January 2002 issue of *Tikkun* magazine.

10. S. Claessens, S. Djankov, and L. H. P. Lang, "Who Controls East Asian Corporations?" (Washington, D.C.: The World Bank, 1999).

11. United Nations Human Development Report 1998, 2.

12. L. Brown et al., "State of the World 2001" (Washington, DC: Worldwatch Institute, 2001).

13. Organization for Economic Cooperation and Development, http://www.oecd.org.

14. W. Bello, "The WTO: Serving the Wealthy, Not the Poor," in *Does Globalization Help the Poor?* (Washington, DC: International Forum on Globalization, 2001), 27.

15. The IMF estimates that the amount in offshore tax havens grew from $3.5 trillion in 1992 to $4.8 trillion in 1997. Other estimates, also badly dated, put the amount as high as $13.7 trillion. See D. Farah, "A New Wave of Island Investing," *Washington Post National Weekly Review,* October 18, 1999; and A. Cowell and E. L. Andrews, "Undercurrents at a Safe Harbor," *New York Times,* September 24, 1999.

16. "Small Business and the Corporation," U.S. Department of State, International Information Programs.

17. See note 2 above.

18. From the U.S. Small Business Administration's Web site, http://www.sba.gov.

19. http://www.bls.gov.

20. "Annual Report on Small Business and Competition," U.S. Small Business Administration, most current document in 2002 written in 1998, Government Printing Office.

CHAPTER 26: *A Democratic Marketplace*

1. U.S. Supreme Court Justice Brandeis in his dissenting opinion on the 1933 *Liggett v. Lee* case that—based on the *Santa Clara* headnote—gave chain stores equal tax rights under the Fourteenth Amendment to "compete" against small, locally owned retailers, and led in part to the loss by local communities of their abilities and rights to regulate chain stores and to have a say in the size of businesses operating in their communities.

2. The information in this section comes from Paul Hawken, *The Ecology of Commerce* (New York: HarperCollins, 1994).

3. Wisconsin law, Section 4489a (Sec. 1, ch. 492, 1905).

4. Jerry Brown, *Dialogues* (Albany, CA: Berkeley Hills Books, 1998).

5. Thomas Jefferson to Dr. Walter Jones, January 2, 1814, http://www.let.rug.nl/usa/P/tj3/writings/brf/jefl226.htm.

6. Harry S. Truman, inaugural address, January 20, 1949, http://www.bartleby.com/124/pres53.html.

CHAPTER 27: *Restoring Government of, by, and for the People*

1. http://www.iiipublishing.com/afd/pa-resol.htm.

2. Al Gore, *The Assault on Reason* (New York: Penguin Books, 2008).

3. Richard Cohen, "Enron: No Taxes..." *Washington Post,* January 21, 2002.

4. Quoting a national radio talk-show host I heard in autumn 2001.

5. John C. Stauber and Sheldon Rampton, *Toxic Sludge Is Good for You* (Monroe, ME: Common Courage Press, 1995). This is an excellent book about the chemical industry's PR machine.

6. Thomas Paine, *The Rights of Man* (1791), http://www.ushistory.org/PAINE/rights/index.htm.

7. Margaret Mead, as quoted in *And I Quote: The Definitive Collection of Quotes, Sayings, and Jokes for the Contemporary Speechmaker,* eds. Ashton Applewhite, Tripp Evans, and Andrew Frothingham (New York: Thomas Dunne Books, 1992).

8. Thomas Jefferson to Nathanial Macon, November 23, 1821, in *The Writings of Thomas Jefferson: Containing His Autobiography, Notes on Virginia, Parliamentary Manual, Official Papers, Messages and Addresses, and Other Writings, Official and Private,* eds. Andrew A. Lipscomb and Albert Ellery Bergh (Washington, DC: Thomas Jefferson Memorial Association, 1903–4): 15:341.

9. All information about the South Sea bubble is from John Carswell, *The South Sea Bubble* (London: Cresset Press, 1960).

10. *Fortune,* July 1934, archived at http://history.sandiego.edu/gen/USPics27/75233.jpg.

11. Journalist Paul Comly French's testimony, quoted in Joel Bakan, *The Corporation* (New York: Free Press Books, 2004).

12. Ibid.

13. Jules Archer, *The Plot to Seize the White House* (New York: Hawthorn Books, 1973), quoted in Bakan, *The Corporation* (see note 11 above).

14. David D. Kirkpatrick, "Health Care Industry Takes Fight to the States," *New York Times,* December 29, 2009, http://www.nytimes.com/2009/12/29/health/policy/29lobby.html.

15. Ibid.

16. Alastair McIntosh, "Defying the Corporate Golem: Lafarge Redland, Corporate 'Human' Rights and the British Constitution," *Foundations* 3:4, Autumn/Winter 2000, 27, http://www.alastairmcintosh.com/articles/2000_golem.htm.

17. Ralph Waldo Emerson, from a lecture at the Masonic Temple, Boston, January 1842.

18. Ibid.

19. John F. Kennedy, inaugural address, January 20, 1961, http://www.jfklibrary.org/Historical+Resources/Archives/Reference+Desk/Speeches/JFK/003POF03Inaugural01201961.htm.

Art Credits

Thaddeus Stevens, p. 6: Library of Congress, Brady-Handy Photograph Collection.

Morrison Remick Waite, p. 15: Library of Congress, Brady-Handy Photograph Collection.

Delphin Delmas, p. 16: portrait from the frontispiece of D. M. Delmas's *Speeches and Addresses* (San Francisco: A. M. Robinson, 1901); original artist uncredited.

J. C. Bancroft Davis, p. 30: National Archives of Canada, photo by Mathew B. Brady.

John A. Bingham, p. 34: Library of Congress, Brady-Handy Photograph Collection.

Roscoe Conkling, p. 34: Library of Congress.

Corrrespondence between J. C. Bancroft Davis and Chief Justice Morrison R. Waite, pp. 37–40: Library of Congress.

Stephen Field, p. 42: Library of Congress, Brady-Handy Photograph Collection.

East India Company flag circa 1707, p. 68: Wikipedia Commons.

Frontispiece and title page, p. 73: *A Retrospect of the Boston Tea-Party with a Memoir of George R. T. Hewes, a Survivor of the Little Band of Patriots Who Drowned the Tea in Boston Harbour in 1773* (New York: S. S. Bliss, 1834); photo by Thom Hartmann.

Every effort has been made to accurately credit the historical origins of the images used, and any misrepresentation is not intentional. We would welcome information from anyone along with evidence of any of the images' original sources and will incorporate this into future printings.

Index

About the Author

Thom Hartmann is the four-time Project Censored Award–winning, best-selling author of more than 20 books in print in 15 languages on five continents and the number one progressive radio and TV talk-show host in the United States, also carried on radio stations in Europe and Africa, syndicated by Pacifica, Dial-Global, and Free Speech TV.

His work has inspired several movies, including one produced and narrated by Leonardo DiCaprio. He has met in personal audiences with, at the invitation of, both Pope John Paul II and the Dalai Lama. He's built several successful businesses and for more than 20 years did international relief work in almost a dozen countries for the international Salem organization based in Germany.

Thom and his wife, Louise, founded a community for abused children and a school for learning-disabled children in New Hampshire, and he has helped launch famine relief, agricultural development, leprosy treatment, orphan care, and hospital programs in Uganda, Colombia, India, and Russia.

About Berrett-Koehler Publishers

Berrett-Koehler is an independent publisher dedicated to an ambitious mission: *Creating a World that Works for All.*

We believe that to truly create a better world, action is needed at all levels—individual, organizational, and societal. At the individual level, our publications help people align their lives with their values and with their aspirations for a better world. At the organizational level, our publications promote progressive leadership and management practices, socially responsible approaches to business, and humane and effective organizations. At the societal level, our publications advance social and economic justice, shared prosperity, sustainability, and new solutions to national and global issues.

A major theme of our publications is "Opening Up New Space." They challenge conventional thinking, introduce new ideas, and foster positive change. Their common quest is changing the underlying beliefs, mindsets, and structures that keep generating the same cycles of problems, no matter who our leaders are or what improvement programs we adopt.

We strive to practice what we preach—to operate our publishing company in line with the ideas in our books. At the core of our approach is *stewardship,* which we define as a deep sense of responsibility to administer the company for the benefit of all of our "stakeholder" groups: authors, customers, employees, investors, service providers, and the communities and environment around us.

We are grateful to the thousands of readers, authors, and other friends of the company who consider themselves to be part of the "BK Community." We hope that you, too, will join us in our mission.

A BK Currents Book

This book is part of our BK Currents series. BK Currents books advance social and economic justice by exploring the critical intersections between business and society. Offering a unique combination of thoughtful analysis and progressive alternatives, BK Currents books promote positive change at the national and global levels. To find out more, visit www.bkcurrents.com.

Be Connected

Visit Our Web Site

Go to www.bkconnection.com to read exclusive previews and excerpts of new books, find detailed information on all Berrett-Koehler titles and authors, browse subject-area libraries of books, and get special discounts.

Subscribe to Our Free E-Newsletter

Be the first to hear about new publications, special discount offers, exclusive articles, news about bestsellers, and more! Get on the list for our free e-newsletter by going to www.bkconnection.com.

Get Quantity Discounts

Berrett-Koehler books are available at quantity discounts for orders of ten or more copies. Please call us toll-free at (800) 929-2929 or e-mail us at bkp.orders@aidcvt.com.

Host a Reading Group

For tips on how to form and carry on a book reading group in your workplace or community, see our Web site at www.bkconnection.com.

Join the BK Community

Thousands of readers of our books have become part of the "BK Community" by participating in events featuring our authors, reviewing draft manuscripts of forthcoming books, spreading the word about their favorite books, and supporting our publishing program in other ways. If you would like to join the BK Community, please contact us at bkcommunity@bkpub.com.